MANAGING THE BUSINESS OF EMPIRE

Essays in Honour of David Fieldhouse

Edited by

PETER BURROUGHS

and

A.J. STOCKWELL

FRANK CASS
LONDON • PORTLAND, OR

First published in 1998 in Great Britain by
FRANK CASS PUBLISHERS
Newbury House, 900 Eastern Avenue
London, IG2 7HH

and in the United States of America by
FRANK CASS PUBLISHERS
c/o ISBS, 5804 N.E. Hassalo Street
Portland, Oregon 97213-3644

Website: http://www.frankcass.com

British Library Cataloguing in Publication Data

Managing the business of empire : essays in honour of
David Fieldhouse
1. Great Britain – Colonies 2. Great Britain – Colonies – Administration 3. Great Britain – Foreign relations 4. Great Britain – Territorial expansion
I. Burroughs, Peter II. Stockwell, A.J.
325.3'41

ISBN 0-7146-4826-4 (cloth)

Library of Congress Cataloging-in-Publication Data

Managing the business of empire : essays in honour of David Fieldhouse / edited by Peter Burroughs and A.J. Stockwell.
p. cm.
Includes bibliographical references and index.
ISBN 0-7146-4826-4
1. Imperialism. 2. Economic history – 19th century. 3. Economic history – 20th century. I. Fieldhouse, D.K. (David Kenneth), 1925–. II. Burroughs, Peter. III. Stockwell, A.J.
JV105.M36 1998
338.9'009171'2 – dc21 98-7267
CIP

This group of studies first appeared as a special issue of *The Journal of Imperial and Commonwealth History*, Vol.26, No.2, May 1998, published by Frank Cass.

Printed in Great Britain by Antony Rowe Ltd., Chippenham, Wilts.

David Fieldhouse

Contents

Preface

This volume of essays has been assembled to honour David Fieldhouse following his retirement in 1992 as Vere Harmsworth Professor of Imperial and Naval History at the University of Cambridge. The contributors have all, at various times and in varying degrees, been associated with him as students, colleagues, and friends. They offer the collection to him with gratitude and warm admiration and as a tribute to his substantial and distinguished contribution to the development of imperial economic history over many decades. The very diversity of subject-matter, time, and place of these articles testifies to the global range of his interests and the formidable expertise he has brought to bear on the history of modern European empires.

The collection opens with a panoramic survey by Peter Burroughs of Fieldhouse's scholarly writings which may also provide a context and point of reference for the ensuing essays. The discussion identifies some of the formative influences which encouraged him to embark on imperial economic history, the major recurrent themes in his work, and the successive stages in his exploration of modern European colonial empires over the past century. Complementary in purpose, the volume ends with two broad assessments of his scholarship and contributions to the development of imperial historiography. Stephen Howe revisits the theory and practice of imperialism, one of Fieldhouse's earliest and persistent preoccupations, and seeks out common ground between his 'conservative' writings on the economic character and effects of colonialism and the recent surge of radical and post-colonialist theorizing about empires. He points to the continuing relevance and power of Fieldhouse's work as a corrective to the weaknesses and wilder excesses of colonial cultural studies, and he discovers several areas of possible complementarity between these dissimilar genres as in the psychology of imperialism, rejection of Eurocentric approaches to the study of empires, and continuities across the past two centuries. Phillip Darby adopts a different perspective but also looks for dialogue and intellectual engagement, particularly between traditional imperial history and post-colonial studies. He notes Fieldhouse's concentration on economic issues to the neglect of cultural and ideational dimensions, but suggests that the distance separating traditional and emergent approaches may not be yawning and unbridgeable. Despite the obstacles erected by disciplinary domains, they share a fruitful interest in the 'spaces' between then and now (empire and after), here and there (metropolis and overseas), public and private (as in such institutions as multinational companies).

A group of essays examines various aspects of imperialism in an elongated nineteenth century. C.A. Bayly takes some of the central themes in Fieldhouse's *Economics and Empire 1830–1914* and projects them back into the previous half-century in order to discover whether this, rather than the late-Victorian era, formed the first age of 'global imperialism'. Like Fieldhouse, he stresses the primacy of political and strategic forces over economic impulses. At a time of fierce international warfare when escalating military expenditures were far outstripping domestic cash resources, Britain seized territories in order to appropriate their revenues to finance imperial 'garrison states', chiefly in Asia but also in Australia and at the Cape. Bayly concludes that British empire-building was driven by the imperatives of local military finance and by the tensions and resistance this provoked in indigenous societies. In his study of Lord Carnarvon's strain of Conservative imperialism, Bruce Knox elucidates British attitudes towards the empire of settlement at a period when a new balance had to be struck between the rival dictates of autonomy and unity. Carnarvon's concern to strengthen tangible ties of co-operation between Britain and the self-governing colonies was unfashionable during the mid-century predominance of Liberal disengagement, and he found himself thrown uncomfortably on the defensive in the 1870s when the epithet 'imperialism' irrupted in domestic politics in condemnation of Disraeli's bellicose foreign policies. As the international climate grew more threatening, Carnarvon championed closer imperial defence, especially in naval matters, and flirted with imperial federation. Structural expressions of imperialism might of course be architectural as well as institutional. Adding a welcome cultural dimension to the collected essays, Jane Ridley enquires whether the location, planning, and design of majestic public buildings in New Delhi symbolized and projected imperial power, as many commentators have argued. Her study of Edwin Lutyens's views and intentions suggests, on the contrary, that he envisaged an aesthetic project that transcended politics and one that would stylistically create a genuine synthesis of East and West. The heated controversies surrounding the ambitious enterprise, then and later, show how simplistic and misleading it can be to apply the catch-all, loaded label of 'imperialism' to pursuits and opinions which demand more subtle analysis.

The same careful discrimination must be practised in examination of the complex linkages between territorial empire and economic growth. Fieldhouse himself made this a central topic in his studies of *Colonialism 1870–1945* and *Black Africa 1945–80* and argued that economic progress was checked or subverted by institutional failures and governmental 'policy factors'. B.R. Tomlinson focuses attention on settlement colonies or neo-Europes, where British colonization initiated a distinctive pattern of temperate economic development and high standards of living, and he enquires why this differential performance occurred. He discounts not only racial, cultural, and institutional factors, but also climatic and ecological considerations. Instead, he emphasizes human agency in terms of the vast European migration overseas 1860–1914, the major impetus given by Europe's demands for primary agricultural products, and the application of technology to the cultivation of expanding areas of virgin land.

Within the non-European, less developed colonies, Fieldhouse has contended, colonialism contained the seeds of its own demise and generated the solvent of decolonization. That disruptive process had both political and economic dimensions; it affected governmental and commercial agencies alike. The complications of adjusting to a new order are illustrated by Sarah Stockwell's study of the creation in the 1950s of national banking and currency systems in the Gold Coast/Ghana. Despite reservations about the wisdom or necessity of such a course, the imperial authorities and metropolitan banks operating overseas faced pressure for financial devolution because of accelerating political change leading to independence. For their part, African nationalist politicians attached significance to the acquisition of national banks and currencies more for political and symbolic reasons than for commercial ones. Politics and economics were also intermingled in Jamaica where the transition from self-government to independence was preceded by public debate about the construction of a national identity, crystallized by government-sponsored festivities in 1955. As Howard Johnson shows, what began as a commemoration of the colony's tercentenary of British rule was transformed into an expression of nationalist aspirations. Embracing self-determination without rejecting the British heritage, politicians and the press looked to the island-wide celebrations to foster cohesion among the diverse sections of the community and a slowly emerging national consciousness. Politicians also harnessed the festivities to long-range economic planning which now aimed at industrialization and attraction of United States capital. Jamaica's statehood, Johnson concludes, was marked by the transition from British colonialism to United States neo-colonialism.

In his essay, A.J. Stockwell approaches the theme of neo-colonialism sceptically in the context of Malaysia and questions the view that political independence masked a continuation of British imperialism by other means. Some commentators have claimed that Malayan decolonization in 1957 and the subsequent creation of Malaysia in 1963 formed a calculated plot to perpetuate British hegemony, especially through the imposition of an unequal military alliance and exploitation of the local economy in collaboration with traditional indigenous elites. Stockwell argues, however, that Britain was not in control of the transfer of power amidst the local forces of communism and communalism. Since strategic security rather than waning economic interests was the overriding priority, British enfeeblement east of Suez necessitated acceptance of questionable Malaysian demands. Moreover, the inauguration of Malaysia served to increase Britain's regional problems, with an armed threat from Indonesia, lukewarm United States support, and communal tension between Malaya and Singapore leading to unwelcome separation in 1965.

Meanwhile, political unravelling of a far different kind was gradually coming to a head in southern Africa. In his account of South Africa's departure from the Commonwealth, Ronald Hyam outlines the choices facing British ministers after 1950. Against the value of maintaining close commercial and defence links and the vulnerability of the High Commission territories had to be set the reality of apartheid, international opinion at the United Nations, and a keenness to lead African countries to independence. Hyam recounts discussions in London during the meeting of Commonwealth prime ministers in 1961 at which South Africa decided to withdraw. He assesses Britain's contribution to this outcome, as symbolized by Harold Macmillan's 'wind of change' speech, and South Africa's reasons for not wanting to remain a member of a marginal institution.

At a time of imperial disengagement in Asia and Africa, it was paradoxical that Britain continued to subsidize emigration to Australia, especially in view of widespread disillusionment with state-assisted migration and acute labour shortages, particularly of skilled workers. As Stephen Constantine explains, repeated renewal of this expensive programme between 1945 and 1972 in part reflected bureaucratic inertia and a surprising parliamentary acquiescence, but the Ministry of Labour calculated that close involvement with the importunate Australians would best prevent damage to the British economy through the indiscriminate recruitment of migrants. Ministers also wanted to sustain the British component in the Australian population, and more generally uphold the power and integrity of the white Commonwealth, though they were also subjected to Australian blackmail with warnings of dire political consequences if the assisted passage scheme was abandoned.

Finally, in acknowledgement of Fieldhouse's interest in commerce and companies, Colin Newbury surveys an accumulating body of writings on business firms active in the Pacific whether involved in general trading, commercial agriculture, or extractive industries. He assesses the place of business history in Pacific studies, and while admitting the limitations imposed by company records and other source material, he identifies several themes which deserve further study. In addition to the connection between business and the administrative partition of the Pacific territories, more needs to be known about the gradual shift from the businessman's activities to the age of managerial capitalism and the replacement of entrepreneurs by professionals operating international companies. The attitudes of expatriate and indigenous businessmen to the devolution of power to local politicians and parties also merit investigation. In black Africa, Fieldhouse himself has shown that politicians could be managed in the initial phase of independence, though not all firms successfully adapted to economic decolonization. Indeed, historians may be more adept than traders at managing the business of empire, as this collection of essays in honour of a distinguished practitioner of the art is designed to demonstrate.

In bringing this project to fruition the editors gratefully acknowledge the enthusiastic co-operation of the individual contributors. They would like to extend special thanks to Howard Johnson, the originator of the whole enterprise, for his invaluable assistance and staunch encouragement.

P.B.
A.J.S.

David Fieldhouse and the Business of Empire

PETER BURROUGHS

David Fieldhouse's career from the early 1950s to the late 1990s has spanned decades of great moment for both the British empire and its historical study. These years have seen the demise of the European colonial empires, followed by probing autopsies, dissections of the imperial experience and scrutiny of imperial legacies. The colonial retreat has helped to stimulate the advance of scholarly investigation, further assisted by the extended release of public documents and the growth of the historical profession. As empire receded from current affairs into recent history, distance has undoubtedly lent enchantment. But intensifying examination of Britain's colonial experience also disrupted the certainties and the unities cherished by previous generations of imperial historians and at first led to a debilitating fragmentation. For a time it looked as though mainstream imperial history was in terminal decline, the victim of area studies. In an inaugural lecture in 1984, Fieldhouse bemoaned the fate of imperial Humpty-Dumpty and doubted that fatal fractures could be mended.[1] His pessimism was premature. As if to prove that there exists life after death, the phoenix of imperial history has arisen from the ashes. In a remarkable reversal of fortune unimaginable in 1984, the discipline has regained collective consciousness and energetic life, swept along in part by renewed public and media interest in the possession and loss of empire, much of it no doubt nostalgic and ephemeral but nonetheless revivifying.

Academically, the subject has not resumed its former deadening unity, single perspective, or common synthesis. Rather, new formulations have become fruitfully diverse, multifaceted, and interdisciplinary in their catholic coverage and unbuttoned enthusiasms. In many respects, this rejuvenation stems from the rediscovery of cultural imperialism and the hypnotic magic of post-colonial discourse analysis. As such it mines territory and chases directions which Fieldhouse himself has not yet shown signs of exploring. For one distinguishing characteristic of imperial history from the early 1950s to the 1990s has been the predominance of economic explanations of the course of empire and the economic preoccupations of its investigators. Symbolically, the beginning of this epoch might be dated from the appearance of Gallagher and Robinson's celebrated manifesto in 1953 on 'the imperialism of free trade' and its demise signalled in 1994 by Cain and Hopkins' study of 'gentlemanly capitalism' in *British Imperialism*. Throughout this heyday, a key figure has been David Fieldhouse, described by more than one recent reviewer as the leading imperial economic historian. Within these auspicious chronological parameters, he progressed from Lecturer in History at the University of Canterbury, New Zealand (1952–57), to Beit Lecturer in Commonwealth History at Oxford (1958–81), and finally to Vere Harmsworth Professor at Cambridge (1981–92).

When Fieldhouse launched his academic career in 1952, the agenda of imperial history was still dominated by constitutional and administrative concerns, the political transformation of empire into commonwealth through successive doses of devolution and enlarging self-government in settler societies. Much of the writing remained anglocentric in perspective, the formulation of policy in Whitehall, the supposed extension of the Westminster model. Here was a global empire of masterful rulers and silent subjects. Beyond the organic family of 'kith and kin' in the white dominions, historians nurtured the ideal of a multiracial commonwealth which would come to fruition in the fullness of time. Writers at Oxford like Reginald Coupland and Margery Perham could thus embrace India and Africa in a historiographical unity, because for them the empire-commonwealth represented moral progress and nobler imperial ethics, based on such enlightened principles as 'trusteeship', 'paramountcy of native interests', and 'indirect rule'. Along with multiracial values and visions went the teleology of an emerging commonwealth. So long as expanding self-determination (and then prospective decolonization) remained the preserve of current affairs, not of history, not only might a study of the past throw illumination on pressing issues of the day, but historians were tempted to project patriotic or moral ideals from the present into the past. Ronald Robinson has provocatively claimed that this propensity or, as some would regard it, failing characterized a distinctively Oxford 'Commonwealth' tradition or 'Liberal Anglican School', with a 'penchant for tracing philosophical antitheses through long historical perspectives, for presenting the imperial record teleologically in terms of an ideal end'.[2] In contrast, the doughty doubters of the Fenlands, who had imbibed Herbert Butterfield's strictures on 'Whig interpretations', shunned such lofty idealism and pursued a pragmatic, even prosaic, investigation of the British imperial experience as part of the wider processes of European expansion.

Such constraints and preconceptions must have been uncongenial to Fieldhouse in the early 1950s, but two separate developments in historical writing at Oxford appear to have shaped and inspired his scholarly inquiries. One was the transition to a more scientific, analytical historiography exemplified by the first volume of Vincent Harlow's *The Founding of the Second British Empire 1763–1793*, published in 1952 when he held the Beit Chair. Rejecting both idealism and interpretations based on hindsight, Harlow studied the imperial record for its own sake, through painstaking documentary research and the massive (and unpruned) accumulation of information. Moreover, he recognized that colonial relations involved, not just constitutional and legal frameworks, but competing economic interests and social divergence. 'The Second Empire', he wrote, 'was predominantly a coloured empire' ruled (allegedly) by 'a strong benevolent bureaucracy directed from London'.[3] As a prevailing principle, Harlow discerned the preference for trade over dominion, and though his notion of a 'swing to the East' has often been questioned, he was the first imperial historian to acknowledge the existence of 'informal empire' and to associate it, through the study of local crises, with the expansion and contraction of the empire of direct rule. Arguing that this process must be examined 'concurrently in the country of origin and in the distant regions affected', he expressly identified the vital interaction of metropolis and periphery. In these various seminal respects, Harlow not only foreshadowed the concerns and agenda that would preoccupy the next generation of imperial historians, Fieldhouse included, but also suggested that a new and more subtle unity might be possible.

Even more significant for Fieldhouse's studies, as he himself acknowledged,[5] were the beginnings of the economic history of modern British colonies, arguably inaugurated by Keith Hancock's landmark *Survey of British Commonwealth Affairs*, published between 1937 and 1942. Commissioned by Chatham House, the work sought to illuminate current imperial problems and influence decisions on future policy. Although the volume on constitutional matters and 'problems of nationality' conformed to the teleology of an emerging multiracial commonwealth, in the two parts of the second volume Hancock burst the shackles of his predecessors by exploring the economic dimensions of empire, hitherto the preserve of anti-imperialists, Marxists, and economists. In this aim, he was hampered by the limitations of his age. Having no economic training himself, he also suffered from the lack of statistics, published official sources, and sophisticated economic concepts, particularly concerning the economics of 'development' and the influential notion of 'growth'. Even so, in his study of economic policy in tropical dependencies, especially the traders' frontier in West Africa, Hancock linked in a comprehensive synthesis the major traditions of imperial history and accommodated within a single historical and conceptual framework the diverse range of British colonizing experience, both impulses from the metropolis and their impact on the societies and economies of regions overseas.

When Fieldhouse arrived at Oxford from New Zealand in 1958, the stolid Harlow was Beit Professor, to be succeeded in 1963 by the effervescent firecracker and jovial polymath Jack Gallagher, following J.C. Beaglehole's inspired refusal of the chair. Although Fieldhouse's earliest articles on New Zealand and Fiji diverged little from the traditional genre of writings on colonial policy and practice, soon after his translation to Oxford he branched away from his colleague Frederick Madden's 'constitutional obsessions' to pursue economic themes.[6] Partly under the influence of the economic historian at Nuffield, Max Hartwell, he first turned his attention to rehabilitating the word 'imperialism', which Hancock had said no self-respecting scholar should use. This proved to be both a congenial subject and a significant pointer to further investigation of broad issues in the general field of imperialism.

With the resolve of a gardener clearing brambles, Fieldhouse's assault on the thickets of 'imperialism' sought to lay bare the dynamics behind the territorial expansion of European empires in the decades after 1870. In the article, 'Imperialism: An Historiographical Revision', *Economic History Review* (1961), and in collected, illustrative extracts from writers on *The Theory of Capitalist Imperialism* (1967), he surveyed assorted interpretations of what to many commentators seemed a surprising and unique phenomenon. Despite devastating analysis by critics, he explained, the predominant dogma of capitalist imperialism had long sustained its spell as a quasi-historical explanation, in part because it offered a straightforward, comprehensive, and plausible answer to a perplexing question. In the inter-war years, it had beguiled historians, more in the United States than at British universities, but its sway was more populist than academic, in that it supplied impressive ammunition for the assailants of empires, not just Marxists and Left-wingers, but also anti-colonial nationalists. 'The impact of the idea was largely polemical', Ronald Robinson has commented. 'Anti-imperial nationalists everywhere adopted the manifesto against exploitation through domination, and hence the idea of capitalist imperialism contributed more to the breaking of empires than to the unities of academic historiography.'[7]

Even so, imperial historians at Oxford and elsewhere had earlier regarded the writings of Hobson and Lenin as a challenge to commonwealth values, and this had sparked a lively, prolonged debate concerning the motives and the degree of moral purpose and economic self-interest underlying imperialism. This running battle, which had swept along Coupland and Perham among others, generated more heat than light. It was not Fieldhouse's prime concern. His attack was grounded in a belief that the theory inhibited a sounder understanding of, and indeed a scholarly inquiry into, the varied impulses which had lain behind the territorial spread of European empires. Although some of his smarting opponents accused him of mounting a crusade and fabricating a caricature or travesty of Marxist ideas the better to slay them,[8] Fieldhouse adopted the stance of the cool, detached observer and disinterested investigator, as against that of a committed participant keen to make a case or ride a hobby-horse.

His critique of capitalist imperialism advanced on two fronts. He exposed theoretical weaknesses by examining its internal premises and logic, and he tested against 'incontrovertible' historical fact its claim that a linkage existed between the export of 'surplus' capital and the acquisition of colonies. As part of his campaign, Fieldhouse condemned a priori reasoning. The theorists were propagating an inductive explanation, derived from a pre-existing body of highly theoretical concepts which they had plundered from the classical economists and tailored to account for historical events, when the objective historian ought to begin with readily observed facts and deduce a thesis from them.

> Instead of starting with a general hypothesis and leaping from there to a general explanation, he is forced to begin with the specific and detailed and then to pace out the way to a broader hypothesis step by step. Treated in this pedantic way imperialism ceases to be a mystical force and becomes the sum of so many established facts. At the same time it is transferred from the speculative field of the historicist and becomes part of the proper study of the historian.[9]

A related objection identified the practice of imposing monocausal interrelations on complex historical developments. Despite the attraction and false sense of certainty these often held out, no single theory or explanation of imperialism could be satisfactory, Fieldhouse contended, whether it focused on European power struggles, commercial rivalry, or jingoistic popular sentiment. To think otherwise was a snare and a delusion.

This is wise counsel, persistently ignored. Imperial history has always been peculiarly susceptible to the imposition of grand concepts, if not overarching theories: 'mercantilism', 'the organic empire', 'the Commonwealth ideal', 'the imperialism of free trade', 'the official mind', 'gentlemanly capitalism'. Their successive proponents have plausibly asserted the value of unifying ideas and the necessity of organizing principles, categories of explanation, and fructifying approaches. But Fieldhouse rightly warned that labels, metaphors, and analogies also contain dangers and distortions; they tend to take on a life of their own. Idiosyncratic concepts of empire and particular analyses of the imperial process inescapably involve partial definitions of the scope, substance, and values of historical investigation, usually reflecting shifting contemporary perceptions of the character of the empire-commonwealth. Too often, writers have started out, or ended up, with a thesis and then selected the evidence to prove it, omitting what did not fit. Fieldhouse stood four-square against such simplism and sleight of hand.

Shunning monocausal explanations and interpretative strait-jackets, Fieldhouse has developed several distinctive and complementary approaches to the study of modern colonial empires. His writings can be conveniently surveyed in three broad chronological spans, which he sees as successive stages in a historical continuum, each given by critics an emotive, controversial label: 'imperialism', or the dynamics of empire-building in the late nineteenth century; 'colonialism', or the subjection of non-European societies by alien rulers in the period 1880–1945; and 'neo-colonialism', or the character and consequences of decolonization since 1945. From the outset, Fieldhouse was one of the earliest writers to recognize that such analyses would have to range beyond the British experience and embrace the colonial activities of other European powers. He first explored this crucial dimension in *The Colonial Empires: A Comparative Survey from the Eighteenth Century* (1966), a volume which he was invited to write for the series, the Fischer *Weltgeschichte*. He also appreciated the need for individual case studies, an agenda which, so it appeared in 1967, promised to be a long, tedious undertaking.

> For the historian who really wants to know why these things happened there is only one possible approach: to begin by studying as fully as possible the general forces operating within Europe and in other parts of the world; to study each particular case of annexation as a special problem; and finally to reach a tentative conclusion about why colonisation occurred in each case. The result will certainly be untidy and often contradictory, but the sum of these multiple investigations is the nearest the historian can come to achieving a general explanation of the tendency of Europe to expand after about 1870. Anything more comprehensive will almost certainly be misleading.[10]

In 1973 Fieldhouse himself fulfilled this commitment with his book *Economics and Empire 1830–1914*. Thematic chapters outlined the various factors that might have fuelled European imperialism, and then diverse patterns of interaction were traced through case studies drawn from Africa,

Asia, and the Pacific, principally involving Britain, France, and Germany. Three underlying themes illuminated these regional chapters: the interplay of economics and politics; the dialogue between metropole and periphery; and the balance between continuity and discontinuity during the nineteenth century. Each of these key components merits further examination.

A central issue of the book concerned the role of economic factors in colonial expansion and their relationship with political action. This perennial puzzle for imperial historians had been given new life and a distinctive twist by Gallagher and Robinson's article of 1953 which asserted *inter alia* that the Victorians had preferred 'informal' economic influence wherever possible and had resorted to 'formal' political control only when necessary. While Fieldhouse occasionally employed this terminology in the book, he elsewhere expressed reservations about regarding informal and formal methods as points along the same spectrum, differing in degree rather than in kind. This was 'a dangerous half-truth' because it overlooked the imperial factor: the power of the metropolis within an imperial commercial system to create a formal framework for economic activity and in some degree determine the character of development.[11] Something more discriminating was required to explain how economic forces might in particular cases have operated to produce formal European rule. It was easy to find commercial grounds for empire; but economic interests did not always necessitate government, a costly liability which countries were anxious to avoid. 'Colonialism was not a preference but a last resort.'[12] This being the case, political reasons for territorial expansion, already stressed in Fieldhouse's earlier writings, now received higher priority and even greater weight as possible alternative or co-ordinate explanations – an unexpected emphasis for an economic historian and somewhat at odds with the book's title.

To measure the balance of forces in any given instance, the linkages and mechanisms had to be exposed whereby economic and other factors impinged on the decision-making process at the highest levels in the European capitals and might, though not necessarily, lead to annexation. This formed 'the hinge of historical interpretation and the main preoccupation' of the book. The regional case studies demonstrated that economic interests were not the major or sole determinant of official policy. On the contrary, the link between economics and empire was 'coincidental and indirect' rather than 'necessary and immediate'.[13] Two patterns emerged. A few territories such as Egypt, the Nile Valley, and East Africa, though scenes of economic activity, were annexed because some political or strategic consideration created a prime national interest that had to be safeguarded. This echoed Robinson and Gallagher's argument in *Africa and the Victorians* (1961); but in a more numerous and instructive group of

African and Pacific territories, Fieldhouse concluded that European commercial enterprise caused insurmountable non-economic problems to which no simple economic solution existed and political control ultimately emerged as the only recourse. In other words, the original economic factors became 'politicized',[14] most often by the obstructive conduct of a rival European power or by chronic local instability.

How and why this should have occurred could not satisfactorily be explained from a 'metrocentric' perspective, and Fieldhouse advised investigators to turn to circumstances and events on the periphery, thus reversing the conventional order of inquiry. This second theme, though foreshadowed in his earlier publications, testified to a shift of emphasis over the previous decade. Traditionally, most commentators had assumed that empire was the result of Europe's needs or impulses radiating outwards, whether those pressures were diplomatic, strategic, or economic. Now historians were coming to realize that circumstances in other parts of the world generated magnetic forces which sucked in the colonial powers and induced them to acquire territory and impose their rule, though this was often connected with the disruptive activities of their own nationals operating on distant frontiers. A 'peripheral' or 'excentric' approach to imperialism was hinted at and boosted by the writings of Gallagher and Robinson, but Fieldhouse arrived independently at this position through research into European enterprise in the Pacific, based on sources available to him in New Zealand which presented a local and 'sub-imperialist' perspective. 'Any historian', he explained, 'who begins a study of colonial history by examining evidence in the one-time colonies rather than in the archives of Europe would find it natural to regard European expansion as the product of peripheral rather than metropolitan developments.'[15] As he later acknowledged,

> While I still believe that late nineteenth-century imperialism was indeed fundamentally a 'political' phenomenon, it now seemed clear to me that the initial impulses to territorial expansion came not from 'the fevered nationalism of Europe', as I had written in 1961, but rather from multiple problems rising on the frontiers of European activity in other continents. Thus those European phenomena on which most accepted accounts were based, including the diplomatic strategems [sic] of statesmen and the violent nationalism of patriotic groups, were secondary or even tertiary factors. Fundamentally, it now appeared, the 'new imperialism' was shorthand for a multiplicity of diverse European responses to urgent and varied problems which happened to arise on the periphery of the world during the last quarter of the nineteenth century.[16]

Now Hobson and other Eurocentric writers seemed irrelevant as well as mistaken. Instead of domestic capital developments pushing governments into seizure of new overseas possessions, 'Europe was pulled into imperialism by the magnetic force of the periphery.'[17]

This constituted a fruitful approach to a historical phenomenon, but not a universal interpretation, Fieldhouse cautioned. By definition, peripheral explanations formed a 'residual category'; involving specific events of time and place, they could not sustain any general theory of imperialism. The most that historians could do was to discern common features and recurrent patterns.[18] Two local causes were much in evidence. One centred in the initiatives and rivalries of Europeans on the spot – officials, traders, missionaries, and other sojourners – and in settler 'sub-imperialisms' of Australians and New Zealanders in the Pacific and Cape colonists in southern Africa. The other stemmed from accelerating European economic penetration which destabilized weak or vulnerable indigenous societies, whether their initial response was resistance or collaboration. This seemed to point to imperialism as being the unplanned reaction to chronic disorder created by increased contact between European civilization and that of other continents.

Nevertheless, if expansionist pressures arose from colonial crises, Fieldhouse argued that the actual decisions to impose political control – or not to do so – were ultimately taken by statesmen and their advisers in European capitals and conditioned by metropolitan patterns of thought. 'In the last resort, therefore, the historian must turn back to examine the working of the official mind in Europe as it reacted to problems flowing in from the frontiers.'[19] Here he embraced the artifice of the 'official mind' which Robinson and Gallagher had belatedly invented in order to provide an overarching interpretation for their old-fashioned diplomatic history of the partition of Africa.[20] Fieldhouse's endorsement of this specious contrivance severely qualified his 'peripheral' approach and tilted the balance again towards metropolitan factors. For stress on the decision-making process brought into the foreground the political puppet-masters of London, Paris, and Berlin. As one reviewer acidly remarked, 'the strategic perceptions of public servants rather than the monetary calculations of private-interest groups appear to determine the pattern of empire'.[21] The 'finance capitalist' was replaced by the 'faceless bureaucrat' in the operations of an autonomous 'official mind', an artificial and mechanistic abstraction. This automaton produced, according to Fieldhouse, not blueprints or planned strategies, but piecemeal solutions to a range of local and dissimilar conditions on the periphery which acquired a collective significance only in retrospect.

The book's third theme was the degree of continuity evident during the nineteenth century. Both contemporaries and theorists had regarded the 'new imperialism' after 1880 as a novel phenomenon marking a significant discontinuity in the historical process. The surge of colonial expansion seemed remarkable in terms of its speed and scale, territories occupied and continents opened up, the number of Powers involved. Imperial historians, too, had long contrasted the 'anti-imperialism' of the mid-century with a post-1870 imperialist fervour. Yet such an abrupt shift and precise demarcation could not be squared with the facts: the rate of territorial acquisition by Britain did not substantially differ and, as Gallagher and Robinson pointed out in 1953, a fundamental continuity of interests, impulses, techniques, and preferences could be discerned throughout the century. Even so, some change of temper and tempo did occur after 1870 if only in the international climate, with more rival Powers engaged in bellicose diplomacy and colonial ambitions inflated by prestige and tinged with jingoistic sentiment.

Fieldhouse endorsed qualified continuity, contending that a peripheral approach to colonial expansion reinforced the case. Whereas metrocentric explanations located the novelty of imperialism in new developments in Europe, study of the outer world exposed long-term factors and continuous economic forces stretching back over many decades and shaping an unfolding interaction between Europe and other continents, though it also revealed, at least in retrospect, conditions in many places already so unstable before 1880 that some far-reaching readjustment seemed likely. Indeed, long-evolving tendencies produced after 1880 a sudden and widespread intensification of so many local problems in so many places that it might collectively be described as a 'general crisis' in relations between Europe and the less-developed world. As such, it differed in degree, but not in kind, from what had previously occurred. Regional studies showed that this heightened tension and conflict flared because the partial or total insulation of Africa and the Pacific from the full force of Europe's impact ended with improved communications and the intrusion of unprecedented numbers of Europeans. Technological advances dramatically destabilized power relationships between Westerners and other peoples; the multiple crises and their timing were thus symptomatic of a profound change in the 'pathology' of international relationships.[22]

This general crisis, Fieldhouse acknowledged, need not have resulted in the rapid spread of colonial rule, since many similar local problems had earlier been solved in other ways. Moreover, policy-makers remained keen to restrict intervention and keep liabilities to a minimum. After 1880, however, they found it convenient or necessary to resort to political control, as the tide of events swept them past all alternative solutions. By the 1890s they had 'become inured' to employing political means to deal with difficulties on the periphery in a changed global environment. While they may have fumbled for piecemeal remedies for individual crises, underlying the general trend Fieldhouse perceived 'an undeniable element of historical determinism', a gloss of inevitability which he had earlier criticized Marxist adversaries for espousing, or at least of retrospective wisdom gained from the collapse of empires. 'Probably', he concluded, 'as the neo-Marxists held, though not for the economic reasons they gave, the whole process was historically inevitable. If so, it was inevitable only as a temporary expedient, to bridge the time-gap between a "modernized" Europe and a pre-capitalist periphery.'[23] Eventually empires generated their own solvent.

Since strictly economic factors played little part in territorial annexation, what was thereafter done during the colonial period to derive advantage from the areas acquired and to promote their development? Fieldhouse addressed this question, first in 'The Economic Exploitation of Africa: Some British and French Comparisons' (1971), and then more fully and provocatively in *Colonialism 1870–1945: An Introduction* (1981), a book originally commissioned for an Italian series of short introductions to major topics written in the format of articles for a large encyclopaedia. With respect to aims and methods, he explained, governments after 1880 sought to justify expansionist policies to 'suspicious publics and parsimonious legislatures' by stressing the substantial commercial benefits of tropical possessions, at least prospectively, especially with the spread of protective tariffs. While the African colonies had to yield an economic return, development was initially left to private enterprise under minimal public control – British chartered companies, French land concessionary companies, and individual entrepreneurs. Except in British West Africa, little concern was yet shown for the interests of Africans: 'exploitation' in the pejorative sense was more typical of the first era than later stages (an accolade Fieldhouse subsequently bestowed on the 1940s). Because excessively optimistic expectations were matched by ignorance of local conditions and of the problems inseparable from extracting wealth from Africa, the initial results were 'economically disappointing and morally disturbing'.[24]

Following a reappraisal of policies in the 1900s, the state undertook a more positive role, both in stimulating economic activity and in balancing European needs against African interests, operating where necessary as protector of Africans against expatriate pressures, a British priority highlighted by Frederick Lugard's emphasis on moral responsibilities. In the inter-war years, while the French regarded the metropolis and overseas dependencies as complementary parts of a single, integrated economy, the British were less consistent, with the African colonies treated as components of a multilateral global commercial system rather than as satellites of Britain. Whatever the prevailing emphasis, governments strove by management to 'open up' dependencies to development by market forces, relying on the dynamics of the capitalist system in an 'open economy' to transform 'backward' into 'modern' societies, and 'thus, by social engineering to wrench each from its geographical setting and integrate it into an imperial economy'.[25]

Again Fieldhouse reiterated his argument that political rule had decisive economic implications. The state used its authority to create a framework for commercial activity and to define the terms of development – externally by controlling trade and currency, and internally by regulating fiscal policy, law, land usage, and labour. Nevertheless, although the imperial factor made African territories more attractive for European ventures, in many places governments restricted potential lines of commercial progress. In the vital issues of land and labour, for example, they had to choose between maximizing economic efficiency or African social stability, as over plantation or peasant production. Different patterns emerged, particularly according to the presence or absence of European settlers, but, Fieldhouse suggested, state paternalism obstructed the changes needed for 'true economic growth'. Allowing for regional variations, he concluded that while government policies 'did not prevent "growth", they were not calculated to promote it, and did so largely by accident'.[26] Overall, the economic reward reaped by Britain and France in Africa during the colonial era fell short of expectations but was compatible with African endowment factors and European endeavours.

A survey of the achievements of colonialism also raised the controversial, problematic issue concerning the balance of advantage enjoyed by colonies under imperial rule. Confronted by the sharply contrasting assessments of commentators, relying more on preconceptions than factual data, Fieldhouse sought to establish the 'balance of probability' in the light of the meagre statistical and documentary evidence currently available, though he also pugnaciously threw down the gauntlet to readers by proposing to 'suggest that there is a viable alternative to the Marxist view of modern colonialism'.[27] He did so by considering separately the political and economic dimensions of subordination.

Alien rule, imperialists contended, was the only way 'backward' countries could have been 'modernized'. Colonialism, critics retorted, had been unnecessary and positively harmful: non-European peoples could have benefited as much or more from contact with Europeans without formal occupation; their innate capacity for self-development and 'modernization' was overlaid or arrested by annexation; instead of acting for themselves, subordination bred a 'colonial mentality' and dependence on aliens for leadership. It was difficult, Fieldhouse acknowledged, to disprove these assumptions but it remained highly doubtful that less-developed countries of the nineteenth-century world would have modernized if left alone and unaided. On the contrary, 'There are many reasons for thinking that the majority would have not been able or willing to adopt the more valuable products of western civilization ... without undergoing the trauma of alien occupation.' To reinforce this judgement, Fieldhouse resorted to the dubious device of counter-factual speculation. If less-developed areas 'had not become European possessions the majority would probably have remained very much as they were' – that is, economically backward, though subject to damaging and uncontrolled commercial incursions – and unlikely to 'have emerged as powerful prosperous societies independent of foreign capitalism'. He conceded that a few Third World countries like Japan and China had proved capable of modernizing themselves, but most colonial territories, especially small, unstable, or fragmented societies, lacked 'the capacity to act as modern states'.[28]

It logically followed, in Fieldhouse's view, that colonialism was, if not a positive experience, 'historically the lesser of two evils facing most indigenous peoples'. Admittedly, 'Alien rule is intrinsically inconsistent with liberal western values; but there are worse things that can happen to any people.' For most societies, 'the realistic alternative to formal imperial rule was widespread anarchy'. Since many indigenous rulers were clear-headed and sensible enough to realize this, the vast surge of colonial acquisitions in the late nineteenth century could be explained as 'a virtually automatic reflex on both sides of the relationship to acute problems of international relations'. If viewed in this light, colonialism could be absolved from the charge of having been 'a deliberately constructed system of international servitude'.[29] Rather, it was a 'largely unplanned' and 'transient phase in the evolving relationship between more and less developed parts of the world in the century after 1870'. Fortunately, too, colonialism contained the seeds of its own destruction: 'imperial disillusionment and moral concern fused with colonial resentment and ambition to generate decolonization'. This was the 'dialectic of colonialism as a historical phenomenon', an outcome as inevitable as spring succeeding winter. Nevertheless, Fieldhouse expressed regret that power passed prematurely to indigenous leaders before their communities had become cohesive national entities. 'The tragedy ... is that the colonial period was for many countries too short for the historical process to reach maturity.' The 'blame' for this state of affairs could be 'apportioned at will' – to conservative, laggardly imperialists or to ambitious, hasty nationalists.[30]

In an analysis of the economic character of colonialism, Fieldhouse addressed the allegation that it was incompatible with true economic development, being primarily a device by rich imperial states to exploit dependencies and thus perpetuate, even create, impoverishment. This conventional charge of radical and socialist writers had led to the extreme position adopted by 'underdevelopment' theorists who contended that alien rule not merely failed to develop colonial societies but actually made them 'poor' and destroyed their inherent capacity to promote growth.[31] Such accusations had not gone uncontested by commentators who emphasized benefits received and moral obligations discharged. For them, colonialism was potentially a beneficial way of assisting pre-capitalist societies to begin the journey to affluence and modernization, even though gains made during the colonial era were often disappointing.

Attempting his own balance-sheet, Fieldhouse admitted that the issue of 'exploitation' was difficult to confront because of inconclusive data on the extraction of 'superprofit' and the 'drain' of resources. Undoubtedly, the achievements of Britain and France in laying the foundations for a Western economy in Africa were paid for chiefly by African labour and resources, as was true of all underdeveloped countries, whether colonial dependencies or sovereign states. 'Under ideal conditions it might have been done better and with less pain to Africans without imperial control, though in the historical context it is difficult to see any practicable alternative.'[32] Since his examination of the actual performance of the economies of British India, French West Africa, and the Belgian Congo showed both a high degree of specialization in agricultural export commodities and limited industrialization, Fieldhouse felt obliged to admit that the 'charge of "lop-sided" economic development cannot be rebutted'. But, in a global economy, complementarity of roles between an industrialized metropole and an agricultural periphery 'would have happened in any case, even without colonialism'.[33]

Besides, the issue was too complex to be explained by 'any one cause, least of all ... the fact of colonial rule'. Colonialism was insufficiently consistent and coherent in its aims over the short time-span between 1870 and 1945 'to justify any such sweeping assertions', and it 'died before it could demonstrate whether it was capable of converting poor into rich societies'. More fruitfully, colonialism might be regarded 'as a factor of limited importance whose main effect was to integrate less-developed societies into the international economy, using whatever techniques of economic control happened to be in vogue at a particular time'.[34] Consequently, 'independence brought little freedom to choose future economic policy ... future development would be in the direction of Western economic systems, whether capitalist, socialist, or mixed. This was the substantive product of exploitation.' Although some might question whether it is the historian's role to judge the record of colonial rule in order to pronounce it morally innocent of charges levelled at it, or 'the lesser of two evils', Fieldhouse concluded that 'colonialism deserves neither the praise nor the blame it has often been given'.[35]

Some of the same issues were addressed in the chapter 'Decolonization, Development, and Dependence: A Survey of Changing Attitudes' (1982), and in *Black Africa 1945–80: Economic Decolonization and Arrested Development* (1986), a book which grew out of a substantial conference paper, the argument of which was subsequently summarized in 'Arrested Development in Anglophone Black Africa?' (1988). Here the chronological focus shifted to the process of decolonization after 1945 and post-independence Africa. The studies examined two crucial and intractable questions: first, the economic dimensions of imperial withdrawal and whether this retreat reflected confidence that the European stake in Africa would be safe without a continued political presence; and second, the consequences of decolonization for the new nations and the reasons why economic development failed to realize the optimistic predictions made by imperial policy-makers, economists, and indeed nationalists in the 1950s and 1960s.

On the former topic, Fieldhouse questioned the standard radical explanation that Europe transferred political power when it no longer needed to govern colonies in order to ensure there opportunity and security for metropolitan capital. During colonialism, so it was argued, the economies of Third World countries were restructured to fit assigned places in a new emergent global system. In the years 1957–65, competent successor rulers appeared, eager to nourish foreign capitalist enterprises. The interests of dominant groups and continuing reliance on Western aid guaranteed that countries would remain embedded within the international economy playing the roles originally allocated them. Thus, neo-colonialism or dependence was the calculated result of decolonization.

Fieldhouse countered this economic argument by again stressing the political dimension – predominant in the long term – as reflected in the collective attitudes of imperial policy-makers and private companies. Admittedly, in the immediate post-war years, colonies were valued as essential elements in Britain's economic recovery and world-power status. As he discussed in another essay, 'The Labour Governments and the Empire-Commonwealth, 1945–51' (1984), tropical dependencies were compelled to subsidize the metropolitan standard of living at a time of severe economic crisis. Paradoxically, Labour's humane rhetoric of economic development was coupled with the reality of intense economic exploitation. Fieldhouse identified three 'abuses': unfair use of the sterling area to support the pound and the British balance of trade; inequitable control of colonial commerce; and manipulation of investment and development projects to suit domestic rather than colonial needs. In explanation of this record, he pleaded benevolent objectives vitiated by ignorance of both business affairs and tropical territories, and by naive faith in the efficacy of socialist intentions and public agencies. Labour ministers also assumed that Britain had ample time to promote modernization through the gradual restructuring of African society; 'development policy was not seen in the context of decolonization at all'.[36]

Nevertheless, Fieldhouse maintained, by about 1952 Britain's economic emergency had passed and thereafter retention of political control over dependencies no longer seemed necessary or desirable. Although expectations and timetables were overtaken by events, the readiness of the 'official mind' to accept the inevitable, if unforeseen, independence of African territories was not directly the result of economic considerations. For its part, British business played a passive role in decolonization. Firms affected by the change appear to have given little thought to preparations, planning, or prospects and to have shown no unease about new regimes and attitudes to foreign capital. As far as both British officials and businessmen were concerned, Fieldhouse concluded, withdrawal from empire was primarily a political rather than an economic phenomenon: if the transfer of power had to come, the main aim must be to forge good relations with the rulers of successor states.

With respect to the second issue, Fieldhouse noted that objective assessment of the economic consequences of decolonization was bedevilled by conflicting assertions and predictions made before, during, and after the events. Insufficient time had yet elapsed, he cautioned, to validate any particular forecasts or verdicts (though he proceeded to give his own). Moreover, it had always been a special feature of the historiography of imperialism that champions and critics of empire alike paraded sweeping generalizations about its economic effects, few of which could be satisfactorily verified or disproved by concrete evidence available at the time – even if theorists were prepared to heed it. Fieldhouse divided recent commentators arbitrarily into two camps: 'optimists' and 'pessimists', the former predominating from the early 1940s until the 1960s, the latter in the ascendant from the 1980s.[37] Optimists included officials and politicians in Britain who expected development to occur because colonies belonged to a benevolent empire and European rule would endure long enough for the basis of economic growth to be securely laid. When these hopes were dashed, a new vein of optimism held that successor regimes would, with assistance, carry on the process begun and along the same lines. From a different perspective, colonial nationalists, European humanitarians, and many economists anticipated that the ending of alien rule would unshackle African potential and generate growth. On the other side of the debate, pessimistic economists disagreed that independent states would follow enlightened policies in the public interest to foster economic development. Marxists and others doubted that democratic regimes in less developed countries could withstand exploitative international capitalism; underdevelopment theorists expected dependency and immiseration.

In his analysis of the economic fortunes of African states after independence, Fieldhouse explored two categories of explanation for their limited performance: 'non-policy' factors which lay outside the control of African governments, chiefly associated with the colonial inheritance, the workings of the global economy, and constraining local conditions; and 'policy' factors relating to the actions and priorities of African regimes. Within this dual approach, he examined four contributory causes of 'arrested development'. First, the initial optimism, as surprising as it was universal, that high growth rates of recent decades would be sustained was grounded on false assumptions which linked independence with rising, unbroken development. The booming 1950s were misleading; apparent promise soon evaporated. The failure of export-led growth and foreign investment led to a misplaced confidence in the nostrums of development economics favouring the type of 'managed' economies that became common in post-colonial Africa. Second, growth was hampered by Africa's entanglement in the international economy and, in the view of the Left, international capitalism. Domestic economies were harmfully exposed to global fluctuations, especially with respect to individual commodities. Third, there existed in tropical Africa to an extent not present elsewhere severe environmental and human impediments to rapid, sustained growth. In predominantly agricultural countries with peasant modes of farming whose productivity failed to keep pace with rising population, it proved difficult to maintain the momentum of economic development or create a modern industrial state.

Fourth, management of these economies was certain to be affected by the nature of the political systems bequeathed by the colonial state and the way in which power was transferred to Africans. These political structures, devised for artificial national entities with arbitrary geographical boundaries, were alien creations, not rooted in traditional authority, legitimacy, and practices but grafted on indigenous societies. Often they lacked viable administrative units; few were 'nations' as the West understood the term. Colonialism in black Africa also left a legacy of 'bureaucratic autocracy', scarcely touched by representative democracy, and 'social pluralism only transiently overlaid by the nationalist myth'.[38] Little was done to prepare for the transfer of power during the brief, foreshortened apprenticeship, to adjust competing groups in new political frameworks, and to legitimate the state's claim to universal obedience from its citizens. Regrettably, Fieldhouse reiterated, independence occurred before African peoples had gained the necessary training or experience to meet the demands of autonomous nation states.

Not only were these countries ill-equipped to provide 'good government', but power passed to self-seeking elites whose incompetent management and corrupt practices were bound to retard, even destroy, the prospects of sustained economic development. The politics of survival forced African leaders, like their counterparts in other former colonies elsewhere, to give priority to their own interests and those of their supporters and to monopolize power in order to preserve viable states. They turned to planned economic development as one method of doing so. Fieldhouse concluded that such interventionist strategies adversely, or at best neutrally, affected economic growth, though international trends from the 1970s accentuated these effects. His case studies of economic performance in Ghana, Nigeria, Kenya, and Tanzania indicated that governments there chose the worst, or least progressive, elements of colonial practice, and compounded this error by adopting expansionist economic policies without the necessary resources, which led to gross overspending, increased reliance on external finance, and heavy indebtedness. Expensive gambles replaced colonial caution and the result was 'arrested development' and 'dependency'. All this lent credibility to the arguments of the 'pessimists', but Fieldhouse contended that when the economic consequences of colonialism and decolonization 'come eventually to be assessed in the light of sufficient time elapsed and evidence available, the verdict will turn not so much on the influence of international capitalism as on whether indigenous African systems were able to master the problem of providing "good government"'.[39]

In addition to scrutiny of public policies and governmental actions, examination of the overseas operations of private companies also throws light on European activities in the less developed world, the nature of colonialism, the impact of decolonization in its political and economic aspects, and the performance of post-independence African economies. Not only did large business organizations operate in territories abroad much like public agencies, but their fluctuating fortunes over the past century afford a striking facsimile or microcosm of broader imperial history as portrayed by writers of Fieldhouse's generation. Commercial concerns of trade and investment predominated; the uneasy relationship between private enterprise and state supervision veered from the 'open' economy to 'management', regulations, and restructuring; economic impulses radiating from Europe outwards gave way to increased decentring and dialogue between metropolis and periphery; willing collaborators were sought, whether local traders, capitalists, politicians, or consumers; business operations rose and then faltered with the challenge of political independence in host countries.

Not surprisingly, Fieldhouse's studies of colonialism and decolonization, especially in black Africa, drew him to investigate the history of multinational companies – both particular enterprises and the general phenomenon as part of globalization. Influenced perhaps by the three-volume classic on the history of Unilever (1954 and 1968), written by Charles Wilson (whose set of rooms at Jesus College Fieldhouse came to occupy), he explored one of the first world-wide international ventures in *Unilever Overseas: The Anatomy of a Multinational 1895–1965* (1978). The development of its external operations over seven decades were analyzed through thirteen case studies of manufacturing and plantation subsidiaries in Africa, Asia, and the South Pacific. Later in *Merchant Capital and Economic Decolonization: The United Africa Company 1929–1987* (1994), he turned his attention to the largest single extra-territorial trading firm active in West and Central Africa, tracing its progress through two phases, as general merchant and then as a restructured business in the post-colonial period. Unlike his earlier writings based chiefly on secondary sources, these books drew on documentary materials, facilitated by access to confidential company papers. What resulted were not conventional business histories but rather portraits of changing relationships between Britain and less developed countries, especially black Africa. As such, they elucidated the nature of colonialism and post-colonial adjustments from a business perspective

As Fieldhouse acknowledged in his study of Unilever, the role of multinational companies occupied a place at the centre of controversy over relations between 'rich' and 'poor' nations, and he aimed 'to test some of the generalised statements made about the character of direct foreign investment in less developed countries'. His investigations suggested partial answers to three broad commercial questions: 'why a capitalist firm should choose to invest in productive enterprises overseas; how its subsidiaries developed and how profitable they proved to their parent; and what effects this investment had on host countries.'[40] On the last point, the two multinationals did not emerge from his detailed scrutiny entirely unscathed. Indeed, the United Africa Company was highly unpopular in the 1930s with British administrators and Africans as an exploitative venture. Overall, however, his assessment pointed to a net benefit for the less developed countries, especially the stimulation of their economies through the efficient and productive use of real resources.

Fieldhouse also sought to discover 'whether colonialism was attractive to a foreign firm contemplating overseas investment and, conversely, whether decolonisation deterred new investment and adversely affected the operations of existing enterprises'.[41] As a general proposition, he argued that for a multinational company like Unilever, manufacturing for local consumers, what chiefly mattered was the type of economic system in being, not whether the particular territory happened to be a colonial dependency or a sovereign state, though he qualified this judgment by conceding the relevance of political factors. Colonialism afforded some obvious advantages for international firms. Usually it guaranteed stability and security; its main 'virtue' was provision of an 'open' economy. At the same time, colonialism in black Africa deterred direct investment in local manufacturing by failing to give protection against external competition. In contrast, Unilever found a favourable milieu when after 1920 India, Ceylon, and Indonesia, though colonies, were allowed to act as quasi-sovereign states and erect protective tariffs against imports from their metropolitan countries.

Decolonization radically altered the business environment. Unstable independent governments, suspicious of foreign companies, were drawn to 'managed' economies, bureaucratic controls, and threats of nationalization. Contrary to the currently fashionable view, especially on the political Left, which charged that international capitalism merely adjusted its devices of domination, Fieldhouse maintained that decolonization had a disruptive impact but that this was not at once apparent with the end of colonial rule. Companies were in fact slow to react to the growth of African nationalism and evolve strategies for dealing with problems arising from rapid political change and altered African consciousness, as in the belated localization of senior management. But with independent statehood they were forced for the first time to recognize the necessity for political calculation, and adopt the role of pressure group with limited clout and no longer enjoying a privileged status with government. A fundamental shift occurred in the relations between foreign business and the host society. Independent states were prepared to exercise their sovereignty as 'virtually their only weapon against international capital'. 'The underlying reality was that by the 1960s the profitability of any particular Unilever subsidiary in a less developed country was likely to be determined less by its efficiency or by the market than by government policy and the way this was implemented by the bureaucracy.'[42] Far from a new imperialist or neo-colonialist system arising, Fieldhouse argued – controversially – that host governments possessed overriding power to regulate, if they so chose; multinationals might be tolerated, even welcomed, but 'the state now holds most of the cards and can determine the rules of the game'.[43]

Unilever and the United Africa Company weathered the politics of decolonization but were less successful in dealing with the economic consequences of the transfer of power and devising a commercial strategy for the post-colonial world. At first, for a decade or so, the companies remained sanguine about economic prospect during what Fieldhouse called 'the golden age of development in independent Africa'. A brief period of post-colonial growth occurred with the introduction of 'managed' economies; the dash for industrialization created wider opportunities and attractive conditions for direct foreign investment. By the 1970s, however, optimism began to fade as Africans sought greater local participation in and tighter control over commercial activities. This was, according to Fieldhouse, 'economic decolonization', when 'African countries, once politically independent, used their sovereignty to cast off, or at least limit, the power of foreign merchant capital'.[44] Firms like the United Africa Company tried to respond by restructuring and diversifying their business operations but the respite was short-lived. The end came with the virtual bankruptcy of most African states, unable to sustain the momentum of development or preserve political stability. Ultimately, foreign trading companies accepted that their traditional activities were no longer viable or relevant in the new environment. The traders' frontier in Africa, which Keith Hancock long ago opened up for imperial economic historians, had finally closed and, fittingly, David Fieldhouse was on hand to record its demise. The business of empire, which he has so illuminatingly traced and incisively analysed, had run its course.

NOTES

1. 'Can Humpty-Dumpty be put together again? Imperial History in the 1980s', *Journal of Imperial and Commonwealth History*, XII, 2 (1984), 9–23.
2. R. Robinson, 'Oxford in Imperial Historiography', in F. Madden and D.K. Fieldhouse (eds.), *Oxford and the Idea of Commonwealth* (London, 1982), 42. On Coupland and Perham, see ibid., 36–9.
3. V.T. Harlow, *The Founding of the Second British Empire 1763–1793*, I (London, 1952), 4. Fieldhouse made a similar sweeping, indeed unguarded, statement: 'Contrary to the assumptions made by most Marxists, officials instinctively and almost invariably put the needs of the subject peoples first.' *Colonialism 1870–1945: An Introduction* (London, 1981), 27.
4. Harlow, ibid., 2. On Harlow, see the comments of Ronald Robinson, 'Oxford in Imperial Historiography', 44–45.
5. D. Fieldhouse, 'Keith Hancock and Imperial Economic History: A Retrospect Forty Years On', in Madden and Fieldhouse, *Oxford and the Idea of Commonwealth*, 144–63. On Hancock, also see Robinson, ibid., 39–41.
6. F. Madden, 'The Commonwealth, Commonwealth History, and Oxford, 1905–1971' in ibid., 23–24, 29.
7. Robinson, 'Oxford in Imperial Historiography', 34.
8. For example, the review by R.D. Wolff, in *American Historical Review*, 80 (1975), 941–2.
9. D.K. Fieldhouse, *The Theory of Capitalist Imperialism* (London, 1967), 193–4.

10. Ibid., 193.
11. D.K. Fieldhouse, 'The Economic Exploitation of Africa: Some British and French Comparisons', in P. Gifford and W. R. Louis (eds.), *France and Britain in Africa: Imperial Rivalry and Colonial Rule* (New Haven and London, 1971), 600–1.
12. D.K. Fieldhouse, *Economics and Empire 1830–1914* (London, 1973), 462.
13. Ibid., 86, 464.
14. Ibid., 466.
15. Ibid., 77.
16. Ibid., Preface to the 1984 edition.
17. Ibid., 463.
18. Ibid., 77.
19. Ibid., 83.
20. See the revealing admission in R.E. Robinson and A. Seal, 'Obituary: Professor John Gallagher', *Journal of Imperial and Commonwealth History*, IX, 2 (1981), 123.
21. R.A. Austen, 'Economic Imperialism Revisited: Late-Nineteenth-Century Europe and Africa', *Journal of Modern History*, 47 (Sept. 1975), 521.
22. *Economics and Empire*, 461.
23. Ibid., 468, 461, 476–7.
24. 'The Economic Exploitation of Africa', 594–5.
25. *Colonialism*, 77.
26. 'The Economic Exploitation of Africa', 641.
27. *Colonialism*, Preface.
28. Ibid., 45, 47–48, 46. For criticism of this counter-factual speculation, see the review by D. Kennedy, *Victorian Studies*, 26 (Autumn 1982), 91.
29. *Colonialism*, 48.
30. Ibid., 8, 49.
31. Ibid., 51.
32. 'The Economic Exploitation of Africa', 640–1.
33. *Colonialism*, 102, 105.
34. Ibid., 102, 104.
35. 'The Economic Exploitation of Africa', 641; *Colonialism*, 105. Also Kennedy's review, *Victorian Studies* 26 (Autumn 1982), 91.
36. D. Fieldhouse, 'Decolonization, Development, and Dependence: A Survey of Changing. Attitudes', in P. Gifford and W.R. Louis (eds.), *The Transfer of Power in Africa: Decolonization 1940–1960* (New Haven and London, 1982), 489.
37. Ibid., 485.
38. D.K. Fieldhouse, *Black Africa 1945–80: Economic Decolonization and Arrested Development* (London, 1986), 57.
39. 'Decolonization, Development, and Dependence' , 514.
40. D.K. Fieldhouse, *Unilever Overseas: The Anatomy of a Multinational 1895–1965* (London, 1978), 3, 556.
41. Ibid., 19.
42. Ibid., 601.
43. D.K. Fieldhouse, 'A New Imperial System? The Role of the Multinational Revisited', in W.J. Mommsen and J. Osterhammel (eds.), *Imperialism and After* (London, 1986), 237–8.
44. D.K. Fieldhouse, *Merchant Capital and Economic Decolonization: The United Africa Company 1929–1987* (Oxford, 1994), 452, viii.

The First Age of Global Imperialism, c. 1760–1830

C.A. BAYLY

Imperialism can be broadly defined as the complex of intentions and material forces which predispose states to an incursion, or attempted incursions, into the sovereignty of other states.[1] General historical works about empires are etiolated and bloodless without the concept of imperialism. They risk becoming little more than a litany of special cases or an elegy of exceptions. Nor does the passive, naturalistic term 'expansion' fill the bill; the word gives no hint of the ruthless drive for dominance in the overseas world which periodically seized metropolitan statesmen, missionaries, soldiers, and sailors.

By that standard, there have been three critical periods of particularly active imperialism in modern European history. One was marked by the Iberian and Dutch conquests in the New World and Asia between 1520 and 1620. These invasions brutally jerked global demography and the international flow of specie in Europe's favour. The second great imperial epoch occurred between about 1760 and 1830 when European empires first seized substantial territory in south and south-east Asia, raced ahead in north America and Australasia, marked out the near east and southern Africa as spheres of dominance, and brought the Atlantic slave system to its peak. The third period culminated with the Partition of Africa after 1878, the Russian conquest of central Asia and the battle for concessions in China.

If we consider the percentage of the world's resources and population seized and redistributed by European powers, the first two imperial epochs were arguably more important, relatively speaking, than the last. The value of the territorial spoils of what is usually considered the age of 'high imperialism' in Africa, the Far East, and the Pacific Ocean after 1878 were relatively small compared with those appropriated during the earlier imperial deluges. Yet, paradoxically, the imperialism of the later nineteenth century has absorbed most of the energies of historians and social theorists. This owes more to recent political controversies than to its overwhelming significance. The age of 'high imperialism' achieved its elevated profile mainly because of its canonical importance in Marxist analysis and because the word 'imperialism' passed into liberal and leftist discourse in British politics. But, as Eric Stokes pointed out in 1969,[2] imperialism was a crucial phase for Marxists because of Lenin's concern with the redistribution of economic resources by capitalist combines *within* Europe, and not so much because Europeans were then appropriating the remaining independent, but relatively insignificant, territories outside Europe.

Of the other two periods of 'high' imperialism, the second, when sophisticated, literate, and commercial cultures of Asia and the Near East were first brought under direct European domination was arguably the most important of all. This neglected period, however, still fits uneasily in broader theorizing about imperialism. It has sometimes been depicted as a precursor of the 'real' imperialism of the later nineteenth century.[3] It has also been seen as one early episode in the longer history of 'the imperialism of free trade'[4] or the imperialism of 'gentlemanly capitalism'.[5] In Vincent Harlow's view it marked, in part, the end of an the older imperialism of mercantilist monopoly and territorial expansion in north America, but also pointed forward to an aggressive search for new markets and trades in the eastern hemisphere.[6]

It is true that several recent syntheses of the history of the British empire have paid some attention to the period and have reached a degree of consensus about its character. Marrying the work of John Brewer and Linda Colley together with that of Indian and Caribbean historians, Peter Cain and Anthony Hopkins designate the period as an important moment in the history of gentlemanly capitalism, characterized by the expansion of what has been called the 'military fiscal state'.[7] This article accepts much of that position. Even in the case of Britain, however, the argument needs to be strengthened. In particular, we need to be more precise about the causal mechanism which linked metropolitan changes in the finance of warfare with territorial acquisitions overseas. We also need to examine the ideology and practice of the imperial state in the periphery and its impact on the societies of subject peoples in the light of this so-called military fiscalism. The effects of imperialism are as much part of its character as its causes.

Secondly, and more important, any theory of imperialism must take into account developments in continental European states and beyond, even if it is trying to explain British imperialism alone. This paper attempts to put the second and, arguably, major phase of European imperialism overseas into the context of the other striking contemporary examples of empire-building during this period, and especially the empire of Republican and Revolutionary France in Europe and around the Mediterranean sea. Putting these two huge waves of international change together, we begin to glimpse a massive and historic redistribution of the world's resources whose common origins still need investigation. What were the underlying preconditions for the new imperialism?

The growth of international trade and finance provides a necessary, but not sufficient, condition for European imperial expansion during the years 1760–1830. One precondition for the later redivision of the world's resources was undoubtedly the tension which arose from the considerable expansion of population, production, and commerce as Europe and parts of east and south-east Asia pulled out of the social and economic crisis of the early seventeenth century.[8] Within Europe proto-industrialization and agricultural specialization had created numerous economic networks which breached the boundaries of the existing dynastic states. The European conflicts of the eighteenth century took on a political form, revolving around matters of alliance and succession. But these political issues seemed important in part because they bore on the control of taxation, towns, and trades. After 1690 the pace of integration in the global economy speeded up dramatically, expanding the scope of the political conflicts between states. New, multi-lateral international trades took off.[9] The influence of colonial mercantile corporations ensured that political stability at home was intimately connected with the success of overseas commerce.[10] No eighteenth-century ministry or economic theorist could ignore threats to resources of trade in the periphery.[11]

Beyond the international expansion of trade and finance, the second element which helps to explain the imperialism of the revolutionary age both within and outside Europe was military finance. The cost of warfare, always the greatest part of state expenditure in the West before about 1830, considerably increased in the course of the eighteenth century.[12] This was a critical determinant of many of the major developments of the era: the emergence of new banking and monetary systems, the collapse of state finance, and European revolution and territorial expansion within and beyond Europe's borders.

Technical developments in warfare were important here, though only in the context of political and social organization. The early part of the eighteenth century witnessed the ousting of the matchlock gun by the flintlock; the middle and later part of the century saw the development of the breech loader, greater sophistication in rifling, and new forms of heavy artillery. The cost of servicing the Royal Navy, for instance, the largest item of government expenditure in Britain was £½m per annum by mid-century and rose steeply thereafter.[13] As John Rule writes, 'The cost of financing the [British] industrial revolution was small beer compared with waging war.'[14] *HMS Victory*, launched in 1785, cost five times more than the fixed capital invested in Ambrose Crawley's ironworks, one of the most celebrated contemporary examples of industrial enterprise.[15]

It was not simply a case of the growing cost and sophistication of the weapons of war themselves. The numbers of men and weapons needed to fight major land battles substantially increased between about 1660 and 1730 and again during the later eighteenth century, particularly after the French revolution. British land armies, in particular, increased substantially during this period. At Minden in 1759 the British deployed 4,400 infantry; at Waterloo in 1815, 21,000.[16] The revolutionary *levée en masse* was a response to foreign invasion of French territory in 1793 and also a statement about revolutionary citizenship. With a rapidly increasing population and a million young men of military age becoming available each year, however, France could easily sustain this level of commitment in its wars of foreign domination.[17] Britain, Russia, and Prussia all had to build much larger armies to meet the challenge. The costs of warfare outside Europe increased by the same degree as new weaponry and techniques filtered into the non-European world two or three generations after they had spread through Europe. The process has been well charted by Geoffrey Parker and David Ralston.[18] European styles of casting cannon and deploying massed infantry fire spread through Russian, to Ottoman, Persian, and Indian rulers in the course of the century.[19]

If military expenditures, the largest item of all state budgets in the age of neo-absolutisms, were expanding exponentially, the sources of income open to most rulers were severely constrained, even falling, especially in the later eighteenth century.[20] There seems little doubt that the rising population of much of continental Europe and of Ireland in the eighteenth century was keeping living standards low, or even reducing them to judge by the constant subsistence crises of the period. These damaged the ability of rural society to pay taxes to the military fiscal states. It also forced them to spend more on internal security.

A more serious brake yet on state expenditure on the military everywhere was the resistance of the landed classes to agricultural taxation. Even in Britain, where national income grew less erratically in the later eighteenth century, governments, faced with greater military bills, were locked out of the new wealth of society.[21] The refusal of the British landed gentry to contemplate a higher land tax scuppered the effort of Lord North's ministry's to retain north America after 1776. Nor could 'breaking windows with guineas' in colonial and European wars, as William Pitt put it, be financed indefinitely from urban excise and trades taxes, given the tendency of eighteenth-century urban populations to revolt and the fragile nature of royal or oligarchic authority in the developing towns. Broadly, industrialization and the expansion of export trades had not yet proceeded far enough to bail out state revenues and finance what was now truly global warfare.

Again, warfare designed to protect or enhance resources usually destroyed them. At the climax of the international crisis of 1793–1815,

Eurasia faced its most serious fiscal blow yet. Across the world soldiers, contractors, and merchants now expected to be paid in coin. But after 1806 Mexico, the world's greatest silver producer, was wracked by settler and peasant wars against Spanish control.[22] This shock was particularly damaging because it followed a long boom in production and export of American silver which had oiled the wheels of commerce from Europe to China. The international specie shortages of the years 1810–30 acted adversely on those very military regimes that had brought about the Mexican crisis, plunging them into yet more frenzied competition for land and silver. Imperialism – territorial expansion within and outside Europe – was centrally driven by the scissors effect which rising military expenditure and stagnant or falling cash revenues put on all the larger regimes, European and non-European. Imperatives of military finance had driven states to strengthen internal control and to projects of external conquest throughout history. But these forces now worked with a global reach and they were reinforced by ways of deploying men, knowledge, and control over physical resources. This speeding up of quantitative changes became, in the later eighteenth century, the forcing house of qualitative change. What was the sequence of events?

The story begins about 1760 in the Americas and Asia. Later, similar techniques of revenue-grabbing were applied to Europe and north Africa by Napoleon. By examining these changes in an international context we can bring together the analysis of imperialism inside and outside the European metropole. The Seven Years War of 1756–63 had been fought on an unprecedented scale. Rebuilding their armies and navies in a period of domestic political uncertainty stretched the European states to their utmost. Indirectly, it initiated the growth of three new world empires: one in Asia and two in the Americas. The two American empires had short lives indeed. The newly energized British empire in the Americas had disintegrated by 1783. In 1776 much of the settler population revolted against the new fiscal burdens imposed on them by a state trying to recoup its military costs, to garrison huge new land areas, and to bail out its monopoly trading corporations. Heavy-handed attempts to reimpose fiscal control from London in the American colonies stirred as much resentment as the flood of alien placemen into a political culture of growing maturity.[23]

The newly invigorated Spanish empire in the southern part of the western hemisphere stirred up similar resentment. But it survived until the shocks of international war and revolution tore away its underpinnings after 1800. Both these empires were brought into being by the attempts of metropolitan statesmen to extract new resources from hitherto lightly-ruled territories in order to finance past defeats or secure the fiscal stability of larger imperial garrisons.

In Spanish America the ministers of King Charles III (1759–88) attempted to repair the financial damage of the defeat by Britain in 1761–62 by exploiting New World resources more effectively.[24] In this 'second conquest of America', they revived the system of heavy-handed state intervention and set the native American population to forced labour with renewed vigour. The result was the great Tupac Amaru revolt of 1780. More significantly, the Crown antagonized the local creole settlers by extending the state tobacco monopoly and directly administering the sales tax, which had hitherto been a lucrative source of income for local men. The Spanish economic theory of *commercio libre*, that is 'free trade' between Spain and its American colonies came to mean in practice the enforcing of a wider imperial monopoly in the interests of the Spanish Peninsula. By these means an economically weak Spain could maintain a larger and more modern army than would otherwise have been feasible in the troubled age depicted by the painter Goya.

While the parallel between north and south America has had much airing in the recent work stimulated by Anthony Pagden and Nicholas Canny,[25] this article emphasizes the common themes which link the Americas with south Asia, the second major domain of empire-building during these years. Indian historians have now shown quite clearly that the predominant, though not the only, motive force behind the English East India Company's massive territorial expansion into India between 1760 and 1856 was the need to finance its army.[26] Of course, the Company stake in Bengal had been created in the first instance by its trading interests and by the informal political influence that it thereby achieved. Certainly, the need to finance the annual investment of Indian goods sent for sale to Britain and uphold the value of the Company's stock remained critical throughout. The mechanism of territorial expansion, however, was driven forward by the relentless and increasing pressure of the military budget and the costs of warfare on the Company's balance sheet. In 1756 it had maintained a mere 3,000 troops in Bengal; in 1766 the number had risen to 26,000.[27] It could not call on the British government for further resources without losing its independence. It had, by law, to pay its dividend in London. It simply had to raise more resources locally, at a period when endemic warfare was damaging its trade in Indian cotton piece goods. Directly or indirectly, the East India Company found ways of grabbing bigger and bigger shares of India's territorial revenues: the revenues paid in silver rupees by peasants and landlords to its indigenous governments. The Indian rulers were forced to pay huge subsidies to service British armies. In time they were forced to cede territory to the Company's direct administration or to revolt against its demands for cash. Either way they lost their independence. J.Z. Holwell remarked: 'new *temporary* victories stimulate and push us to grasp new acquisitions of territory. These call for a large increase in military force to defend them, and thus we shall go on grasping and expanding.' [28]

A similar point can be made about the continued expansion of the borders of the south Asian empire and in Ceylon after 1815. Ronald Robinson and John Gallagher in their celebrated 1953 article, 'The Imperialism of Free Trade', pointed to the early nineteenth century annexation of the Indian peripheries – Berar, Punjab, the Sindh – as proof that free trade was compatible with imperialism.[29] Yet it appears that the imperialism was much more in evidence than the free trade in all these cases. These border annexations actually sprang from conflict on the colonial frontier caused by a domineering British military presence and from officials' desire for new tranches of land revenue.[30]

Quite apart from strategic imperatives – scorned by modern historians – and the desire to secure revenues to balance military expenditure, the large and politically influential armies in the 'garrison states' of southern Asia created their own powerful momentum for domineering and conquest. Douglas Peers is quite right when he discounts strictly commercial motives for the wars against Nepal (1814–16) and against Burma (1824–26). There was some interest in the teak of the Burmese coast and people were mesmerized by the hope for a great new China trade, of course. But, in the words of Peers, 'war arose because Anglo-Indian militarism demanded it'.[31] Hundreds of bored and discontented British officers, the under-employed detritus of the Waterloo generation, demanded action, abetted by a rabid Anglo-Indian press in Calcutta.

At this point we run into the major methodological problem of global history-writing. Single-cause explanations look simplistic; but, on the other hand, an excessive stress on difference and complexity reduces analysis to mere description. There is, of course, a danger that the analysis advanced here is too monolithic. Many interests and pressure groups deplored or tried to slow the expansion of territorial empire. Many other factors, besides the fiscal requirements of local forces, were certainly involved in local territorial expansion. After 1800, for instance, evangelical Christian opposition to the slave trade created African interests for the Royal Navy.[32] In the case of Sierra Leone, on the African coast, it had created a colony. The interests of commerce were the main impulse behind the territorial ambitions of the Hudson's Bay and North Western Companies in Canada,[33] though it has been argued that the long military struggle with the French and, later, the Americans ensured that the imperial state in the north of the American continent was always more powerful and military in character than it had ever been in the colonies to the south.[34] Most important, in the

Caribbean, still the major British colonial trading zone until 1800, purely commercial concerns certainly appear to have reigned predominant. It has been estimated, for instance, that the West Indies trades and associated investment accounted for seven to ten per cent of Britain's annual national income,[35] and an even higher percentage of France's. Yet even here commercial concerns were ever more closely linked with fiscal and military ones. George III had earlier remarked that 'if we lose our sugar islands, it will be impossible to raise money to continue the war'. In 1797 Pitt was able to raise further resources for war mainly because of the continued buoyancy of West Indian trades in slaves and sugar.[36]

Thus we ought to take heart from William of Occam who warned against the needless proliferation of categories. It is still possible to argue that the central thrust of British empire-building over these years was determined by the needs of local military finance and provision and by the tensions and resistance this created in indigenous societies. For the imperial garrison state also took root outside British Asia. The first Australian colonies were run as naval and military despotisms built on convict labour until the 1840s.[37] Convict colonies reduced the cost of the domestic security budget. Again, at Versailles Lord Castlereagh bargained fiercely to hold onto the Cape colony, St. Helena, and Mauritius not 'for their commercial value' but 'because they affect essentially the engagement and security of [British] dominion'.[38] By 1808 the British garrison at the Cape had increased to 5,000 from the mere 1,500 maintained there by the Batavians during the Peace of Amiens of 1803.[39] Most of the economic measures of British government on the Cape before 1830, and in particular the tying of African Khoikhoi labour by pass laws, derived from the need to finance and service the garrison and transiting ships.[40] Even the corn and grain resources of the Cape were developed to meet the exigencies of Napoleon's Continental Blockade. By a final irony, the presence of the large garrison guarding the defeated French Emperor on St. Helena between 1815 and 1821 significantly increased the demand for all Cape produce.[41]

It is to Napoleon Bonaparte that the article now turns. For unless we are to argue determinedly for English exceptionalism, any worthwhile 'theory' of imperialism must take into account other empires, and also the origins and consequences of the imperial drive for Europe itself.[42] Napoleon's empire was as vast as the empires the British and Spanish lost in the New World and the British created in Asia. In intention, the short-lived but radical transformation of Europe and its frontiers by Napoleon arose from the strategic and ideological needs of the French revolutionary wars against Austria, Prussia, Russia, and Britain.[43] Napoleon's empire, however, soon developed its own momentum. In the first place, the enormous indemnities and subsidies demanded from conquered or cowed territories and the allied armies they raised helped to offset the enormous cost of the war to France itself.[44] Secondly, the control of foreign economic resources made possible by French conquest was felt to compensate France for its colonial and military losses.[45]

The methods of fiscal extraction used by the First Empire to pay for its armies and reward its military aristocracy were various, but everywhere summary. First, Napoleon demanded huge indemnities from defeated enemies: perhaps 6,000,000 francs from Venice in 1797,[46] excluding looted works of art; millions of francs from Austria at the peace of Aix la Chapelle. Next, the territories of conquered states were reorganized to pay for the upkeep of French garrison troops and for the expansion of the huge federal forces which Napoleon required for his big pushes against Austria and Russia. During his brief but epochal conquest of Egypt from 1798 to 1801, 1,000,000 francs per month were needed to keep the occupation force supplied.[47]

Finally, Napoleon had to fuse his new military order, which included Poles, Austrians, and Italians as well as Frenchmen, with the restive pre-revolutionary aristocracy and to provide the new imperial military class with an income.[48] He developed a system of 'donations' and 'entails', or cash provisions, in the conquered territories on which he settled his commanders and bureaucrats. For instance, a condition of the cession of Venetia, northern Italy, to the Kingdom of Italy was that one-fifth of its revenues and national properties to the value of 30,000,000 francs were attached to these new fiefs.[49] A further 1,200,000 francs were set aside for distribution to generals, officers, and soldiers designated by the Napoleon. By 1814 he was making grants of this sort to 5,000 people at a cost of 30,000,000 francs per annum.[50] This system was highly corrupt as well as exploitative. Napoleon might well have said, echoing Robert Clive of India, that he was 'astonished by his own moderation'. But those around him profited handsomely. The military contractor and state financier, J.G. Ouvrard, first sought to attach himself to the First Consul's family by servicing the massive debts of his wife, Josephine.[51] He then moved on to create a ramshackle army of sub-contractors and clients in military and financial supply across the empire and as far as Spanish America.

Ironically, lacking the flexibility of the domestic British paper money and credit system,[52] Napoleon's methods bore a striking resemblance to the techniques introduced by the British, or adapted from the former Mughal rulers in India. The fact that one set of practices was applied to Indians and another to southern Europeans should not bother us. Indian peasant incomes were not far short of those of southern Italians at this period and cultural patterns were highly localized in both regions. The conceptual boundaries of Europe and Asia had yet to be set firmly. The moral distance between Paris and Eboli in southern Italy was not very much greater than that between London and Faizabad in north India.

In economic policy and practice the Napoleonic Empire, like the British empire, garnished a state and army-driven logic of economic integration with the rhetoric of free trade. It is true that the Republican and Imperial regimes tried everywhere to break down tariff barriers and dispossess ancient commercial corporations. They drew on the free-trading language of the French and Scottish political economists, Quesnay and Adam Smith. In practice, however, state-direction of the economy remained universal and the underlying drive was to create an imperial monopoly, not to introduce free trade.[53] This impulse culminated in the policies of the Berlin Decree and the Continental Blockade after 1806 which sought to seal off continental Europe from British imports and create a tied and dependent market for French goods east of the Rhine and south of the Alps. To paraphrase Lenin, the imperialism of military fiscalism also turns out to be the imperialism of the highest stage of monopoly. Even the beginnings of the new French empire in north Africa after 1830 were indirectly connected with the earlier practices of military supply during the wars of the Republic and First Empire. Algeria was seized in 1830 as the distant consequence of a long-running dispute between the French and the Dey which had originated in an arrangement for grain supplies for the Republican armies.[54] Nostalgia for the great age of Napoleonic conquest also played its part.

In the Russian empire, too, the expansion of the garrison state was a powerful contributory factor to territorial acquisition, even though Catherine II and Alexander I both justified their conquests by reference to the development of trade. In the Crimea in the 1760s and 1770s military colonies of veterans drove forward the pace of Russian advance. The impact of these military colonies, ruled by reason and benevolence, and planted in the midst of foreign populations of Europeans and Asians, bears a close resemblance to the Invalid Thanas (colonies of retired soldiers) planted by British India on its fringes.[55] In the eastern Caucasus, during the years 1804–5, a Russia now heavily militarized as a result of the European wars confronted an Iranian Qajar regime which was attempting to reclaim the lands and revenues of an area which had once belonged to the great Safavid Empire.[56] In all these cases, the long expansion of the garrison state with its demands on finance and personnel caused distortions in the European peripheries and brought about waves of secondary conquest in their train.

All classic theories of imperialism built ideology into their formulations. In the Marxist theories and, to some degree, in formulations of the imperialism of free trade, ideology was a mask behind which lurked the brute urge to power of states and classes. In theories of 'Orientalism' which have flowed from the work of Edward Said, imperial discourse has similarly been absorbed into the fabric of domination. By contrast, in arguments such as Joseph Schumpeter's on empire as a manifestation of a reinvented aristocratic desire for glory or Cain and Hopkins' on 'gentlemanly capitalism', the role of ideology is more complex. It acts as an aspect of class formation. Can we say that any ideology or cluster of ideologies was typical of the imperialism of 1760–1830, and if so, how far did it affect material and moral outcomes?

Certainly, the view that this period saw the beginnings of the imperialism of free trade must be heavily modified. Even in the case of Britain, protectionist legislation remained in place until the early 1840s and the aim of governments, especially in the periphery, was generally to engross trade, labour, and production, though sometimes in the name of free trade. Similarly, while the Christian evangelical movement at home was instrumental in the anti-slave trade agitation as early as 1793, it played a muted role in European empire-building overseas until after 1830, except to some degree in the heart of the British 'white settler colonies'.[57] In fact, the Protestant Christian impulse within the British empire was viewed with great ambivalence between 1770 and 1815. It could hardly serve as an integrative force in an embattled empire ruling over Quebec and Maltese Catholics, Cape Dutch Calvinists, Hindus, Buddhists, and Muslims.

In the French empire the case is even more clear-cut. During his invasion of Egypt, Napoleon had the brio to portray himself as a Muslim who had despoiled the Papacy. He famously declared that his aim was to govern peoples as they wished: 'It was by making myself Catholic that I won the war of the Vendée, by making myself Muslim that I established myself in Egypt, in making myself Ultramontain that I won men's hearts in Italy. If I were to govern a Jewish people, I would re-establish Solomon's Temple.'[58] The rhetoric he used in addressing the Islamic powers of the near east was a kind of Muslim millenarianism, or Mahdism, which stressed the renovation of state and universal religion. Neither Napoleon's later concordat with the Papacy nor the Restoration of the Monarchy served to revivify the French commitment to imperial evangelization. This awaited the Second Empire of Napoleon III after 1850. Even in Imperial Russia, the cry to Christianity in arms was ambivalent. Both Catherine and Alexander used it to rally Georgia and Armenia against the Ottomans. But many of the Tsarist allies in expansion, such as the Crimean Tartars, were themselves Muslims.

Instead, the dominant ideologies of the imperial projects of the period were informed by its military and aristocratic character. They comprised first the institution of scientific data-collection, often by military officers.[59] Secondly, they were infused by a rhetoric of benevolence in the name of universal religion, deism,[60] which could appease and integrate the huge variety of native leaders and soldiers who served in the imperial armies. Though Charles Dickens's character, Sidney Carton, would have been outraged, the difference between the British Christian deists who governed India before 1813 and the post-revolutionary French deists who governed Paris, Egypt, and southern Italy was not very great. Both elites perceived room for the existence of non-Christian religions and conservative indigenous patriotisms within their wider imperial orbits. Napoleon came to liberate Germany, Italy and Egypt from the petty tyrants who had despoiled them.[61] James Tod, the British commissioner in western India, similarly believed he could incorporate the aristocratic warrior patriotism of the Hindu Rajputs within the expanding British empire.[62] Even in north America, the Johnsons and other leading lights of the Indian Department after 1750 'went native' with abandon, donning their eagle-head-dresses and siring children by tribal women.[63]

For the military gentlemen and gentlemen soldiers who ruled these revived multi-ethnic empires, the engrossing of trade might be the first object of economic domination, but what has been elsewhere called 'agrarian patriotism' was the guarantee of their long-term stability.[64] Only by measuring, settling, and making the land pay could military defence or expansion be maintained and the rule of benevolence expanded. For the French in Europe and north Africa as for the British in India and southern Africa, the land survey – developed out of earlier military surveys – became the chief engine of agrarian knowledge-gathering. This in turn generated a massive data-bank of information about indigenous peoples and their respective positions on the ladder of civility and martial virtue. The huge French scientific effort invested in the *Déscription de l'Egypte*[65] was mirrored by efforts at data collection throughout French Italy, Spain, and central Europe. But the aristocratic scientific ideology was also in evidence in the wide circles of the connection of the botanist, Sir Joseph Banks, throughout the British empire. If the naval exploration of Captain Cook's generation had initiated such data collection in the age of blue-water expansion, land expansion in Asia and Africa gave their heads to military surveyors and antiquarians in search of universal human knowledge and good artillery sitings.

These enterprises affected outcomes in broadly analogous ways. Studies of Napoleonic Egypt, Spain, and Italy have shown how the brief French and French-installed military governments sought to simplify systems of landholding and land tax. The holdings of old corporate bodies, notably the Catholic Church[66] in Europe and the Mameluke Turkish military elite in Egypt,[67] were stripped away along with venal fiscal intermediaries. This, it was hoped, would raise production and revenue because a proper landed class and a proper peasantry would co-operate in maintaining an effective rural hierarchy. Such measures were demanded both by the notion of a sphere of benevolent public activity and by the voracious demands of the garrison state. The ideologies and practices of the Napoleonic government of Sicily charted by John Davis[68] are immediately recognizable to the historian of British India.[69] The same language of benevolence was used in rural settlements to benefit certain types of landholder and yeoman to the disadvantage of earlier office-holders, holders of corporate rights, and the older bodies of warrior predators.

The subordinates of the Napoleons and Wellesleys from Spain to Capetown and Jamaica to Jogjakarta adopted similar policies to make the supply of labour both more rational and supposedly more benevolent.[70] The slave trade was formally abolished and slavery as an institution was purged of some of its worst excesses throughout the British and French empires. But just as the European enlightened despots had baulked at the ending of serfdom, so the enlightened imperialists also expanded the boundaries of other types of unfreedom. The supply of labour to the estates which supported the imperial garrison state was rigidly controlled. So slavery, both formal and informal, was perpetuated by all manner of means. Probably, the years 1760–1830 saw the highest peak of slave trade and slave exploitation in world history, if we put together the still powerful currents of the Atlantic slave trade,[71] the trade in African slaves to the near East and India to build harbours and fortresses, and the multifarious systems of bonding labour adopted in the growing European empires.

It is important to reiterate that the picture of empires over this long period and vast area should not be monolithic even if one overriding cause drove their expansion. In time, commerce and the interests and attitudes of the first generation of white settlers played a significant role from Albany in south Africa to Adelaide in Australia. The desire of officials and missionaries to stamp British law and sovereignty on ‘ungodly and barbarous peoples’ from the Indian Thugs to the American Iroquois was a vital motive, especially after 1830. The myth of civilian, as opposed to military, control remained important in the British empire, and was reinforced in the 1830s. Soldiers and civilians tussled for power and office. Missionaries and settlers had begun to influence counsels. Legislatures argued with autocratic governors in Canada and the Cape. These other interests and agendas, however, were heavily influenced by military and naval requirements and patterns of thinking. As Michael Mann has argued,[72] military bureaucracy was at the leading edge of state-formation in most European countries from 1760 to 1830. Similarly, economic organization was heavily imprinted by patterns of warfare. Global capitalism, like the modern state, emerged out of the skin of military fiscalism in the extra-European world as well as in Europe. Thus commercial houses of agency plying the China and south-east Asia opium trade were bloated with the salaries of Bengal Army officers. The opium trade itself was the main guarantee of Indian government finances, which were now crushed by the costs of the Burma and Afghan wars. Martin Daunton has argued that the interests of provincial industrialists were as important in the second British empire of the period 1760 to 1860 as those of London's 'gentlemanly capitalists'. But what were the commercial interests selling? Weapons and garrison stores remained a key item in their export schedules to overseas dependencies which were only dwarfed by textile exports after 1830. The massive new military and naval presence sometimes facilitated the expansion of trade. Sometimes, by contrast, the agents of military fiscalism stifled the entrepreneurs and drove them outward to find new trades and resources. Gentlemen and capitalists were as often in contention as in collusion in the periphery. The argument, then, must be that military attitudes, military finance, intentions, and structures tied together the fabric of the European empires of this period, not that there was nothing beyond these interests.

So far this paper has concentrated on the metropolitan context of expansion and of its agents in the periphery. Any serious theory of imperialism must also take into account non-European empire building and those changes in the societies of the dominated peoples which facilitated or impeded the creation of European empires. The history of non-Europeans and the colonized fits into the picture of the new imperialism of the years from 1760 to 1830 under two broad categories: state-building and resistance. First, state-building by non-European peoples, anticipating and responding to the new imperialism, set up conflicts of interest and policy which engaged the attention of the expanding empires towards them.

Before 1790 it was the old empires and states of Eurasia which first felt the pressures of the military-fiscal scissors, mentioned earlier: the Chinese, Mughal, Safavid, and Ottoman empires. Within the frameworks of all these old dominions there had already arisen a variety of new states, semi-independent provinces, and reformed bureaucracies which attempted to grapple with the problems of defence and revenue. From the rulers of early eighteenth-century Bengal to Ali Bey in late eighteenth-century Egypt, from the Gurkha, Sikh, or Burmese states of conquest to the late Qing China the imperatives were the same.[73] All major non-European powers of the period were attempting to squeeze out more resources to provide for expensive armies from societies vulnerable to population growth, declining productivity, and fiscal venality. Higher land tax, more rigorous labour services, state monopolies and, above all, external conquest of new resources were the desperate expedients they hit on.

It was certainly the aggressive states of northern and western Europe which provided the prime compulsion behind the new global imperialism. Their determined war-making and territorial expansion were, however, redoubled in their effects by conflict with the restless new military monarchies which they encountered in the periphery. Muhammad Ali's empire in the near east and north Africa or the Durrani Afghans and Nepalis in south Asia prefigured later European spheres of conquest.

Secondly, the very resistance of subject peoples encountering novel forms of extraction and compulsion provided a significant encouragement to war and expansion. This was as true of the British campaigns in north America, Ireland, or India as it was of the revolts against French rule in Cairo, southern Italy, and Spain.[74] Local armed resistance summoned up more vigorous policies of suppression and exploitation which either entrenched imperial power more deeply, as in the case of India and the Cape, or drew firm limits to it, as in the case of Napoleon's European and African satellites. In the longer term, again, this phase of European imperialism, created inside and outside Europe, if not nationalism, then energized forms of local patriotism. It is very instructive to read the works of Guiseppe Mazzini, the Italian liberator, alongside those of Raja Ram Mohan Roy, the great Indian reformer. Many features of the new imperialism of the European powers during the revolutionary and Napoleonic wars persisted well into the nineteenth century.

Undoubtedly, the inexorable trend upward and outward of the garrison was broken, or slowed down, in the larger European countries by 1840. The huge forces of the wartime era could not be supported even by European states now benefiting from the first stage of industrialization. Moreover, the distortions caused by the swelling of the 'old corruption' of military finance and jobbery would not be born by financial markets and by newly enfranchised middle class constituencies in Britain and France. Free trade, free settlement, and the paring down of military costs were not just a doctrine, but increasingly a reality, especially in Britain, where the government's proportion of GDP declined steadily between 1825 and 1870, as Harling and Mandler have demonstrated.[75] Nevertheless, the sudden death of the military-fiscal state can be greatly exaggerated on the peripheries of empire. A large tranche of the fiscal-military costs of the British empire was transferred permanently onto the backs of the Indian peasant tax-payer. The pressures of military modernization in France were in part exported to north Africa and later Indo-China.

Much scholarly energy has been spent over the past century in analysing or refuting the 'new imperialism' of the later nineteenth century. If that phenomenon ever existed, then it is plainly important to consider what might have impelled the 'old' territorial conquests of the late eighteenth and early nineteenth century against which, by implication, it has always been measured. If on the other hand, imperialism was a steady and persistent force surviving through from that earlier century or before, then the significance of the huge territorial conquests of the era still needs to be put into a global context.

We are now generally agreed that British expansion during the years from 1760 to 1830 was something or other to do with wars and finance. This essay has suggested that we need now to be more precise about the connection between military finance and that territorial expansion. We need also to confirm or modify the thesis of British exceptionalism by considering other European and non-European powers. This paper has argued, unusually for today's academia, that Lenin and Schumpeter got it right in part. The great age of imperialism was, indeed, a stage in the history of capitalism, when powerful and well-armed bodies of aristocrats and financiers struggled to redivide the resources of the whole world, as Lenin argued. These struggles brought a generation of mass warfare and propelled the collapse of whole civilizations into revolution or servitude to foreigners. My main modification of Lenin's position is that he was, in general, reviewing a past even in 1916 a hundred years behind him, rather than revealing the present and future.

In the same way, Joseph Schumpeter considered the imperialism of the 1890s to be a product of the atavism, or social nostalgia, of the rising middle classes seeking to explore the martial values of the old aristocracy in extra-European settings. But Schumpeter's new imperialism was also past its climactic moment. It was represented, not by Rhodes or Gulbenkian, the arms traders and adventurers of the 1890s and 1900s, but by Napoleon's marshals enjoying their revenue-fiefs in Hungary and by the Duke of Wellington's Anglo-Irish and Scottish companions who sought to 'repair their fortunes' with Indian blood and Indian silver.

NOTES

This paper has benefited from the effective criticism of seminars and lecture audiences in Cambridge, the University of British Columbia, Vancouver, the University of Victoria, British Columbia, and Tufts University, Medford, Massachusetts. Among individuals I must single out for thanks: Professor David Fieldhouse himself, a master of incisive criticism; also Robert Travers, Maya Jasanoff, Dr L.A. Quayson, Dr Ronald Hyam, whose forthcoming essay on the 'primacy of geo-politics' develops related themes for a longer period, Professor James Belich, Dr C.M. Clark, Dr Nuala Zahedieh, Professor Martin Daunton, Prof. Sugata Bose, Dr David Washbrook.

1. P. Cain and A.G. Hopkins, *British Imperialism: Innovation and Expansion, 1688–1914* (London, 1993), 43.
2. Eric Stokes, 'Late nineteenth-century colonial expansion and the attack on the theory of economic imperialism: A case of mistaken identity?', *Historical Journal*, 12, 2 (1969), 285–301.
3. George Lichtheim, *Imperialism* (London, 1971); Bernard Semmel, *The Rise of Free-Trade Imperialism: Classical political economy and the rise of the empire of free-trade imperialism, 1750–1850* (Cambridge, 1970).
4. Vincent Harlow, *The Founding of the Second British Empire, 1763–93*, II, *New Continents and Changing Values* (Oxford, 1964), 1–6.
5. Cain and Hopkins, *British Imperialism*, I, 75–9.
6. Harlow, *Second British Empire*, II, 782–800
7. John Brewer, *The Sinews of Power: War, Money and the English State 1688–1783* (London, 1989); L. Colley, *Britons: Forging the nation 1707–1837* (London, 1993). For a position which continues to stress the importance of economics and trade, M.J. Daunton, 'Home and colonial', *Twentieth Century British History*, 5, 3 (1995), 344–58, and earlier, F. Crouzet, 'Towards an Export Economy: British Exports during the industrial revolution', *Explorations in Economic History*, 17 (1980), 48–93; R. Davis, *The Industrial Revolution and British Overseas Trade* (Leicester, 1979).
8. Ralph Davies, *The Rise of the Atlantic Economies* (London, 1973), 194–230; for the same concept applied to east and southeast Asia see, A. Reid, *Southeast Asia in the Age of Commerce*, I (Yale, 1988); William Atwell, 'Some observations on the "seventeenth century crisis" in China and Japan', *Journal of Asian Studies*, 45, 2 (1986), 223–4.
9. Davies, *Atlantic Economies*, 250–300; J.C. Vives, *An Economic History of Spain* (Princeton, 1969), 564–5, for new Spanish monopoly trading companies; growth of French trade with Egypt before the invasion of 1798, J. Julliany, *Essai sur le Commerce de Marseille* (2nd ed.), II (Paris, 1842), 351, cited Roger Owen, *Cotton and the Egyptian Economy, 1820–1914* (Oxford, 1970), 14–16; K.N. Chaudhuri, *The Trading World of Asia and the English East India Company, 1660–1760* (Cambridge, 1978), 191–208, on Indian Ocean trades.
10. Vives, *A Economic History of Spain*, 564–5; Catherine Manning, *Fortunes à Faire: the French in Asian trade 1719–48* (Aldershot, 1996); Lucy S. Sutherland, *The East India Company in Eighteenth Century Politics* (Oxford, 1962).
11. Anthony Pagden, *The Lords of All the World: Ideologies of empire in Spain, Britain and France, 1500–1800* (London, 1995), 156–95.
12. J. Black, *European Warfare 1660–1800* (London, 1994).
13. John Rule, *The Vital Century: England's developing economy, 1714–1815* (Harlow, 1992), 276.
14. Ibid.
15. Ibid.
16. Ibid., 285; Charles Tilly provides the following grim statistics; great power battle deaths during the War of the Austrian Succession: 359,000; for the French revolutionary and Napoleonic wars: 2,532,000, Charles Tilly, *Coercion, Capital and European States, AD 900–1992* (revised edn., Cambridge, Mass. 1992), 165; to this should be added the lives of at least 1 million non-European peoples and several million slaves between 1793 and 1815.
17. Black, *European Warfare*, 168–89.
18. D.B. Ralston, *Importing the European Army: The introduction of European military techniques and institutions into the extra-European world, 1600–1914* (Chicago, 1990); G. Parker, *The Military Revolution: Military innovation and the rise of the West, 1500–1800* (Cambridge, 1988).
19. See, R.G.S. Cooper, 'Cross-cultural conflict analysis: The reality of British victory in the Second Anglo-Maratha War, 1803–5' (unpublished PhD Diss., Cambridge, 1992); P. Spear, *Master of Bengal: Clive and his India* (London, 1975), 166–71; for military adaptation by native peoples in north America cf. R.S. Allen, *His Majesty's Indian Allies: British Indian Policy in the Defence of Canada, 1774–1815* (Toronto, 1992).
20. See, F. Aftalion, *The French Revolution: An Economic interpretation* (Cambridge, 1990), 'the state had been living beyond its means since the beginning of the seventeenth century'

but the crises of tax-farming, war, and growing poverty of the poor pushed it over the edge, 11, 17–20, 31–43; in Spain agrarian crises persisted to mid-century with scarcities and a plague of locusts in 1755–6, thereafter reform and technical innovation slowly improved the economy, but not quickly enough to bail out the state, Vives, *Economic History of Spain*, 505–7; W. Abel, tr. O. Ordish, *Agrarian Fluctuations in Europe from the Thirteenth to the Eighteenth Century* (London, 1980), 215–22, sees a general depression in European agriculture from 1801–17 and on into the nineteenth century, following a patchy revival in the eighteenth. South Asia was similarly plagued by famines from 1769–1804.

21. P.K.O' Brien, 'The political economy of British taxation', *Economic History Review*, 41 (1988). P. Mathias and P.K. O'Brien, 'Taxation in Britain and France, 1715–1810, *Journal of European Economic History*, 5 (1975), 604–5.
22. John Lynch, *The Spanish American Revolutions 1808–26*, 14, 328–9; for the importance of imported bullion in, for example, China, see P. Kuhn, *Soul Stealers: The Chinese Sorcery Scare of 1768* (Cambridge, Mass., 1990), 30–49.
23. I.R. Christie and B.W. Labaree, *Empire or Independence: A British American dialogue on the coming of the American Revolution* (London, 1976), 1–46; R.R. Palmer, *The Age of the Democratic Revolution*, I (Princeton, 1959), II (Princeton, 1964).
24. John Lynch, *Bourbon Spain 1700–1808* (London, 1989), 328–74; J. Lynch, *The Spanish American Revolutions 1808–26* (New York, 1973), 7–20; Vives, *Economic History of Spain*, 547, 561; French techniques of fiscal extraction and 'internal colonialism' were contemporaneously developed in the case of Corsica after 1763, see Pierre da Passano, *Histoire de l'annexation de la Corse* (Le Coteau/Roanne, 1990).
25. N. Canny and A. Pagden, *Colonial Identity in the Atlantic World 1500–1800* (Princeton, 1987), 267–78.
26. See for example, R. Barnett, *North India Between Empires: Awadh the Mughals and the British, 1720–1801* (Berkeley, 1980); D.A. Washbrook, 'Progress and problems: south Asian economic and social history, c. 1720–1860', *Modern Asian Studies*, 22, 1 (1988), 57–96; C.A. Bayly, *Indian Society and the Making of the British Empire* (Cambridge, 1987), chs. 2 and 3; for a nuanced account which demonstrates the dialogue between trading and fiscal interests, P. J. Marshall, *Trade and Conquest: Studies in the rise of British dominion in India* (Variorum, London, 1993); but note that Africa and Asia did not significantly grow in importance as sources or destinations of British trade, see Crouzet, 'British overseas trade'; Davis, *Industrial Revolution*.
27. H.V. Bowen, *Revolution and Reform: The Indian problem in British politics, 1757–1773* (Cambridge, 1991), 12.
28. Cited ibid., 105.
29. R. Robinson and J. Gallagher, 'The imperialism of free trade', *Economic History Review*, 2 ser., 6, 1 (1953), 1–15.
30. D.J. Howlett, 'An end to expansion: Influences on British policy in India c. 1830–60' (unpub. PhD dissertation, Cambridge University, 1981).
31. D. Peers, *Between Mars and Mammon: Colonial armies and the garrison state in India, 1819–1835* (London, 1995), 150; cf. J. Pemble, *The Invasion of Nepal: John Company at War* (Oxford, 1971).
32. R. Furneaux, *William Wilberforce* (London, 1974), 120–6; cf. P.M. Martin, *The External Trade of the Loango Coast, 1576–1870* (Oxford, 1972), 138–9 for the impact of the Anglo-French wars.
33. E.E. Rich, *The Hudson's Bay Company*, III, (London, 1965)
34. E. Mancke, 'Another British America: A Canadian model for the early modern British Empire', *Journal of Imperial and Commonwealth History*, 25, 1 (1997), 1–36.
35. M. Duffy, *Soldiers, Sugar and Seapower: The British expeditions to the West Indies and the war against revolutionary France* (Oxford, 1987), 17, ch. 1, *passim*.
36. Ibid., 285.
37. A. Atkinson, *The Europeans in Australia: A History*, I, *The Beginning* (Melbourne, 1997), 37–78; for Bligh, ibid., 271–90; J. Ritchie, *Lachlan Macquarie* (Melbourne, 1986); R. Hughes, *The Fatal Shore: A history of the transportation of convicts to Australia 1787–1868* (London, 1987), 414–34; L. Ryan, *The Aboriginal Tasmanians* (Brisbane, 1981); land and

commercial policy in Australia was run largely to maintain the convict settlement's self-sufficiency until the 1830s, P. Burroughs, *Britain and Australia 1831–1855: A study in imperial relations and Crown lands administration* (Oxford, 1967), 1–10.

38. Cited in S. Newton King, 'The labour market of the Cape Colony, 1807–28', in S. Marks and A. Atmore, *Economy and Society in Pre-Industrial South Africa* (London, 1980), 172, cf. 173, *passim*; L.C. Duly, *British Land Policy at the Cape* (London, 1964), 186; R. Elphick and H. Giliomee, *The Shaping of South African Society, 1652–1840* (rev. edn., London, 1989); cf. J. S. Galbraith, *Reluctant Empire. British Policy on the South African Frontier, 1834–54* (Berkeley, 1963); A.K. Millar, *Plantagenet in Africa: Lord Charles Somerset* (Capetown, 1965).
39. Newton-King, 'Labour market', 176.
40. Ibid., 163.
41. Ibid.
42. For a general background to European state formation see Charles Tilly, *Coercion, Capital and the European States AD 990–1992* (rev. edn. Cambridge, Mass., 1992).
43. See O. Connelly, *Napoleon's Satellite Kingdoms* (New York, 1965).
44. Stuart J. Woolf, *Napoleon's Integration of Europe* (London, 1989), 133–84; J. Tulard (ed.) *Dictionnaire Napoléon* (Paris, 1988), 'contributions', 507–10 and 'finances publiques', 732–5.
45. F. Crouzet, 'Wars, blockade and economic change in Europe, 1792–1815', *Journal of Economic History*, 24 (1964).
46. F. de Bourrienne, *Mémoires de Napoléon Bonaparte* (Paris, 1836), English trans. E. Sanderson (ed.), *Memoirs of Napoleon Bonaparte* (London, 1904), 54.
47. R. Owen, *Cotton and the Egyptian Economy, 1821–1914* (Oxford, 1969), 16.
48. J-P Bertrand, 'Napoleon's officers', *Past and Present*, 112 (1986).
49. Woolf, *Integration*, 182.
50. Ibid., 183.
51. L. Bergeron, *Banquiers, Negociants et Manufacturiers Parisiens du Directoire à l'Empire*, (Paris, 1975), esp.156–8; for Napoleon's circle's finances, Bourrienne, *Memoirs*, 141–2; on Ouvrard, ibid., 304–8.
52. Charles P. Kindelberger, *A Financial History of Western Europe* (2nd. edn. Oxford, 1993), 101–3
53. Woolf, *Integration.*
54. H.I. Priestley, *France Overseas: A study of modern imperialism*, 23–31; this conquest was a straightforward looting operation; about Fr. 100 million of the Algerian treasury reached France of which half went to the French treasury and the rest was pocketed by military officers, J. M. Abun-Nasr, *A History of the Maghrib* (Cambridge, 1971), 238.
55. Seema Alavi, 'The Company army and rural society: The invalid thanah 1780–1830', *Modern Asian Studies*, I (1993), 147–78; John Keep, *Soldiers of the Tsar: Army and Society in Russia 1462–1874* (Oxford, 1985), 275.
56. Muriel Atkin, *Russia and Iran 1780–1828* (Minneapolis, 1980), 92, *passim.*
57. Furneaux, *Wilberforce*; cf. A.K. Davidson, *Evangelicals and Attitudes to India, 1786–1813* (London, 1990).
58. J. Tulard (ed.), *Dictionnaire Napoléon* (Paris, 1987), 451; elsewhere he remarked: 'I respect, more than the Mamelukes, God, his Prophet and the Alcoran', Bourrienne, *Memoirs*, 71; cf. S. Boustany, *The Journals of Bonaparte in Egypt, 1798–1801* (Cairo, 1971), I, *passim.*
59. For France, S. Woolf, 'Statistics and the modern state', *Comparative Studies in Society and History*, 31, 1989; *Napoleon's Integration*, 133–43; Woolf, 'The construction of a European world view in the revolutionary-Napoleonic years', *Past and Present*, 137 (1992), 72–101; for Britain, M. Edney, 'The patronage of science and the creation of imperial space', *Cartographica*, 30, I (1993), 61–7; 'British military education, map-making and military "map-mindedness" in the late enlightenment', *Cartographic Journal*, 31, I (1994), 14–20; Edney, *Mapping an Empire* (Chicago, 1997); R.H. Phillimore, *Historical Records of the Survey of India* II, *1800–1815* (Dehra Dun, 1950).
60. P.J. Marshall and G. Williams, *The Great Map of Mankind: British perceptions of the world in the Age of Enlightenment* (London, 1982). For one example see, F. Wilford, 'On Egypt and

Other countries adjacent to the Coli River or Nile of Ethiopia from the ancient books of the Hindus', *Asiatick Researches*, III (1799), 295–9 ff; for background, Frank E. Manuel, *The Eighteenth Century Confronts the Gods* (Cambridge Mass., 1959), and for the deeper deist tradition, R. Cudworth, *The True Intellectual System of the Universe* (London, 1678); David Hume, *Natural History of Religion* (Edinburgh, 1757).

61. Woolf, *Napoleon's Integration*, 206–9.
62. Norbert Peabody, 'Tod's *Rajast'han* and the boundaries of imperial rule in nineteenth century India', *Modern Asian Studies*, 30, 1 (1996), 141–70; cf. S. Woolf, 'French civilisation and ethnicity in the Napoleonic Empire', *Past and Present*, 124 (1989), 96–106.
63. Allen, *His Majesty's Indian Allies*.
64. C.A.Bayly, *Imperial Meridian: The British Empire and the World, 1780–1830* (London, 1989).
65. *Déscription de l'Egypte* (2nd. edn.), I (Paris, 1824).
66. Woolf, *Napoleon's Integration*.
67. S.J. Shaw, *Ottoman Egypt in the Age of the French Revolution* (Cambridge, Mass., 1964).
68. J.A. Davis, 'The Napoleonic era in southern Italy: an ambiguous legacy?', *Proceedings of the British Academy*, 80 (1991), 133–48.
69. For example, the proceedings of Jonathan Duncan whose revenue settlements of the Banaras territories in the 1790s displayed all these features; Duncan also founded a college in the city to collate the knowledge of its Brahmin priests, see A. Shakespear, *Selections from the Duncan Records*, 2 vols (Banaras, 1873).
70. For example, P.R.B. Carey, 'Waiting for the *ratu adil*: the Javanese village community on the eve of the Java war', *Modern Asian Studies*, 20, 1 (1986); Newton-King, 'The labour market of the Cape colony'.
71. John Iliffe, *Africa: The history of a continent* (Cambridge, 1995), esp. 130–1, *passim*.
72. Michael Mann, *The Structure of Social Power*, I (Cambridge, 1986).
73. Bayly, *Imperial Meridian*, 16–74; cf.S. and E.K. Shaw, *The History of the Ottoman Empire and Modern Turkey* (Cambridge, 1977), II, 256–70; Victor Lieberman, *Burmese Administrative Cycles: Anarchy and conquest c. 1580–1760* (Princeton, 1984); Kumar Pradhan, *The Gorkha Conquests: The Process and Consequences of the unification of Nepal with particular reference to eastern Nepal* (Delhi, 1991); Indu Banga, *The Agrarian System of the Sikhs: Late eighteenth and early nineteenth century* (Delhi, 1978); J.S.Grewal, *The Sikhs of the Punjab* (Cambridge, 1990). Peter Perdue has recently shown how the eighteenth-century Chinese Emperor Chi'en Lung tightened his grip on central Asia, increasing his dominion's flows of tribute and revenue, P. Perdue, 'Military mobilisation in seventeenth and eighteenth century China, Russia and Mongolia', *Modern Asian Studies*, 30, 4 (1996), 757–94.
74. Woolf, *Napoleon's Integration*, 226–9, for resistance to Napoleonic tax squeeze; C.A. Bayly, 'The British fiscal-military state and indigenous resistance: India 1750–1820', in Lawrence Stone (ed.), *An Imperial State at War: Britain from 1689 to 1815* (London, 1994), 322–55; C. Esdaile, 'War and politics in Spain, 1808–1814', *Historical Journal*, 31, 2 (1988), 295–317.
75. P. Harling and P. Mandler, 'From fiscal-military state to laissez faire state, 1760–1850', *Journal of British Studies*, 32, I (1993), 44–70; cf. C.A.Bayly, 'Returning the British to South Asian History: The limits of colonial hegemony', *South Asia* 17, 2 (1994), 1–25.

The Earl of Carnarvon, Empire, and Imperialism, 1855–90

BRUCE KNOX

The adoption of the word 'imperialism' into the English language, with, for the first time, an English meaning, began in the 1870s.[1] The fourth Earl of Carnarvon was amongst the first to draw attention to the process and to use it in relation to British imperial experience. In so doing, Carnarvon invested 'imperialism' with an idealistic and forward-looking meaning strictly associated with the empire. His contribution was individual, but significant in our continuing attempts to understand the place of empire and imperialism in British history. Carnarvon's imperialism was very different from that attributed in the late 1870s to his party's leader, Benjamin Disraeli. 'Beaconsfieldism' (for Disraeli became Earl of Beaconsfield in 1876) became a target of the Conservative party's opponents, and the party acquired an 'imperial' reputation. In particular, W.E. Gladstone and Robert Lowe wrote powerfully against it, and they were arguably responsible for establishing a distinctly derogatory view of imperialism in the British canon. Carnarvon's views are thus worth juxtaposing with those of Gladstone and Lowe.

Carnarvon's career spanned the thirty years which saw, first, what has been called 'the nadir of Conservatism',[2] then the recovery of the 1870s, and the triumph brought to the party by Gladstone's ill-managed attempt to carry Home Rule for Ireland in the mid-1880s. In that time he held ministerial office on four occasions, first as under-secretary for the colonies (1858–59), then secretary of state (1866–67 and 1874–78), and finally lord lieutenant of Ireland (1885–86). It was a distinguished career, though marked ultimately by failure as well as by obvious achievement; for, while Carnarvon possessed great abilities and was notably high-minded, his capacities were more intellectual, imaginative, and administrative than political, so that he more than once over-reached himself. From perhaps the middle of the 1860s, Carnarvon increasingly devoted most of his political energy to the affairs of the colonial empire. Eventually, in 1885–86, he extended himself to the problem of Ireland which he believed might be solved, or at least greatly ameliorated, by treating it as a near analogue of relations between Britain and the self-governing colonies. The apogee of Carnarvon's commitment to colonial affairs was reached in his secretaryship of state in 1874–78. Yet there was nothing about his imperialism which might to be assigned to some recent transformation. Both critics and exponents of imperialism in later years were prone to locate its beginning in or about 1870.[3] For Carnarvon, however, 'imperialism' was inseparable from the colonial empire and its long existence. Certainly, the Franco-Prussian war of 1870–71 intensified his concern with the defence, not just of the British Isles, but of the empire as a whole; and that concern persisted to the end of his life, as was appropriate during a period in which the British sense of security was seriously diminished.

But the beginning of his preoccupation may be found in the sixteen months he spent in 1858–59 as parliamentary under-secretary for the colonies in the second of Lord Derby's three minority Conservative administrations. This was in the nature of a happy accident. It is possible that Carnarvon was introduced to the affairs of colonies during his time at Eton in the late 1840s, where his housemaster had been Edward Coleridge, who had considerable colonial associations. But whether Coleridge had passed on anything of his interests to his pupils, including not only Carnarvon but his cousin and contemporary Robert Herbert, is a matter of speculation.[4] Nothing in Carnarvon's time at Christ Church is known to suggest such interest. After Oxford, he travelled in the Levant and, though he visited Malta and Corfu, colonies were but incidental to his itinerary. His maiden speech in the House of Lords included an earnest appreciation of those colonies which had contributed to the Patriotic Fund since the start of the Crimean War.[5] There is no reason, however, to suppose that in late February 1858 Derby was moved by anything more than the need to recruit promising men to his ministry from a Conservative party allegedly wanting in talent; Carnarvon was one of the 'secondary appointments' of whose quality Disraeli boasted.[6]

Carnarvon himself showed no special enthusiasm for the post he was offered. He even put it in doubt by trying to exact an assurance from Derby that he would not proceed with the Conspiracy Bill which had brought down the Palmerston ministry:[7] a kind of omen in one who was to resign a cabinet post three times. But in the Colonial Office Carnarvon discovered an aptitude for official, bureaucratic work and a taste for governance. He found interesting and competent colleagues in the departmental officials. Lord Stanley, the secretary of state, he already knew. Carnarvon learnt from him (as one might expect) not ideas or enthusiasm, but efficient and relentless habits of work. That work was decisive. He found it 'severe and heavy', but, to his surprise, full of interest, for so many colonial problems threw up 'large questions of government & principle'.[8] He found himself not merely reading the voluminous papers which came in despatches and inter-departmental letters, but doing what amounted to serious research in past papers so as to understand current issues. He made summaries of this research, keeping much for reference. He learnt to write the minutes for which the Colonial Office has become justly famous: and of these also he kept copies for reference or, conceivably, for posterity.[9] The minutes were, of course, offered as advice to the secretary of state. It is a comment on Stanley, as well as on Carnarvon's inexperience, that his advice seldom seemed to be particularly wanted.[10]

Stanley was secretary of state for a mere three months. His successor was important in the making of Carnarvon. When Derby was forming his ministry, he had first offered the Colonial Office to Sir Edward Bulwer Lytton, who had to decline because his re-election in Hertfordshire would have been opposed. Now he was brought in. Lytton was, no doubt, 'a versatile and accomplished politician',[11] but he was better known as a highly successful novelist. Of official work he had had no experience: according to Disraeli his only claim to a cabinet post stemmed from a 'too gracious' remark made by Derby in 1855.[12] Disraeli might have been right, insofar as Lytton proved to be an incompetent administrator and a troublesome colleague. 'Life to him is a novel and ... may be said to come out in serials', noted Gathorne Hardy, after hearing from Spencer Walpole about Lytton's behaviour in cabinet; and Disraeli would happily have got rid of him by Christmas 1858.[13] But Lytton had credentials, whether or not Derby consciously took them into account. He was the author of *The Caxtons* (1849), one of the most successful novels of the past decade, which contained a carefully researched and thoughtful exposition of a 'philosophy of colonising'.[14] This did not make Lytton a satisfactory secretary of state in practical terms, but it did mean that he brought to the office imagination and, as Gladstone acknowledged, warmth: better these, surely, than the radical theories for which Sir William Molesworth – briefly colonial secretary of state in 1856 – had long been known. During his twelve months in office, Lytton's dilatoriness, his carelessness with documents, his obsessive attention to some matters to the virtual exclusion of others, and his verbosity, were problems in the department. His basic enthusiasm, however, was such that the wry observation that Lytton thought he could 'reform the whole colonial empire'[15] was not quite without foundation.

For Carnarvon, Lytton's assets as well as his shortcomings provided a stimulating environment, a source of ideas, and, just as importantly, an opportunity. Stanley had been so much 'master of his work' that Carnarvon felt that he himself could evade making decisions in the face of 'superior workmanship'. When Stanley left his position was 'materially altered'; he felt it necessary now 'to understand and to advise on every question wh. arises. I feel that my opinion is looked for and that it is important in its effect upon the ultimate decision'.[16] Indeed, he believed that his advice would almost always be accepted. Colonial Office papers as well as his own show the benefit gained from his first three months in office. This is not to say that Lytton was somehow a *roi fainéant*, but his work as secretary of state should be judged by his great efforts in relation to four or five special problems in South Africa, in British North America, and, oddly but importantly, the Ionian Islands.[17] His decisions in other matters were generally prompted by a combination of advice from Herman Merivale (the permanent under-secretary) and Carnarvon. Moreover, from early February 1859 Lytton's health (and temperament) caused him to spend long periods at home at Knebworth or taking the waters at Buxton. Carnarvon's Journal records that he was left in 'entire control' of the Colonial Office as a result.[18] Though Derby and other senior ministers kept a watch on sensitive matters, there is no doubting Carnarvon's grasp of official business, the affairs of the colonies, and the nature of the colonial empire. It is small wonder that he acquired a taste for exercising both his expertise and his talents. But he owed something to Lytton in quite another, and more significant, way. By his own account, in addition to their official contact, he had much satisfying conversation with Lytton as a frequent guest at Knebworth. The author of *The Caxtons* appears, in fact, to have done much to form Carnarvon's enthusiasm for those colonies in which were established 'a constitution and a civilization similar to our own'.[19] Upon those colonies – in British North America and Australasia – his 'imperialism' was primarily based.

Following this initiation, Carnarvon was able to contribute authoritatively to questions and debates on colonial topics in the House of Lords. In July 1866, when Derby formed his third ministry, the sometime under-secretary was offered the secretaryship of state. Because he resigned the following March over the Reform Bill he was in office a mere eight months, but his interest in colonial issues was deepened and consolidated. Chief of these in mid-1866 was the projected confederation of the British North American provinces. Carnarvon's predecessor, Edward Cardwell, had worked to bring this to fruition, as Carnarvon never failed to say. He set out, practically from the first moment in office, to ensure that the work was not wasted. By the time he introduced the British North America bill into the House of Lords in February 1867, he had been engaged almost continuously with the issue and with the Canadian and other delegates who had come to London. The whole experience focused Carnarvon's thoughts on three great matters. First, this joining together of separate colonies was an enhancement of responsible government which, in his view, had been brought to pass by a combination of the energy and the vision of colonists, indispensably stimulated and encouraged by the imperial government, and guaranteed by the sovereign authority of parliament. Second, far from sharing the not uncommon belief that such a development would lead to the separation of the new Dominion from the empire, Carnarvon was convinced that it not only saved Canada from absorption by the United States but strengthened the link with Britain. He saw no incompatibility between the creation of a 'colonial nation' with 'aspirations' of its own and imperial unity.[20] These two modes of understanding thenceforward dominated his approaches to colonial relations and suggested to him, perhaps too powerfully, a way of solving problems which were otherwise intractable. The third area in which his ideas were advanced was that of defence. Confederation seemed to Carnarvon to afford to British North America the political strength and the resources which would enable a true sharing of defence responsibilities between the colony and Britain. His resignation deprived him of much chance to try to put this idea into effect. On the other hand, in 1866 he concluded an arrangement with a colony at the other end of the world. The government of Victoria had sent a minister to London to negotiate naval defence with the imperial government. Thanks to Carnarvon, the mission was successful, and Victoria obtained a brand-new ironclad as a gift, in return for guaranteeing advanced docking facilities in Melbourne for ships of the Navy.[21] To him it represented the first step in putting colonial defence on an equitable footing for the first time since Earl Grey's initiative of the late 1840s, by which colonies – those in Australia at least – were required to pay for any portion of their imperial garrisons beyond what the British government decided was necessary for 'imperial purposes'.[22] Again, Carnarvon had no time to follow it up, for, with General Peel and Lord Cranborne (shortly to be Marquess of Salisbury), he resigned from Lord Derby's cabinet in March 1867, outraged by Disraeli's apparent willingness to see the constitution overwhelmed by what they regarded as excessive and unjustifiable numbers of the urban working classes.[23] Two years later, any attempt Carnarvon might have hoped to make to resume his initiative was made extraordinarily difficult by the new Liberal government.

In 1869–70 the colonial policy of Lord Granville, with Gladstone's full approval, abrogated what Carnarvon had tried to consolidate in 1866–67 – the maintenance of military relations between Britain and the self-governing colonies on a new level of mutuality. This involved especially those continuing responsibility of the imperial government for the defence of the whole empire, but with those colonies having responsible government increasingly sharing the cost and organization of their particular defences. The Liberal approach, partly a delayed response to the selfish behaviour of

New Zealand during the 1860s, partly the consummation of a doctrinaire view, was to end all possibility of dispute by removing every regular British soldier from Canada, Australia, and New Zealand. Carnarvon uttered a passionate protest at what appeared to be this misguided colonial policy. To his mind it struck at the integrity of the empire; he feared that it might indicate that the government was, as had been suggested, truly wishing to 'get rid of' the colonies by at least the appearance of withdrawing from their defence. He could hardly have been reassured by Gladstone's assertion, during a debate on colonial relations in the House of Commons, that he could see no reason to maintain any 'political or administrative connection' with Canada and its like.[24] Carnarvon's anxiety was real, and it may well have intensified his sense of responsibility for colonial relations: Canadian ministers were chief amongst those who encouraged him.[25] It presumably also increased his distance from the Liberals, and, although the ordinary processes of party readjustments were strong, it might have helped his return to the Conservative front bench, with Salisbury, at about the same time as his speech in February 1870 attacking Granville's policy.[26] Equally crucial was the connection which we can make with Disraeli. A condition of the return of Carnarvon and Salisbury to the party fold was that they need not acknowledge Disraeli as leader, for they had not forgiven him for 1867.[27] Two years later, however, Disraeli consolidated his claims to leadership with two famous speeches, both of which contained significant, if brief, references to the empire. The second of these, at the Crystal Palace in June 1872,[28] famously contained a scathing attack upon 'the attempts of Liberalism to effect the disintegration of the Empire of England'. Disraeli was wildly unjust in claiming that disintegrationist policies had been in place 'since the advent of Liberalism, forty years ago'. But he referred also to 'the moral and political aspects' of empire. It was precisely these which, in Carnarvon's view, the Liberals had not only neglected but, by their 1869–70 policies, positively weakened. He could hardly have failed to be attracted by Disraeli's dictum, that 'no Minister in this country will do his duty who neglects any opportunity of reconstructing as much as possible our Colonial Empire'. We may reasonably suppose that the Crystal Palace speech helped to reconcile Carnarvon to the prospect of Disraeli as leader, so that he, rather more than Salisbury, was willing and anxious to accept office as secretary of state for the colonies in 1874. It is even possible to speculate as to whether Disraeli drew on Carnarvon's 1870 attack on Granville.

The Conservative victory in the February 1874 general election seemed to promise well for the work of a vigorous and imaginative minister, for the party's majority was large, and the first since 1846. Carnarvon's own reputation was high both at home and abroad, and his appointment was welcomed, even by some Liberals.[29] Carnarvon was moreover in touch with colonial affairs, not only because he had enjoyed some correspondence with, especially, members of the Canadian government after 1867, but because his cousin and confidant, Robert Herbert, had been a senior official in the Colonial Office since 1870 and permanent under-secretary since May 1871: it is difficult to over-estimate the significance of that relationship in preparing Carnarvon, in a very practical sense, for the work he would undertake in 1874–78.[30] At the beginning of the ministry, even more important in easing Carnarvon's path was the new prime minister: disillusionment came later.

Carnarvon approached his prospects most earnestly. One of the most illuminating utterances in the Carnarvon archive is in a letter written early in February 1874. Not for the first or last time, Carnarvon took a kind of prompt from an Australian colonist: in this case, Edward Wilson, proprietor of the Melbourne *Argus*, sometime radical but by 1874 one of the chief defenders of 'property and intelligence' against 'democracy'. Though he claimed higher motives, it was chiefly in that role that Wilson wrote urging that whoever took the Colonial Office in the new administration, it must not be Sir Charles Adderley, an aspirant to the post, and well known for his 'Colonial Reform' theories antagonistic to any imperial initiative in relation to the self-governing colonies.[31] That much was no doubt clear to Carnarvon, as Adderley had been his under-secretary in 1866–67, had recently published a valuable work on colonial policy, and had welcomed the Liberals' colonial military policy. He had no need to delve into Wilson's hidden meanings,[32] but, in the wake of 1869–70, no one was more alive to what appeared to be the possibility of separation provoked, not by a colony but by the British government itself. It was thus appropriate for Carnarvon to reply to Wilson with words expressing his general view more positively than was his wont. Whether or not he became secretary of state, he wrote, 'I know & care enough about Colonial connection to spare no pains myself & to render any assistance in my power to others to maintain unimpaired that which I prize so highly the integrity of the Empire'.[33] The theme of 'the integrity of the Empire' was to bedevil Carnarvon just over a decade later, when he attempted his final (as it turned out) contribution to the good governance of that same empire as lord lieutenant of Ireland. But, entering the Colonial Office in 1874, he believed that his task was to repair the damage to 'colonial connection' which he considered had been wrought under the Liberals. It is this which gives us the best clue to Carnarvon's next four years of colonial policy.

Bulwer Lytton in 1858 might have believed, as it was said, that he could reform the colonies. Carnarvon was less ambitious in 1874, but he nevertheless undertook one task which was arguably impossible, and another which was certainly so. In each case his own ambition and over-estimation of his political capacities had something to do with the disappointments which he suffered. Carnarvon was susceptible not, as Disraeli thought, to flattery[34] but to high-flying optimism. To this extent, it was not necessarily his good fortune that during 1874 he was approached on colonial subjects by James Anthony Froude, the essayist and historian, and Sir Charles Gavan Duffy, former Young Ireland rebel and then a politician in Victoria. Their contributions to Carnarvon's future were very different, but of mixed merit in each case. Carnarvon was well acquainted with Froude,[35] whose articles in the first issues of the new series of *Fraser's Magazine*, of which he was editor, in 1870, linked concern for the colonies with patriotism. Duffy, on the other hand, was unknown to Carnarvon when he presented a letter of introduction from the governor of Victoria in June 1874,[36] and his importance in Carnarvon's life dates from a visit to Highclere in August. Froude and Duffy had basically common concerns, at least to begin with. Almost as soon as the new government was in office, Froude told Carnarvon that he intended to visit Australia to look into the practical aspects of encouraging closer relations, probably to do with defence.[37] Later Carnarvon persuaded Froude to go first to South Africa, on what turned out to be the famous 'secret mission'[38] in connection with Carnarvon's design to solve the sub-continent's problems by federating the colonies and states. Duffy also had defence in mind and spoke about it at great length at Highclere and in a subsequent memorandum of great eloquence and expanded ideas (and flattering to both Carnarvon and the Conservatives).[39]

In any more comprehensive study it would be unfair to both Carnarvon and the affairs of the British empire to give exclusive attention to these two individuals or the episodes with which they are connected. Yet separately and together their relations with Carnarvon have much to do with his hopes and policies then and later. South Africa furnished him with his greatest project during 1874–78, and the complications it presented, his falling short of success, are largely to do with Froude and with Carnarvon's reliance on him for assessments on the spot. Froude's activities in the Cape Colony, his capacity to antagonize both its governor and its ministry, were a nice demonstration of how unwise it might be to send a 'literary gentleman' on a delicate, indeed supposedly secret, political mission. We might well share the wonderment of Lord Blachford (formerly Frederic Rogers of the Colonial Office) that Robert Herbert, 'with his Australian experience', and the understanding which he certainly had of colonial sensitivity to English 'interference', agreed to it.[40] We might just as well wonder what possessed Carnarvon to make his choice. The answer points to one or more of his flaws – a tendency to be unduly impressed by ideas, and by the prospect of large views and reason prevailing over prejudice and pettiness.

In very different circumstances, Duffy brought out some of this failing in Carnarvon: for it was Duffy who gave Carnarvon reason to hope that, in a reversal of the Liberal policy of 1869–70, the self-governing colonies might again accept British garrisons. Carnarvon had, as he put it, 'always resented' the withdrawal of the troops, and resented even more the manner in which it was carried out; and he believed in the superior value of 'the older and … better system of the Empire'.[41] If the restoration could be achieved, it would be a coup, for it would undo what the Liberals had done, but on the basis of a new arrangement which would fully engage the colonies in their own defence, with hardly any imperial expense. This time, 'his Australian experience' enabled Herbert to warn Carnarvon about Duffy's standing in Australia, and thus against placing too much reliance on his optimism.[42]

Carnarvon proceeded very cautiously, but extended the idea to include Canada. In what may be called the highest point of his appreciation of Disraeli, he explained his 'notions' to the Prime Minister and received his 'heartiest support'. According to Carnarvon, Disraeli (who was, conceivably, hardly aware of the existence of Australia) 'wanted to send "the bearskin" back to Canada to represent the visible sovereignty of the Empire'.[43] Carnarvon went ahead with a very discreet inquiry into the possibilities, but seems to have been prepared for the generally discouraging responses he received. But there came, in November 1875, a surprise request from Victoria for 'two or more Batteries of artillery & one wing or more of Infantry'.[44] Carnarvon eagerly took it up. One of his bitterest disappointments followed. Disraeli at first gave what seemed to be the most enthusiastic support. 'I look upon the restoration of our military relations with our Colonies,' he wrote, 'as a question of high policy, which ought never to be absent from our thoughts. The question involves social, & political, as well as military, considerations, & you may rely on my earnest support of any steps, on your part, to accomplish this great end'.[45] Gathorne Hardy, secretary of state for war, on the other hand, fobbed off the proposal for technical reasons; but the real problem was political. Hardy was 'quite in favour of drawing the Colonies closer by all means', but reminded Carnarvon that 'the self-defence of Colonies is upheld by many of our friends as well as opponents'.[46] Disraeli gave Carnarvon no help in cabinet. The Victorian request was accordingly rejected; and the discovery that Disraeli's interest in the colonies was so marginal as to be nugatory was, as much as anything, the beginning of Carnarvon's second estrangement from the Conservative leader.[47]

Duffy and Duffy's ideas had yet more influence. In his memorandum on imperial defence he elaborated also his belief that the general political relations of the colonies with Britain could be drawn much closer by means of an imperial council, and that Carnarvon was the man to bring it to pass.[48] Again, Carnarvon was cautious and, under Herbert's advice, did nothing about it. Still, the idea was attractive and helped to turn his mind in the direction of imperial federation. More than this, Duffy appeared to Carnarvon as a great example of the value of 'colonial connection', for here was a former Irish rebel, having held high office under the Crown in Victoria, so far removed from disaffection as to be remarkably anxious to consolidate the imperial connection.[49] A decade later, as we shall see, this was to have a further impact on Carnarvon's statesmanship.

The 'Beaconsfieldism' attacked by Gladstone with such effect in 1879, and the 'imperialism' to which Robert Lowe was to refer in a savage 1878 article, were not of Carnarvon's making, nor was it really to do with colonies. For all his patriotism, and although he approved of, for instance, the coup by which 'the gate of the Eastern empire'[50] was secured by the assertion of control over the Suez Canal, Carnarvon had no stomach for the kind of aggressive stance which formed so much of Beaconsfield's Eastern policy in 1876–78. In January 1878, Carnarvon, written off by Beaconsfield-Disraeli as 'a weak enthusiast dreaming over the celebration of High Mass in St. Sofia', in the company of various 'priests and professors',[51] resigned from the cabinet because his idea of empire had ceased to coincide with Disraeli's. It remains the case, however, that when Gladstone attacked 'the ambition of Lord Beaconsfield', he did so not only on account of Afghan villagers and the movement of Indian troops into the Mediterranean, but because of the annexation of Fiji and the Transvaal, of which he made much in his Midlothian campaign. For those annexations Carnarvon was responsible. Were these akin to 'Beaconsfieldism', or the 'imperialism' into which, as Gladstone put it, Lord Beaconsfield wished to lead the country? There are indicators besides the rhetoric of a political opponent.

Carnarvon's undertakings in 1874–78 were a curious, but not a haphazard, mixture.[52] For instance, no doubt the partition of West Africa can be said to have begun as early as the annexation of Lagos in 1861, but the acquisition of the Gold Coast protectorates in 1875 seems to have been simply the consummation of two old-fashioned policies – to rationalize and limit West African commitments, and to strike at the institution of slavery. The Perak war of 1875, brought on in the Malay peninsula by ambitious local officials, extended 'the imperial frontier in the tropics', but Carnarvon accepted it reluctantly as the unwelcome fruit of the activities of the men on the spot. Elsewhere it was different. In justifying the acceptance of the cession of Fiji, he cited the need for 'an English government' not only to control 'English crime' in the South Pacific, but to safeguard communications between Sydney and North America. His cousin and chief official, Robert Herbert, was sceptical of this, and lamented that New Guinea was not annexed instead, because, especially in view of German movements, it bore much more on the interests of the Australian colonies, and therefore of the empire.[53] But it was Fiji for which Carnarvon could clearly justify imperial expenditure.

Carnarvon's South African undertaking had a much larger geopolitical aspect to it: he was deeply impressed with the value of the Cape to British world trade and strategy. We should be wary, however, of seeking to assimilate the annexation of the Transvaal in 1877 to the partition of Africa – and thus, however pedantically, to imperialism in the sense established by J.A. Hobson or even Robinson and Gallagher.[54] Carnarvon's policy better fits with a view of the problems of the sub-continent which dates back to the 1850s, problems which Carnarvon hoped to bring to an end by confederating British colonies with 'Dutch' republics. Certainly an unusual use of the power of the state, the annexation harked back to Sir Harry Smith – though not to Sir George Grey's scheme of 1858[55] – rather than forward to the 'scramble'. The Froude mission, moreover, despite its disastrous reality, was part of Carnarvon's wish to persuade Cape Colony ministers, through the governor in the first instance, in effect to emulate their Canadian counterparts of a decade earlier, by recognizing the utility of federation and using their pre-eminent weight in the sub-continent to lead a movement towards it.[56] But, when the Cape ministers resisted such overtures, Carnarvon publicly undertook a confederation campaign. Privately he became willing, even after a time anxious, to challenge a self-governing colonial ministry who obstructed a policy 'of great [imperial] importance'. Indeed, he boasted to Disraeli of the victory he foresaw for the secretary of state, of a kind which had not been seen for a generation.[57] It was a curious aberration in the behaviour of one who was, in general, so optimistic about the compatibility of colonial self-government with 'the integrity of the empire'.

But then, Carnarvon saw the future of the empire as partly dependent upon an active role for the imperial government. In an important address in November 1878, which will shortly be examined in more detail and which can be safely regarded as a considered utterance, he referred to the need of 'great colonies endowed with free and responsible self-government' to continue to look for 'the help of the Home Government' to settle 'great constitutional questions'.[58] He was cautious, though not cautious enough, in applying this dictum. His attitude to the Victorian political and constitutional crisis of the late 1860s had been a case in point. In office in 1866–67, he kept clear of the local dispute, but he maintained the imperial government's need to supervise and if necessary control the actions of the governor: a subject on which, by a speech from opposition in the Lords in 1868, he was made an object of hostility and of ridicule in the Victorian legislative assembly.[59] His view was further indicated in the speech with which he introduced the British North America Bill in the House of Lords in 1867, and explains his intervention in the Canadian dispute about the Dominion's obligations to construct the trans-continental railway which had been the price of British Columbia's entry to the confederation.[60]

Similarly, in the very carefully composed letter by which in 1874 he drew the attention of Victorian and New South Wales governments to his hopes for co-operation in military defence, he described the presence of a British garrison in the colonies as, amongst other things – an echo of Disraeli here – 'an external symbol of Empire'. This is of particular importance. As affecting his hopes for a restoration of military relations, and for the 'message' which could be read into it, it might have been unwise. His words were by no means intended in any but a benign sense, but they were open to misinterpretation. Hence perhaps the response of Henry Parkes, premier of New South Wales. He was shortly afterwards to assure Carnarvon that 'every step that tends to make [the Colonies] more consciously a part of the Empire will be a great national gain'. But, giving his views on the garrison proposal, he referred to the withdrawal of the troops as having been 'popularly regarded here as the acknowledgement by Great Britain – not only of the political freedom of the colonies, but of their innate power to provide for themselves; as the removal of the last symbol of Imperial authority in the management of Australian affairs.'[61] Such a combination of words was inauspicious for Carnarvon's hopes.

We have, then, a context for Carnarvon's Address on 'Imperial Administration' to the Edinburgh Philosophical Society on 5 November 1878. Ten months earlier, by resigning from the Beaconsfield ministry, Carnarvon had ended four years as colonial secretary. His address was very much that of an Englishman for whom it was difficult to conceive of colonial relations except in terms of the continued prosperity and pre-eminence of England – 'and, thank God, in the word England is included Scotland',[62] he said, perhaps less than tactfully in the circumstances – upon which indeed the viability of the empire depended. This created, as we have just seen, problems for his ideas of mutuality between Britain and the self-governing colonies. Yet that self-government coupled with continuing imperial effectiveness, is essential to his remarks on 'imperialism'. This he described in this speech as a 'new word ... which has crept in amongst us'. A new word it was, in a British context,[63] but it was no new phenomenon for

Carnarvon. If in what he said there is a touch of a vision of a 'new' age, it was not of the kind which J.A. Hobson was to saddle with the word 'imperialism'. Considering the 'new word', he said: 'I have heard of Imperial policy, and Imperial interests, but … [i]n one sense the British Constitution knows nothing of Imperialism. It would be unfair, however, to deny that the British Constitution recognises much that partakes of an Imperial character.'[64] He was therefore prepared to accept 'imperial' and 'imperialism' so long as they could be properly understood as referring to authentic elements of the British experience of empire. He proceeded to distinguish between 'a true and a false Imperialism', first 'by ascertaining what it is not'. Alarmed by the sight of 'vast standing armies – great empires casting their colossal shadow over the smaller States' in Europe, he emphasized that true imperialism was not 'Caesarism… that base second-hand copy of continental despotism–that bastard monarch begotten in the slime of political and financial corruption'.[65]

For Carnarvon, these were exceptionally strong words. But he was mindful not merely of the military perils which the German triumph in 1870–71 had so much increased, for, he continued, Englishmen must themselves take care. They needed to remember that, if there were to be such a thing as English imperialism, it could not override the constitutional need for parliament and the crown 'to act in concert and in reference to each other' – that is, parliamentary government. If this was a veiled reference to Disraeli's recent policies from which (as Gladstone emphasized) parliament had been largely excluded, so also, considering one of the most famous phrases in the Crystal Palace speech, Disraeli might have been his target when he deprecated 'the words, "A great England and a little England"', and warning that imperialism was not 'mere bulk of territory and multiplication of subjects'. It is of a kind with Carnarvon's distaste for adding, in 1876, 'Empress of India' to the Queen's titles, partly because the new Royal Titles Act was not drawn so as to include the colonies, partly because the title had associations which were 'at least barbarous'.[66]

So much for what imperialism was not. Carnarvon was less comfortable in ascribing a positive meaning to imperialism, 'if indeed it has meaning'. He mentioned obligations owed beyond the seas, and 'a common unity' akin to an individual's patriotism. But he cited Canning and Walpole in warning that patriotism too could be true or false, and concluded that the truth in each case depended on acknowledging that 'we cannot with impunity divorce our system of politics from our system of morals'. One might say that this was a little vague, and Carnarvon turned with apparent relief to 'the great empire of England'. Here he found 'the true strength of our Imperialism', chiefly 'the self-government of the great Anglo-Saxon Colonies'. He allowed himself to dream of 'a great English-speaking community, united together in a peaceful confederation'. He dreamed further of 'a picture so vast and noble that the mind loses itself in the contemplation of what might be under the beneficent rule of Great Britain'. In a sense which is today indiscriminately disapproved, Carnarvon's reference was to the 'our native fellow-subjects – races struggling to emerge into civilization', to whom 'it is our part to give wise laws, good government'. Fulfilling our duties to such people, he said, was also true imperialism. Given peace and sufficient funds, much could be accomplished. How? By using the existing structure of the empire. 'To me', he said, 'the Colonial Empire of Great Britain seems one of the most magnificent pictures of administration that the labours of man have ever created, or that the eye of man has ever seen.' Only one precedent existed, 'the great Empire of Rome'. From Rome he drew precedents and illustrations: discordant nationalities; conflicting religions; the great problem of having to try to reconcile 'the Western and Oriental elements of the Empire' – which, he desponded, they had failed to do, as had the English; and especially, the difficulty of 'how to maintain, extend, or modify their frontiers'. He ended his discourse with the warning that nothing could be accomplished unless the body politic of England, 'the heart of the Empire', were kept healthy.

Carnarvon's disquisition on imperialism was the concluding part of his Edinburgh address. There was much more to it, chiefly describing in some detail the duties of the colonial secretary and the work of the department. We may neglect most of this for present purposes. But Carnarvon had begun his speech with a hint that, much as he would wish to avoid politically controversial remarks, he might not be able to do so. Nor did he, for only in part could his views on imperialism and the empire have been congenial to either his late colleagues or Gladstonian Liberals. His references to administration and, most startlingly, to Rome were surely anathema to such as Robert Lowe and Gladstone. Shortly after the Edinburgh address was delivered, Lowe – a friend since the Reform controversy of mid-1866 – wrote to Carnarvon congratulating him, with a rather awkward reservation. 'I have but one difference with it', he acknowledged 'I want to make the term "Imperial" a term [of] reproach as "a spirited Foreign Policy" has become and not as a term of praise for anything however good that thing may be in itself.'[67] Carnarvon could hardly have agreed. 'Imperial Administration' looks indeed, rather like a mild reply, perhaps rebuke, to Lowe. Both he and Gladstone had recently published their views on imperialism and Britain's imperial character.[68] These were undisguised attacks on the Beaconsfield ministry, a foretaste of Gladstone's shortly forthcoming Midlothian campaign. Small wonder that Lowe demurred at Carnarvon's acceptance of 'imperial', let alone 'imperialism', for his own views were uncompromisingly hostile. 'What does Imperialism mean?', he wrote, 'It means the assertion of absolute force over others ... the triumph of Imperialism is most complete when power is most clearly manifested; ... Imperialism is the apotheosis of violence.'

We need not here inquire into the accuracy of Lowe's account of recent and more remote history, but it is no injustice to him to represent his conclusions by this selection. Imperialism for him had nothing to do with the self-government of Anglo-Saxon colonies; and he contrasted the colonies with the Roman empire which fell because Rome, itself scrupulous about freedom, kept conquered provinces in subjection. 'No doubt', he explained to Carnarvon, 'when we governed the Colonies from Downing Street of which I have had some experience [in New South Wales in the 1840s] we were acting imperially but when we allowed them to govern themselves we became something much better than imperial.'[69] Gladstone's article had much in common with Lowe's. He was a trifle less extreme in his language, though no less anxious to draw a distinction between the 'free congenital communities' comprising the 'transmarine Colonial Empire', and the 'territorial aggrandisement, backed by military display' which was, he alleged, the Tory party's 'imperialism'. Though not unwilling to refer to 'the Imperial State of the United Kingdom', he dwelt on the colonies, restating his long-held view that they were best regarded in the light of ancient Greek colonization, and deprecating those (the Conservatives) who wished to maintain them by 'administrative connection, and the shadow of political subordination'. No wonder that Carnarvon so emphatically praised the administrative character of the empire, and that he linked it with the duty of offering government and improvement to other races, something which Gladstone quite omitted from his view of 'England's Mission'.

Carnarvon's commitment to the colonial empire and the meaning it had for him continued to occupy much of his political life. He willingly accepted, from the new Liberal government, chairmanship of the Royal Commission on Colonial Defence of 1879–81. Carnarvon had become more than ever convinced that Britain's future was inseparable from her connection with the colonies. He increasingly inclined towards the idea of an imperial federation; and he continued to be willing to contemplate such territorial expansion as would secure the interests of colonies, provided those colonies were willing to bear a financial burden in the process. More than that, about to visit Canada in 1883, he expressed the belief that English politics had reached a stage when 'some at least of our most perplexing questions may perhaps be better read by the light of Colonial than our domestic experience'.[70] He was unspecific, but one such question is easily identified. Beginning in 1883, a renewed correspondence with Gavan Duffy was to do more than anything else to form Carnarvon's belief that the union of England and Ireland could be – and, in the interests of 'the Empire overseas' as well as the United Kingdom, ought urgently to be – saved by applying colonial experience; and he pressed such thoughts on Salisbury.[71] He may again have been misled by the very virtues of his belief, and what seemed to him and to others its rational possibilities. His Irish administration of 1885–86, during which his desire to make a cautious exploration of some form of Home Rule became apparent, is largely to be explained in these terms. Nor did his conviction diminish when he was (as Robert Herbert put it) 'shunted into a siding'[72] as a result of that administration. But there is nothing more tragic in his career than the rebuff which Lord Salisbury delivered to him in the name of the 'mandate' which he had from the party and the country about Ireland. It was sustained even unto their last exchange of letters before Carnarvon's death in 1890, and arose (again) from misinterpretation of a phrase. Salisbury excluded him from the Tory cabinet of July 1886 for having earlier referred to a desire to satisfy Irish 'national aspirations'. This was incompatible, in Salisbury's opinion, with that very integrity of the empire to which Carnarvon was so much attached.[73] Carnarvon never again held office. As an illustrious private individual, extending his experience despite a serious decline in his health, he visited Australia in 1887–88, calling at the Cape on the way; and this episode, at once lengthier and more profoundly moving than his earlier tour of Canada, produced a great deal of perceptive commentary and reflection.[74]

It seems, then, that Carnarvon's 1878 address on 'Imperial Administration' pretty well defined him as an 'imperialist' of what Henry Parkes later called 'the better sort';[75] nor would he have denied the label, and he fitted well with the ideas associated with such as Sir John Seeley, whose *Expansion of England* lectures were published just a few years later in 1883.[76] Gladstone and Lowe were decidedly 'anti-imperialist': and it is specially ironical that Gladstone, as prime minister in 1882, was responsible for that quintessentially representative act of the 'new imperialism', the occupation of Egypt. In 1878, unlike Carnarvon, their horror of what they perceived as the cast of mind characteristic of Lord Beaconsfield, and the brand of patriotism with which he associated himself, was so great that they could get no further than party contest in deploying the 'new word'. Carnarvon was not far from them in deprecating Beaconsfieldism; but neither of them exhibited anything like the breadth of his consideration of empire, or the uses which he believed had been served, and could be better served, by it. Thus did they invest 'imperialism' with a narrow and polemical use. At this, the end of the twentieth century, respect for empire, even as represented by the true colonies, seems practically to have disappeared; 'post-colonialism' prevails, and most understanding of 'imperialism' accords with the harsh views of the Gladstonians. It may be, however, that Carnarvon's ideas and ideals, now relegated, have a good deal more to tell us about the practice of imperial governance, not only in his own experience of twenty-odd years before 1878, but of the years from which imperialism is supposed to have sprung, and those during which, variously described, it flourished. What, if anything, they tell us about the long reputation of the Conservatives as the party of empire, is a consideration outside the scope of this essay.

NOTES

1. See R. Koebner and H.D. Schmidt, *Imperialism: The Story and Significance of a Political Word 1840–1960* (Cambridge, 1964).
2. Robert Stewart, *The Foundation of the Conservative Party 1830–1867* (London, 1978), 272. See also: Richard Shannon, *The Age of Disraeli, 1868–1881: The Rise of Tory Democracy* (London, 1992); E.H.H. Green, *The Crisis of Conservatism: The Politics, Economics and Ideology of the British Conservative Party, 1880–1914* (London: New York, 1995).
3. Probably the latest consideration of the topic is John Legge, 'A New Imperialism in the Late 19th Century? Revisiting an Old Debate', in Brook Barrington (ed.), *Empires, Imperialism and Southeast Asia* (Melbourne, 1997). The essay gives large attention to David Fieldhouse's contributions to the study of imperialism.
4. Cf. Bruce Knox (ed.), *The Queensland Years of Robert Herbert* (St. Lucia, 1977), 5–6.
5. 3 *Hansard*, 130 (31 Jan. 1854), col.9.
6. W.F. Monypenny and G.E. Buckle, *The Life of Benjamin Disraeli* (6 vols., London, 1910–1920) (hereafter, M&B), IV, 119.
7. Journal, Feb. 1858, Add.Mss. 60892, fos.19–20. References to the two collections of Carnarvon Papers will be as follows: the collection in the Public Record Office, Kew, is in PRO 30/6, which will be rendered here as CP (followed by the volume number). The papers in the British Library will be cited (as in this note) by their Add. Mss. numbers.
8. Ibid., fos.20–22.
9. See CP 131–2.
10. Journal, Feb .1858 and Aug. 1858, 22–36. Add.Mss. 60892, fos.19–20.
11. M&B, III, 569.
12. Disraeli to Derby, 25 Feb. 1858, M&B, IV, 118, III, 569; 3 *Hansard* 136 (8 Feb. 1855) cols. 1337–8.
13. Diary of Gathorne Hardy, 12 Jan. 1859, A.E. Gathorne Hardy (ed.), *Gathorne Hardy, First Earl of Cranbrook* (London, 1910), I, 126; Disraeli to Derby, 20, 27 Dec. 1858, Papers of the 14th Earl of Derby (Liverpool City Libraries), Box 145/5.
14. *The Caxtons* (any edition), Part XII, chap. VI; see also, Part XVII.
15. J.R. Godley to C.B. Adderley, 21 Aug. 1858, W.S. Childe-Pemberton, *Life of Lord Norton* (London, 1909), 172.
16. Journal, Aug. 1858, Add. Mss. 60892, fos.22–36.
17. See, for example, Bruce Knox, 'British Policy and the Ionian Islands, 1847–1864: Nationalism and Imperial Administration', *English Historical Review*, XCIX (1984), 503–29.
18. Journal, 1 July 1859, Add. Mss. 60892, fos.57–8 and *passim*.
19. Ibid., 68–70; T.H.S. Escott, *Life of Edward Bulwer, 1st Baron Lytton* (London, 1910), 303 (citing an interview with Lord Carnarvon). The quotation is from *The Caxtons* (Knebworth edn, London, 1874), 327.
20. See Bruce A. Knox, 'Conservative Imperialism 1858–1874: Bulwer Lytton, Lord Carnarvon, and Canadian Confederation', *International History Review*, VI (1984), 333–57.
21. See Victorian application, Carnarvon's Cabinet circular, and replies of colleagues, in CP 166.
22. See, for example, D.C. Gordon, *The Dominion Partnership in Imperial Defense, 1870–1914*

(Baltimore, 1965), 2–4.
23. Stewart, *Conservative Party*, 362. See evidence of bitterness: Add. Mss. 61070, fos.209–11; Diary, 9 July 1867. Add. Mss. 60899.
24. Bruce Knox, 'Imperial Consequences of Constitutional Problems in New South Wales and Victoria 1865–1870', *Australian Historical Studies*, 21 (1985), 515–33; 3 *Hansard*, 199 (14 Feb. 1870); Add. Mss. 60901, Diary, 12 Dec. 1869; 3 *Hansard*, 200, col.1905.
25. See, for example, correspondence in CP 171; Diary, *idem*.
26. The process of rejoining is recorded in Add. Mss. 60902, Diary, beginning 4 Feb. 1870.
27. See, ibid., esp. 25 Feb. 1870.
28. Extract in M&B, V, 194–6.
29. See, for example, R. Herbert to Carnarvon, 9 Feb. 1874. T.B. Potter, A.J. Mundella to Carnarvon, 19 Feb., 21 Feb. 1874, Add. Mss. 60791, fos.39–43. Add. Mss. 60854, fos.94, 97–8. On the significance of the change, however, cf. C.C. Eldridge, *England's Mission: The Imperial Idea in the Age of Gladstone and Disraeli* (London, 1973).
30. Carnarvon's Diary shows close contact with Herbert in 1870–74, including political consultation: Add. Mss. 60791, 60792, *passim*.
31. Edward Wilson to Carnarvon, 9 Feb. 1874, Add. Mss. 60854, fo.89; unaddressed draft by Carnarvon, 12 Feb. 1874, ibid., fo.92. Cf. similar request from Secretary of the Colonial Institute, encl. in Gathorne Hardy to Disraeli, 15 Feb. 1874, Bodleian Library, Disraeli Papers, B/XX/Ha/68.
32. Cf. Knox, 'Imperial Consequences'. Wilson and others were to be disappointed in this respect when Carnarvon failed to intervene in the Victorian crisis of 1877: see A.G. Serle, 'New Light on the Colonial Office, Sir George Bowen and the Victorian Constitutional Crises', *Historical Studies*, 13 (1969).
33. Unaddressed draft by Carnarvon, 12 Feb. 1874, Add. Mss. 60854, fo.92.
34. M. Corry to Sir Henry Ponsonby, 13 May 1878, M&B, VI, 419–20.
35. Diary, 5 Feb. 1870, Add. Mss. 60902; Diary, 2 Nov. 1871, ibid., 60903.
36. Duffy to Carnarvon, 24 June 1874, CP 43, fos.211–212.
37. Froude to Carnarvon, 4 March 1874, A.H. Hardinge, *The Life of ... Carnarvon* (3 vols, London, 1926), II, 176.
38. Diary, 3 May 1874, Add. Mss. 60906; Carnarvon to Sir Stafford Northcote, 15 Aug. 1874, CP 7, fos.27–8.
39. Add.Mss.60906, Diary, 20 Aug. 1874; Memorandum by Sir G. Duffy, 16 Sept. 1874, on the organization of the Colonial Empire. Add. Mss. 60812, fos.193–213.
40. Blachford to Sir Henry Taylor, 28 Dec. 1875, G.E. Marindin, *Letters of Frederic Lord Blachford* (London, 1896).
41. Draft letter Carnarvon to Sir William Stawell, acting-Governor of Victoria, 18 Nov. 1874, CP 47, fos.57–61. He addressed Sir Hercules Robinson (New South Wales) in identical terms.
42. R. Herbert to Lord Carnarvon, 25 Sept. 1874, Add. Mss. 60791, fos.123–31.
43. Diary, 29 Sept. 1874, Add. Mss. 60906. See also, ibid., 30 Sept. 1874.
44. A. Michie (Victorian Agent-General) to CO, 29 Nov. 1875, CO 309/113, fo.382. Cf. earlier, similar request, G. Verdon (Victorian Agent-General) to CO, 21 Oct. 1870, referring to 'reciprocal obligations of Great Britain and her Colonial Possessions'. CO 309/96, fos.347–51.
45. Disraeli to Carnarvon, 8 Dec. 1875, CP 11, fo.108.
46. Hardy to Carnarvon, 13 Dec. 1875, CP 12, fos.133–6. Cf., Canadian prime minister, Alexander Mackenzie's impression, in June 1875, of the untoward views of 'the commercial interests, the landed classes, and the general public', cited in Richard A. Preston, *Canada and 'Imperial Defense': A study of the origins of the British Commonwealth's Defense Organization, 1867–1919* (Durham, N.C., 1967), 76.
47. Cf. Carnarvon to Duke of Cambridge, 22 March 1876, CP 13; Hardinge, II, 77.
48. See above, fn. 39.
49. See ref. in 'Imperial Administration', Address by Lord Carnarvon to the Edinburgh Philosophical Institution, 5 Nov. 1878, in R. Herbert (ed.), *Essays, Addresses and Translations by ... Carnarvon* (3 vols., London, 1896), III, 6.
50. CP 11, fo.100, Carnarvon to Disraeli, 29 Nov. 1875.

51. Beaconsfield to the Queen, 6 Oct. 1877. Royal Archives, B53/19; 3 Nov. 1877, ibid., B53/36, Cabinet Reports of Prime Ministers to the Crown 1868–1916 (microfilm: Harvester Press, 1974).
52. See W.D. McIntyre, *The Imperial Frontier in the Tropics, 1865–1875* (London, 1967); C.F. Goodfellow, *Great Britain and South African Confederation, 1868–1881* (Cape Town, 1966); Eldridge, *England's Mission.*
53. Herbert to Carnarvon, 10 April 1874, Add. Mss. 60791.
54. R. Robinson and J. Gallagher, with Alice Denny, *Africa and the Victorians: The Official Mind of Imperialism* (London, 1965)
55. See minute by Carnarvon on this, 7 Jan. 1859, CO 48/390, fos.499–505.
56. See correspondence with Sir Henry Barkly (Governor of the Cape) during 1874 in CP 32, esp. Carnarvon to Barkly, 27 May, 24 June, 22 Aug., Barkly to Carnarvon, 6 July.
57. Carnarvon to Barkly, 4 Aug. 1875, CP 32; CP 11, Carnarvon to Disraeli, 15 July, 2 Sept. 1875.
58. 'Imperial Adminstration', in *Essays and Addresses*, 9.
59. Knox, 'Imperial Consequences', 515 and *passim.*
60. See C.W. de Kiewiet and F.H. Underhill (eds.), *Dufferin–Carnarvon Correspondence 1874–1878* (Toronto, 1955), *passim*, esp. Carnarvon to Dufferin, 17 June, 30 July 1874.
61. Parkes to Carnarvon, 31 July 1875, CP 46, fo.64; H. Parkes to Sir Hercules Robinson, 26 April 1875, enc. in Robinson to Carnarvon, 7 May 1875, CP 25, fos.212–17. See also, Sir W. Stawell to Carnarvon (Secret & confidential), 24 Feb. 1875, CO 309/113, fos.35–40.
62. *Essays and Addresses*, 29.
63. Ibid., 21–2. See, Koebner and Schmidt, *Imperialism.*
64. *Essays and Addresses*, 22.
65. Ibid., 23.
66. Carnarvon to Disraeli, 21 Feb. 1876,. CP 11, fo.117.
67. Lowe to Carnarvon, c.10 Nov. 1878, Add. Mss. 60854, fos.146–7.
68. W.E. Gladstone, 'England's Mission', *Nineteenth Century*, (Sept. 1878), 560–84; R. Lowe, 'Imperialism', *Fortnightly Review*, CXLII, New Series (Oct. 1878) 453–65.
69. Lowe to Carnarvon, c.10 Nov. 1878, Add. Mss 60854, fos.146–7.
70. Carnarvon to Sir J. Macdonald, 17 July 1883, National Archives of Canada, Macdonald Papers, Vol.395, pt. 1.
71. Add. Mss. 60821 (Duffy–Carnarvon correspondence), Carnarvon to Salisbury, 25 Dec. 1884; Add. Mss. 60760, fos.13–14, draft of letter by Salisbury, 21 March 1885, ibid., fos.18–21, 5; Duffy's MS., 'Ireland's Place in the Federation of the Empire', ibid., fos.31–36.
72. Herbert to Carnarvon, 9 Jan. 1886, Add. Mss 60795, fo.73.
73. Salisbury to Carnarvon, 25 July 1886; Add. Mss. 60760, fos.112–14; Salisbury to Carnarvon, 27 March 1890, ibid., fos.140–7; Carnarvon to Salisbury, 2 April 1890, ibid., fos.147–[50].
74. Diaries, 1887–8, see Add. Mss. 60929, 60930; Notes on the Cape and Australia, 1887–9, Add. Mss. 60809; notes and drafts, Add. Mss. 60957, fos.82–117, esp. for 'Australia in 1888', *Essays and Addresses,* 97–143.
75. A.W. Martin, *Henry Parkes: A Biography* (Melbourne, 1980), 325.
76. He was, however, wary of the Imperial Federation League formed in 1884: Herbert to Carnarvon 11 Nov. 1886, Add. Mss. 60795, fos.116–18.

Edwin Lutyens, New Delhi, and the Architecture of Imperialism

JANE RIDLEY

Edwin Lutyens's New Delhi is one of the few pieces of imperial architecture which has achieved critical acclaim. Praise from the critic Robert Byron in *Country Life* (1931) was echoed by A.S.G. Butler, in the memorial volumes, *The Architecture of Sir Edwin Lutyens*, and by Lutyens's biographer Christopher Hussey.[1] Robert Irving's *Imperial Summer* gives a fully documented account of the building of the new city; it is essentially an architectural critique.[2] But New Delhi is also a political symbol, and both right and left agree on its meaning. Both see it as a statement of imperial despotism. Driving up Kings Way in 1931 Robert Byron hailed the red, pink, and cream dome of the newly-built Viceroy's House as 'a shout of the Imperial suggestion … an offence against democracy, a slap in the face of the modern average man'.[3] For Christopher Hussey, writing in the aftermath of the Emergency, it was 'the last splendid assertion of European humanism before the engulfing of its ideals in racial and ideological confusion'.[4] One fact must be borne in mind when discussing New Delhi, wrote Colin Amery: 'The design of the city was concerned with the architecture of power.'[5] For this very reason it is criticized by the left. A younger generation of Indians see Lutyens's 'arrogant' domes as symbols of alien imperial rule. Marxists stigmatize Delhi as an expression of the dominance-dependence relationship of colonialism.[6] Tom Metcalf has argued that Lutyens's New Delhi failed to provide an architectural response to the political problems of British India.[7] It is the purpose of this article to evaluate these views and to suggest alternative ways of looking at Lutyens's New Delhi. Preoccupation with the projection of power has obscured Lutyens's aesthetic project at New Delhi: the creation of a genuine synthesis of east and west.

Anthony King in *Colonial Urban Development* (1976) provides a Marxist critique of Delhi. New Delhi, according to King, is a textbook example of the modern colonial city, showing clearly 'how the power structure inherent in the dominance-dependence relationship of colonialism influenced urban development'.[8] The colonial city of Delhi consists of four clearly differentiated areas. Old Delhi, the native city, built in the seventeenth century, is crowded, with narrow streets and traditional crafts, dependent on animal energy. In the colonial city of New Delhi, the population density is far lower; this is a city of wide, tree-lined roads designed for cars fronted by bungalows where a significant proportion of space is allotted to visual and ceremonial or symbolic areas. The third zone is the cantonment or imperial military camp, to the south. Fourthly, there is the fringe, the squalid, unplanned shantytown of rural migrants clinging to the city's skirts.[9] These four types of space are characteristic of the colonial city, and King shows how the cantonment and colonial city shifted during the course of British rule. Colonial cities are essentially planned cities, more so than western cities, as vested interests play little or no part; instead of a compromise between vested interests and planning authorities, the city is imposed by the dominant power upon the dependent.

During the first half of the nineteenth century, while the British coexisted in Delhi with the titular Mogul emperors, they maintained a relaxed presence in Delhi. The cantonment, initially established inside the old city when Delhi was conquered from the Mahrattas in 1803, was removed three miles outside in 1828, to a site which Europeans found healthier, distanced from the squalor of the native city. After the military emergency of the Mutiny the British presence was significantly tightened. The Emperor Bahadur Shah, who had been captured by the British crouching in the magnificent tomb erected by Akbar to his father Humayun (1562–75), was exiled and the Royal Palace confiscated. British troops occupied the Palace, which they renamed Delhi Fort; a belt of native housing 500 yards wide around the high red walls of the fort was cleared, sharply emphasizing the British military presence, and the shift from 'acquiescence' of the Mogul Emperor to subjugation of the colonial culture. The civil lines were laid out to the north, with armed force, the ultimate source of power, located at their rear. The native city was crowded into the area bounded by the old city wall.[10]

The colonial city, in King's analysis, is an expression of 'the colonial third culture', the culture of the European colonial community in India. ('Colonial' is here used in spite of the fact that most of the European community was not permanently settled in India.) The third culture is defined in distinction from the 'first' or metropolitan culture and the 'second' indigenous culture. The third culture results from contact in the colonized country between the indigenous culture and the metropolitan culture or, more precisely, elements which are selected 'by a socially and regionally selected set of cultural agents recruited mainly from the middle classes of the metropolitan society'.[11] There is an area of overlap between the second and third cultures; but the strongest input to the third culture is from the metropolis. In addition the third culture acts as a diffusion channel, conveying culture from the second culture back to the third.

The notion of cultural overlap implies a two-way flow between the indigenous and colonial cultures. Initially the area of overlap contained only basic needs such as dress, diet, and language; over the period of colonial rule, the area broadened to include aspects of government, administration, knowledge systems, cultural artefacts.[12] The colloquial language of Anglo-India, collected and explained by H. Yule and A.C. Burnell in *Hobson-Jobson* (1903), documents the area of overlap. Words were evolved to describe spaces within the city: cantonment (military camp), civil lines, or bungalow.[13] But there were always aspects of the third culture which remained unique to Europeans: 'particular social groupings, social and political ideologies, literature, perceptions about the natives and aspects of lifestyle'.[14] The historic landscape was defined in terms of the history of the English in India, not the indigenous culture. The Ridge to the north of Delhi, for example, an area of heavy fighting during the Mutiny, became almost hallowed ground.

King argues that the model of the colonial city applies equally to New Delhi. The distribution of power within New Delhi ensured the replication of the characteristic tripartite arrangement of 'native city', 'cantonment', and 'civil station'.[15] The layout of the city was based on two 'culturally-controlled decisions', that is, decisions controlled by the colonial third culture. The first of these was the decision on the site. 'Although a small group of metropolitan "planning" specialists were available,' wrote King, 'the final decision on siting was made at the local source of colonial power' – that is, by the viceroy. Second, no attempt was made to integrate the new city to the old Delhi. 'Conforming to earlier colonial urban models, the civilians lived outside and away from the "native town", with the ultimate source of power, armed force, located slightly to their rear.'[16] What distinguished the new city from its predecessor were the technological assumptions underlying its construction. New Delhi was a city planned for the motor car, the telephone, and the printing press, and it soon adapted to the cinema, radio, and aeroplane. 'In this sense New Delhi, both in its functioning as well as its layout, represented a dependent, technological appendage of a Western industrial state. Without this technology it could function only by substituting manpower for tasks designed for machine.'[17] King is dismissive of Lutyens and Baker, the two architects of the New Delhi, and the 'baroque' ideas and 'garden city' principles they allegedly followed. 'The use of these terms is misleading in the bi-cultural framework in which Delhi developed. So-called "garden city" principles represent a rationalised application of the underlying values which had characterised conceptual models of settlement in the colonial society at least since the eighteenth century.'[18]

The notion of the colonial third culture and its relation to the built environment is a useful one, a reminder of the extent to which New Delhi was the product of traditional power structures. Style should not blind us to the underlying dynamics. But King is a prisoner of his own model, bending the evidence to fit a pattern. The decision to move the capital of India to Delhi was, as King admits, taken within 'the power structure of colonialism', meaning the metropolis; but so were many of the decisions about the siting, planning, and design of the new capital which he locates within the colonial third culture. New Delhi was shaped more by the metropolitan culture and less by the third culture than he allows. To King's insights about the third culture must be added further layers of explanation. The indigenous culture was of greater importance than either King or the architectural critics suggest.

The transfer of the capital was announced by George V at the Coronation Durbar in Delhi in December 1911. The decision had been kept a closely guarded secret, and the announcement was intended as a surprise; but it was a predictable response to the tensions and disaffection created by Curzon's ill-advised partition of Bengal in 1905. Bengal was the homeland of the moderate Hindu nationalists, and by destroying the existing Bengal legislature and creating a predominantly Muslim province of East Bengal, Curzon alienated the Hindus, driving them into a new extremism and terrorism. It was an act of breath-taking arrogance and contempt for Indian opinion; to Hindus it seemed 'a deliberate blow aimed at the growing solidarity and self-consciousness of the Bengalee-speaking population'.[19] Calcutta seethed with anti-British agitation, sedition, and terrorism.

The Liberal government's first response was constitutional reform, associating more Indians with the colonial administration. When the Morley-Minto reform failed to appease the nationalists, Crewe, who succeeded Morley as Indian Secretary in 1911, was forced to address the problem directly. Lord Hardinge, who was appointed Viceroy in 1910, proposed to reverse the partition and reunite Bengal. But the seat of government was to be transferred from Calcutta to Delhi. As the centre of Bengali nationalism, Calcutta was an inappropriate imperial capital; if the provinces of India were to receive self-government, it was 'essential', in Hardinge's view, to dissociate the supreme government from any particular provincial government. Because Delhi was the historic capital of the Mogul Emperors, the move was calculated to conciliate the Muslims, who may have seen the reunification of Bengal as a concession to Hindu pressure.[20] Delhi was also a city with strong imperial associations for the British. It had been the site of epic fighting during the Mutiny, and in 1877 Lord Lytton had chosen to hold the first of the Durbars there. The new capital was an essentially imperialist project; a bold assertion of British rule over an increasingly disaffected India. It was nevertheless opposed vociferously by Curzon, the champion of centralized autocracy, who objected to Hardinge's proposal to create a federation of self-governing states.[21]

The decision on the siting of the new capital was made in 1912. Here too metropolitan influences prevailed. In March 1912 a committee of experts was appointed with a brief to report to the viceroy on the site of the new city and its general planning. The Delhi Planning Committee consisted of J.A. Brodie, Borough Engineer of Liverpool, Captain George Swinton, Chairman of the London County Council, and the architect Edwin Lutyens, architect of Hampstead Garden Suburb (1908–11). Surveying the city and its environs from the back of an elephant, the committee narrowed down the choice to two. The first was the site north of the old city on the Ridge. For the British this was hallowed ground, burned into their memories by the fighting of 1857; in Christopher Hussey's words, 'a concentrated chronicle of blood and fire eclipsing for them the blurred annals of as many centuries of lurid Pathan pomp and the majesty of the Moguls long disintegrated into dusty ruin'.[22] Here the British had built their civil lines after the Mutiny, and here George V had laid the foundation stone in December 1911. The second site was south of the old city, on the west bank of the River Jumna, with views, as Lutyens wrote, 'across old Delhi to that wilderness of ruined tombs that form the remains of the seven older Delhis'.[23] In spite of sentimental and emotive pressure to build on the Ridge or northern site, the Committee reported overwhelmingly in favour of the southern site in June 1912. The Ridge, they insisted was cramped and unhealthy; land was expensive because of existing suburban development. The southern site, and especially the hills around Raisina, offered more scope, height, and space.

Lord Hardinge alleged in his memoirs that it was he who insisted on the south site, and King cites this as evidence that the colonial third culture dictated the site, overruling the 'experts' from Britain.[24] In fact, the Delhi Planning Committee, and especially Lutyens and Brodie, consistently urged the southern site and opposed the Ridge. Hardinge initially supported the south, but he was unpredictable and inconsistent, the more so after he was injured by an assassin's bomb on entering Delhi in December 1912. 'The Viceroy changes his mind every time I see him', complained Lutyens.[25] Bowing to public criticism, he ordered a reconsideration of the northern site, which the Committee again rejected. Acknowledging perhaps that British experts had been appointed 'in an effort to secure knowledge and a breadth of vision absent in Indian officialdom', Hardinge acquiesced in the southern site.[26]

Nor was the plan itself quite so heavily determined by the colonial third culture as King suggests. The layout of the city, which Lutyens designed, comprises two elements. There is, firstly, the imperial, beaux-arts city. The basic design for an impressive Government House flanked by secretariat buildings forming the climax of a grand processional axis was sketched by Lutyens as early as May 1912.[27] In India for a second time in the winter of 1912–13, Lutyens sketched a more detailed layout with the Government House located, at the Viceroy's suggestion, on Raisina Hill, south of old Delhi. In early drafts the hill was occupied solely by Government House. After the arrival of Herbert Baker, who joined Lutyens as architect early in 1913, the Secretariat buildings, which he was to design, moved up onto the Ridge at his insistence. Baker and Lutyens persuaded Hardinge to accept the idea of an acropolis, or Great Place, crowned by Government House and Secretariats.[28] Government House was the climax of three axes: one processional route from the new railway station, a second (Kings Way) looking straight towards the ancient city of Indrapat, and a third vista looking towards Humayun's Tomb. The siting of the buildings of power on an acropolis deliberately echoes the Capitol in Rome; and so did the placing of the Secretariats before Government House. 'The imagination is led,' the Planning Committee reported, 'from the machinery to the prime moving power itself.'[29] The core of the new city echoes the beaux-arts planning of Haussman's Paris and perhaps also the plan of Washington. Here is the geometry of power; the monumental baroque city with its rectangular grid, straight axes, central vistas, wide boulevards, and processional routes; the acropolis which intimidates and threatens as much as it impresses.

But New Delhi is not an orthodox baroque city. The processional route of King's Way is lined not by houses but by trees and open spaces and canals. Superimposed upon the rectangular grid is a second, distinct geometrical system, composed of two overlapping hexagons. Their points of intersection coincide with the east-west axis of King's Way. The hexagons, which are in turn divided into smaller hexagons, which themselves are divided into triangles, define the limits of the residential city.[30] Here the roads are wide and tree-lined, sometimes curving and lined by bungalows set back from the road and surrounded by leafy gardens. The geometry of the hexagons is blurred by leafiness, a juxtaposition of the natural and classical of the kind which Lutyens's gardens had evolved since 1890. Similarly, the combination of rectangular grid with hexagon combines the circulating plan with the classical axes typical of Lutyens house plans.[31] Lutyens's decision to build a garden city has been linked to his experience at Hampstead Garden Suburb, where he had been architect since 1908. This had brought him into contact with Raymond Unwin, and progressive ideas on town planning, which stressed the combination of incongruities. The Parker-Unwin plan for Letchworth (1903) contains features which prefigure Lutyens's New Delhi: 'the grand approach which bisects the symmetrical plan, and connects the centre to the regional transportation route, the "monumental" centre and "rural" city, the variety of vista, and the interpenetration of the landscape and city'.[32] Important though the garden city was in shaping Lutyens's thinking, bungalows, compounds, trees, grid layouts are, as King points out, typical of the colonial city. New Delhi's physical separation from the old city, made possible by the motor car, is a measure of the British distancing themselves from the Indians in a way that was new for Delhi, where the pattern had been one of dual authority and co-existence.

New Delhi contains another layer of meaning which critics have ignored. In a recent study of the history of Delhi since prehistoric times, A.K. Jain suggests that criticism of New Delhi by Indian and Western scholars as 'a Western transplant is superficial and limited to its direct contrast and comparison with [the Mogul city of] Shahjahanabad'.[33] Jain has identified striking parallels between Lutyens's Delhi and the prehistoric city of Indrapat. Like Indrapat, New Delhi is located on the western bank of the river Jumna. That Lutyens was very much aware of the prehistoric city is suggested by his alignment of the east-west vista from Government House, which terminates at Indrapat.[34] He always marked Indrapat on his city plans. The layout of New Delhi coincides with the principles of vedic architecture, the quasi-mystical system which inspired the planning of the vanished city of Indrapat (1000–1800 BC). Thus Government House faced east, the aspect dictated by vedic art to capture the cooling breeze and morning sun. Lutyens's city plan of rectangular grid and superimposed hexagonal system recalls the ancient Indian vedic plan, which consisted of a square or rectangle inscribed within a circle. The qualities of a vedic plan were symmetry, a centre, and cardinal points. The centre of the square was the spiritual zone, consecrated to Brahma. At the central crossing of Kings Way and Queens Way, Lutyens placed cultural institutions, museums, and record offices. As in vedic planning, the residential area was carefully zoned for different classes.[35] Lutyens's drawings distinguished areas of settlement for 'rich whites', 'thin whites', and 'thin blacks'.[36]

Lutyens was himself dismissive of traditional Hindu architecture. He laughed at superstitions and Sanskrit writings which warned against a lion-shaped house (a house with a front wider than its back) and commended as lucky a cow-shaped house with a front narrower than its back.[37] But the similarities between Lutyens and vedic planning are not entirely fanciful. It is conceivable, as Jain suggests, that both classical and vedic planning stem from a common Indo-European culture, which was possibly brought to India from Greece by Alexander.[38] In his quest for the elemental geometry of classicism, Lutyens, unconsciously perhaps, moved back to the very origins of Indian civilization.

Lutyens achieved a similar effect at the Cenotaph or Great War Stone, designed in 1919–20. His design for the finely proportioned horizontal stone block uses the Greek method of entasis. By making verticals slightly out of plumb and curving surfaces imperceptibly, entasis creates an anti-optical illusion. Buildings appear more square than they look to the naked eye. At the Cenotaph, Lutyens used entasis to imply a secret form, a sphere, the perfect shape which had been his first idea for the monument. Drawings show that 'he intended the vertical sides to taper to meet at a point 1000 ft in the air and the horizontal lines to be part of a circle with a centre 900 ft below ground'. Entasis gives the Cenotaph a tactile quality characteristic of Greek architecture, which was intended to be read by the hand, as much as the eye.[39] Lutyens probably arrived at this through geometry, rather than study of the Greeks. He was interested to learn that the method used by the ancient Egyptians for setting out the angle of the great pyramid was 'the same as what I used and thought I had discovered for the setting out of my roofs'.[40] By the use of elemental geometry, Lutyens achieved the strangest feats of architectural empathy. The Cenotaph, stark, non-denominational, and non-triumphalist, captured the subdued and sombre mood of post-Great War Britain. Perhaps New Delhi's geometry performed a similar feat, transcending the transient imperatives of imperialism to evoke an ancient pre-Mogul past.

The architectural style of the principal buildings of New Delhi, Government House and the Secretariats, was the subject of fierce debate, in India and in Britain. The European community in India favoured on the whole a purely western renaissance style. Most commentators in Britain, too, preferred a western style. A minority called for an Indian style. King George V, surprisingly perhaps, advocated Mogul architecture as the style for the new capital. Architects such as Lanchester and Voysey supported him. Hardinge, the viceroy, urged an Oriental style combined with European classical elements. So did the influential Curzon, a powerful critic of the transfer of capital, who insisted that the new capital, if built it must be, should be in an Indo-European style.[41]

Evidently the style of the new capital was not merely an aesthetic issue. Aesthetic judgements were coded political positions. There were other layers of meaning, too, but these are ignored by Anthony King, whose study of Delhi deliberately avoids 'what is normally called "architecture" … as generally having too limited an application'.[42] The 'so-called "Classical" architecture preferred by the Europeans in India King dismisses in language which suggests an observer from another planet. The Europeans, he says, placed high value on 'historically derived canons of "aesthetic" taste derived from past civilisations of Greece and Rome'. This led them to superimpose upon their bungalows 'symbolic "architectural" features transposed from interpretations of Roman and Greek built form'.[43] King's dismissal of architecture as part of the status baggage of the third culture blinds him to its cultural significance. Architectural style was as much a language as the Anglo-Indian argot collected in Hobson-Johnson. The debate about the style of the new capital reveals much about the third culture; it was characteristic that Europeans in India should favour a western, alien style of architecture. But the advocates of a mixed Indo-European style surely do not conform to King's model. Most of these were in the metropolis; yet they did not insist on imposing metropolitan culture, even though men like Curzon and George V were strong apologists of empire. Clearly something else is going on here. One way of reading this debate is given by Edward Said's concept of Orientalism.

For Edward Said, Orientalism is a form of cultural dominance. The consequence of knowledge in the west about the east which had grown ever since the eighteenth century, it assumes an absolute demarcation between East and West. Knowledge is power; and within Oriental-European relations, 'Europe was always in a position of strength, not to say domination'. The Oriental was seen as depraved, irrational, childlike. He lived 'in a different but thoroughly organised world of his own ... Yet what gave the Oriental's world its intelligibility and identity was not the result of his own efforts but rather the whole complex series of knowledgeable manipulations by which the Orient was identified with the West ... Knowledge of the Orient, because generated out of strength, in a sense *creates* the Orient, the Oriental and his world.'[44] The European judges the Oriental in law courts, disciplines him in schools or prisons, studies him in Universities; the Oriental is '*contained* and *represented* by dominating frameworks'. Orientalism divides men into 'them' and 'us'; it is an instrument for exerting western control over the east.[45]

Historians are uncomfortable with discourse analysis, and Said has been criticized for the 'unidirectional' cultural flow he postulates from west to east and for his concentration on elite texts.[46] Where the Battle of the Styles is concerned, however, Said is a useful guide. The debate was conducted within the British elite, and Indians were not consulted. Hardinge and Curzon, the protagonists of an 'Eastern' style, called for an architecture which would contain Indian motif within the framework of western classicism. In *The Times* Herbert Baker envisaged a new style which would reflect British rule in India; 'a blend of the best elements of East and West'. The dome, the open court of audience, the colonnade, and arcade should be combined with southern European classicism. The 'crux', Baker told the viceroy, was use of the column, the leitmotif of classicism.[47]

Baker's politically correct Orientalism forms a marked contrast with the sentiments expressed privately by Lutyens. In letters home to his wife, written in 1912, he excoriated India and its architecture. The natives were 'children'. 'The very low intellects of the natives spoil much and I do not think it is possible for the Indians and whites to mix freely and naturally.'[48] Indian architecture was 'the building style of children'. India makes one 'very Tory and pre-Tory feudal!'[49] Mogul architecture he condemned as 'cumbrous ill-constructed building covered with a veneer of stone or marble and very tiresome to the western intelligence'. 'Personally I do not believe there is any real Indian architecture or any great tradition. There are just spurts by various mushroom dynasties with as much intellect in them as any other *art nouveau*.'[50]

No doubt Orientalism saw Indians as 'them', as children, but Lutyens's contempt is as frank as it is distasteful. These letters have done more than anything to damage his reputation with the post-Independence generation of Indians. Anthony King quoted this material to show that Lutyens shared the attitudes of the colonial third culture, which he expressed in his architecture.[51] These are the redneck, chauvinistic attitudes described and explained by Kipling and later satirized by Forster in *Passage to India*. To William Dalrymple, Lutyens's intolerance suggests the Wagner paradox: 'how could someone with so insular a vision have managed to produce such breathtaking works of art?'[52] Not that Lutyens admired the Indian Civil Service. Initial enthusiasm turned swiftly to disillusionment as, bruised and obstructed by interminable committees, he realized that even despotism could only achieve the second best. For Anglo-Indian aesthetic taste, moreover, he had only contempt. Of the tin-roofed buildings of Simla he wrote, 'if one was told the monkeys had built it all one would have said what wonderful monkeys, they must be shot in case they do it again'.[53]

We do not need the post-structuralists to remind us that letters, especially private letters, are expressions of the moment; true, perhaps, to the feelings of one moment and one relationship, but not true for all time, capable of being contradicted and loaded with subtext. The letters Lutyens wrote from India in 1912–13 are angry, coloured by despair at the failure of his marriage and his wife's insistence on ending marital relations. Emily Lutyens had become converted to Theosophy, Mrs Besant's Indian-inspired creed which urged chastity; she was platonically obsessed with the young Krishnamurti, whom the Theosophists acclaimed as the reincarnation of Jesus Christ; and as a supporter of the women's movement, she had been taught to see sex as a form of male exploitation. Small wonder that Lutyens was bitter; the more absorbed his wife became in eastern, esoteric philosophy, adopting vegetarianism and meditation, the more angry he became towards India and the Indians.

In any case, Lutyens's letters offer no easy clues to his work. Quite the contrary; it was his belief that art could not be expressed in words. 'I think an art begins where words fail it', he wrote. 'An art has to be something which it alone can express in its own medium.'[54] True art must express itself in its own terms; it was not the vehicle of literary or political sentiment. That was the trouble with the Pre-Raphaelites and with Ruskin. To 'read' Lutyens's architecture in terms of his letters, is too simplistic; to condemn the work because one dislikes the letters is unfair. Truly to understand Lutyens's project at New Delhi we need to proclaim the death of the architect; to look at the work in its own terms.

Artistic philosophy was at the heart of the quarrel between Lutyens and Herbert Baker. Lutyens complained endlessly about Baker's sloppiness, about his willingness to compromise and take short cuts. Lacking a public-school education himself, Lutyens sneered at Baker's prosiness, envying and despising his easy ways with committees and bureaucrats. Baker, he grumbled, was no artist but an imperialist lackey: 'his world is bound by the range of a pom-pom gun'.[55] 'His work all centres round and [is] built on phrases that will sound well with his Round Table friends', growled Lutyens. 'A little more of the T square and a little less of the Round Table.'[56] Nor did Lutyens's complaints lack substance. In South Africa, where he had worked for Cecil Rhodes and associated with Milner's Kindergarten, Baker had earned a reputation as the architect of imperialism. The mission of the architect, he believed was to give expression to Britain's national ideals; to provide a framework of architectural order analogous to the law and order provided by colonial rule. In India, Baker was essentially an Orientalist, imposing a Western framework upon native skills. 'The controlling mind must heat and weld into his orderly conception all that India has given him of subtlety and industry in craftsmanship', he wrote.[57] He was a Victorian in his belief that the purposes of architecture were moral and didactic; public buildings, he believed, should convey meanings, as churches did, expressed in symbols, decoration, and mottoes. His Secretariats are, as Gavin Stamp wrote, 'Edwardian Baroque with Indian details'.[58] Over the entrance Baker inscribed a motto which even the Viceroy Lord Hardinge found 'rather pointed':[59]

LIBERTY WILL NOT DESCEND TO A PEOPLE;
A PEOPLE MUST RAISE THEMSELVES TO LIBERTY;
IT IS A BLESSING WHICH MUST BE EARNED BEFORE IT CAN BE ENJOYED

Baker and Lutyens endured long, feuding winters together, quarrelling on board P & O liners and in the Delhi office which they shared, known as 'Raisina Mill'. Baker was no match for Lutyens's verbal wit, and he was easily demoralized by Lutyens's sneers, jibes, and disparagement. Young architects remembered painfully awkward dinners, when the two rivals sat in ostentatious, hostile silence at either end of a long table.[60] Baker gained his revenge with the gradient, the inclined rise in Raisina Hill which he flattened in order to allow access between the Secretariat buildings, thus obscuring the vista along Kings Way towards Viceroy's House. Lutyens, immersed in the intricate labour of repeatedly reducing his elaborate plans to scale, had failed to notice the significance of the gradient drawings. It was an astonishing oversight, his 'bakerloo', as he called it. 'It is bad design', he raged, 'to terminate an architectural vista with a disappearing target.'[61] For six years he campaigned to reverse the decision. But Lutyens was no match for Baker in dealing with officialdom, the more so as changing the gradient would have entailed extra expense, and his efforts achieved nothing. He had failed to foresee the implications of moving the Secretariats up to join Government House onto the acropolis, a decision made at Baker's instance to which he had willingly agreed.[62] For Lutyens the quarrel did not end there. In 1931, when the new city was inaugurated, Robert Byron reported on New Delhi for *Country Life* and the *Architectural Review*. Briefed and charmed by Lutyens, Byron devoted four rapturous articles to Viceroy's House; but to Baker's chagrin, the Secretariats received only a single article.[63]

Lutyens's persistent belittling and carping about his rival seem vindictive and wilful. Certainly, he succeeded in destroying Baker's confidence. Never again did Baker design with the assurance he had shown in South Africa. Yet, as Christopher Hussey perceived, Lutyens's behaviour needs to be seen in terms of his artist's morality. For Lutyens, wrote Hussey, 'ethical virtues were of value only so far as they corresponded with aesthetic virtues; when they diverged, ethics ceased to count; the purpose of life was the embodiment of divine order in finite form, and when a man fell short in this endeavour, he fell from grace, became a bad man.'[64] Judged by these lights, Baker was a traitor to his calling; he committed the cardinal sin of compromising his art for political advantage. Lutyens was ruthless in pursuit of his art; it was for him the supreme good, transcending politics and ethics. To this extent, he conformed to the character of the aesthete, delineated by Alasdair MacIntyre in his *tour d'horizon* of *fin-de-siècle* morality; but unlike MacIntyre's rich hedonistic aesthete, Lutyens was driven by a dedication to work which was positively puritanical.[65]

In his book *Imperial Vision*, a study of Indian architecture and the Raj, Tom Metcalf has endeavoured to 'read' Viceroy's House as a political statement. While conceding its aesthetic value, Metcalf criticizes Lutyens's work at

New Delhi for failing to provide an architectural solution to the political problems of British India. Fundamentally, it had nothing to offer the Indian middle classes. Not only were they not consulted, but Metcalf asserts that the initial design contained no provision for a legislative chamber, which was included only as an afterthought, to accommodate the 1919 reforms; and by locating the circular parliament building, which Baker designed, below the acropolis and to one side of the central axis the British underlined its unimportance.[66] The sheer size of Viceroy's House Metcalf sees as 'a device to mask a growing insecurity by shouting forth an assertive magnificence'.[67] Nor did the stylistic synthesis of east and west achieved by Lutyens at Viceroy's House offer a solution to Britain's problems. Lutyens rejected Indo-Saracenic, the style which, in the hands of architects like Swinton Jacob, implied a political aspiration of Anglo-Indian co-operation, with the British as latter-day Mogul emperors. Instead, he incorporated Buddhist elements into his design, most notably in the dome, inspired by the *stupa* at Sanchi. But Buddhism had no followers in India, and by adopting Buddhist forms, says Metcalf, Lutyens side-stepped the Hindu–Muslim divide, acknowledging that Britain had 'abdicated its claim to a superior knowledge of India's peoples and its past'.[68] This was an architecture which had nothing to say to the Indian middle classes. 'Confined within the classic traditions of European imperialism, it led, inevitably, nowhere.'[69] Metcalf begs the question that it is the role of the architect to provide political *solutions*. Following an agenda influenced by Marxism and by Edward Said, he assumes that architecture in an imperial context is necessarily concerned with the projection of power. By reading Lutyens's architecture in terms of the language of power, Metcalf commits himself to a partial and limited view of its significance.

Today, Viceroy's House, now the President's House, or Rashtrapati Bhavan, occupies a silent, lonely eminence on Raisina Hill, and the real hurly-burly of Indian politics takes place down below in the parliament. But Metcalf is wrong to say that 'no provision at all was made in the original plan for a parliament building'.[70] Lutyens's early plans located an Imperial Legislative Council inside Government (rather than Viceroy's) House, as it was then called. Only after the Montagu-Chelmsford reform in 1919 was the India Office persuaded of the need for a separate building, and the parliament moved down the hill.[71] The inclusion of a council chamber inside the Viceroy's House was one reason for its size: its ground area is bigger than Versailles.[72] Lutyens had no illusions about the permanence of British rule in India. 'I am not sure but that the only gentlemanlike thing we can do is to leave India', he wrote in 1913, contemplating the nationalist movement. 'Poor India, she will have some iron-shod foot across her throat.'[73] 'Is it our swan song?' he mused of the building work required under the Montagu-Chelmsford reform. 'I only hope it may be a good tune well sung to our and India's dignity.'[74] Sustained by nightly reading of Gibbon's *Decline and Fall*, he was conscious that he was designing a memorial for British India, a building which India could inherit. Perhaps Viceroy's House should be seen in the same light as the war memorials which he was designing in the early 1920s: as a gigantic mausoleum. The Durbar Hall, the circular space beneath the dome at the centre of the square, is clearly inspired by the Parthenon in Rome; but it recalls also the circular inner chamber beneath the dome of a Moghul tomb: like Humayun's tomb (1562–75), built by Akbar for his father, the Durbar Hall depends for its drama upon moving from shade to the bright Indian sunlight.

Pace Metcalf, Lutyens did not ignore Muslim and Hindu forms. True, he rejected Indo-Saracenic. But this was on aesthetic grounds, rather than political. It was, for him, an excrescence of Victorian gothic, epitomizing the 'innate and ignorant vulgarity' of British building in India.[75] Lutyens was far more learned in Indian architectural forms than most western critics recognize. For all his sarcastic criticism of Indian architecture, he absorbed a remarkable amount, observed on the tours which Hardinge arranged. His background as an Arts and Crafts architect taught him how to absorb a vernacular, how to analyse and recreate it, achieving a paradoxical synthesis between vernacular texture and the forms and geometry of classicism. Indian architecture, he once wrote, is 'what a Surrey cottage *ornée* is to Westminster Abbey'.[76] It is a telling phrase. For the Surrey cottage was the source of the Lutyens-Jekyll Arts and Crafts aesthetic; and with Viceroy's House he achieved a beaux-arts palace which was also an Arts and Crafts masterpiece.

Take the chujjah, the cornice which projects eight feet around the building, forming a shield against the sun and throwing deep, dark shadows. It is, the critics explain, a characteristic feature of Mogul architecture. Beneath the chujjah is a bold lozenge-like design, pink against black, and this the critics do not explain. It is a pipal leaf, a characteristic Mogul pattern. The Public Works Department has preserved a complete set of 8,500 Delhi working drawings, and this archive contains a full-scale drawing of the pipal leaf, plotting the precise angles needed to take the leaf design around a corner while maintaining the illusion of constant size. In the Mogul garden of Viceroy's House, Lutyens designed a pergola. Unlike his English pergolas, whose brick pillars are crowned with timber beams, the New Delhi pergola is built entirely of red sandstone. The inspiration is surely Fatepuhr Sikri, Akbar's ruined city, where Lutyens saw stone beams, used like wood in tension. Mogul architecture, Lutyens realized, was tents in stone; Akbar's palace is decorated with carved chains, tassels, and bells. Hence the so-called Delhi order which Lutyens designed for his classical columns, decorated with bells of stone which, it was said, could never toll the end of a dynasty. 'Chattris', wrote Lutyens, 'are stupid useless things'; but chattris march along the roofline of Viceroy's House, punctuating the sweeping horizontals of red sandstone in a way that is intended to recall the Red Fort in Delhi.[77] The Taj Mahal, he said, 'is wonderful but it is not architecture'; rather it was veneered joinery in stone.[78] Yet the floors of Viceroy's House are laid with marble patterns, intricately cut in the fashion he had noticed at Agra. The house is built of red and cream sandstone, quarried from Dohlpur, where the Moguls took their stone.

'I must say to my own undoing,' wrote Lutyens ruefully, 'that Indians understand me quicker than Englishmen and object less to my methods of persiflage by which I find it easier to convey my ideas.'[79] Because of its identification with British imperialism, critics and historians have underestimated the Indian elements in Lutyens's synthesis. Yet that element was central to his enterprise. Perhaps, like Forster's project of Anglo-Indian friendship, Lutyens's Indian vision was ultimately flawed; perhaps the last word should be Forster's:

> 'Why can't we be friends now?' said the other, holding him affectionately. 'It is what I want. It's what you want.'
>
> But the horses didn't want it – they swerved apart; the earth didn't want it, sending up rocks through which riders must pass single file; the temples, the tank, the jail, the palace, the birds, the carrion, the Guest House, that came into view as they issued from the gap and saw Mau beneath: they didn't want it, and they said in their hundred voices, 'No, not yet,' and the sky said, 'No, not there.'[80]

NOTES

1. Robert Byron, 'New Delhi', *Architectural Review*, 69 (Jan. 1931), 1–30; Robert Byron, 'New Delhi' I–IV, *Country Life*, 69 (1931), 708–16, 754–61; 782–9, 808–15, A.S.G. Butler, *The Architecture of Sir Edwin Lutyens*, 3 vols. (London, 1950), II, 28–44; Christopher Hussey, *Life of Sir Edwin Lutyens* (London, 1950), 237–327, 405–32, 495–524.
2. Robert Grant Irving, *Indian Summer: Lutyens, Baker, and Imperial Delhi* (London, 1981).
3. Quoted in Clayre Percy and Jane Ridley (eds.), *The Letters of Edwin Lutyens to his Wife, Lady Emily* (London, 1985), 257.
4. Hussey, *Edwin Lutyens*, 238.
5. E.F.N. Ribiero and A.K. Jain (eds.), *Proceedings of the Seminar on the Future of New Delhi* (Delhi, 1984), 7.
6. Anthony D. King, *Colonial Urban Development* (London, 1976).
7. Thomas R. Metcalf, *An Imperial Vision: Indian Architecture and Britain's Raj* (Berkeley, 1989), 236–43.
8. King, *Colonial Urban Development*, xiii.
9. Ibid., 6–8.
10. Ibid., 210, 212–13.

11. Ibid., 64–5.
12. Ibid., 65–6.
13. Ibid., 68–96.
14. Ibid., 65–6.
15. Ibid., 230.
16. Ibid., 236.
17. Ibid., 237.
18. Ibid., 238.
19. R.J. Moore, *Liberalism and Indian Politics* (London, 1985), 78–80; Judith M. Brown, *Modern India: The Origins of an Asian Democracy* (Oxford, 1985), 174.
20. Moore, *Liberalism and Indian Politics*, 101–5.
21. Ibid., 105.
22. Hussey, *Edwin Lutyens*, 251.
23. Quoted in Irving, *Indian Summer*, 46.
24. King, *Colonial Urban Development*, 235.
25. Percy and Ridley, *Lutyens Letters*, 276.
26. Irving, *Indian Summer*, 52. See Hussey, *Edwin Lutyens*, 243.
27. Irving, *Indian Summer*, 53–6.
28. Ibid., 67–8.
29. Quoted in ibid., 73.
30. Allan Greenberg, 'Lutyens's Architecture Restudied', *Perspecta*, 12 (1969), 138.
31. Ibid., 142.
32. Ibid., 144.
33. A.K. Jain, *The Cities of Delhi* (Delhi, 1994), 101.
34. Ibid., 13.
35. Ibid., 19.
36. See Irving, *Indian Summer*, 78.
37. Percy and Ridley, *Lutyens Letters*, 242.
38. Jain, *Cities of Delhi*, 101.
39. Andrew Crompton, 'The Secret of the Cenotaph', *A A Files* (forthcoming).
40. Percy and Ridley, *Lutyens Letters*, 335.
41. Irving, *Indian Summer*, 103–6.
42. King, *Colonial Urban Development*, 18.
43. Ibid., 48.
44. Edward W. Said, *Orientalism* (1995 edn), 40.
45. Ibid., 40–5.
46. John M. MacKenzie, *Orientalism: History, Theory and the Arts* (Manchester, 1995), 8–15.
47. Irving, *Indian Summer*, 105.
48. Percy and Ridley, *Lutyens Letters*, 247.
49. Ibid., 231.
50. Ibid., 251.
51. King, *Colonial Urban Development*, 238.
52. William Dalrymple, *City of Djinns* (London, 1993), 84.
53. Percy and Ridley, *Lutyens Letters*, 245.
54. Ibid., 311.
55. Ibid., 291.
56. Ibid., 378.
57. Irving, *Indian Summer*, 277.
58. Arts Council, *Lutyens: The Work of the English Architect Sir Edwin Lutyens* (London, 1981), 38.
59. Irving, *Indian Summer*, 290–1. William Dalrymple wrongly ascribes the inscription to Lutyens, citing it as evidence of the architect as bully: *City of Djinns*, 83.
60. Herbert Ward, *An Eccentric Odyssey: The Early Life of the Rev Herbert Ward* (London, 1988), 82.
61. Irving, *Indian Summer*, 154.
62. See ibid., 67–8, 142–63.

63. I am grateful to James Knox, who is currently writing Robert Byron's biography, for information on this point.
64. Hussey, *Lutyens*, 244.
65. Alasdair MacIntyre, *After Virtue: A Study in Moral Theory* (London, 1985 edn), 40–1.
66. Metcalf, *Imperial Vision*, 240–1.
67. Ibid., 236.
68. Ibid., 293.
69. Ibid., 239.
70. Ibid., 241.
71. Irving, *Indian Summer*, 294–5.
72. Butler, *Architecture of Sir Edwin Lutyens*, II, 30.
73. Percy and Ridley, *Lutyens Letters*, 276–7.
74. Ibid., 387.
75. Ibid., 397; Irving, *Indian Summer*, 125.
76. Percy and Ridley, *Lutyens Letters*, 388.
77. Ibid., 281.
78. Ibid., 250, 279–80.
79. Ibid., 344.
80. E.M. Forster, *A Passage to India* (1961 edn), 317.

Empire of the Dandelion: Ecological Imperialism and Economic Expansion, 1860–1914

B.R. TOMLINSON

The linked issues of empire, economic growth, and welfare in the non-European world underpin much of David Fieldhouse's work on the imperial and global economy of the last two hundred years. In considering the importance of economic motives for imperial expansion, the costs and benefits of empire to Britain, the constraints on economic development in imperial and post-imperial territories, and the interaction of imperial firms with local institutional structures, Fieldhouse has produced a wide-ranging and consistent set of empirical studies that stress the complexity of causal links between imperial contacts and the lack of smooth economic progress in non-European lands. His work suggests strongly that institutional failures in Asia and Africa, both in the public and the private sphere, undermined the potentially dynamic effects of European agents in colonial and post-colonial economies, while Britain itself derived few unique economic advantages from its imperial role.

The question of 'why isn't the whole world developed?' – why growth rates and welfare levels have differed so markedly over the last two centuries between those parts of the globe inhabited chiefly by Europeans, and those inhabited by other races – is one that has exercised many scholars with a wide range of assumptions and preconceptions. Imperial economic historians have often approached these issues through the classic debate about global change in the nineteenth century – the sluggish and apparently often perverse response of large areas of the world to the impact of European capitalism, and the technology and institutions that were transforming Western economies and societies at the time. Fieldhouse has given one set of answers to such questions; other authors have produced alternative explanations based on different intellectual traditions and geographical perspectives. This is a continuing debate in which no uncontested conclusions may ever be reached.

The relationship between imperialism (direct and indirect) and the economic progress of non-European territories has been investigated most thoroughly in the 'lagging' areas of the international economy, where underdevelopment has been the pre-dominant characteristic. The purpose of this essay, however, is to consider the issue in a rather different perspective, by focusing instead on those parts of the world in which imperial expansion, characterized by physical colonization, initiated a distinctive pattern of economic growth that brought clear welfare benefits to those who rapidly became the majority of the inhabitants. These were the colonies of settlement in the western hemisphere and Oceania, which enjoyed some of the highest per capita incomes and rates of economic development during the second half of the nineteenth century. Their success was based largely, but not entirely, on agricultural growth. While the United States was the only economy outside western Europe to have begun exporting industrial goods before 1914, there were also significant manufacturing sectors, in terms of output per head, in Canada, Australia, and New Zealand.[1] The inhabitants of these countries also enjoyed comparatively high incomes and per capita rates of economic growth during the last third of the nineteenth century, with the United States and Canada achieving the largest absolute and per capita growth rates in the world after 1870.[2]

Many contemporary accounts of settler-economy exceptionalism in the late nineteenth century stressed racial and cultural factors to explain the apparent dynamism of temperate economies and the contrasting torpor of tropical peoples. Classic work in this genre was undertaken by the American geographer Ellsworth Huntingdon, whose *Civilization and Climate* (1915) used an original research methodology to investigate the phenomenon. Huntingdon conceded that race, culture, and institutions (religion, education, and government) were all important in explaining differential economic performance across the globe, but argued that physical environment – especially climate – was a crucial additional factor in its own right. His method was to create a definition of civilization, and then to map the regions of the globe in which such characteristics appeared. The higher elements of civilization, Huntingdon argued, could be measured by:

> the power of initiative, the capacity for formulating new ideas and for carrying them into effect, the power of self-control, high standards of honesty and morality, the power to lead and control other races, the capacity for disseminating ideas … . These qualities find expression in high ideals, respect for law, inventiveness, ability to develop philosophical systems, stability and honesty of government, a highly developed system of education, the capacity to dominate the less

> civilized parts of the world, and the ability to carry out far-reaching enterprises covering long periods of time and great areas of the world's surface.[3]

After receiving the opinions of 50 eminent 'experts' across the world (mainly geographers, anthropologists, and 'travellers'), Huntingdon concluded that climate, human energy, and the ability of races and peoples to make 'an impression on the world'[4] were all closely linked, so that climatic conditions explained the distribution of civilization in the world more accurately than variations in racial distribution, religion, or forms of government.

Several of the contributors to *Climate and Civilization* pointed out inconsistencies in Huntingdon's definition of civilization, with one correspondent (described as an 'English anthropologist') pointing out that '"the power of self-control, high standards of morality, … high ideals, respect for law" are eminently characteristic of many savage and barbarian peoples, notably the North American Indians, and in my opinion these latter stand very much higher than the average American citizen, but the latter lead in "the power to lead and control other races, and capacity for disseminating ideas … inventiveness, highly developed systems, etc."' Huntingdon admitted that his concept of civilization was 'a European definition'; since 'the reason for regarding the standard set forth as European is that Europe is today its great exponent'.[5] Given these assumptions, it is no surprise that Huntingdon's world-map of the distribution of civilization showed western Europe (excluding Ireland and Iberia), the eastern United States, California, the coastal region of south-western Australia, and New Zealand as having 'very high' levels of civilization, with 'high' levels in Iberia, Ireland, and European Russia, the rest of the United States, the River Plate region of Latin America, the south-western hinterland of Victoria and New South Wales, Japan, and Korea.[6] As he concluded,

> The geographical distribution of health and energy depends on climate and weather more than any other single factor. The well-known contrast between the energetic peoples of the most progressive parts of the temperate zone and the inhabitants of the tropics and even of the intermediate regions … is largely due to climate.[7]

Such arguments, which stressed that Europeans who lived in the tropics were likely to suffer considerable degeneration over time, were vigorously contested by some white-settler communities – notably in northern Australia.[8] Unperturbed, Huntington expanded and refined his arguments in a series of publications until the 1940s, culminating in *The Mainsprings of*

Civilization (1945), and attracted a number of collaborators and disciples. Typical of these was S.F. Markham who established, to his own satisfaction, an explicit link between climatic conditions and economic performance, as measured by levels of GNP and export trade per capita, and concluded that such tests 'prove that civilization and energy depend to no little degree on climate and man's control of it'.[9]

It is easy to mock the assumptions of Huntingdon and his followers, and to expose the limitations in a methodology which, as later critics pointed out, had the 'regrettable' consequence that 'from an isolated study of associations a full-blown gospel of climatic determinism rapidly emerged'.[10] Donald Denoon has memorably employed the same technique of simple correlation to construct a 'Big Bird theory of development' that links high standards of living for setters in 1900 AD with the existence of large flightless birds in 1000 AD.[11] Yet despite these obvious flaws, the common sense explanation that the success of European settler societies have their origins in some innate characteristic of Europeans have had a long shelf-life, and continue to haunt the literature on comparative economic development in a number of forms. In the modern literature on the North–South divide, and the comparative economic history of 'modernization' in Europe and Asia, attempts are still made to identify underlying cultural, societal, or institutional factors that provide the essential foundations for economic progress. While noone would now argue that the flower of civilization can only flourish in temperate climes, a map of global differences in indices of GNP per capita, the physical quality of life or human development – which many would identify as implicit indicators of measures of human progress – show the same boundaries as Huntingdon's map of the distribution of civilization.[12] As one team of economic geographers has concluded, measurements of economic, demographic, and socio-economic characteristics give a valid indication of the 'attainment' of different countries; by these criteria the former British colonies of settlement in the temperate zones again clearly out-score former European colonies of conquest in the tropics.[13]

At first sight, Alfred Crosby's *Ecological Imperialism* (1986) provides a useful way of taking the problem of settler-economy exceptionalism one stage further by substituting a much broader set of environmental considerations for the dubious categories of race, culturally determined institutions, and climate. Crosby's argument seeks to remove the human element from the centre of the explanation by invoking instead a much broader process in which nature, rather than mankind, provided the dynamic force. This account of the expansion of Europeans ('a division of

Caucasians distinctive in their politics and technologies, rather than their physiques') into the temperate regions of the non-European world sets out to answer a deceptively simply question – 'European emigrants and their descendants are all over the place, which requires explanation', with European peoples making up the great majority of the populations of distinctively 'neo-European' countries scattered throughout the globe – the settler-colonies of the continental United States, Canada, Argentina, Uruguay, Australia, and New Zealand.[14] For Crosby, the most striking feature of this phenomenon is that those parts of the world that are today the most like Europe in their population and culture, and that produce the largest amounts of European agricultural produce, are all far away from Europe, and have indigenous faunas and floras that are very different from those of Europe. Despite this, European plants and animals, not just humans, have adapted to their new environment with tremendous success: 'perhaps European humans have triumphed because of their superiority in arms, organization, and fanaticism, but what in heaven's name is the reason that the sun never sets on the empire of the dandelion?'[15]

Crosby's resolution of this paradox depends on identifying a distinctive process of ecological imperialism, through which the wealth of today's neo-Europes has been based on the success of a 'portmanteau biota' consisting of European humans, plus the plants, animals, pests and pathogens that they brought with them.[16] What distinguished the neo-Europes from the rest of the non-European world, in this analysis, is simply that they were the areas where such a biota could flourish, and expand through a Darwinian process of competitive evolution. The neo-Europes were areas with similar climates to that of Europe, and with similar levels of light intensity and photosynthesis. The indigenous biota of these regions were simpler and less diverse than those of Eurasia before contact took place, partly because human settlement had occurred significantly later there than in Eurasia. Thus local species (including pests) were less adapted to a human presence, which was rarely as dense anyway. The coming of the first human settlers to the neo-Europes, especially in the western hemisphere, caused mass extinctions of large mammals; their land-management systems by use of fire (notably the creation of prairies for buffalo in North America, and the clearing of the bush for hunting grounds in Australia) created ecosystems that European organisms could later adapt quite easily for their own purposes. European settlers brought with them domesticated livestock and food-plants, and also weeds, pests, and diseases, that had long developed in close association with human settlement, and had achieved a symbiotic relationship with humans, and with each other. This process was especially marked in European plants, which had evolved many means of reproduction and spread: European grasses adapted well to grazing by domestic animals, and were tolerant of close-cropping, bare soil, and constantly being trodden on; European weeds were well adapted to colonizing bare soil, to being spread by domestic animals (burrs), to overcoming constant reaping (hay meadow plants), and to the frequent turning of the soil in ploughing. Indeed, many – such as poppies – required these conditions to propagate. As European-style agricultural activities spread throughout the new world, so did the distinctive flora associated with them, eradicating less well-adapted plants along the way when set in a traumatized ecosystem. These factors, taken in conjunction, explain dandelion imperialism and, with it, the success of the European settler – 'the purposeful but often drunken ringmaster of a three-ring circus of organisms'[17] – in the neo-European lands.

Crosby's identification of the process of ecological imperialism creates a neat and seductive argument, which makes intuitive sense to anyone who has visited regions where European-style landscapes have been created out of an alien environment. This can be seen most clearly in plant-distributions, since flowers, grasses, bushes, and trees shape such landscapes most clearly for European sensibilities. Such transformations have been particularly marked in Australia, where about ten per cent of the current flora has been introduced since European settlement, with up to twice that figure in the most densely settled regions in the south-east of the continent.[18] For food-crops – the staple of European colonization – the distinction is even more stark. None of the food-crops currently grown in Australia is native to the region, while only 0.1 per cent of the acreage in North America is now given over to native crops, as opposed to 50 per cent to crops that had been naturalized in Europe before they were transplanted to the new world.[19]

As the distinctive sub-discipline of imperial environmental history has developed, however, doubts have been raised about the significance of such simple correlations.[20] Crosby's assumption of an inherent evolutionary advantage attached to the Eurasian biota can be questioned by studying the history of the expansion of new world plants, pests, and diseases – such as eucalyptus, Colorado beetles, Dutch elm disease, Phylloxera, and syphilis – that have engaged in a reverse process of ecological imperialism. The destructive impact of migrants on indigenous ecosystems was not an exclusively European phenomenon, as the effect of Polynesian settlement in Hawaii demonstrated. For historians of imperial expansion the problem of human agency, and the phenomenon of discontinuous change over time, are particularly significant. Much of the apparently 'natural' expansion of plants and pathogens that occurred in the neo-Europes was closely linked to the process of human colonization and conquest. In particular, the mass extinctions of the indigenous populations of the Americas and Oceania through exposure to diseases such as smallpox, measles, malaria, and tuberculosis resulted largely from the degraded socio-economic conditions to which non-European peoples were exposed by the process of capitalist expansion. As Eric Wolf has pointed out, 'the advent of pathogens ... does not in itself furnish an adequate explanation of what happened. One must ask also about the social and political conditions that permitted the pathogens to proliferate at so rapid a rate.' The unfortunate effects of such changes were particularly marked in the case of the 'great dying' that accompanied Spanish and Portuguese expansion in the Caribbean and Central and South America after 1500, a process that fundamentally changed the access to land, rewards for labour, and freedom of movement of the local inhabitants. Disruptions to the indigenous socio-economic, political, and cultural systems of the indigenous populations of North America that resulted from European interventions in the fur trade in the seventeenth, eighteenth, and early nineteenth centuries, and the later search for land and gold on the prairies and elsewhere, had a similar effect.[21]

While the 'emptying' of non-European lands in the new world through contact with European expansion began in the sixteenth and seventeenth centuries, the expansion of European settlement, and the creation of a global economy dominated by economic activity in the neo-Europes, lagged some way behind. European participation in the global economy of the pre-industrial era was centred on trade and extraction in Asia and Africa rather than on the production of European commodities in settler economies. Until the end of the eighteenth century Europe's imports from overseas consisted largely of bullion, tobacco, and furs from the new world, plus spices, sugar, coffee, tea, and manufactured fine textiles from Asia. The most important international economic exchanges were the regional trade networks that linked Europe with West African slaves, Caribbean sugar, and South American bullion; and with Indian textiles, South-East Asia spices, and Chinese tea and silk.[22] Between 1500 and 1800 the process of European colonization, which was central to the shaping of the archetypal neo-European environments of North America, Oceania, and the River Plate countries of South America, was slow, with only 4 per cent of ethnic Europeans resident outside Europe by 1800.[23] The most economically significant European settlements overseas were in the Caribbean, where they made little use of an imported European biota, being based on use of non-European plants (sugar, cotton, tobacco), grown by non-European labour (black slaves) in an agricultural system of plantations that was alien to Europe.

During the course of the nineteenth century these regional distributions of economic activity altered fundamentally, as the dynamics of large-scale industrialization changed patterns of demand and supply in Europe and overseas, leading to a far more intense process of global economic expansion than anything which had gone before. The needs of European manufacturers and consumers now centred on primary products that were best produced in temperate climates, grown by European settlers using familiar technologies, crop-types, and farming methods. Wheat and meat, the chief agrarian products of the settler-economies, became the staples of mass consumption in the world's industrial cities. As a result, by 1913 the most successful, wealthiest, and most rapidly-growing regions outside Europe were those that had been settled by Europeans.

It was during the nineteenth century, and especially in the fifty-odd years from 1860 to 1914, that Crosby's central problematic becomes significant. This was the period when European expansion, measured as the expansion of peoples as well as of regions of political control, became the clear, dominant force in global economic and environmental history. In 1800 the colonial population of North America consisted of less than 5 million whites and about one million blacks, South America had a European population of less than half a million, Australia about 10,000, and New Zealand almost none. In 1914, by contrast, more than one fifth of ethnic Europeans lived outside their home region, and the percentage of the world's population of European descent had increased from around one quarter of the total in 1750 to two-fifths.[24] Once we refine the chronology of European expansion in this way we can also see that Crosby's key question needs to be modified somewhat. The problem to be explained is not simply that 'European emigrants and their descendants are all over the place' but rather that European emigrants and their descendants are all over the place and have enjoyed, in the aggregate, a higher standard of living than any other race in the world for the last two hundred years. Are these two phenomena related?

Conventional explanations of the exceptional levels of economic growth and welfare enjoyed by European settlers in temperate economies during the nineteenth century have singled out demand factors as the most significant area of explanation. World trade in primary produce tripled in both value and volume between the 1880s and 1913, and doubled between the 1890s and 1913.[25] By 1900 the economies of North America and Oceania were supplying almost one-fifth of world exports by value, equal to that of the rest of the non-European world in total, with by far the highest per capita export figures outside western Europe.[26] Coupled to such demand stimuli, there was also an increase in the supply of crucial factors of production, especially cultivated land. One recent estimate suggests that the world's croplands increased by 272 million hectares between 1700 and 1850, and by a further 376 million hectares between 1850 and 1920 – a rise of 70 per cent in seven decades.[27] As Figures 1 and 2 make clear, the absolute and relative increases were concentrated particularly in areas of the globe settled by Europeans. In 1700 Europeans farmed about 43 per cent of the world's cultivated land, almost all of it within Europe itself (including Russia), in 1850 they farmed 56 per cent, three-quarters within Europe, and by 1920 they farmed 62 per cent, almost half of which was now in areas of overseas settlement. Put another way, about half of the new croplands opened up in the world between 1850 and 1920 were in the European-dominated regions of North and South America and Oceania, and on these lands depended a considerable amount of the economic activity and new wealth of such regions. While significant increases were recorded in Russia and Latin America between 1700 and 1850, and in Australia, New Zealand, and Latin America between 1850 and 1920, by far the largest absolute and relative increases in the area of cropped land during both periods occurred in North America, which contained a negligible amount of the world's croplands in 1700, less than one tenth in 1850, and as much as two fifths in 1920. In global terms, the story of European ecological imperialism must chiefly be the story of the expanding agricultural frontier in the United States and Canada.

At first sight, it is striking that most of the new land opened up by European agriculture in the settler economies resembled that of western Europe in significant ways. According to the classificatory system of world regions developed by Warren Thornwaite, the essential climatic variables of 'precipitation effectiveness' (the ratio of rainfall quantity to temperature), 'temperature efficiency' (a mean temperature above 32°F), and the seasonal distribution of rainfall in the south-eastern and south-western tips of Australia, the Cape area of South Africa, the whole of New Zealand, the regions of the United States and Canada east of the Mississippi and south of the Great Lakes, plus the Pacific coastal strip from California to Vancouver were similar to those in Europe west of the Urals.[28] This reinforces the general point that European colonization was successful in regions that could most easily support European-style agriculture, but it does not endorse any simple models of ecological imperialism. In the first place, European settlers did not find this land ready-prepared for agricultural activity – it had to be cleared of bush, prairie, and forest, as well as of any indigenous inhabitants whose activities obstructed these operations. Secondly, even after the land had been cleared it often resisted colonization by European plants and animals quite vigorously – especially in the harsh conditions of rural Australia, where an 'intimate relationship' between science and politics was thought necessary until well into the twentieth century to change nature in appropriate ways for European agricultural activity. Here, in the 'restive fringe', the frontier could not be expanded unless science and technology were actively 'harnessed in the interpretation

FIGURE 1
DISTRIBUTION OF WORLD CROPLANDS, 1700–1920, IN PERCENTAGES

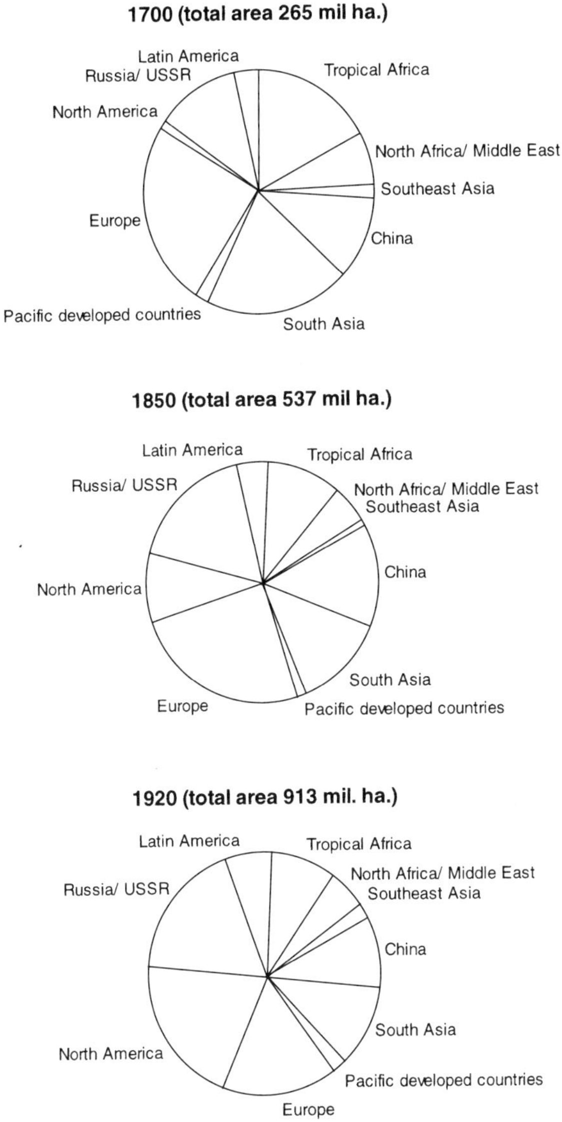

Source: Calculated from data in B.L. Turner II *et al.* (eds.), *The Earth as Transformed by Human Action: Global and Regional Changes in the Biosphere over the past 300 years* (Cambridge, 1990), Table 10-1.

FIGURE 2
DISTRIBUTION OF WORLD CROPLANDS, 1700–1920, BY AREA

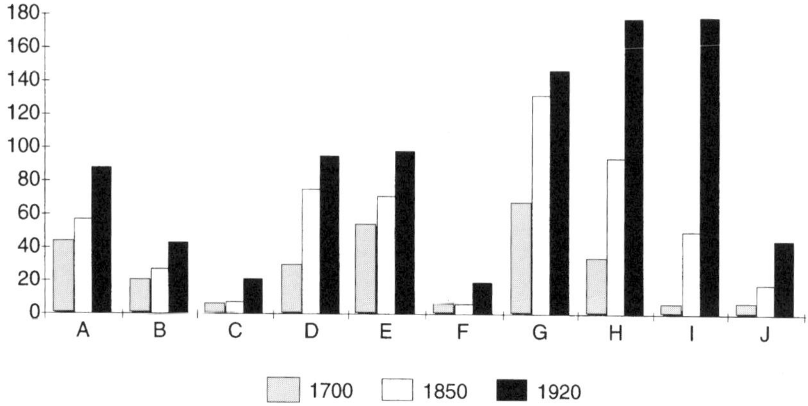

Note: In millions of hectares. A = Tropical Africa; B = North Africa and the Middle East; C = Southeast Asia; D = China; E = South Asia; F = Pacific Developed Countries; G = Europe; H = Russia/USSR; I = North America; J = Latin America.

Source: As Figure 1.

of primary environmental challenges and the associated development of economic and social adaptations'.[29]

It is not possible to make any consistent or revealing comparisons between levels of agricultural productivity in the regions of European settlement and those elsewhere in the world during the nineteenth century. However, there is little to suggest that settlers in the temperate zones outside Europe displayed any unique achievements in this area. The methods of farming in the corn-hog belt of the American mid-west in the nineteenth century were 'not very good', and yields were low, with little increases achieved between 1860 and 1930.[30] The expansion of wheat production in the United States which followed the opening up of the prairies was striking – from zero hectares in 1860, to 8.4 million in 1870, to 18.4 in 1910[31] – but agricultural methods left much to be desired:

> The cultivation of these vast areas [of America west of the Mississippi] was rapidly becoming mechanically elaborate, though it remained agriculturally primitive. No manure was used: none was available for use. The seed was drilled into a shallow furrow and left to grow. After one or two crops, a bare fallow was allowed to restore to the soil such fertility as it might.[32]

Industrially derived technology was used to transport and store grain and other agricultural produce, and to substitute machinery for labour in the clearing and exploitation of the land. The integration of storage and transport made it possible to expand wheat cultivation away from coastal areas rapidly.[33] In North America generally, with capital and labour scarce, and land free, or virtually so, much agriculture remained extensive, content to harvest low yields per acre while facing persistent problems of low rainfall and recurrent drought which depressed yields still further.[34] Even where labour was relatively cheap, investment remained low and the socio-economic structure of land-ownership limited productivity once more. Thus in Argentina the Italian tenant-farmers, used to open up the wheat lands in the 1890s, left the plains as empty as they had found them forty years before, so that, as one contemporary critic complained, 'the landowner could turn the land back to cattle, to sheep, or to the wilderness as easily as he had called it into wheat production'.[35]

In these circumstances, the crucial technological input to settler-agriculture was that which cleared the land, and enabled large areas to be prepared for cultivation and harvested quickly. The steel Deere plough solved some of the problems of prairie agriculture, while in Australia the stump-jump plough was developed to cope with the difficulties of clearing *mallee* land.[36] Advances in adapting mechanization to ploughing faster than to logging switched land-clearance for agriculture in the United States to the western prairies and away from the wooded states of the Great Lakes from the 1860s, although improvements in stump-clearing technology reduced the labour requirement for clearing forest significantly and tipped the strategic balance in the 'war on the woods' in states such as Ohio.[37] The McCormick reaper, developed in the 1830s, was the first of a generation of machines that revolutionized the harvesting and processing of standing crops in North America and Australia. By contrast, technical developments that fostered intensive cultivation lagged far behind. No hybrid varieties of maize that might improve productivity were developed in the United States before the 1930s; new wheat varieties were developed – such as the drought-resistant *Federation* in Australia in 1902, and *Red Fife* and *Marquis* in Canada which could cope with a shorter growing season – but these simply allowed existing crop-production techniques to be spread over a wider area.[38] It is symptomatic of the mechanically elaborate but agriculturally primitive nature of much neo-European agriculture that perhaps the crucial technological breakthrough on the prairies was the invention of barbed wire, patented in 1873.[39] Settler-agriculture prospered by the application of industrial technology to virgin lands, which enabled European farming techniques to bring economic gains, however inefficiently they were practised. It was the availability of such land, and of the machines to farm with European crops, that made man–land ratios so much more favourable in the temperate colonies of settlement than in the tropics in the nineteenth century.

The ability of farmers across the world to respond to new patterns of demand from industrial Europe was not unique to European settlers in temperate zones. The tropical agriculture of Asia and Africa also played its part in the expansion of world trade in the second half of the nineteenth century, supplying raw materials such as rubber and vegetable oils, and formerly exotic foods (sugar, coffee, cocoa, tea) that had now become staples. As in the neo-Europes, economic expansion in the tropics in the nineteenth century was chiefly based on movement of capital, goods, and people, and the opening up frontier regions such as Assam, the Outer Islands of Indonesia, and the Kenyan highlands. Farmers in Asia and Africa proved adept at adopting or adapting new and existing crops and agricultural technologies to meet changed circumstances. This was particularly marked in Japan, where the agricultural development of the nineteenth century – popularized in the *Meiji Noho* methods of the 1890s and 1900s that amounted to a proto-industrial form of the green revolution in food production – was based largely on the breeding of new strains of rice, and the adopting of new techniques in sericulture and riziculture. Similar developments took place, in a less intense form, elsewhere in Asia and Africa – in wheat and cotton cultivation in India, and in cocoa production in West Africa, for example.[40] However, it is significant that the agricultural technologies associated with European industrialization were of very limited use to African and Asian peasants. While imperial governments invested in botanical gardens and agricultural research stations to facilitate the introduction of plants from elsewhere in the world, the tools of empire that were transforming the neo-Europes were not applied in the tropics. Mechanized agriculture could not easily be transported to the different ecological and social conditions of the non-European world; successful advances in agricultural technology there were based on existing indigenous traditions of invention, not on the knowledge-base of industrial Europe.

Identifying the phenomenon of ecological imperialism has improved our understanding of the transformation of the world that has taken place as a result of European expansion over the last four centuries. The colonization of large parts of the globe by animals, plants, and other organisms that accompanied transoceanic settlement by European migrants in the western hemisphere and Oceania represents an aspect of the history of imperialism that deserves further study. However, the significance of this process needs to be specified more carefully than has sometimes been the case so far. The extensive colonization of neo-European lands was a phenomenon that took place chiefly in the nineteenth century, and in response to the conditions of economic demand and supply generated by European industrialization. 'Empty' lands suitable for European-style cultivation and colonization, an ample supply of migrants, adequate capital inputs and strong demand stimuli were all important, coupled to the use of industrially derived machine technology that could clear the land and exploit its produce. For these reasons the most successful countries of the non-European world by 1914 were those in the temperate zones where European tastes and technologies had provided the essential stimuli for economic expansion through production of the primary goods that were the essential inputs for the industrial processes of the day. This expansion was the product of particular circumstances, rather than of a fundamental evolutionary process.

The empire of the dandelion was never secure. It was always under threat from large fluctuations in demand, and from the technical problems of transporting European agricultural techniques to lands with different rainfall patterns and reserves of fertility. It flourished in the late nineteenth and early twentieth centuries despite these constraints, but it came to an abrupt end in the 1930s with the twin disasters of the Great Depression and the Dust Bowl. Since then the economic fortunes of the neo-European lands have depended on more complex patterns of activity, and the utilization of new sources of knowledge, and human and physical capital. If the conditions for successful ecological imperialism are understood correctly, we can also see that the response of the peoples of Africa and Asia over the last two hundred years to the difficult challenge of achieving economic growth – the issue with which David Fieldhouse's work on imperial economic history has been chiefly concerned – cannot properly be measured against the attainments of the European colonies of settlement in the nineteenth century.

NOTES

1. W. Arthur Lewis, *Growth and Fluctuations 1870–1913* (London, 1978), Table 7.1.
2. A.G. Kenwood and A.L. Lougheed, *The Growth of the International Economy* (London, 1992), 19–21.
3. Ellsworth Huntington, *Civilization and Climate* (New Haven, 1915), 150.
4. Ibid., 163.
5. Ibid., 163–4. His contributors were also strongly Eurocentric – 25 Americans, 7 British, 12 other Europeans, and 6 from Asia.
6. Ibid., Figure 31.
7. Ibid., 453.
8. See, for example, R.W. Cilento, *The White Man's Burden in the Tropics* (Melbourne, 1925), which argued that Queenslanders suffered no disability other than 'the faulty circumstances

of social environment which are inseparable from the opening up of a new country for the purpose of primary production' (168).

9. S.F. Markham, *Climate and the Energy of Nations* (Oxford, 1944), 129.
10. D.H.K. Lee, *Climate and Economic Development in the Tropics* (New York, 1957), 8.
11. Donald Denoon, *Settler Capitalism: The Dynamics of Development in the Southern Hemisphere* (Oxford, 1983), 9.
12. For a convenient map of this type, see Paul Knox and John Agnew, *The Geography of the World Economy – An Introduction to Economic Geography* (London, 1994), figure 2.1, which shows that only western Europe, the United States, Canada, Australia, and New Zealand had a GNP of more than $11,000 per capita in 1989.
13. N. Ginsberg, J. Osborn, and G. Black, *Geographic Perspectives on the Wealth of Nations* (Chicago, 1988). This work constructs 'world standard distance scales' to show that the United States, western and central Europe, Australia, Canada, New Zealand, Japan, and some minor island states have the highest measures.
14. Alfred W. Crosby, *Ecological Imperialism: The Biological Expansion of Europe, 900–1900* (Cambridge, 1986), 2–3.
15. Ibid., 7.
16. Ibid., 270.
17. Alfred Crosby, *Germs, Seeds and Animals: Studies in Ecological History* (New York, 1994), xiii.
18. I.G.Simmons, *Changing the Face of the Earth: Culture, Environment, History* (Oxford, 1989), 126–7.
19. D.B. Grigg, *The Agricultural Systems of the World: An Evolutionary Approach* (Cambridge, 1974), 27.
20. See, for example, Tom Griffiths, 'Ecology and Empire: Towards an Australian history of the world', in Tom Griffiths and Libby Robin (eds.), *Ecology and Empire: Environmental History of Settler Societies* (Keele, 1997), ch.1.
21. Eric Wolf, *Europe and the People Without History* (Berkeley, 1982), chs.5–6. The passage quoted is on p.133.
22. For a recent summary of intercontinental trade patterns since 1492, see Patrick Karl O'Brien, 'Intercontinental Trade and the Development of the Third World since the Industrial Revolution', *Journal of World History*, 8 (1997), 75–133.
23. Dudley E. Baines, *Emigration from Europe, 1815–1930* (Basingstoke, 1991), 11–12.
24. Ibid., 11–12; B.L. Turner II and others (eds.), *The Earth as Transformed by Human Action: Global and Regional Change in the Biosphere over the Past 300 Years* (Cambridge, 1990), Table 6-1.
25. Lewis, *Growth and Fluctuations*, Table A.12. The index numbers (1913 = 100) were: 1881– value 36.4, volume 37.8; 1893 – value 39.9, volume 49.6; 1899 – value 50.4, volume 63.2.
26. John R. Hanson II, *Trade in Transition: Exports from the Third World, 1840–1900* (New York, 1980), 13–31, 129–34.
27. Turner, *Earth Transformed*, Table 10-2.
28. For Thornwaite's system see C.W. Thornwaite, 'An Approach toward a Rational Classification of Climate', *Geographical Review*, V (1948), 55–94. A convenient set of maps showing this typology is found in Colin Clark, *Population Growth and Land Use* (London, 1967), 144–7.
29. J.M. Powell, *An Historical Geography of Modern Australia: The restive fringe* (Cambridge, 1988), esp. ch. 5; the quoted passage is on p.121. See also Griffiths and Robin, *Ecology and Empire*, chs. 2–7, 11–13.
30. Grigg, *Agricultural Systems*, 182, 184.
31. Ibid., Table 44.
32. G.E. Fussell, 'Growth of Food Production' in Charles Singer and others (eds.), *A History of Technology Volume V: The Late Nineteenth Century, 1850– 1900* (Oxford, 1958), 5–6.
33. Avner Offer, *The First World War: An Agrarian Interpretation* (Oxford, 1989), 141–2, 148–9.
34. These characteristics of settler agriculture survived well into the twentieth century – in the 1960s wheat yields per hectare in most of the neo-Europes were about one-third of those in western Europe. Grigg, *Agricultural Systems*, 257.

35. Quoted in Denoon, *Settler Capitalism*, 97.
36. Grigg, *Agricultural Systems*, 262–3.
37. Michael Williams, *Americans and Their Forests: A Historical Geography* (Oxford, 1989), 353–7.
38. Grigg, *Agricultural Systems*, 265.
39. Ibid., 262.
40. On these developments, see T.C. Smith, *Agrarian Origins of Modern Japan* (Stanford, 1959), P. Francks, *Japanese Economic Development: Theory and Practice* (London, 1992), B.R. Tomlinson, *The Economy of Modern India, 1870–1960* (Cambridge, 1993), and A.G. Hopkins, *An Economic History of West Africa* (London, 1973).

Instilling the 'Sterling Tradition': Decolonization and the Creation of a Central Bank in Ghana

S.E. STOCKWELL

Among the most important and contentious debates around the history of European decolonization is that concerning the significance in imperial policy-making of calculations of metropolitan economic interest and the consequences of colonial rule for post-colonial economic experiences. Such questions have been key preoccupations in much of David Fieldhouse's work.[1] Economic decolonization is also a central theme in his monumental history of the United Africa Company (UAC), which is consequently among the best case studies through which to approach these issues at a micro-level, one which any future synthesis of the subject will have to take fully into account.[2] The economic dimension of decolonization is just one of the many topics provocatively highlighted in a widely discussed, recent general interpretation of British imperialism. In *British Imperialism*, P.J. Cain and A.G. Hopkins argue that developments in British colonial policy after 1945 are best understood in the context of the changing fortunes of sterling.[3] Yet key aspects of the economics of decolonization await detailed investigation from historians of the kind Fieldhouse has now afforded UAC. Of particular significance is the disengagement of the colonies from the financial institutions of empire, and the creation of national banking and currency systems.[4] The following essay aims to make a modest contribution to our understanding of this issue.

This disengagement was central to economic decolonization, because at the end of the Second World War, on the eve of African decolonization, the colonial empire remained tightly bound into an imperial financial system. Indeed, for British colonies in Africa these ties were greater in the late colonial period than ever before, for the introduction of controls during the war had brought about a transformation of the sterling area from a loose association of countries basing their exchange rates on sterling into a highly regulated system. In 1945 British colonies, as members of the sterling area, jointly applied exchange control on transactions with outside countries, and maintained a common reserve of gold and dollars held in London. Colonial currencies were issued by regional currency boards: in the West African colonies of Nigeria, the Gold Coast, Gambia, and Sierra Leone by the West African Currency Board, established in 1912. These boards acted as money changers, exchanging sterling for local currencies issued at fixed exchange rates, and guaranteeing convertibility between colonial currencies and sterling. The boards also supervised the investment of the reserves backing each colonial currency, typically invested in British government securities and constituting in effect a loan to the British government.

Decolonization called into question this whole system. Although most colonies pledged to remain in the sterling area at independence, they withdrew from the colonial currency boards, establishing their own central banks with currency-issuing functions. Thus equipped, Britain's former colonies were free, should they wish, to end convertibility with sterling, to withdraw their funds invested in British securities, and to secede from the sterling area. Interesting comparisons can be drawn here between French and British decolonization, for former French colonies in sub-Saharan Africa chose to maintain much more of their colonial system, for example creating regional rather than national central banks, and retaining the CFA currency system as members of the franc zone. These contrasting choices have had long-term economic consequences for post-colonial African states. In the case of Ghana (the Gold Coast), with which this paper is concerned, some studies, drawing comparisons with the Ivory Coast in Francophone West Africa, have identified the creation of national banking and currency institutions as contributing to Ghana's economic problems in the 1960s and 1970s. Released from the constraints of the colonial system, it is argued, successive governments in Ghana were led down the path of over-valuation and sought central bank credits to finance expenditure deficits.[5]

Aside from their long-term economic importance, the creation of these national banks and currencies raises interesting questions for historians. How much significance did African nationalists attach to the acquisition of national banks and currencies, and for what reasons? What considerations governed British policy on banking and currency? What was the impact of these developments on the British banks, which, in the absence of central banks in the colonies, had acted as bankers to governments and which largely dominated commercial banking in the empire? This article considers these questions in relation to the establishment of, first, a national bank, and secondly, a central bank with currency-issuing functions, in the Gold Coast. This offers an especially interesting case because the Gold Coast was one of the first British African colonies to attain independence, the first to establish its own central bank, and, by virtue of its export earnings, one of the most valuable colonial sterling-area members. Comparisons will be drawn in the conclusion with other recently published studies addressing similar questions with reference to other parts of the colonial empire.

By the Second World War the Gold Coast was considered to be the most politically advanced of Britain's African colonies. The colony's first political party campaigning for self-government, the United Gold Coast Convention (UGCC), was formed in August 1947 under the leadership of professionals and merchants. In late 1947 they arranged for Kwame Nkrumah, the general secretary to the West African National Secretariat in London, to return to the Gold Coast to take up the post of party secretary. The following year rioting broke out in the colony, resulting in the appointment of a commission of enquiry under the chairmanship of Aiken Watson, and subsequently the Coussey Committee on constitutional reform. This led in 1951 to the creation of an African assembly and partial African self-government. These years also saw significant developments in Gold Coast nationalist politics, as a split emerged between, on the one hand, the Gold Coast Convention leaders, and on the other hand, Kwame Nkrumah, as he began to develop a following among the youth element of the party. In June 1949 Nkrumah finally broke with the UGCC forming his own party, the Convention People's Party (CPP), and in 1950 the new party, in alliance with a variety of organizations in the colony including farmers'associations and trade unions, branded the Coussey Committee's proposals for constitutional reform insufficient, and launched a Positive Action campaign to coerce government into conceding 'self-government now'. Contrary to official expectations, the CPP won the first elections to the new assembly, necessitating Nkrumah's release from jail where he had been imprisoned for his part in the Positive Action campaign.

From the outset opposition to the financial structures of colonialism constituted a significant element to this nationalist challenge to British rule. African politicians argued that development in the Gold Coast was constrained by the obligations sterling-area membership entailed. Colonial dollar-earnings were pooled in London (for which the colonies received an allocation of sterling), and since ceilings were placed on purchases by sterling-area members from the dollar area, this mechanism allowed Britain to extract maximum advantage from the dollar-area trading activities of the colonies. The colonies were net contributors to the sterling area; the Dominions and Britain drew from the sterling area's dollar pool. The accommodation of Gold Coast import policies to those of the area as a whole and the colony's inability to gain access to all the dollars it contributed to the sterling-area were especially resented by African politicians.[6]

By the late 1940s British banks in the colony had also become the target of African opposition. Two British banks, the Bank of British West Africa (BBWA) and Barclays Dominion Colonial and Overseas (DCO), exercised a virtual monopoly over banking in the colony. There were no African banks – local companies had been prevented from entering into banking business since 1906 – although a co-operative bank was formed just after the Second World War.[7] There were several aspects of the British banks' operations which came in for criticism. For a start, the overwhelming mass of their business was with other expatriate companies, with both banks reluctant to lend to African customers they considered unable to offer adequate or reliable security,[8] provoking allegations of discriminatory lending policies which, it was held, deprived local enterprises of capital. It was also alleged that the banks'charges were too high.

The creation of some form of state-aided or national bank was envisaged by African politicians as one solution to these individual and national credit requirements. In May 1948 J.B. Danquah, a founding member of the UGCC and member of the legislative council, gave notice of his intention to apply for leave to introduce a bill for the establishment of a bank. The bill was described by Robert Scott, the Gold Coast colonial secretary, as more a statement of policy than a serious draft of legislation.[9] Although Gold Coast politicians argued that a bank was an essential vehicle of development, their campaign was as much based on political considerations as economic, as Danquah was subsequently to admit.[10]

This campaign marked the beginnings of the sustained pressure in the colony for reform, forcing the Colonial Office to consider the future of banking in the colony at a time when there was still little anticipation of the speed with which the Gold Coast would achieve independence.[11] Moreover, agitation in the Gold Coast occurred in a period in which the thrust of British colonial policy was towards greater, rather than reduced, imperial economic integration as the most comprehensive moves yet were being made to develop the resources of the empire sterling-area for Britain's benefit. In summer 1947 Britain attempted to end exchange controls on transactions with countries outside the sterling area but the ensuing disastrous run on sterling between July and August 1947 resulted in the restoration of controls and the suspension of free convertibility on 20 August. In the consequent financial crisis, the British government pressed for increased colonial production of dollar-earning export commodities in order to relieve the sterling-area's deficit with the dollar area. The post-war years also saw, as a result primarily of the boom in commodity prices, the growth in colonial sterling balances leading to fears that rapid withdrawal by the colonies from these reserves, should they obtain sufficient freedom to do so, could destabilize the British economy.[12] It has been calculated that the currency reserves constituted approximately one third of all colonial sterling balances.[13]

If moves towards financial devolution in the Gold Coast ran counter to wider imperial policy in the late 1940s, the Colonial Office was also sceptical from the outset about the wisdom of establishing any form of government-sponsored bank in the Gold Coast. Particular concern was expressed about the possible dangers of extending credit into spheres where apparently the commercial banks had not thought it 'appropriate to venture'.[14] Furthermore, although the nationalist campaign was at this stage for a 'state-aided' or 'national' bank rather than one with currency-issuing functions, it none the less raised the spectre of the possible transformation of a state bank into a full central bank.[15]

The criticism of existing banking facilities, however, coming so soon after the Accra disturbances, left the British government – at least in the opinion of the Gold Coast colonial government – with little choice but to respond. The Colonial Office was warned by Scott that failure to do so would be read as 'another manifestation of the European's desire to perpetuate "exploitation"'. It emerged, moreover, that the colonial government had itself been contemplating new departures in the banking field. Scott informed the secretary of state for the colonies that an informal committee of officials, members of the legislative council, and Africans involved in commerce, had been formed in August 1947 with a view to considering ways in which greater African participation in trade and commerce could be encouraged. One of its recommendations was that consideration be given to the establishment of a state bank to provide greater facilities for Africans seeking financial assistance for trade and industry. Scott now suggested that the colonial government seize the initiative from Danquah and introduce its own bill prepared as a result of these discussions.[16] Further, it transpired that, in the charged political atmosphere of the time, the colonial government, acting precipitately, had already indicated to nationalists its willingness to contemplate the creation of a new institution in the form of an agricultural bank. In July 1948 the colony's financial secretary, R.P. Armitage, admitted that his government was 'deeply committed in principle' to taking some action and 'would find it difficult to retreat'.[17] Given these circumstances, it was arranged for an adviser on banking issues to visit the Gold Coast. The man chosen, G. D. Paton, was recommended by the Bank of England and was already acting as an adviser to the Nigerian government on banking issues.

Paton's report, submitted to the colonial secretary on 4 December 1948, recommended various changes including the amendment of the legislation restricting the formation of local banking companies and an extension to the recently established co-operative banking system. On economic grounds alone, Paton found there was little need for a new state bank, but concluded that it might be politically desirable to establish one.[18] These findings did little to persuade the Colonial Office, which informed the governor of the Gold Coast that it viewed proposals for a state bank 'with considerable doubt'.[19] The colonial government now agreed that the establishment of a state bank would be premature and preferred to concentrate on other means of funding development, perhaps via the creation of an agricultural loans board,[20] but in view of the sustained pressure they were still facing from J.B. Danquah, officials were unable to let the issue drop and concluded that the appointment of a select committee to consider the report further was unavoidable. As the colonial government reported to the Colonial Office, it 'had headed Danquah off this subject on several occasions', but was unable 'to keep the matter out of public debate any longer'. Nonetheless, it still hoped to prevent nationalist demands going any further. Armitage, chair of the committee appointed to consider the possibility of establishing a national bank, endeavoured 'to get the Committee to narrow the field and discard certain types of banking particularly that of a Commercial Bank and of Reserve Bank'. He was unable, however, to persuade the committee, the members of which included Danquah as well as a representative of expatriate business, the UAC's Patrick Fitzgerald, to do anything other than recommend that further advice be sought on the suitability of different banking systems.[21]

By this time the CPP's success in the 1951 elections to the colony's new legislative assembly had relegated Danquah to the opposition benches, where he and other former members of the UGCC formed the Ghana Congress Party in 1952. Although the campaign for a national bank had originated with those who were now opposition members, the CPP had also taken up the issue, advocating the establishment of a national bank in its election manifesto.[22] Indeed, in London, officials at the Bank of England expressed concern at the impact the CPP's electoral success might have on the banking issue. They had found Danquah 'a difficult customer but clever', who was '*relatively* speaking, moderate and sane'; Nkrumah and his associates, it was feared, were, 'not unnaturally, after the Stabilisation, etc., Funds'.[23] In fact the CPP leadership proved to be more accommodating than some initially anticipated, but from the outset there was continued pressure on the CPP from both its own backbenchers and from opposition members to press on with the creation of national banking and currency institutions. As one Bank of England official observed, among the backbenchers were those who 'behave most rationally in the Legislative Assembly and then go out to their constituencies and stir up trouble by making promises directly contrary to their own Government Policy';[24] while opposition members continued to challenge Nkrumah's government to grasp the nettle of financial reform, calling not just for a state bank, but for the creation of a full central bank which would be able to issue currency.[25]

On assuming office, the CPP proceeded to approve the recommendation made by the Gold Coast committee that further investigation of the banking issue be undertaken, and Sir Cecil Trevor, former deputy governor of the Reserve Bank of India, was selected for the task. The appointment of this second inquiry in 1951 seems to have been regarded in London as little more than a paper exercise. Trevor's name was one of several put forward by the Bank of England. Officials at the Bank observed that the individuals suggested 'may look too good for such a fruitless enterprise', but noted that it was regarded as important to send 'someone who looks pretty responsible'.[26] Yet contrary to these expectations, Trevor's report signed in 1951 did recommend the establishment of a national bank,[27] dividing opinion within the Colonial Office: while some officials were unable to agree with its conclusion in favour of the establishment of a bank, others viewed it more sympathetically.[28] Whatever its reservations the Colonial Office's hand had been forced by the report in which Trevor appeared to have committed himself to the establishment of a bank before discussing the issue with the Colonial Office, but it was conceded in London that Trevor had acted legitimately, as he was technically employed by the Gold Coast government.[29] With acceptance by the Gold Coast executive council of Trevor's recommendation to establish a national bank, the necessary legislation was prepared, and in May 1953 the Bank of the Gold Coast opened for business, under the management of A. Eggleston, formerly employed at the Imperial Bank of India.

The Colonial Office, Bank of England, and Treasury hoped that by agreeing to the establishment of the bank they would succeed in winning the initiative and head off demands for further change. Thus as Henry Bourdillon, assistant secretary at the Colonial Office, acknowledged while considering the Trevor Report, it was 'much better to make a start on a modest scale now, and to learn from a modest failure if this cannot be avoided, than to be obliged to give way later to some dangerous and far-reaching proposal'.[30] Commenting retrospectively on the establishment of the Bank of the Gold Coast, the Bank of England recorded that, 'the real purpose was to deflect African pressure for the creation of a central bank'.[31] In this context it was noted that the vacuum in commercial banking facilities, which the Bank of the Gold Coast was allegedly brought into existence to fill, did not in fact exist. For a short while it looked as if this strategy had succeeded, but it was apparent that calls for further reform would follow. During the reading of the ordinance for the establishment of the Bank of the Gold Coast in 1952, several speakers including Danquah had expressed their disappointment at the absence of any provision for the new bank to develop automatically into a central bank.[32]

If the Colonial Office was aware that the Gold Coast was unlikely to be content with a mere commercial bank, considering whether 'anything can or should be done now in anticipation of any ultimate change',[33] it nevertheless preferred to tinker with existing currency board arrangements rather than envisage the colony's withdrawal from the colonial currency system altogether. Proposals for admitting greater West African representation and localization into the organization of the WACB were floated before the Board and the West African governments in 1952,[34] with the Colonial Office canvassing the idea of separate note issues administered by commissioners in the Gold Coast and Nigeria. Even in this respect, however, officials stated that 'our strong inclination is to do nothing'.[35] The Colonial Office's stand, described at the Bank of England as the strongest 'ever seen in regard to reservation of currency matters',[36] was generally welcomed by the Treasury and the Bank of England, although reservations were expressed by officials at both. Some at the Treasury doubted whether it would prove politically possible to hold this line,[37] and at the Bank Jack Fisher, adviser to its governors, stressed the importance of training Africans in currency management in preparation for the further changes which would inevitably come.[38]

Colonial officials in Accra were more disapproving, pressing, as they had done in the late 1940s, for a more progressive policy.[39] Metropolitan proposals for minor adjustments to the colonial currency system were criticized as insufficient, and if there was to be change it must be – in the Colonial Office's own words – 'more than a palliative'.[40] Thus from Accra Reginald Saloway, ex-officio chief secretary and minister of defence and external affairs, argued that the Gold Coast 'must move in the direction of a Bank of Issue', and alleged that if the British government were to do nothing, 'we will arrive at the day when – out here at all events – we shall be entirely weaponless against such an attack'. He advised that they 'do everything possible now to create good will by anticipating the demand which we know must come'.[41]

It is possible that the impact of this appeal may have been weakened by news, received shortly afterwards from the governor, that Nkrumah appeared to be willing to delay the issue of a Gold Coast currency until the country obtained independence in order that it could be issued under the country's new name of Ghana.[42] For the Colonial Office, still reluctant to concede control of monetary and currency matters, introduced only minor changes into the regulations of all currency boards. Limited investment of currency reserves and a small fiduciary issue were permitted, but with the currencies of the colonies remaining fully backed by, and exchangeable with, sterling[43] – a departure which can be traced back to discussions held during the Second World War, when the merits of allowing the colonies to use a small proportion of their currency funds for local development purposes had been considered.[44]

As it turned out, negotiations for a central bank began within two years of the opening of the Bank of the Gold Coast, swept along by further political change in the colony. The creation of a central bank featured in campaigning for a second general election in the Gold Coast in June 1954,[45] and Kenneth Tours, economic adviser in the colony, suggested that if the CPP were returned to office, and once a new constitution had come into operation conceding full internal self-government, the CPP would move on the matter of the bank.[46] A month later the officer administering the government in the Gold Coast wrote to the Colonial Office requesting advice on a local currency issue to coincide with full independence for the colony.[47] Following his party's success in the elections, the new CPP minister of finance, Komlo Gbedemah, at a meeting with the secretary of state for the colonies in December 1954, confirmed his government's wish to disengage from the currency board.[48] By this stage political pressure in the Gold Coast was coupled with growing international interest in colonial currency arrangements when World Bank missions to Nigeria and Malaya in the 1950s reported in favour of the establishment of central banks in each colony.[49]

While accepting that the colony would now secede from the WACB, officials in London hoped that Gbedemah had been dissuaded during discussions in late 1954 from proceeding with the immediate transformation of the Bank of the Gold Coast into a full central bank. Instead, as papers prepared in London for an abortive conference in spring 1955 on the future of the WACB showed, it was expected that the Gold Coast would opt for an intermediary settlement of a banking and currency commission.[50] However, these hopes were dashed when, in late summer 1955, examples of the country's new notes were received and it became apparent that the CPP government intended they should be issued by the Bank of the Gold Coast.[51]

The Bank of England, criticizing the handling of the banking question, recognized the extent to which it – like the Colonial Office and Treasury – had repeatedly failed to keep pace with opinion in the Gold Coast. In August 1955 J.B. Loynes, an adviser at the Bank of England, complained that 'Both Whitehall and ourselves have been to some extent on the wrong foot since Trevor's unfortunate report of 1952.'[52] A week later Jack Fisher criticized the apparent lack of communication between Gbedemah and Eggleston on the one hand, and the Colonial Office on the other, annotating a memorandum with the comment 'the CO seem quite unable to keep themselves properly informed about what is going on'.[53]

The Colonial Office for its part had found its handling of the banking issue undermined by the tendency of some of the personnel despatched to the colony to attach themselves to the nationalist banking cause: while Trevor had committed himself to the establishment of a national bank without consulting London, so Eggleston, new managing director of the Bank of the Gold Coast, was now suspected of harbouring his own ambition to transform his bank into a central bank. The introduction of full internal self-government after the 1954 elections and the appointment of a CPP figure as minister of finance also made it more difficult for the Colonial Office to stay informed. In November 1954, for instance, the department had been surprised to learn that Gbedemah was in London holding discussions with various banks. His activities were discovered only when British officials were alerted to the fact that he had failed to turn up to a cocktail party arranged in his honour by the Gold Coast commissioner in London.[54] Commenting on the difficulty of dealing with Gbedemah, the Colonial Office lamented the fact that 'the ambitious Mr Eggleston has the ear of the GC Govt. [sic] and we have not'.[55]

Bowing to what now appeared to be the inevitable creation of a bank of issue, representatives of the Treasury and the Bank of England sitting on the WACB realized that they must co-operate with the colony in order to achieve a successful central banking system, 'to cut our losses and press for the establishment of the Bank as a full Bank of Issue forthwith'.[56] The Colonial Office also recognized the necessity of ensuring that the currency arrangements were successful: 'the basic essential, in fact, is to ensure that the Gold Coast government does not set up a Frankenstein'. It was important to both the Gold Coast and to Britain that the establishment of a bank of issue and the introduction of a new currency be done in such a way that commercial confidence in the Gold Coast would not be diminished. The Colonial Office acknowledged that 'we in the UK have a vital interest in seeing that disruptions in monetary mechanisms inside the sterling area do not occur if they can be avoided'.[57]

Although British officials and the Bank of England had expressed disappointment at their failure to stall demands for a central bank, they now sought to exercise control over subsequent developments leading to the creation of the bank and the colony's secession from the currency board. The Colonial Office, at the suggestion of the Bank of England, was careful to 'avoid pressing a reluctant Mr Gbedemah to go to the Bank of England for advice: we must rather get him to ask for it'.[58] After its repeated failure to control the development of agitation on the banking issue, the Colonial Office now appeared to have been successful. At a meeting between Gbedemah and the Governor of the Bank of England they agreed that the Bank's J.B. Loynes should henceforth act as adviser to the Gold Coast government. Loynes was charged, above all, with securing the Gold Coast's government's acceptance that commercial and central banking functions be distinct: any other arrangement would allow the Bank of the Gold Coast to compete with other commercial banks with the help of state funds, as well as with the deposits the other commercial banks would be obliged to hold with the bank.

Under Loynes' guidance two bills were prepared: one to amend the Bank of the Gold Coast ordinance, with a view to making the Bank of the Gold Coast into a purely commercial banking institution, the Ghana Commercial Bank; and the second to provide for the creation of a central bank, to be known as the Bank of Ghana. The Bank of Ghana was intended to be the issuing authority of the new national currency; to be responsible for the investment of the government's externally held reserves; to act as a banker and adviser to the government; and, as the ultimate banking authority, to hold accounts of the other commercial banks in the country.[59] As Loynes saw it, 'my aim has been to give the people here something which looks fairly imposing but which, if applied, should not be too dangerous'.[60] Loynes was presumably referring to the 'danger' of creating a banking system which, if too complicated or without the necessary safeguards, would have been open to mismanagement and abuse.

In a public relations initiative, advance production of the new currency was financed by WACB purchase of Gold Coast government treasury bills,[61] while the Royal Mint bid for the task of minting the new currency.[62] Bank of England personnel were appointed to senior positions, including that of Deputy Governor, Manager of the Issue Department, and Manager of the Bank Department, ensuring that further links were forged between the two banks. This was, as a Conservative party research paper commented, a natural means through which to instill 'the sterling tradition'.[63] In addition, an account was opened by the new Bank of Ghana with the Bank of England (although in common with most Commonwealth countries, it also opened a dollar account with the Federal Reserve Bank of New York).[64]

The Bank of Ghana opened its doors in 1957. Its new currency units were made equivalent to sterling, with only a limited fiduciary issue permitted. The degree to which the Gold Coast still at this stage appeared to be tied to sterling became a focus of some criticism during the passage of legislation to establish the new Bank of Ghana.[65] WACB currency remained legal tender in Ghana until July 1959. By 1961 the imposition of exchange control in Ghana had ended free convertibility of the new currency with sterling. In 1965 when the last of the four British West African colonies, the Gambia, obtained independence, the Board was wound up.

From 1948, then, sustained nationalist agitation for changes to the colony's banking and currency arrangements resulted in, first, the creation of a national bank and, secondly, the establishment of a central bank and the Gold Coast's withdrawal from the colonial currency board. What was the impact of these developments on the British banks? Even before the establishment of the Bank of the Gold Coast, British banks were adversely affected by the nationalist campaign. Both banks, Barclays DCO and BBWA, had already attempted to effect some improvements in their operations generally in the colonial empire: Barclays DCO established a financial intermediary, Barclays Overseas Development Corporation, to provide funds for local development, and BBWA had modified its lending policy.[66] However, the extensive criticism of both banks in the Gold Coast in the late 1940s encouraged the Bank of England to reconsider its relations with the two banks over West African issues. Its officials contended that the British banks had been given 'special treatment' in West Africa in the past as the region was acknowledged to be one likely to yield only low overall banking profits. Now, not only was this no longer justified given relative boom conditions in West Africa in this period,[67] but both were encouraged to reduce charges. This, it was argued, would 'have quite an effect in stealing the thunder of ill-disposed or ill-informed people in West Africa'.[68] In response, DCO and BBWA offered to reduce their internal remittance rates, but claimed they were unable to reduce their London-West Africa rates without incurring considerable loss of income.[69]

The establishment of the Bank of the Gold Coast in 1953 presented British banks with a new competitor. A desire to establish branches in advance of the new bank may have been one factor behind the rapid expansion both banks embarked upon in the early 1950s: between 1952 and 1962 the number of BBWA and DCO branches in the country rose from 15 to 54 and 12 to 60 respectively.[70] This expansion, however, also occurred in a period in which the retreat of European trading companies, which had previously advanced cash to African traders, farmers, and buying agencies, from general retailing and cocoa buying to more specialist and wholesale merchandizing left a vacuum into which the banks could move.[71] Nevertheless, the establishment of an institution intended specifically to solve the problem of rural credit-supply may have also been welcomed in so far as it effectively relieved BBWA and Barclays DCO from some of the responsibilities of lending to Africans against what was considered to be inadequate security.[72]

The campaign for the development of national bank and currency institutions also raises interesting questions about the nature of Gold Coast nationalist politics. Although nationalists argued that indigenous banking institutions would contribute to the colony's economic development, the campaign originated as much from political as economic considerations. Once the campaign was underway, some African nationalists appear to have been persuaded by arguments that first, a national bank, and secondly, a central bank were unnecessary on economic grounds. However, by appropriating the issue of banking for their cause, politicians of all persuasions created a political constituency which would not be satisfied by half-measures. Thus Armitage had reported in 1949 that although members of the select committee established to consider Paton's report were aware that certain types of banking were inappropriate for the Gold Coast, the 'Committee wanted to save its face'.[73]

From 1951 the CPP in particular could ill afford to take a soft line on an issue flagged by their 'moderate' opponents. It is striking that, allegedly, the two men most informed on banking issues – Gbedemah, minister of finance, and Eggleston, managing director of the Bank of the Gold Coast, opposed Nkrumah's decision to go ahead with the establishment of a full central bank. The final decision to proceed with the establishment of a central bank had apparently be taken at a private meeting between Nkrumah, Gbedemah, and Kojo Botsio, minister of state, overruling the decision reached shortly before at a full cabinet meeting.[74] It was no doubt inevitable that opposition members would seek to make political capital out of the banking issue, and for them as for the CPP the bank was a political symbol, but even allowing for this, and the fact that it was Nkrumah's government which introduced all relevant legislation, the association from the outset of politicians usually regarded as more 'moderate'than their socialist CPP counterparts with the campaign for autonomous banking and currency institutions nonetheless raises interesting questions about the nature of 'radical' and 'moderate' African nationalism. Opposition members' association with banking issues may reflect the differences in composition of Gold Coast nationalist parties: Richard Rathbone has shown that African businessmen, deprived of opportunities under the colonial government, first found a voice in the UGCC.[75] The interest shown by Danquah as well as that of another prominent campaigner for banking reform, his nephew Ofori Atta, may also have derived in part from Ofori Atta I's interest in establishing an African bank in the 1930s.[76] One might also speculate as to why the advocacy of such radical policies is not reflected in the conventional designation of this group of nationalists as 'moderates'. The explanation is surely that British observers were ultimately less concerned with the implications of the nationalists' economic policies for the imperial financial system, however significant, than with the geopolitical consequences of Nkrumah's political radicalism.

For its part, in the face of sustained nationalist pressure, the Colonial Office had from 1947 fought a rearguard action on the banking issue, attempting to moderate nationalist demands, and to delay Gold Coast secession from the colonial currency board and the establishment of a central bank. How can officials' reluctance to see the Gold Coast establish a national and then central bank be explained? In part, the department's stance reflected the range of other, often conflicting, considerations which had to be reconciled with any initiatives taken in respect to the issue of currency in the Gold Coast. These included government obligations towards the International Monetary Fund, where Britain was considered responsible for the currency policies of its colonies, and the need to consider all four British West African colonies together. The views of other West African governments on the future of the WACB had been sought early in 1953 when the question of the Gold Coast's continued membership was raised, and the governors of Sierra Leone and the Gambia came down strongly against any change to the current system. Concern was also expressed at the possible reaction from Sir Godfrey Huggins, prime minister of Southern Rhodesia, should developments in banking and currency in the Gold Coast outstrip those in the white settler colony or those contemplated for the proposed Central Africa Federation.[77]

The Colonial Office's reluctance to introduce radical changes to colonial currency arrangements may additionally have reflected the view that changes to the currency system were unnecessary on economic grounds. Some support for these views could be found, as we have seen, in the reports commissioned to enquire into the colony's banking arrangements as well as in other contemporary studies of the sterling area and colonial currencies. In 1953, for instance, in a survey of colonial monetary conditions published under the auspices of the Colonial Office, Ida Greaves argued that possession of an independent currency would not necessarily increase a colony's prosperity,[78] although it should be noted that there was little consensus as to whether or not the colonial currency system imposed a burden on the colonies.[79]

There is little evidence that the British government aimed at any point at creating dependency; indeed the Colonial Office deplored the possibility: 'The world is strewn with unsatisfactory Central banks and shaky currencies and the combination of the two in any country is simply to replace political dependence by economic dependence, exemplified in [the] form of foreign aid.'[80] Moreover, as we have seen, while British officials and the Bank of England were in a position to influence the form of central banking and currency adopted in the colony, it would be unrealistic to assume that they could have further stalled nationalist demands for either monetary or political independence.

Although Britain's reluctance to see the establishment of a central bank does not seem to have been determined by a desire to retain control of its former colony whilst transferring political power, the nationalist campaign did commence at a point at which the economic development of the colonies was considered vital to British recovery. By the time the central bank was established, the empire sterling-area was of diminishing value to Britain,[81] and the percentage of the colony's external trade conducted with the United Kingdom declining.[82] Nevertheless, British policy addressed the interests of the sterling area as a whole, seeking to preserve the existing financial ties between Britain and the Gold Coast and to avoid the disruption within the sterling area which West African financial instability would produce. Once it had become clear that Gold Coast ministers intended proceeding with the immediate creation of a central bank, British officials and the Bank of England co-operated with Nkrumah's government in a manner which corresponds to Cain and Hopkins's thesis that the Bank of England sought to keep the Commonwealth 'sterling-minded', if not, as officials' resistance to changes to the Gold Coast banking system illustrates, their claim that the formation of central banking in the colonies was actually 'encouraged' in the later 1950s.[83]

Above all, the issue of central banking and the country's membership of the sterling area was conceived in political, as well as financial, terms. It was of 'great political significance to the free world that the GC [sic] should attain full independence as an indisputably going concern'.[84] Several years later, whilst advising the chancellor of the exchequer, John Selwyn Lloyd, in advance of a meeting with Gbedemah to discuss rumours that Ghana proposed withdrawing from the area, the Bank of England argued that, 'Mr Gbedemah will hardly need reminding that the most important aspect of the question is the political aspect'. It would be the first time that any Commonwealth country had left the sterling area, and officials feared that Ghana's departure 'would certainly give the outside world the impression that Ghana wished in some sense to draw away to some extent from the Commonwealth'.[85]

On a wider front, parallels can be drawn between the transition to central banking in the Gold Coast and the experience of the other British colony which achieved independence in 1957, Malaya. In the latter case, Schenk also found that Britain resisted Malayan monetary independence, and went on to argue, as this article has done, that this did not represent an attempt on the part of the British government to move from formal to informal empire.[86] A recent study of banking in Nigeria by Ugochukwu Uche also offers interesting comparisons: it shows that the Bank of England was reluctant to see the establishment of a central bank in Nigeria, and attempted to persuade the World Bank to abandon its support for such a move.[87]

Nevertheless, as this paper has shown, the evolution of post-colonial financial institutions can be properly understood only in terms of their more immediate political context. Viewed from the 'local'perspective, colonial policy in relation to an issue often held to be at the crux of Britain's post-war relationships with its colonies was characterized by confusion and an inability on the part of the Colonial Office to keep abreast of developments in the colony. African nationalist pressure and, additionally, international pressure in the form of World Bank recommendations forced the dissolution of the West African colonial currency system. Yet, the British government did in the end succeed in exercising a supervisory role over the creation of the Bank of Ghana and at independence Ghana remained within the sterling area, retaining a fixed exchange rate with sterling. While this was of significance to Britain, it was above all the political aspect of the banking issue which concerned British officials. In this respect, this article bears out David Fieldhouse's contention in his broad survey of development in Anglophone Africa that, 'as more evidence becomes available, it will become clear that decolonization was primarily a political rather than an economic phenomenon so far as British officials and businessmen were concerned'. It also illustrates his conclusions reached for nineteenth-century British imperialism that economic factors, while important, were ultimately subordinate to the political imperatives of metropole and periphery.[88]

NOTES

I am very grateful to Colin Newbury, Catherine Schenk, Richard Rathbone, and Arthur Burns for their helpful comments on an earlier version of this article, and to the archivists of the Bank of England, and to Barclays Bank of Ghana, the Standard Chartered Bank of Ghana, and interviewees for their assistance.

1. D.K. Fieldhouse, *Black Africa 1945–1980: Economic Decolonization and Arrested Development* (London, 1986); 'Arrested Development in Anglophone Black Africa?', in P. Gifford and W.R. Louis (eds.), *Decolonization and African Independence: The Transfer of Power, 1960–1980* (New Haven and London, 1988); 'Decolonization, Development, and Dependence: A Survey of Changing Attitudes', in P. Gifford and W.R. Louis (eds.), *The Transfer of Power in Africa: Decolonization, 1940–1960* (New Haven and London, 1982).
2. D.K. Fieldhouse, *Merchant Capital and Economic Decolonization: The United Africa Company 1929–1987* (Oxford, 1994).
3. P.J. Cain and A.G. Hopkins, *British Imperialism*, II, *Crisis and Deconstruction 1914–1990* (London, 1993), ch.11.
4. This article is based on research undertaken for S. Stockwell, 'British Business, Politics and Decolonisation in the Gold Coast c. 1945–1960'(University of Oxford D.Phil, 1993).There is a limited discussion of the creation of the Ghanaian central bank in Y. Bangura, *Britain*

and Commonwealth Africa: The Politics of Economic Relations, 1951–75 (Manchester, 1983), 46–53, and a survey of colonial monetary and banking systems in post-war Africa in W.T. Newlyn and D.C. Rowan, *Money and Banking in British Colonial Africa* (Oxford, 1954). The relevant company histories, Sir J. Crossley and J. Blandford, *The DCO Story: A History of Banking in Many Countries 1925–71* (London, 1975) and R. Fry, *Bankers in West Africa: The Story of the Bank of British West Africa Ltd.* (London, 1976), say little about the creation of the Bank of the Gold Coast or the Bank of Ghana. For other regions of the British colonial empire, see C. Schenk 'The Origins of a Central Bank in Malaya and the Transition to Independence, 1954–59', *Journal of Imperial and Commonwealth History*, XXI (1993), 409–31; and C. Ugochukwu Uche, 'Bank of England vs the IBRD: Did the Nigerian Colony Deserve a Central Bank?', *Explorations in Economic History*, 34 (1997), 220–41. Since this article was written a piece published by Ugochukwu Uche has been brought to my attention: 'From currency board to central banking: the Gold Coast experience', *South African Journal of Economic History*, 10, 2 (1955), 80–94. Although addressing the same subject, there are significant differences of scope and approach between our two articles.

5. F. Teal, 'The Foreign Exchange Regime and Growth: A Comparison of Ghana and the Ivory Coast', *African Affairs*, 85 (1986), 267–82; D. Rimmer, *Staying Poor: Ghana's Political Economy, 1950–1990* (Oxford, 1992), 205–6.
6. Although Gold Coast politicians argued that these arrangements were constraining the colony's development, as Schenk has shown the colonies in fact consistently underspent their allocation for dollar imports: C. Schenk, *Britain and the Sterling Area: from Devaluation to Convertibility in the 1950s* (London,1994), 62, table 3.2.
7. G.D. Paton, *Report on the Development and Control of Banking and Agricultural Credit Facilities in the Gold Coast* (Accra, 1949), 4–5, paras.16, 23.
8. See R. Scott, Gold Coast, to secretary of state for the colonies, 26 May 1948, Public Record Office (PRO), London, Colonial Office (CO), CO 852/767/6, no 1. See also Fry, *Bankers*, 182; and Newlyn and Rowan, *Money and Banking*, 211–12. It is debatable whether or not this was in fact the case. Newlyn and Rowan argued, ibid., 212, 'A frequent complaint is that the banks' advances policy is racially discriminatory. In our view this is not the case. The expatriate banks are not adapted to providing the type of finance (usually medium term) which Africans demand.' It is also interesting in this respect that the Bank of England commented that the Gold Coast Bank's first managing director believed that there were in fact few commercial grounds for establishing the Bank of the Gold Coast: Bank of England note on the Bank of the Gold Coast, 10 Sept. 1954, Bank of England (BoE), London, OV 69/3, no 35. It has also been argued recently that British overseas banks were not as conservative as has traditionally been assumed: F. Bostock, 'The British Overseas Banks and Development Finance in Africa after 1945', *Business History*, XXXVIII (1991), 157–76.
9. R. Scott to the secretary of state for the colonies, 26 May 1948, CO 852/767/6, no 1.
10. Paton, *Report*, 3, para.12.
11. The report of the Watson Commission had not, for example, been published at the time of Scott's 26 May letter to the Colonial Office: *Report of the Commission of Enquiry into Disturbances in the Gold Coast, 1948* (London, 1948).
12. A. Hinds, 'Imperial Policy and Colonial Sterling Balances 1943–56', *Journal of Imperial and Commonwealth History*, XIX (1991), 37. Schenk argues that the extent to which the balances constituted a threat to British financial stability has been exaggerated: Schenk, *Britain*, ch.2.
13. Schenk, *Britain*, 22.
14. W.G. Boss to J.St.J. Rootham, 27 July 1948, BoE, OV 69/1, no 157.
15. 'Gold Coast, Draft Ordinance for the establishment of a state-aided bank – "The Gold Coast Bank"', 12 Aug. 1948, BoE, OV 69/1, no 63.
16. R. Scott to secretary of state for the colonies, 26 May 1948, CO 852/767/6, no 1.
17. R.P. Armitage to A. Cohen, 20 July 1948, CO 852/767/6, no 6.
18. Paton, *Report*, 3–5, paras. 14, 19, 23.
19. Secretary of state for the colonies to officer administering the government of the Gold Coast, 17 June 1949, CO 852/767/7, no 3.
20. R. Scott to secretary of state for the colonies, 3 Aug. 1949, CO 852/767/7, no 8.

21. R.P. Armitage to L.H. Gorsuch, CO, 16 Jan. 1951, enclosure to W.G. Hullard, CO, to W.J. Jackson, BoE, 2 Feb. 1951, BoE, OV 69/1, no 206B.
22. Convention People's Party, General Election Manifesto, 1951, reproduced in G.E. Metcalfe (ed.), *Great Britain and Ghana: Documents of Ghana History 1807–1957* (Oxford, 1994 edn.), document 508.
23. 'Gold Coast Banking', 6 Feb. 1951, BoE, OV 69/1, no 210; 'Gold Coast', 29 March 1951, BoE OV 69/1, no 213. In this instance the evidence does not support Krozewski's suggestion that 'the change in British policy away from the "liberal" U.G.C.C. towards the "radical" C.P.P. was prompted in part by the latter's lenient position on matters which were of vital importance to the sterling area': G. Krozewski, 'Sterling, the 'minor'territories, and the end of formal empire, 1939–1958', *Economic History Review*, XLVI, 2 (1993), 257.
24. S.W. Payton (accompanied Trevor during 1951 enquiry into Gold Coast banking) to O'Brien, 7 July 1951, BoE, OV 69/2, no 3.
25. See, for example, W.E. Ofori Atta, 2 April 1951, Gold Coast, *Legislative Assembly Debates*, 1951, no 1, 60.
26. 'Gold Coast', memo by H.C.B.M[ynors], 2 April 1951, BoE, OV 69/1, no 216.
27. C. Trevor, *Banking Conditions in the Gold Coast and on the Question of Setting up a National Bank* (Accra, 1952).
28. Minute by H.T. Bourdillon on Trevor report, 11 Sept. 1951, CO 537/6982.
29. 'Gold Coast Banking', 24 Aug. 1951, BoE, OV 69/2, no 13.
30. Minute by H.T. Bourdillon on Trevor report, 11 Sept. 1951, CO 537/6982.
31. BoE note on the Bank of the Gold Coast, 10 Sept. 1954, BoE, OV 69/3, no 35.
32. J.B. Danquah, 8 Oct. 1952, Gold Coast, *Legislative Assembly Debates*, 1952, no 3, 214–16.
33. E. Melville to governors of Nigeria and Gold Coast, 21 Nov. 1952 (copy), BoE, OV 67/2, no 29A.
34. 'Possible Changes in the West African Currency System', prepared by R.N. Kershaw, 17 Oct. 1952, BoE, OV 67/2, no 19.
35. E. Melville to governors of the Gold Coast and Nigeria, 21 Nov. 1952 (copy), BoE, OV 67/2, no 29A.
36. 'West Africa' memo by W. Jackson prepared for J.L. Fisher, adviser to the governors at the BoE, 18 May 1953, BoE, OV 67/2, no 29G.
37. A.K. Potter, Treasury, to E. Melville, 27 May 1953, CO 1025/5A, no 42.
38. J. Fisher to E. Melville, 19 May 1953, CO 1025/5A, no 41.
39. Personal secretary to the Gold Coast minister of finance to CO, cited in E. Melville to A.K. Potter, Treasury, 8 Aug. 1952, BoE, OV 67/2, no 11.
40. E. Melville to governors of Nigeria and the Gold Coast, 21 Nov. 1952 (copy), BoE, OV 67/2, no 29 A.
41. R. Saloway to E. Melville, 20 March 1953, CO 1025/5A, no 27.
42. Sir C. Arden-Clarke to E. Melville, 30 May 1953, CO 1025/5A, no 43.
43. Bangura, *Britain*, 47–8.
44. S. Caine, CO, to Lord Keynes, 14 May 1943, PRO, Treasury (T), T 236/4090. The CO, Treasury, and BoE were by 1945 largely agreed upon the need for colonies to be given access to their accumulated sterling balances for development purposes, but no firm decision was reached over this issue in view of continuing concern about the possibility of the balances being liquidated against imports from either Britain or the dollar area.
45. CPP election manifesto quoted in 'The Bank of the Gold Coast', BoE memo, 5 May 1954, BoE, OV 69/3, no 14.
46. K. Tours to E. Melville, 20 April 1954, CO 1025/39, no 4.
47. Officer administering the government of the Gold Coast to the secretary of state for the colonies, 15 May 1954, CO 1025/39, no 7.
48. R.J. Vile note for A.N. Galsworthy, 21 Dec. 1954, BoE, OV 69/3, no 40D.
49. 'West Africa – Central Banking and Currency', 23 Nov. 1954, BoE, OV 69/3, no 39A.
50. Memo by D.M. Benuson-Butt to Miss Dalton, 3 May 1955, T 236/3983, no 24. It was thought that a Nigerian currency might be issued either by a board, banking commission (as an intermediate stage), or a bank of issue, and that Sierra Leone and the Gambia would share a common currency probably run by the remainder of the WACB.

51. 'Gold Coast', BoE memo, 30 Aug. 1955, BoE, OV 69/3, no 55a.
52. Ibid.
53. 'Gold Coast', memo by J. Fisher, 6 Sept. 1955, BoE, OV 69/3, no 55c.
54. BoE minute of telephone call from the CO, 18 Nov. 1954, BoE, OV 69/3, no 38B.
55. 'Gold Coast Currency and Banking', CO notes prepared for a meeting with the Treasury and BoE, 14 Sept. 1955, CO 1025/42, no 29.
56. Minute by W.G. Wilson, 5 Sept. 1955, CO 1025/42.
57. 'Gold Coast Currency and Banking', CO memo for a meeting with the Treasury and BoE, 14 Sept. 1955, CO 1025/42, no 29.
58. Brief for the secretary of state for the colonies on his meeting with K. Gbedemah, 15 Sept. 1955, BoE, OV 69/3, no 55G.
59 See BoE, OV 69/4.
60. J.B. Loynes to Hawker, 7 March 1955 [should be 1956], BoE, OV 69/3, no 61H.
61 J. Fisher to R.J. Vile, 16 Nov. 1956, BoE, OV 69/4, no 47c.
62. Deputy Master of Mint, Sir Lionel Thompson to A.N. Galsworthy, 11 July 1955, CO 1025/42, no 14.
63. 'Future of the Sterling Area', April 1957, Bodleian Library Oxford, Conservative Party Archive, CCO 507/3/1: CCC 103, 4.
64. See notes and correspondence on BoE, OV 69/8.
65. See, for instance, M.K. Apaloo, 13 Feb. 1957, Gold Coast, *Legislative Assembly Debates*, Vol. 3, 850.
66. See Bostock, 'British Overseas Banks', 161–66.
67. 'West African banks remittance charges', memo by W.Jackson, BoE and sent to R.N. Kershaw, Nov. 1951, BoE, OV 67/1, no 199. Jackson stood in for Kershaw as BoE representative on the WACB when the latter was not available.
68. 'West African Currency', memo by R.N.K[ershaw] for the governor of the BoE, 19 Dec. 1951, BoE, OV 67/1, no 202.
69. DCO claimed that they had made a net loss of income on their West African business in the five-year period ending 1940, and that it was only in the last two years that they had begun to make a reasonable return: R.N. Kershaw to Sir Harold Downie, Crown Agents for the Colonies, 3 Jan. 1952, CO 537/7624, no 1.
70. Fry, *Bankers*, 197.
71. 'West Africa: the British Banks', note by J.B. Loynes, 6 April 1956, BoE, OV 67/2, no 80/1; Fry, *Bankers*, 183, 186, 195.
72. A point made to me in three interviews conducted with former personnel of the Ghana National Bank and the two expatriate banks: Mr. T.E. Anin (formerly with the Ghana National Bank), London 9 Aug. 1991; Mr R. Mensah (formerly of DCO), Accra 1 Oct. 1991; Mr. C.Lamptey (formerly of BBWA), Accra 19 Sept. 1991.
73. R.P. Armitage to L.H. Gorsuch, CO, 16 Jan. 1951 (copy), BoE, OV 69/1, no 206B.
74. Minute by W.G. Wilson on his meeting with Hepburn Smith, Permanent Secretary to Ministry of Finance in the Gold Coast, A.N. Galsworthy, and D.M.B. Butt, Treasury, 26 Sept. 1955, CO 1025/42. This account may, however, be suspect in view of the ambitions British officials believed Eggleston had for the bank.
75. R. Rathbone, 'Businessmen in Politics: Party Struggle in Ghana,1949–57', *Journal of Development Studies*, IX, 3 (1973), 391–401.
76. A point made to me by Richard Rathbone. On earlier campaigns for African banks see: A.G. Hopkins, 'Economic Aspects of Political Movements in Nigeria and in the Gold Coast 1918–1939', *Journal of African History*, VII, (1966), 133–52.
77. The governors of Sierra Leone and Gambia to CO, 5 Jan. 1953 and 28 Jan. 1953, CO 1025/5A, nos. 12 and 19. Minute by Sir H. Poynton, 20 April 1953, CO 1025/5A.
78. Ida Greaves, *Colonial Monetary Conditions* (Colonial Research Studies, no. 10, HMSO, 1953), 92.
79. See, for instance, the debate between Ida Greaves and Arthur Hazlewood: A. Hazlewood, 'Sterling Balances and the Colonial Currency System', *Economic Journal*, LXII (1952), 942–5; I. Greaves, 'Sterling Balances and the Colonial Currency System. A Comment', *Economic Journal*, LXIII (1953), 921–3.

80. 'Gold Coast Currency and Banking', CO notes for a meeting with the Treasury and Bank of England, 14 Sept. 1955, CO 1025/42, no 29.
81. See, for instance, Cain and Hopkins, *British Imperialism*, II, *Crisis and Deconstruction*, 281.
82. From 62.8 per cent to 39.7 per cent between 1939 and 1957: calculated from G.B. Kay, *The Political Economy of Colonialism in Ghana* (Cambridge, 1972), 341–2, table 22a.
83. Cain and Hopkins, *British Imperialism*, II, *Crisis and Deconstruction*, 288–89. Comparisons can also be made with the establishment of central banks in the Dominions in the interwar period: see ibid., 65–6, 91–2, and P.J. Cain, 'Gentlemanly Imperialism at Work: The Bank of England, Canada and the Sterling Area, 1932–1936', *Economic History Review*, XLIX, (1996), 336–57.
84. 'Gold Coast Currency and Banking', CO notes for a meeting with the Treasury and Bank of England, 1 Sept. 1955, CO 1025/42, no 29.
85. Memo by D.E.F.R., 16 Sept. 1960, BoE, OV 69/5, no 66.
86. Schenk, 'The Origins of a Central Bank in Malaya', 427–28.
87. Ugochukwu Uche, 'Bank of England vs the IBRD', *passim*.
88. Fieldhouse, 'Arrested Development', 141–2. For British expansion in the nineteenth century see, for instance, *Economics and Empire 1830–1914* (London, 1973), 463–77.

The 'Jamaica 300' Celebrations of 1955: Commemoration in a Colonial Polity

HOWARD JOHNSON

In 1955 government-sponsored, island-wide festivities commemorated Jamaica's tercentenary as a British colony. Initially announced in 1954 as a celebration of 'the three hundredth anniversary of British rule in Jamaica', the commemorative activities were later described as marking 'three centuries of Jamaican history' and 'three hundred years of association' with Britain. These changes in the description of the celebrations reflected the public debate about what should be commemorated. This anniversary, coming only seven years before Jamaican independence, provides an opportunity for examining the nature of Jamaican nationalism, the construction of a national identity, and the political uses of these commemorative activities especially in the context of long-range economic planning.

The idea of commemorating the tercentenary of British rule in Jamaica was first mooted by Donald Sangster, minister of finance in the Jamaica Labour Party (JLP) government, after a visit to New Zealand in 1950 where he had seen the centennial celebrations marking the founding of the city of Christchurch. Sangster was especially struck by the potential of commemorative celebrations (and the publicity which accompanied them) as a mechanism for advancing the political and economic agenda of their organizers. In the Jamaican context, the tercentenary year provided the occasion rather than the reason for celebrations. As Sangster explained in a House of Representatives debate in September 1954, 'It happened that 1955 was chosen … because it was necessary to have a date within this decade. And 1955 was chosen because of the period when the English-speaking life began in Jamaica. It could have been made to be an anniversary of Columbus' coming.'[1] Although ostensibly about the past, the tercentenary celebrations, which Sangster proposed, were intended to serve the political and economic objectives of the JLP administration.

In February 1954, the point at which the planning for the tercentenary celebrations began in earnest, Sangster's main objectives were to expand the industrial sector by attracting external investment capital and increase the island's tourist trade. Since 1950, tourism, bauxite-alumina production, and secondary industries had been primarily responsible for the rapid economic growth which Jamaica had experienced. Faced with the chronic problems of unemployment and underemployment, the JLP administration had adopted a policy of positively encouraging industrial development as a major component of its economic strategy. In 1952, for example, the government had established the Industrial Development Corporation 'to stimulate, facilitate and undertake the development of industry'.[2] The role of the celebrations in promoting those economic activities was best articulated by Wendell Malliet, a columnist in the colony's leading newspaper, the *Daily Gleaner*: 'Jamaica's Tercentenary should be used to show the world our need for aid, our determination to improve our lot and raise our standard of living, and our responsibility to faithfully discharge obligations assumed. Every effort should be made to bring thousands of visitors to the Island where they may see for themselves what we have to offer as an area for sound and profitable investment and a tourist paradise.'[3]

In the early stages of planning for the tercentenary, Sangster envisaged the celebrations as a commemoration of British rule. The report of a meeting held on 8 February 1954 (attended by senior civil servants and representatives from the agricultural, tourism, and commercial sectors) which was designed to canvas opinion on the form of celebrations should take, stated: 'The Minister of Finance told the meeting that it was planned to celebrate the three hundredth anniversary of British rule in Jamaica and special promotions were planned.' By that stage, Sangster had definite ideas on the nature of the commemorative events. An important aspect of his plan for using the celebrations as 'a marketing device' for Jamaica's manufacturing industry and tourism was to invite foreign dignitaries to visit the colony during the tercentenary year; such visits would direct welcome foreign attention to Jamaica and enhance its reputation overseas. At that meeting, Sangster announced that both Princess Margaret and President Paul Magloire of Haiti had been invited to the island during 1955 in connection with the celebrations. Sporting events were regarded as an essential feature of the commemorative activities. Sangster reported that he had contacted several local sports organizations which had promised to stage special events during the anniversary year and that the Australian cricket team would undertake its first tour of the British West Indies in connection with the celebrations.[4]

With the initial emphasis on celebrating three centuries of British rule (despite Sangster's preoccupation with a contemporary political agenda) several of the early proposals for commemorative activities were oriented towards the British past, British precursors, and the British heritage. An early example of this trend was the proposal, made in February 1954, that a pageant should be staged depicting the 300-year history of Jamaica as a British territory. Proposals for celebratory events tended to be concentrated on a three-month period with a focus on 10 May, the anniversary date of the British conquest of Jamaica. In May 1954, by which time the planning for the celebrations was the responsibility of an executive committee chaired by Sangster, the Jamaica Historical Society (dominated by the resident British) outlined plans for a historical festival scheduled for 10 May 1955 to coincide with the date of the arrival of the English in the island. As late as August of that year, the emphasis remained on the British connection. Thus Sangster announced in an informal meeting with members of the press on the progress of the tercentenary preparations: 'Highlight month will be May when a ceremony and pageant at Port Royal will depict the British landing at Passage Fort.' A proposal to 'ascertain and invite to the celebrations relatives of Admiral Penn and General Venables' who had commanded the English forces which landed in Jamaica in 1655 reflected this attitude.[5] Opposition politicians would later explain the pro-British bias referring to the fact that the committee was not 'representative of Jamaica' – probably a reference to its white (sometimes expatriate) members.[6]

Sangster's insensitivity to the incompatibility of the British-oriented proposals for commemorative activities with nationalist aspirations reflected, in part, the early and lingering position of the governing JLP on the question of self-determination. Unlike the opposition People's National Party (PNP), in which nationalism formed 'the principal ideological underpinning', the JLP led by W. A. Bustamante had throughout the 1940s adopted an anti-nationalist stance.[7] In the 1944 general elections, for example, Bustamante had denounced self-government as 'brown man rule'. Richard Hart has argued that 'the fact that he [Bustamante] was able to manoeuvre his massive working class following into hostility to the concept, in 1944, undoubtedly delayed the growth of Jamaican nationalism'.[8]

A nationalist perspective on the activities which would be appropriate for the tercentenary year was provided in April 1954 by a sub-committee of the Kingston and St. Andrew Corporation (KSAC), the PNP-dominated municipal body. In a list of recommendations which they drafted for submission to the committee planning the celebrations, the members of the sub-committee chose to emphasize the emergence of Jamaica to nationhood rather than a commemoration of British rule. Their divergent approach to commemorative activities was evident in the recommendation which stated: 'The celebrations to be directed towards showing the emergence of Jamaica as a Nation at the national level and on the municipal level, the establishment and growth of Kingston as the premiere metropolis in the

British Caribbean.' The sub-committee also proposed the 'Enshrining of national heroes e.g. Marcus Garvey and William Gordon.'[9]

The proposals of the KSAC constituted one of the earliest critiques of the direction which plans for the tercentenary had taken to that point. Subsequent criticisms focused on the tendency to celebrate the military conquest of Jamaica by Penn and Venables and pointed to the institution of slavery as the defining feature of British colonialism.[10] The editor of the *Daily Gleaner*, Theodore Sealy, in a subtle criticism of the planning committee's orientation toward the past, wrote of Jamaica's '300 years of progress and development as a member of the British Commonwealth of Nations'. 'In many respects, Jamaica is a different place today to the somewhat rude island that Penn and Venables took over. Industrially and socially we have come on in the world. Politically and constitutionally, we are progressing along national lines to the development of a full democratic system within the Commonwealth.'[11]

Over time these kinds of criticism changed perceptibly the nature of the celebrations planned for the tercentenary year. This shift in approach was evident from the comments of the governor, Sir Hugh Foot (who had been involved in the planning process) in his communications with the Colonial Office. On 31 May 1954, he reported the establishment of an executive committee which would be responsible for 'detailed arrangements for celebration of Jamaica's 300th anniversary under the British Flag'.[12] In the following month, Foot explained at a meeting at the Colonial Office that: 'The theme would be three centuries of Jamaican history rather than commemoration of the conquest of Jamaica by Penn and Venables.'[13] It is significant that 'Celebrating 300 years of History' had been the title of the *Daily Gleaner* editorial which had criticized the planning of commemorative events earlier in May.

The executive committee in charge of planning responded to criticisms by reorienting aspects of its programme. In July 1954, the *Daily Gleaner* reported that the committee had decided on three principal objectives. These included attracting tourists to the island in record numbers (familiar from earlier discussions) and involving every section of the population in the festivities. Most important was 'to get Jamaicans better acquainted with the history of their island'. The committee intended to select only the positive aspects of the British historical record in Jamaica, editing out the negative features of the colonial past. In the words of the newspaper report, it would involve 'the discarding of the bad things in the history of the past 300 years and the preservation and passage into our modern life of the good things'.[14] It is probable that this form of amnesia was a response to those individuals who had pointed out that the British colonial record included slavery and the slave trade. The committee's commemoration of the tercentenary involved what Michael Billig has described as 'the complex dialectic of remembering and forgetting'.[15] This approach remained central to the commemorative activities even when the composition of the planning committee, changed with the election of a PNP government in January 1955. Thus J. J. Mills, a retired educator, who in 1955 became chief administrative officer of the Jamaica Working Committee stated in a foreword written for the Jamaica 300 supplement of the *Daily Gleaner*:

> In personal experience we seem to remember best those things which most deeply stirred our emotions. Fortunately, as a people we quite easily put aside resentment. We forget easily what has caused pain, and turn readily to good humour, goodwill and pleasantness. There have been some dark spots in our history and failings in our community life which we must live down and forget.

It may have been this deliberately edited version of the colonial past which allowed the Sugar Manufacturers Association of Jamaica to place an advertisement in the same supplement without a trace of irony and with no reference to the institution of slavery. Under the heading '300 Years of Sugar Production', the advertisement read in part: 'The Sugar Industry is an outstanding example of National Progress, achieved by an enlightened and wise policy of planned production, carried out co-operatively by the Primary Producers who constitute the Sugar Manufacturers of Jamaica.'[16]

The reorientation of the commemorative celebrations from the British past to the Jamaican present and future became clearly discernible after the JLP administration was forced on the defensive about the purpose of the celebrations in the House of Representatives in September 1954. Hitherto, the event had been treated primarily as a government initiative rather than an occasion which needed bipartisan approval. However, members of the opposition had an opportunity to express their opinions during the consideration of the Second Supplementary Estimates 1954–55 which provided for £25,000 towards the cost of the celebrations. The members' main concern was that the publicity had emphasized the commemoration of three hundred years under British rule at a time when they regarded the achievement of self-government as imminent. As Florizel Glasspole (PNP Eastern Kingston) who raised the issue observed, 'I am 100% for Jamaica's existence in the British Commonwealth of Nations but I don't want to perpetuate British rule.' Percival Broderick (PNP North-eastern Clarendon) expressed the view that nations did not celebrate their conquest but accomplishments. 'The English don't celebrate the time when the Picts and the Scots used to over-run England or the time when the hordes of Austria used to sweep across the Channel.' Kenneth Hill, the National Labour Party member for Western Kingston, suggested that the celebrations be undertaken 'with a motif and theme that we have got where we are in spite of Great Britain; in spite of imperialistic rule and colonialism … and we are emerging in spite of handicaps with which we have been faced for three hundred years'.[17]

Faced with these criticisms, the government ministers asserted their commitment to self-government and the tercentenary commemoration as a celebration not of conquest, but, in the words of Edwin Allen, Minister of Education and Social Welfare, 'our development, achievement and culture'. Sangster claimed that his aim had been to gain popular support for 'some celebration or thanksgiving or activity to focus the mind of Jamaica on what has been achieved and what is possible in the future'.[18] These government statements were transparently face-saving exercises but they helped to reduce the ambiguity which had surrounded the tercentenary celebrations. It was thus possible for the editor of the *Daily Gleaner* to write in December of that year: 'the celebrations can have great political significance, especially as the keynote had already been settled as commemorating an epoch in national progress rather than a piece of colonial conquest and history'.[19] In January 1955 Sangster, as the chairman of the Tercentenary Celebrations Committee, stated that the celebrations would mark 300 years of 'progress and development as a junior partner with Britain in her vast Colonial enterprise'.[20] With the change of government later that month, the Chief Minister, N. W. Manley indicated that he regarded the tercentenary year as one 'dedicated to the growth and development of our young national spirit'. As he observed: 'Jamaica 300 in any other terms would be inconsistent with the historical moment that we are in'.[21]

With the change in government, the tercentenary celebrations developed an overtly nationalist orientation under the influence of Manley and the PNP administration. In December, Manley claimed: 'this year, 1955, has witnessed the development of national feeling; the development of national energy; and the development of national determination to tackle the problems of Jamaica which must surely make this year unique in all the annals of our history'.[22] This heightened national consciousness reflected the efforts of Manley who, as Chief Minister, had increased opportunities to foster the nationalist agenda and of the Jamaica 300 Working Committee which had publicized the commemorative events as celebrating the birth of a nation.

Although this nationalist stance received its most enthusiastic support from PNP adherents, the JLP had, by that stage, accepted the goal of political self-determination. In 1954, for example, JLP ministers had expressed the hope that the tercentenary celebrations would be accompanied by the grant of self-government. In October, there was unanimous bipartisan support for the proposals of a constitution committee of the House of Representatives to amend the constitution to provide full internal self-government as soon as possible after the general elections. In introducing the resolution endorsing those recommendations, Sangster (Leader of the House and chairman of the committee) had spoken in nationalist terms reminiscent of Manley. 'I am saying that we are meeting in Jamaica as a group of people who are witnessing the birth of a Nation, aiming at Dominion status in the near future.'[23]

The national consciousness of this period was paradoxically anti-colonial yet pro-British. Jamaican nationalism was anti-colonial only in the limited sense that the politicians (whose views on this issue are most accessible) were opposed to the continuation of Jamaica's status as a colonial dependency. There was bipartisan support for the idea that Jamaica had successfully served a political apprenticeship, mastering parliamentary government under the watchful eye of the Colonial Office, and therefore deserved political advancement. In October 1954, for example, Sangster had based his expectation of the early achievement of Dominion status on the fact that 'over the past few years we have demonstrated in this country, quite clearly that we have the capacity for governing ourselves'. On that occasion, Manley had expressed the opinion that 'if we handle ourselves with wisdom and honesty, nothing shall stop us from achieving Dominion status within the next few years'.[24] Politicians even suggested that the surveillance of the British and the need to conform to metropolitan standards of parliamentary democracy extended to electioneering. In a speech to his constituents, the PNP candidate for Central Kingston exhorted them to conduct a clean election campaign. 'I want it clean because the people of Great Britain are watching us to see if we are fit for full self-government and by God's grace and with your health and co-operation we shall prove our fitness.'[25]

A rejection of colonial status did not involve either a rejection of the British heritage or a loosening of ties to the British monarchy. Manley was careful to distance himself from the idea of the tercentenary commemoration as 'a celebration of three hundred years of colonialism', though he was prepared to admit Britain's salutary and pervasive influence on Jamaican life. 'All the principles of Law and order, justice and right in this country derive entirely from our association with England, and no other country has been influenced by Britain to a greater extent.'[26] The expectation of constitutional advancement served, as the *Daily Gleaner* suggested in February 1955, to strengthen Jamaican ties to the British Crown which was regarded as the symbol of the colony's membership in the British Commonwealth of Nations.[27] The unchanging position of the British monarchy, despite the nationalist impulse, was reflected in the effusive welcome extended to Princess Margaret by a government minister who had remained untouched by the earlier discussions on the nature of the commemoration. 'On behalf of this gathering I wish to assure Your Royal Highness of our deep and abiding loyalty and most humble and sincere affection to the Throne and to the illustrious members of the Royal Family. It seems most fitting that at a time when we are discussing Three Hundred Years of British Rule in Jamaica, that a member of the Royal Family should deign to honour us with her gracious presence.'[28] An index of the continued importance of the British monarchy was the symbolic significance which a newspaper reporter (who had followed Princess Margaret's progress through the British Caribbean) attached to her arrival at a reception flanked by the Chief Minister and Mrs Manley. 'At previous receptions during the tour – Trinidad, Tobago, Grenada, St. Vincent, Barbados, Antigua, St. Kitts – Her Royal Highness arrived at the official receptions escorted by the respective Governors and Commanders-in-Chief of the islands; never was she attended by an Administrator, never by a political personage. Jamaica's tall stature in the evolution within the British Commonwealth, was emphasized in yesterday's twilight as the white gowned, youthful Princess, appeared at the top of the stairway walking between Mr. and Mrs. Manley.'[29]

Manley's efforts to project the tercentenary commemoration as a celebration of nationhood was aimed, in part, at the mass of the population who, he was aware, had remained largely unaffected by the national spirit. As he had admitted in September 1954 'there is a large section in this country that does not understand yet the aspirations summed up in the expression National Jamaica'.[30] The slow pace with which nationalist sentiment had spread among the rural population can be explained by their preoccupation with bread-and-butter issues. Bustamante's hostility to the concept of political self-determination also delayed its acceptance among his large working-class following. The main focus of the working people's loyalty remained the British monarchy which was associated with slave emancipation. This was a loyalty which was further encouraged by the educational system and the Empire-day celebrations of the twentieth century. A *Daily Gleaner* editorial of 26 November 1953 provides an insight into Jamaican working-class attitudes to the British monarchy in that period: 'Abiding and unshakeable devotion to the Throne has been a traditional feature of West Indian and Jamaican political life for well-nigh three centuries. If Governors fell short of the people's expectations it was because the Sovereign was unaware of their actions. If they fulfilled every expectation, it was only a fulfillment of the will of the Monarch.'[31] Given the strength of that loyalty, the main challenge was to make these colonial subjects into involved citizens of an emerging nation-state.

The promotion of a national consciousness among the colony's working class during this period was a matter of some urgency, for the evidence suggests that it was expected to mask the race, colour, and class divisions which were becoming increasingly apparent in Jamaican society. A *Daily Gleaner* editorial of 31 December 1953 appealed to political leaders to attempt 'to reconstruct and re-establish goodwill between all classes in the community'. It argued that both the socialism of the PNP and the populism of the JLP had led to increased class and racial tensions. The result had been hostility directed against those who made 'substantial contribution to the national wealth and revenue'. In the following year a columnist in the same newspaper, noting the existence of sharp disparities in wealth and racial bitterness, suggested that nationalism could function as an integrative force: 'there was, and is, a great psychological need for a phase of nationalism; for without this feeling our people are unlikely to become a united whole. Colonial territories are faced with a lot of necessary paradoxes. You have to unite people and get them to feel a part of one another.'[32]

This desire to create a national cohesiveness may explain the emphasis, during the planning and execution of the tercentenary celebrations by a bureaucratic and cultural elite, on the involvement of the wider society. As Wycliffe S. Bennett, the general organizer of the Jamaica Festival of the Arts, writing late in 1954 observed, 'It has been conceived as a spontaneous national offering, in which all sections of the community will be able to play a great part.'[33] Theodore Sealy, as chairman of the Jamaica 300 Working Committee, also stressed popular involvement in the festivities. He was anxious to stage events which would 'communicate widespread enthusiasm and emotion for the occasion throughout the populace'.[34] Without popular participation in the celebrations, the working classes would invest no emotional capital in the new national venture. The planners must have been gratified by the newspaper report of the prize-giving concert of the Westmoreland Festival of Arts, held in the public square in Savanna-la-Mar, which stressed the momentary egalitarianism of an enthusiastic audience. 'Lawyer stood beside maid-servant, doctor beside gardener boy and landowner beside labourer. People had gathered from the corners of the parish to see and hear the best artistic Talent the month-long Westmoreland Festival of the Arts had discovered.'[35] At the conclusion of the National Festival of the Arts in December 1955, Sir Hugh Foot referred to the high level of response and participation of every parish in the celebrations 'with the result that the ties which bind the parishes together in a national unity have been permanently strengthened'.[36]

The three-century milestone and the emphasis placed on Jamaica as an emergent nation in the tercentenary celebrations led members of its educated elite to muse on the constituent elements of the national identity –

the features of its distinctiveness.[37] The identity which church, political, and cultural leaders constructed for Jamaica was a non-racial one which affirmed, in a society where significant racial, class, and colour differences persisted, a commonality which transcended those divisions. Commentators claimed that Jamaica had succeeded as a society in achieving a relative harmony and mutual tolerance among the diverse peoples who formed its population. They also generally suggested that this achievement was without parallel in the contemporary world. The views expressed by the Rt. Rev. P. W. Gibson, Suffragan Bishop of Kingston, at the interdenominational religious service which marked the beginning of the Jamaica 300 celebrations, were typical:

> Jamaica stands as a witness to the world that in Christ it is possible for people of every race and culture to meet in one body around the Lord's Table. It is possible for a country to embrace within her borders European and African, Chinese and Syrian and Indian without clash, without cleavage, without hatred and rancour, without those sharp divisions which have made the names of certain countries a byword for ignorant prejudice and malignant strife.[38]

Commentators sometimes suggested that the interaction of the disparate elements had resulted not only in racial harmony but also a distinctive creole lifestyle – an embryonic form of the creole society paradigm. Wycliffe S. Bennett, providing a rationale for tercentenary celebrations, observed in 1954 that 'our ancestors came at different times from lands as distant and different as Africa, Europe, India and China. It is from their mixing and living together in a common habitat during the past three centuries, suffering the same heartaches and reverses and sharing the same joys and accomplishments, that they have developed a common point of view, a common outlook, a common way of thinking, that is the very essence of being a people'.[39] Not all contemporary commentators took as sanguine a view of the much-vaunted tolerant society. As Theodore Sealy admitted, 'a society has evolved in Jamaica which is tolerant of differences in origin even if still broken down into many units, ostensibly tolerant, but often offensively exclusive'.[40]

The perception of Jamaica as a model of 'inter-racial fraternalism' was, in the 1950s, not new.[41] Writing in 1917, significantly for a United States audience, T.H. MacDermot, the white Jamaican poet and editor of the *Jamaica Times* had observed of Jamaica that 'although the creation still bears marks of human imperfection and incompleteness, a community has been brought into being in which the racial elements, in such fierce and embittered antagonism elsewhere, are gradually, but surely, blending into a whole of common citizenship'.[42] In the following decades, this conception of Jamaican identity was challenged by the influence of Marcus Garvey who affirmed the African identity of the black majority. The insistence on a non-racial national identity can be seen as a rejection of the black racial counter-identity which threatened to exclude other racial groups including the dominant white minority. The comments of W. Adolphe Roberts, the white Jamaican historian and pioneer of the movement for political self-determination, in 1954 on what constituted 'Jamaicanness' was clearly a response to the continued influence of Garveyite views:

> I condemn doctrines of racism in connection with Jamaican nationalism. They are meaningless and harmful. National cultures are not founded upon race, but upon a synthesis of the strains involved. Let us leave it to the Hitlers to attempt to revive the myth of race as a unifying virtue. It is as mischievous to argue that Jamaica is a Negro country as it would be patently silly to say that it is Anglo-Saxon. Jamaica is itself.[43]

The view of Jamaica as a uniquely harmonious inter-racial community came to acquire 'the status of an official myth', eventually inspiring the national motto of the independent nation – 'Out of Many One People'.[44]

Another aspect of the process of national self-definition in the tercentenary year was the identification of a pantheon of national heroes. This was an idea which predated the celebrations. In 1952 F.B.L. 'Slave Boy' Evans, the leader of the United Negro Party, had moved a resolution in the House of Representatives which called on the government to declare the birthdays of Marcus Garvey and J.A.G. Smith (a leading politician of the Crown Colony Government era) national holidays on the grounds that they were national heroes. Although the resolution was supported in the House, no further action was taken.[45] The timing of that resolution suggests that it might well have been a response to the publication in that year of W. Adolphe Roberts' *Six Great Jamaicans: Biographical Sketches*. This book was an early example of the search for a usable colonial past which culminated in the government's declaration of National Heroes after independence.[46]

As noted earlier, the issue of national heroes was raised in 1954 by members of a sub-committee of the KSAC which recommended the 'enshrining' of national heroes such as Marcus Garvey and George William Gordon. This proposal evoked a response from an English columnist in the *Daily Gleaner* who supported the idea of establishing 'memorials to people who have deserved well of this country' but opposed such an honour for Garvey. As he commented, referring to the trek of Jamaican migrants to Britain, 'what did Marcus Garvey ever do for this country, beyond taking a good deal of money out of it, and then going to live in England, thus becoming one of the early pioneers of the exploitation of Britain now so popular with Jamaicans'.[47] This column prompted a series of letters to the newspaper supporting the idea of honouring Garvey. Among them was one from Edna Manley, the sculptor and wife of N. W. Manley, who wrote that 'Mr Garvey was a great pioneer for his people – he did important work in fighting for the equal recognition of black and brown with white. A job that someone had to do in the British West Indies.'[48]

In the following year, the KSAC returned to the issue when it proposed in February that the Emancipation Day holiday on 1 August be replaced by 'Patriots Day'. The resolution argued that the celebration of Emancipation Day perpetuated 'the feeling of inferiority born of the gratitude of the slave to the master for giving him freedom' and noted that the removal of this sense of inferiority was 'essential to the psychological growth and development of a people seeking self-government'. Patriots Day, it pointed out, would commemorate 'those Jamaicans who dedicated their lives to the gigantic task of awakening in the minds and hearts of the children of ex-slaves the feeling of social equality with the children of ex-slave owners i.e. the late Marcus Garvey, George William Gordon and others'.[49] This resolution suggests that the official policy of selective amnesia and the competing claims of a non-racial Jamaican identity had not erased the racial memory of the island's black majority.

Although the KSAC's recommendation was not implemented, the idea of national heroes was supported by prominent figures in Jamaican society. Thus P. M. Sherlock, the vice-principal of the University College of the West Indies, endorsed the decision of the KSAC to honour the memory of Garvey who, he noted, 'the history of the past 50 years showed had more than any other single West Indian, given to the Negro a sense of pride in himself and his forefathers'. In an editorial of October of that year, Theodore Sealy drew attention to the idea of national heroes and went as far as suggesting that leaders of slave revolts might be included in that pantheon – an idea which would receive official sanction only in the 1970s. 'There is, however, an almost unpardonable failure to discover, collect or preserve anything connected with the lives of those who might be termed great Jamaican patriots – the leaders of the slave risings, William George Gordon, Marcus Garvey and the late J.A.G. Smith, to name only a few random examples.' So widely acceptable was the idea of national heroes that the English rector of the Kingston Parish Church observed in his sermon at the annual Constitution Day service that 'In this year of Jamaica 300 we have been looking back over the centuries, calling to mind the history of our land, remembering with gratitude our national heroes'.[50]

The discussion to this point has established that the planning and execution of the commemorative events of 1955 quickened the nationalist impulse, prompted the construction of a national identity, and initiated the process of decolonizing Jamaican history by focusing on indigenous rather than the metropolitan heroes of the colony's textbooks. Yet the tercentenary celebrations also constituted an integral part of the PNP's economic strategy (shared by the previous government) of developing closer economic ties with the United States. Ironically the movement towards decolonization (celebrated in the tercentenary festivities) coincided with a process of United States neo-colonization.

The PNP's economic strategy marked a change in the party's approach to the role of foreign capital in the island's economic development which was evident before the 1949 general elections. As Richard Hart (a participant in the discussions) has noted, the party leadership had hitherto 'viewed the direct investment of foreign capital with a distrust bordering on hostility'. However, the prospect of holding office (which seemed then a real possibility) and having to deal with the high levels of unemployment in Jamaica led N.W. Manley to revise his ideas on the question of foreign capital. He adopted a policy of industrialization on the basis of direct foreign investment. The PNP's Statement of Policy, adopted after some opposition within the party, acknowledged the new direction in economic policy on which Manley had decided. 'General measures and inducements to attract the direct investment of private foreign capital in aid of our development programme will be adopted after careful study of the particular enterprise.'[51]

The PNP did not win the 1949 elections but it remained committed to a policy of industrialization. In a speech in 1954, Manley noted that he was aware of the urgent necessity to provide employment for a rapidly growing population. 'Here in Jamaica where there is a population of 15,000 every year seeking to be employed, it is not possible that this labour force can be supported entirely through agriculture.'[52] It is clear that the PNP also anticipated a closer economic relationship with United States investors should they come to power. As Wills O. Isaacs, the PNP candidate for Central Kingston in the 1955 elections, pointed out, 'When the People's National Party gets into power although we propose to remain always within the British Commonwealth of Nations we would desire to draw closely economically to the United States of America and expand our trade to that country.'[53] The PNP had, by that time, prepared for that eventuality by expelling the left-wing of the party in 1952 and publicly rejecting in 1953 the approach of the Jagan government (in British Guiana) whose members intended to initiate, with popular support, reforms which would have an adverse impact on foreign investors.[54] Aware of Cold War sensibilities, Manley hastened to assure the wary both at home and abroad that his earlier commitment to left-wing policies had ended. Thus his speech on the party's victory in 1955 was reassuring. 'I am not going to take away anything from anybody except for proper purposes and with proper compensation. I am not going to steal away the rich man's money nor am I going to take the poor man's goats … I am not going to tax any class out of existence … I am not going to run anybody out of the country. On the contrary the aim must be to create conditions under which people will stop wanting to run away.'[55]

At the time he assumed office, Manley was faced with the urgent problem of a rapidly increasing population with which the efforts to create new jobs could not keep pace. The enormity of the problem was suggested by a report on conditions in Jamaica by Sir Hugh Foot in April 1955. 'It is impossible to turn to the question of future prospects without first looking at the problem which overwhelms everything else – the problem of population … If nothing can be done to check the increase then in the end all our development projects and all our efforts to provide social services will one day look like sand castles before the advancing tide.' As Foot noted, the steady migration of Jamaican workers to Britain in the previous year was less than the annual increase in the labour force. At that point, both Foot and the new administration anticipated that the problems of economic development would be alleviated by the Colonial Development and Welfare grants. Thus Foot had expressed the view that 'the task ahead cannot possibly be achieved on the scale or in the time required without large-scale assistance from Great Britain. That assistance will no doubt continue in the form of generous Colonial Development and Welfare Grants.'[56] In the following month, however, those expectations were disappointed when the grants allocated to Jamaica were significantly lower than anticipated. The government could not hope to finance economic development from increases in revenue in a colony which was already one of the most heavily taxed or from floating a loan on the London market where interest rates were high. It was in these circumstances that Manley turned increasingly to the United States for private capital investment.[57]

The tercentenary celebrations served to direct the attention of foreign investors on Jamaica during 1955. This, as suggested earlier, had been one of the primary objectives of the JLP administration. However, the PNP used the selection of foreign dignitaries for visits during the course of the celebrations to legitimize economic policies on which the administration had decided and to indicate that Jamaica was open to United States investment. Governor Luis Muñoz Marín's visit in June was especially significant, for this Puerto Rican leader had faced similar problems to Jamaica. His approach to the economic problems of Puerto Rico combined an emphasis on industrialization, primarily by United States capital, with an intensive programme of agricultural development. This reflected Manley's latest thinking on the way forward. By June 1955, he had realized that the results from industrialization, which was capital rather than labour intensive, would not be immediate and that the agricultural sector would remain crucial in achieving improved conditions for the Jamaican people. The parallels between the two countries were remarked on by the *Daily Gleaner* in that same month:

> Puerto Rico has an even more desperate pressure of population than does Jamaica. Migration to the United States has been an aid and perhaps a problem in just the same way as the present wave of migration to Britain has been providing a temporary solution for Jamaica, yet fraught with problems. So that there are a great many things in common between Jamaica and Puerto Rico in their political aspirations, in their industrial ambitions and activities and in their agricultural predominance and pre-occupations.[58]

In September that year, Adlai Stevenson's visit to open the Industrial Fair, sponsored by the Jamaica Manufacturers Association, gave both Manley and Foot an opportunity to present in public the case for additional United States investment in Jamaica. Using the phrase coined by Stevenson, 'the revolution of rising expectations', Manley pointed out in his speech that 'Our people, the people of Jamaica, the people of the Caribbean Area, are no longer content with a mean and narrow life of grinding poverty.' It was in the light of those rising expectations that he declared in unequivocal terms the government's intention to provide a stable business environment for United States capital:

> Certainly I do not have to repeat that this Government is pledged to do everything in its power to assist in the drive to industrialisation and to maintain the general conditions that will bring new capital to our shores. I repeat the pledges and assurances of the utmost good faith to those who come and affirm our determination to maintain stable political situations and sensible and balanced conditions where labour and industrial relations are concerned.

Sir Hugh Foot, as the representative of the British government, was equally welcoming in his remarks to the visiting United States politician. Thus he indicated the openness to foreign capital, encouraged by his own government. 'Tonight, in the name of Jamaica, I welcome with sincerity and enthusiasm United States assistance – and United States investment. Nowhere in the world will the assistance be more appreciated, nowhere will the investment be more safe.' He pointed out Jamaica's continued allegiance to English traditions, institutions, and loyalty to the Queen but indicated that the association was no longer exclusive. This plea for United States investment ended with a reference to Jamaica's special suitability for productive foreign investment. 'With our English tradition on the one hand and our American geographical position on the other, we believe that nowhere in the world should the advantages of practical Anglo-American co-operation be more apparent or more productive than here in the island of Jamaica.'[59] This appeal to United States investors substantiates the claim of Wm. Roger Louis and Ronald Robinson that 'there was no conspiracy to take over the Empire. American influence expanded by imperial default and by the invitation of nationalists'.[60]

Originally conceived as a commemoration of three hundred years of British rule, the tercentenary celebrations eventually looked, not backward at the British record as colonizers, but forward to Jamaica's emergence as a nation state. The PNP administration used the commemorative events to extend a national consciousness beyond the traditional middle-class constituency and as an integrative device in a divided society. Jamaicans were thus asked to imagine themselves as members, in Benedict Anderson's phrase, of the 'deep horizontal comradeship' of the nation despite the existing inequalities and the hostilities which they generated.[61] The commemoration with its nationalist orientation led to the construction of a non-racial identity, shaped by an educated elite, which rejected the racial counter-identity of Jamaica's black majority. In its most overtly political function, the 'Jamaica 300' celebrations promoted what was essentially a bipartisan economic programme to industrialize by attracting United States private capital investment to the island. It was this economic strategy which eased the transition from British colonialism to United States neo-colonialism in Jamaica.

NOTES

1. Donald Sangster, 23 Sept. 1954, *Jamaica Hansard* (House of Representatives), Session 1954, no.1, 251.
2. Owen Jefferson, *The Post-War Economic Development of Jamaica* (Kingston, 1972), 132.
3. 'Tercentenary of Jamaica's History', *Daily Gleaner*, 20 April 1954.
4. *Daily Gleaner*, 10 Feb. 1954. The phrase 'a marketing device' is William M. Johnston's, *Celebrations: The Cult of Anniversaries in Europe and the United States Today* (New Brunswick, 1991), 50.
5. See reports in *Daily Gleaner*, 10 Feb., 20 May, 6 Aug. Governor Sir Hugh Foot later proposed that the direct descendant of Christopher Columbus, the Duke of Veragua, Lord of the Ocean Seas and Marquis of Jamaica, should be invited to Jamaica during the anniversary year, 'From many points of view including that of our tourist publicity the first visit of a Marquis of Jamaica to Jamaica for over three hundred years would be an event of some importance.' H.M. Foot to W.I.J. Wallace, 25 May 1955 (Conf.), file no.608/6/01, Public Record Office (PRO), London, Colonial Office (CO), CO 1031/1976.

6. Percival Broderick, 23 Sept. 1954, *Jamaica Hansard* (House of Representatives), Session 1954, no.1, 249.
7. Trevor Munroe, *The Politics of Constitutional Decolonization: Jamaica, 1944–62* (Kingston, 1972), 39.
8. Richard Hart, 'Jamaica and Self-Determination, 1660–1970', *Race*, XIII (1972), 286.
9. *Daily Gleaner*, 9 April 1954.
10. See comments by Armistead Lee, economic officer in the American Consulate General at the Columbus Day celebrations, *Daily Gleaner*, 18 Oct. 1954.
11. See editorial, 'Celebrating 300 Years of History', *Daily Gleaner*, 16 May 1954.
12. See extract from Savingram to the secretary of state for the colonies from the governor of Jamaica, no.636, 31 May 1954, file no.608/6/01, CO 1031/1976.
13. See 'Draft Note of a Meeting held in Mr Rogers' room in the Colonial Office', 22 June 1954, file no.608/6/01, CO 1031/1976.
14. *Daily Gleaner*, 3 July 1954.
15. Michael Billig, *Banal Nationalism* (London, 1995), 37. For recent useful discussions of history and memory see John R. Gillis (ed.), *Commemorations: The Politics of National Identity* (Princeton, 1994); Michael Kammen, *Mystic Chords of Memory: The Transformation of Tradition in American Culture* (New York, 1991). See also Geneviève Fabre and Robert O'Meally (eds.), *History and Memory in African-American Culture* (Oxford, 1994).
16. *Daily Gleaner*, 10 May 1955.
17. See 23 Sept. 1954, *Jamaica Hansard* (House of Representatives), Session 1954, no.1, 248–9.
18. Ibid., 251.
19. *Daily Gleaner*, 21 Dec. 1954.
20. Ibid., 3 Jan. 1955.
21. Ibid., 17 Jan. 1955.
22. See remarks by N. W. Manley at the ceremony of the lighting of the Christmas tree in Kingston, ibid., 17 Dec. 1955.
23. See report on 'Historic Day in the House', ibid., 20 Oct. 1954.
24. Ibid.
25. Ibid., 27 Oct. 1954.
26. See Manley's speech at dinner to welcome the British representatives of the Commonwealth Parliamentary Association, ibid., 8 Aug. 1955. Also Manley's speech in connection with the tercentenary celebrations of the Church of England in Jamaica, ibid., 17 Nov. 1955. Cf. John Darwin, *Britain and Decolonisation: The Retreat from Empire in the Post-War World* (Basingstoke, 1988), 220.
27. See editorial 'Fare Thee Well', ibid., 24 Feb. 1955.
28. Report on the opening of the Morant Bay Hospital, ibid., 23 Feb. 1955.
29. See news item, 'Proud Moment for Jamaica', ibid.
30. N. W. Manley, 23 Sept. 1954, *Jamaica Hansard* (House of Representatives), Session 1954, no.1, 251.
31. For a parallel with the British North American colonies, David I. Kertzer, *Ritual, Politics, and Power* (New Haven, 1988), 161.
32. Comments by Thomas Wright, *Daily Gleaner*, 15 Sept. 1954.
33. See Wycliffe S. Bennett, 'Why Celebrate?', *Pepperpot*, IV (1954), 8.
34. See editorial, 'Jamaica 300', *Daily Gleaner*, 29 March 1955.
35. See news report, '5,000 at Westmoreland 300', ibid., 1 Nov. 1955.
36. Ibid., 16 Dec. 1955.
37. For excellent discussions of this theme, Lyn Spillman, *Nation and Commemoration: Creating National Identities in the United States and Australia* (Cambridge, 1997), and Heidi Tarver, 'The Creation of American National Identity: 1774–1796', *Berkeley Journal of Sociology*, XXVII (1992), 35–99.
38. *Daily Gleaner*, 17 Jan. 1955.
39. Wycliffe S. Bennett, 'Why Celebrate?', *Pepperpot*, IV (1954), 8. For an excellent discussion of the creole society paradigm, O. Nigel Bolland, 'Creolization and Creole Societies: A Cultural Nationalist View of Caribbean Social History', in idem, *Struggles for Freedom:*

Essays on Slavery, Colonialism and Culture in the Caribbean and Central America (Kingston and Belize City, 1997), 3–36.

40. See editorial, 'Forward', *Daily Gleaner*, 10 May 1955.
41. The phrase is Gordon K. Lewis's, *The Growth of the Modern West Indies* (London, 1968), 192.
42. T. H. McDermot, 'From a Jamaica Portfolio', *Journal of Negro History*, II (1917), 147.
43. See news item, 'Jamaica should have had self-govt. 100 years ago', *Daily Gleaner*, 5 July 1954. For a discussion of the idea of counter-identity, Johnston, *Celebrations*, 41.
44. Lewis, *Growth of the Modern West Indies*, 190.
45. See 'Political Report on Jamaica for the month of July 1952' (Secret), file no.58/118/01, CO 1031/132.
46. W. Adolphe Roberts, *Six Great Jamaicans: Biographical Sketches* (Kingston, 1952).
47. G. St. C. Scotter, 'Today', *Daily Gleaner*, 6 July 1954.
48. See letters by Edna Manley and Guy F. Dobson, ibid., 8 July 1954. Also letter by P. Alexander Wauka, ibid., 23 July 1954.
49. Ibid., 12 Feb. 1955.
50. Ibid., 10 Nov.; editorial on 'The Past', 13 Oct.; report on the sermon, 22 Nov. 1955.
51. Hart, 'Jamaica and Self-Determination', 288–90.
52. See speech at the Jamaica Manufacturers Association's exhibition, ibid., 3 Aug. 1954.
53. Ibid., 27 Oct. 1954.
54. See statement by the PNP on the abrogation of the British Guiana constitution, ibid., 16 Oct. 1953.
55. Quoted in Philip Sherlock, *Norman Manley* (London, 1980), 158–9.
56. H.M. Foot to Alan Lennox-Boyd, 12 April 1955 (Conf.), file no.58/156/01/B, CO 1031/133.
57. See statement by N. W. Manley on Jamaica's Colonial Development and Welfare allocation, *Daily Gleaner*, 4 May 1955. For a useful discussion of Manley's early attempts to attract private foreign investment, Munroe, *Politics of Constitutional Decolonization*, 99–100.
58. See editorial, 'Welcome', *Daily Gleaner*, 8 June 1955. For an authoritative assessment of Muñoz Marín's economic policy, see James L. Dietz, *Economic History of Puerto Rico: Institutional Change and Capitalist Development* (Princeton, 1986).
59. See report on the opening of the fair, *Daily Gleaner*, 16 Sept. 1955.
60. Wm. Roger Louis and Ronald Robinson, 'Empire Preserv'd: How the Americans put Anti-Communism before Anti-Imperialism', *Times Literary Supplement*, no.4805, 5 May 1995, 16.
61. Quoted in Tarver, 'Creation of American National Identity', 60.

Malaysia: The Making of a Neo-Colony?

A.J. STOCKWELL

David Fieldhouse has written: 'Neo-colonialism, like colonialism, is a term of opprobrium. It came into general use only in the 1950s as a consequence of the withdrawal of political control from an increasing number of European colonies; and its implication is that for a less developed country the normal end of colonialism does not necessarily result in genuine independence.'[1] As used by Marxists, the term denotes economic subjugation: just as colonialism had resulted in economic exploitation, so neo-colonialism led to under-development, making former dependencies still poorer. This economic subservience continued after the end of formal colonial rule because foreign companies maintained their domination in alliance with the new indigenous rulers. Non-Marxists, too, have concluded that decolonization was the pursuit of imperialism by other means, but, in addition to economic considerations, they have taken into account political and strategic factors. They have also pointed to the 'metropolitan infirmity' which limited the Europeans' capacity to shape developments to their own liking. As David Fieldhouse has written with regard to Africa, 'the fact that economic links between the one-time metropolises and the new states … remained close after independence' does not necessarily mean that 'such results were expected and that these expectations encouraged officials and capitalists to look forward to decolonization without fear'.[2] Some have argued that after 1945 Britain was not in a position either to control the colonial empire or to direct the process of decolonization and that, where empire remained, it did so under new, American-dominated management.[3]

The manner of Malayan decolonization and the subsequent creation of Malaysia suggest neo-colonialism at work. On 31 August 1957, Tunku Abdul Rahman proclaimed 'Merdeka' (independence) and Britain transferred power to the Federation of Malaya. On 16 September 1963 Malaya merged with the former British colonies of Singapore, North Borneo (now Sabah), and Sarawak to achieve what the Tunku claimed was 'the end of colonialism' in Southeast Asia. To the Tunku's opponents both at home and abroad, however, Malayan independence was a sham while the making of Malaysia was a neo-colonial conspiracy. Between 1957 and the late 1960s, it is alleged, Britain maintained hegemony in Malaya/Malaysia, not by formal rule or coercion, but by an unequal military alliance, the management of market forces, and cultural infiltration.

This assessment, however, fails to take into account Britain's enfeeblement in the area: the government was unable to command either the transfer of power in 1957 or the negotiations leading to Malaysia in 1963 and ministers frequently accepted Malayan demands against their better judgment. Moreover, the inauguration of Malaysia did more to aggravate Britain's problems than enhance Britain's influence in the region. The case for neo-colonialism, with its emphasis upon economic dominance, is further undermined by ministers' preoccupation with strategic issues and their apparent indifference to business interests in Malaysia.

According to the proponents of neo-colonialism, a single feature which the constituent parts of Malaysia shared was experience of British rule. Its form varied. Until 1942 Britain's empire in Southeast Asia comprised: the colony of the Straits Settlements (Singapore, Penang and Malacca), nine protected Malay states (four of which had federated in 1896), the kingdom of Sarawak under the Brooke raj, and chartered company administration in North Borneo. After the Second World War, Singapore, Sarawak, and North Borneo became crown colonies, while Penang and Malacca joined the Malay states to form the Malayan Union in 1946 and the Federation of Malaya in 1948. It was British rule which determined national and international boundaries, joining Malay and Borneo states and separating them from the wider Malay world of Indonesia, which created a state structure centred upon Kuala Lumpur, which opened the country to western capitalism, which shaped the emergence of a so-called 'plural society' where ethnic differences were reinforced by the separate economic functions and political status of the principal communities, and which, further, manipulated communalism to impede Malayan nationalism and retard class affiliations. The success of the British in winning, maintaining and, finally, transferring power depended on the close collaboration of traditional leaders of Malay society in particular. In the Malay states princes and peasants grew to depend upon British 'protection', while Asian immigrants were crucial to the growth of a 'modern' Malaya of tin-mining, plantation agriculture, towns, and services. 'To describe this process as one of "development" of Malaya is an obvious circumlocution';[4] rather, the structure of British rule was basically 'the vehicle for British exploitation of the Malayan economy'.[5] Colonialism established relationships and institutions which perpetuated British influence over the post-colonial state. In short, British rule led to the making of a neo-colony.

The timing and manner of decolonization appear to endorse this verdict.

The easy transition of Malaya from formal dependency to independent member of the Commonwealth was marked by a phased transfer of power to Malayan elites committed to maintain colonial institutions, advance capitalism, and counter communism. It is true that the communist insurrection (1948–60) tied down large numbers of British and Commonwealth forces and severely stretched Britain's defence budget, but, on balance the British calculated that Malaya was an asset worth fighting for. It is also true that insurgency forced the pace of Britain's withdrawal, but the beneficiaries were safe nationalists rather than communists who were in retreat militarily and marginalized politically. In Caldwell's view,

> Britain had carefully steered things to a point at which it seemed imminently safe to delegate to the well-trained and well-constrained puppets cultivated for many years the responsibilities of 'independence'... 'Merdeka' (Independence) was officially proclaimed to the satisfaction both of the elites of the Malay and Chinese communities and of the cream of British businessmen so deeply entrenched in the economy of this hand-made neo-colony. The latter could enjoy the freedom celebrations with particular gratification: at independence, 75 per cent of all rubber plantation acreage was in European (mostly British) hands, along with 61 per cent of all tin production, and 75 per cent of all services and trade. The expense and ferocity of the 'Emergency' had paid off.[6]

Furthermore, the independence settlement of 1957 included, firstly, a defence treaty by which Britain continued to use military bases in Malaya and to assist in internal security operations, secondly, Malayan membership of the Commonwealth and sterling area, and, thirdly, the employment of British expatriates in key government positions. In addition, Britain and Malaya shared responsibility for the internal security of Singapore. Thereafter, 'Malaya stayed on the course on which the British had launched it: a free enterprise community in which economic growth proceeded rapidly.'[7] Small wonder that Tunku Abdul Rahman (Prime Minister of Malaya/Malaysia, 1957–70), who, unlike Nehru, Nkrumah, Kenyatta, or Sukarno, had not acquired through detention in a colonial gaol the laurels of a nationalist martyr, was dismissed in some quarters as a British stooge.

The creation of Malaysia appears to fit the same pattern of Anglo-Malayan relations. On 27 May 1961 Tunku Abdul Rahman announced his 'grand design' for 'Greater Malaysia' – the merger of the independent Federation with Britain's dependencies of Singapore, Brunei, North Borneo, and Sarawak.[8] The initiative did not come as a surprise to the British; nor did it clash with their long-held objectives. In the 1930s the British governor and high commissioner, Sir Cecil Clementi (whose wife drove Noel Coward 'dementi'), had worked in vain towards the closer association of British dependencies in the region. In August 1941 Churchill had despatched Duff Cooper, chancellor of the Duchy of Lancaster, to Singapore to examine co-ordination between the various British civil and military authorities in the area. He recommended the appointment of a commissioner-general for the Far East based at Singapore. After Pearl Harbor in December, he himself was made resident minister in an abortive attempt to withstand the Japanese onslaught. Regionalism was a key feature of wartime planning for post-war Southeast Asia, with the result that in 1946, after Mountbatten's South East Asia Command was wound up, a governor-general (later commissioner-general) was appointed to the area. In turn, Malcolm MacDonald (governor-general 1946–48, commissioner-general 1948–55), Robert H. Scott (commissioner-general 1955–59), and Lord Selkirk (1959–63) co-ordinated Britain's foreign, colonial, and defence policies in Southeast Asia.[9] As in Central Africa and the West Indies, the federation of proximate, if disparate, territories was believed to carry administrative, economic, and strategic advantages. From 1948, after Lord Killearn completed two years as special commissioner with particular responsibility for economic matters, strategic considerations dominated British thinking about Southeast Asia: it was felt that colonial fragmentation had contributed to the military debacle of 1941–42 and could not be allowed to jeopardize Britain's position in the Cold War.

Although divergent local developments resulted in Malaya's achieving independence in isolation from both Singapore and the Borneo territories, Britain's commitment to their merger did not diminish. On the contrary, it was heightened by three factors. The first of these was political unrest in Singapore. In 1959 the island-colony had gained internal self-government under Lee Kuan Yew who played a major part in convincing the Tunku of the urgency of merger on grounds of security. In July 1961 the radical left-wing split from Lee's People's Action Party to form the Barisan Sosialis (socialist front) in opposition to the neo-colonial Malaysia scheme. Consequently, the PAP's working majority was endangered, Lee Kuan Yew was forced to 'ride the tiger' of socialism, and Singapore was dubbed the 'Cuba' of Southeast Asia. The second factor was the status of Britain's Borneo dependencies.[10] Ministers and officials accepted that the crown colonies of Sarawak and North Borneo and the sultanate of Brunei were unlikely candidates for separate nationhood, yet, because of their political and economic under-development, their closer association with the peninsula should not be rushed. An added complication was the constitutional position of the sultan of Brunei who had concluded a treaty with Britain in 1959, whereby his kingdom acquired internal self-government, without democratic or even representative institutions. Thirdly, apart from Dutch New Guinea (surrendered to Indonesia in 1963) and Portuguese Timor (incorporated within the Republic of Indonesia in 1976), Singapore and British Borneo were the last remnants of European colonialism in Southeast Asia and were a source of increasing embarrassment to Britain in the United Nations and in its relations with the United States.

Six months after the Tunku announced his plan, Anglo-Malayan exploratory talks were held in London which resulted in a joint statement (23 November 1961) accepting 'Greater Malaysia' in principle, providing for the continued use by Britain of the Singapore base, and promising a commission to assess the views of Borneo peoples for whom Britain had direct responsibility.[11] Early the following year a Malaysian Solidarity Consultative Committee, meeting in Kuala Lumpur, declared in favour of merger. In February 1962, the commission of inquiry (chaired by Lord Cobbold and consisting of two British and two Malayan members) arrived in Borneo to sound opinion in Sarawak and North Borneo.[12] The Cobbold Report concluded that about one third of the population in each territory strongly favoured Malaysia; that another third supported the project but asked for various safeguards; and that the remaining third either preferred continuity of British rule or the achievement of independence in advance of the formation of Malaysia.[13] On the basis of these findings, Macmillan and the Tunku reached an agreement for merger on 31 July 1962. In the next twelve months details were negotiated with respect to the interstate relations of the new federation as well as arrangements to assist the transition of Sarawak and North Borneo from colonial rule to self-government within Malaysia. The Sultan of Brunei wavered in his support for the scheme. In July 1962 Sultan Sir Omar Ali Saifuddin announced that he accepted in principle Brunei's future within Malaysia, but in December supporters of A.M. Azahari's Party Rakyat (people's party) revolted against Malaysia and in favour of a separate state of North Borneo (Brunei, Sarawak and Sabah). This rebellion, which the Gurkhas put down, convinced the British of the need to draw Brunei into Malaysia, if necessary by force or by cultivating the support of detained Party Rakyat leaders.[14] Alarmed by the revolt, however, the sultan decided in July 1963 not to enter Malaysia but to remain a British protected state. Despite the Brunei revolt and the hostility of Indonesia and the Philippines (whose opposition delayed plans while the United Nations conducted a further survey of opinion in Borneo), Malaysia was inaugurated on 16 September 1963.

Communist parties and the governments of the Philippines and Indonesia condemned Malaysia as 'a British-sponsored neo-colonialist plot'. The Philippines laid claim to Sabah, on the basis of an interpretation of the 1878 agreement whereby a British commercial syndicate had acquired a concession from the Sultan of Sulu. President Sukarno's hostility was more threatening. A nationalist with socialist leanings and many contending groups to square in Indonesia, Sukarno had at first accepted the Tunku's proposal but a desperate need for the support of the Indonesian Communist Party swung him into virulent opposition. Attacking Malaysia principally on the grounds that it perpetuated British power in Southeast Asia and divided the Malay world of Indonesia, the Philippines, and Malaya, Sukarno embarked upon nearly three years of 'Konfrontasi' or Confrontation with the new state.[15] Sukarno had first used the term 'Confrontation' in June 1960 to register Indonesia's opposition to the Dutch claim upon the western half of New Guinea (Irian Jaya). This dispute was settled through the intervention of the United States which, because it was anxious that the Indonesian Communist Party should not have the opportunity to exploit the issue in order to destabilize Sukarno's regime, arbitrated in Indonesia's favour. Once again, this time with respect to Malaysia, Sukarno confronted a European colonial power. On the day after Malaysia Day a mob sacked the British embassy in Jakarta.[16] As Indonesian forces made forays across the border, British and Australian troops were brought in to defend the one-thousand-mile frontier between Malaysian Borneo and Indonesian Borneo (or Kalimantan). Whether or not Malaysia would sustain British influence in the area in the long term it appeared in 1963 that Malaysia's immediate survival depended upon Britain's military assistance.

Liberation from neo-colonialism was a long time in coming. The first milestone was reached at the end of the 1960s and was marked by two unrelated events: the decision by the Wilson government to withdraw from east of Suez by 1971 and the bloody, racial conflict triggered by Malaysia's elections in May 1969. Indeed, the '13 May incident' appeared to do more than the inauguration of Malaysia six years earlier or the achievement of Malayan independence six years before that to arouse a sense of national identity. Following this unrest, principles of state (*Rukunegara*) were promulgated, the New Economic Policy which has shaped national planning ever since was launched, the anglophile prime minister (Tunku Abdul Rahman) resigned, and Malaysia's relationship with Britain was adjusted. The second milestone was passed in 1981 when Dr Mahathir became prime minister. The first non-aristocratic and locally educated Malay to lead the country, Mahathir launched a 'dawn raid' upon the London Stock Exchange to secure control of the Guthrie Corporation, Sime Darby, Dunlop, Harrisons and Crosfield, and other major companies as a prelude to the first of his 'buy British last' campaigns.[17] Dismayed by western decadence and discounting as irrelevant liberal criticisms of Southeast Asia's authoritarian regimes, Mahathir preferred to 'look east' and advanced 'Asian values'.

Throughout the 1980s and 1990s he railed against westerners whom he saw clinging to political, economic, and intellectual hegemony in Southeast Asia. When, in 1994, the *Sunday Times* revealed a connection between British aid for the construction of the Pergau dam and Malaysian arms orders, Mahathir retaliated angrily against the 'colonialism' of the British press. The British government and British business feared a return to 'buy British last'. Their consternation demonstrated, in the words of another Sunday paper, that the 'Malays are masters now as Britons have to grovel'. 'The painful truth is that we [British] need them [Malaysians] more than they need us. For many Malaysians, Britain has at last found its proper place in the world.'[18] At last the age of colonialism was dead.

Though a plausible thesis, neo-colonialism is flawed so far as Anglo-Malayan relations are concerned. A preliminary review of the government record indicates a number of weaknesses regarding its application to the period from the coming of independence to the formation of Malaysia.[19] First of all, it was not the case, as neo-colonialism suggests, that the British were in command of the transfer of power to Malayans in the years 1955–57. The Malayan Alliance (consisting of the United Malays National Organization or UMNO, the Malayan Chinese Association or MCA, and the Malayan Indian Congress or MIC) forced them to proceed faster and further than they intended. In so doing, the British government abandoned three key and publicly stated preconditions for independence. The first of these was that the state of emergency, or state of undeclared war against the communists, should have ended before the grant of independence. This principle had been proclaimed perhaps most vigorously by Oliver Lyttelton (Conservative secretary of state for the colonies 1951–54) but there was cross-party agreement over it and Attlee had declared in April 1949 that the Labour government 'had no intention of jeopardising the security, well-being and liberty of these peoples, for whom Britain has responsibilities, by premature withdrawal'.[20] By October 1955, however, ministers were prepared to retreat from the position that a continuation of the shooting war was 'an obstacle on the road to self-government'.[21] They did so, not so much because of their evident success in that war, as because they wished to prevent the Tunku from advancing his own cause by the adoption of the high-risk strategy of negotiating a political deal with communists. Had the Tunku's Malay supporters been kept waiting in the wings much longer, there was the danger that they might have grown restive, perhaps forcing him to make more radical demands or abandoning his essentially constitutional methods in favour of greater militancy. So it was that the independence of Malaya preceded the end of the emergency by exactly three years.

The second principle which was compromised under the weight of Malayan politics was the British commitment to hand over power to a genuinely multiracial movement. The British wartime plan, which was embodied in the Malayan Union experiment of 1946–48, to lay the foundations for a multiracial nation through administrative centralization and a generous scheme of common citizenship was thwarted by Malay communalism in the form of the United Malays National Organization. Subsequent attempts to launch non-communal parties, notably the Independence of Malaya Party in 1951, fizzled out. In their place emerged the Alliance of three communally exclusive parties (UMNO, MCA and MIC) which the British mistrusted as the institutionalization of racial divisions. The Alliance's landslide victory in the federal elections of 1955, when it won 51 of the 52 electable seats, convinced the British of the coalition's popular foundations and persuaded them to accept its legitimacy. By no stretch of the imagination, however, did the Alliance electoral success demonstrate a genuinely multiracial support. It was carried to victory in 1955 on the votes of Malays who, because of the citizenship law, accounted for 84 per cent of the electorate even though they numbered less than half of the total population of the Federation.

The third precondition of independence had been merger with Singapore, and preferably with the British Borneo territories as well. Though a principle of British policy since the 'new imperialism' of the wartime planning era, this, too, was overtaken by events. The speed of political advance on the peninsula was accelerated by the ebb and flow of insurgency and counter-insurgency. Notwithstanding Malcolm MacDonald's enthusiasm for closer association and despite his optimism in the willingness of peninsular and island elites to combine in a common endeavour, ingrained Malay distrust of Chinese-dominated Singapore deterred the British government from pushing ahead with merger in what were generally seen to be unpropitious circumstances.

Not only were the British not in command of the process of decolonization, they also had misgivings with respect to the reliability of the leader of the emergent nation-state. Some recognized in the Tunku the qualities of Jawaharlal Nehru, which might bode ill for British defence strategy in the region. Others doubted his political acumen and his ability to master a brief; they wondered whether he would be able to rein in the more extravagant aspirations of his supporters or protect his ministerial colleagues from the corrupting effects of power. Neither of these assessments suggests that the British regarded him as their poodle. Anxiety concerning the future stability, prosperity, and dependability of the new Malaya is revealed by questions raised in a position paper produced in the office of the commissioner-general a few months before independence.[22]

Would the Tunku be able to moderate Malay hostility to the Chinese community, or, on the other hand, contain Chinese communism and prevent Malaya falling under the domination of the People's Republic of China? Would he guard against administrative decay and cope with post-emergency problems such as resettling the thousands of Malays who had been involved in counter-insurgency operations? How reliable an ally would he turn out to be in international affairs, given his refusal to join the South East Asia Treaty Organisation?

The charge of neo-colonialism also suggests that Britain continued to have major economic interests in Malaya, which required protection. Officials stressed at the time of transfer of power that the country was a source of essential raw materials and a substantial dollar-earner.[23] Though this litany was regularly repeated in succeeding years, Malaya's economic importance for Britain was on the wane in the decolonization era and its aftermath. As Nicholas White has shown, 'British capital in Malaya was losing its bargaining power with both imperial and colonial governments ... The tensions of the [post-war] reconstruction era ... had the effect of alienating business from government.' In support of his argument that 'late colonialism in Malaya served British capitalism badly', White has demonstrated that business leaders were 'marginalized within metropolitan policy-making circles by the 1950s'. Even more significant was the change in Malaya's pattern of trade. 'Pan-Malayan rubber exports to the dollar area fell from 53 per cent of total export volume in 1947 to 33 per cent in 1950, to 21 per cent by 1962.' The world was consuming less and less natural rubber and more and more synthetic rubber with the result that Malaya's market share dropped from 40 per cent on the eve of the Pacific war to about 20 per cent in 1957. A similar trend towards substitution affected Malayan tin exports. Meanwhile, as the importance for Britain of Malaya's dollar earnings diminished and interest faded in commercial development within the sterling area, so Malayan investment groups diversified into western economies. In short, by the time of transfer of power, 'Malaya was declining in economic significance for the UK and, as a result, the British business lobby was more and more peripheral.'[24] Furthermore, British exports to the region fell off conspicuously by the early 1960s and this state of affairs was brought to the prime minister's attention by the commissioner-general in his regular reports. By the end of his term as commissioner-general, Selkirk had reached the conclusion that 'Our interest [in Southeast Asia] is not so much in the extent of our economic investments and trade as in our vested interest in world peace.' He continued: 'If we can accept this as the basis of our policy in the Far East, I believe our whole position would become more natural and understandable to the people of the area.'[25] Indeed, although the prime minister went out of his way to meet Sardon Jubir, Malaya's minister of transport, when he visited London in May 1961, in the hope that he would be induced to spent at least some of his purse of £17 million on British manufactures,[26] Macmillan's overriding interest in Malaya was as a front-line state in the Cold War.

For ministers and senior officials Malaya's strategic value outweighed its economic value. Its importance to Britain was 'as a base for defence purposes' and 'as a symbol of British influence in the area'.[27] With diminished resources, however, the British government sought to achieve peace on the cheap. Robert Scott's reports to Eden regularly returned to a single, simple theme: reduced capacity necessitated the concentration of limited resources on the peacetime offensive rather than preparations for war.[28] Eight weeks before Nasser nationalized the Suez canal, Scott recommended the integration of British defence policies with those of the United States, Australia and New Zealand.[29] In mid-December 1956 he argued that the Suez debacle had confirmed his view that Britain should reduce its obligations instead of cutting the resources devoted to a constant number of obligations. 'Cut commitments', he stressed, 'not the means to discharge them.'[30] Selkirk took up the refrain, urging the Macmillan government to focus on economic aid, trade, and teaching English, not defence expenditure.[31] A world role came with a price tag, and ministers and senior officials were looking for ways to cut the cost of Britain's presence in Southeast Asia.[32] Indeed, the enthusiasm with which Selkirk welcomed the Tunku's 'grand design' indicated the extent to which British power had declined in Southeast Asia.

Macmillan generally accepted Selkirk's assessment of 'the difficulty of shaping a satisfactory British policy for South East Asia'. He agreed that 'our limited resources and our growing commitments elsewhere make it essential that we should gradually reduce our military and colonial responsibilities in South East Asia'.[33] The government's ability to maintain British influence for peace in the area – which was the cabinet's paramount consideration – was reduced, first of all, by disagreements with local leaders. For, although it made financial sense to devolve formal power and draw emergent nation-states into systems for regional security, commitments to colonial self-government and regional defence in the Malaysia area posed the sort of dilemma already encountered in Egypt and Cyprus. On the one hand, military bases antagonized local nationalists; on the other, national independence placed constraints upon the use of bases. While Malayan and Singaporean leaders played down their significance for fear of inflaming domestic criticisms, Britain wanted to publicize the bases for deterrent effect as well as to demonstrate solidarity with the Americans and Australians in the region.[34] Australia and New Zealand, however, showed an increasing tendency to rely upon the United States which more and more doubted Britain's capacity to sustain global influence. On 15 December 1961, three weeks after the Anglo-Malayan exploratory talks in London, Philip de Zulueta (the prime minister's private secretary) advised Macmillan:

> … the arrangements for Greater Malaysia are bringing to a head the question of whether Australia and New Zealand should look even more in future to the Americans for their defence in war and therefore for their supplies in peace. No doubt the Americans will be delighted to encourage this tendency as part of their view of this country as a minor European power. It may be that we shall have to acquiesce in this change because our strength is not great enough to play a serious role in the Far East, but this is clearly a question which ought to be looked at very carefully.[35]

The decline of British power in Southeast Asia was only too apparent when set in the context of developments elsewhere in the years 1961–63. Macmillan may have cultivated the pose of a world leader, especially in his avuncular relationship with J.F. Kennedy, but his government was shaken by the stop-go policy of the chancellor of the exchequer (Selwyn Lloyd), the drastic cabinet reshuffle in the 'night of the long knives' (July 1962), and the Profumo crisis. Despite a public sang-froid, Macmillan was dogged by a dark foreboding made all the more apocalyptic by the Cuban missile crisis and China's offensive against India in October 1962. Wounded by Dean Acheson's jibe (delivered coincidentally at the time of the Brunei revolt in December 1962)[36] that Britain had lost an empire but had yet to find a role in the world, Macmillan grappled in vain with Britain's bid to join the European Economic Community, which de Gaulle vetoed in January 1963, and with the problems of Central Africa, which, he admitted, were never absent from his mind.[37] Indeed, ministers drew parallels between the Central African Federation and the Greater Malaysia scheme: both had a strategic importance and made economic sense, yet both were plagued by secessionism and complicated by the involvement of an array of Whitehall departments.

Institutional fragmentation occasionally threatened to sabotage Britain's Malaysia policy. The perspectives of officials in Southeast Asia varied with the office which they held and the careers they had followed. Sir Geofroy Tory, formerly of the Commonwealth Relations Office, served as the high commissioner in Kuala Lumpur from 1957 to 1963. Performing a diplomatic as opposed to a colonial role, he closely monitored the activities of Tunku Abdul Rahman and the federal government. Like Sir Glyn Jones in Nyasaland (1961–64) and Sir Evelyn Hone in Northern Rhodesia (1959–64), on the other hand, Sir Alexander Waddell, governor of Sarawak

1960–63, and Sir William Goode, governor of North Borneo 1960–63, represented the 'colonial tradition' of protecting the interests of indigenous peoples. Waddell had joined the colonial service in the late 1930s and Goode, having entered the Malayan Civil Service in 1931, had been governor of Singapore in 1957–59. By contrast again, Selkirk had been first lord of the Admiralty before his posting to Singapore. Like his predecessors as commissioner-general, he was exercised by the lack of coherence in the regional management of Britain's foreign, colonial, and military affairs and advocated the creation of a unified command structure.[38] In Whitehall, the principal departments involved in Malaysia policy were the Commonwealth Relations Office (under Duncan Sandys from July 1960 to October 1964), the Colonial Office (under Reginald Maudling from October 1961 until July 1962 when Sandys combined the office with the CRO), and the Ministry of Defence (under Harold Watkinson from September 1959 to July 1962 and Peter Thorneycroft from July 1962 to October 1964). Macmillan was impressed by Duncan Sandys: 'cool as a cucumber, methodical; very strong in character, has gradually mastered the art of Parliamentary speaking, tremendously hard working; not easily shaken from his course – ambitious, and rather cruel ...'[39] A former minister of defence (1957–59) and a tough negotiator with Roy Welensky of the Central Africa Federation, Sandys had the credentials to take charge of Britain's Malaysia policy. Even so, as late as February 1963 de Zulueta still felt the need to draw to the prime minister's attention to the worrying diffusion of responsibility across Whitehall and the lack of executive direction. By May, however, he was more confident that daily meetings of a Cabinet Office committee were imposing effective inter-departmental co-ordination.[40]

The dictum, that 'the aim of British policy in Asia should be to encourage and persuade and help Asian countries to conduct their own affairs in an orderly, efficient, and peaceful way', was easier said than done.[41] In fact the British travelled a bumpy road towards the formation of Malaysia and jostled with their fellow travellers, sometimes at the risk of breakdown. Apart from tensions within the British government, there were marked differences of approach adopted by Britain, Malaya, and Singapore. First of all, the priorities of the various parties to the process differed. London was principally concerned to achieve the merger of Singapore and Malaysia. This was regarded as crucial to the security of both the island and the broader region. In the British view, because they were geographically distinct and less developed economically and politically, entry of the Borneo territories might take longer and require a transition period of British administration. The Tunku, on the other hand, had no wish to be left 'holding the Singapore baby' without the inclusion of those non-Chinese inhabitants of Sarawak, North Borneo, and possibly Brunei to cushion

Malaya from the impact of Singapore's Chinese majority.[42] Indeed, at times (for example when the internal security problems of Singapore eased as a result of the detention in February 1963 of over one hundred potential subversives) Lee Kuan Yew feared that the Tunku might abandon Malaysia altogether. While this did not happen, discussions between Malaya and Singapore regarding their respective financial contributions to Malaysia were hard fought and Lee Kuan Yew threatened to arrogate sovereign powers in advance of Malaysia Day.[43]

The second matter causing friction between Malayan and British negotiators was the status of Sarawak and North Borneo. The Tunku demanded the early cession of British sovereignty. Malayans would not tolerate transitional arrangements whereby the British presence would be prolonged much after Malaysia Day; such a relationship would surely compromise Malaysian independence. Britain for its part had a deep-rooted commitment to protect the interests of the Borneo peoples. The Colonial Office and administrators on the spot felt that the resources of the Federation were already stretched and might not run to the provision of satisfactory administration of Sarawak and Sabah for which, in any case, Malayans had little real sympathy. Moreover, colonial officials suspected that Kuala Lumpur, for all its hostility to any hint of British neo-colonialism, was itself embarking on a bout of empire-building in Borneo. These views were shared by the British members of the Cobbold Commission, Abell and Watherston, both of whom had had careers in the colonial service. They proposed an arrangement whereby sovereignty (including control over defence) would be transferred to Malaysia, but British governors would remain for several more years to provide administrative continuity.[44] The last Rajah of Sarawak and Bertram Brooke also wrote to the prime minister about Britain's historic obligations to the peoples of Sarawak.[45] While colonial officials were incensed by what they took to be the Tunku's manipulation of the mission to the disadvantage of the Borneo peoples,[46] the Tunku complained that British officials in Borneo were sabotaging Cobbold's inquiry.[47] Macmillan, nervous that these disagreements might derail the Malaysia plan, grew impatient with what appeared to be the unrealistic sentimentality of the Borneo lobby. Alerted to a telegram from Sir William Goode, who protested against Malayan aggrandisement towards Borneo, Macmillan scrawled his worries to Sir Norman Brook, secretary to the cabinet:

> I am rather shocked by this telegram & the attitude it reveals. Does he [the governor of North Borneo] realise (a) our weakness in Singapore (b) our *urgent* [*sic*] need to hand over the security problem there. The whole mood is based on a false assessment of our power. If this is [the] C.O. point of view we shall fail. What shall we do?[48]

When the Tunku sent a message to Macmillan rejecting Cobbold's recommendations and proposing a postponement of Malaysia until Borneo was ready for merger, Macmillan replied by return, distancing himself from the British members of the commission and inviting Abdul Rahman to London for further talks which resulted in both prime ministers signing the agreement for merger.[49] Constitutional safeguards for North Borneo and Sarawak were then negotiated by the Inter-Governmental Committee (chaired by Lord Lansdowne, minister of state for colonial affairs) which was formed in August 1962 and reported in February. It was on the basis of its recommendations that the first elections were held in North Borneo and Sarawak.

The third sticking-point in the Malaysia talks was defence. One aspect of this was the future of Singapore's bases. The British sought guarantees for their continued use for regional and Commonwealth defence as well as for SEATO purposes, though fastidiously pointed out that they would not be SEATO bases. On the other hand, ever on their guard against radical protests at home, both Tunku Abdul Rahman and Lee Kuan Yew were reluctant to enter into a well-publicized commitment to the British on the use of bases. Another aspect of the defence issue concerned the extent of British military aid to Malaysia. These discussions, in which the Treasury offered £12.5 million while the Malayan delegation held out for more, resembled the bargaining that had taken place six years earlier on the eve of the transfer of power to Malaya.[50]

British negotiators were, therefore, impeded by the intransigence of the Tunku Abdul Rahman particularly over the status of Sarawak and North Borneo, the vulnerability of Lee Kuan Yew to domestic unrest, and the intractability of the Sultan of Brunei. The weeks leading up to Malaysia Day were particularly tense: Sultan Omar Ali Saiffudin decided not to join the federation; Lee Kuan Yew threatened to arrogate sovereign powers in advance of the inauguration of Malaysia; Tunku Abdul Rahman announced his intention to merge with only North Borneo and Sarawak. The 'brinkmanship' of Lee placed him on a 'collision course' with the Tunku. Another dimension to the crisis was local irritation with Kuala Lumpur's insistence on the appointment of Malay governors to Sarawak and Sabah, rather than nominees from Borneo ethnic groups. Meanwhile, as Indonesia grew more menacing by the day, the military implications of Malaysia for Britain appeared unavoidable. Although the Malaysia Agreement was signed on 9 July 1963 by representatives of Britain, Malaya, Singapore, North Borneo, and Sarawak, it was touch and go whether it would come to fruition. Inauguration day, scheduled for the anniversary of the independence of Malaya on 31 August, was postponed by a fortnight to allow the United Nations to conduct a further survey of opinion in Borneo.

Its conclusion in favour of Malaysia only intensified Indonesia's guerrilla operations. During the first half of September, Duncan Sandys laboured in Kuala Lumpur desperately struggling to keep Malaysia on course. Not the most emollient of men, he nonetheless succeeded in arbitrating between Malaya and Singapore. It was with evident relief that Macmillan received Sandys' telegram of 11 September announcing: 'I think we can now be reasonably confident that Singapore will join Malaysia on 16 September peacefully and constitutionally and that we shall not be faced with the ugly situation which seemed only too likely when I sent you my last report on 5th September.'[51] Five days later Malaysia was inaugurated and immediately encountered Indonesia's Confrontation.

This essay has identified a number of flaws in the term neo-colonialism when applied to Britain's relations with Malaya in the period from independence to the formation of Malaysia. It has become clear, first of all, that during the mid-1950s the British were deflected from their plans for the transfer of power to Malaya by powerful, local forces of communism and communalism. The second point to note is that any attempt to shift from formal to informal empire or to substitute neo-colonialism for colonialism would have been gravely handicapped by Britain's reduced circumstances. Simply, Britain lacked the power locally to secure control over its continuing interests in the post-colonial period. Thirdly, British interests were themselves changing. The record establishes that what was uppermost in the official mind at this time was not British investments, nor the dollar-earnings of rubber, nor the reactions of plantation and mining companies, but the security of the region. Senior officials, ministers, and the prime minister himself were committed to the 'Greater Malaysia' scheme on account of the solution it seemed to offer to a particularly knotty problem of maintaining regional stability at minimum cost to the British taxpayer. Fourthly, while regional consolidation was an established British objective, the initiative in this instance 'came largely from the Tunku and the original inspiration was almost certainly Lee Kuan Yew's'.[52] Britain followed their lead but never commanded the heights from which it might assert mastery over the planning and execution of the 'grand design'.

Finally, whatever long-term benefits it promised, the creation of Malaysia immediately saddled Britain with burdens and problems. The first of these was Indonesian Confrontation. In January 1963 Selkirk warned Macmillan that 'we will have to recognise that our military assistance to Malaysia during the formative stage may have to be larger and last longer than we had previously thought would be the case'.[53] A few months later Macmillan informed the foreign secretary of his anxiety regarding the problem of defending 'this new child of ours': it was a huge gamble, risking the armed opposition of Indonesia and the Philippines and eliciting nothing but lukewarm support from the United States and Australia.[54] Moreover, the secretary to the cabinet pointed out the political disadvantages of giving Malaysia military assistance which 'could easily be represented as thinly disguised "neo-colonialism"'.[55] Indonesia's campaign to 'crush Malaysia' lasted until the two states concluded a peace agreement on 1 June 1996, which was ratified by the two governments on 11 August. While the operation was not costly to Britain either in numbers of men deployed (17,000 at the peak) or in casualties (114 British forces were killed), its success depended upon extensive air and naval support. It was not until Confrontation had ended that the British government was free to plan the withdrawal from east of Suez.[56]

A second, potentially harmful consequence for Britain was the impact which military assistance to Malaysia had on Anglo-American relations. The prime minister's private secretary noted in February 1963 that 'the Americans are now becoming luke warm about Malaysia because they do not wish to be involved with the Indonesians.'[57] The United States administration was particularly anxious to safeguard the interests of American oil companies. In one of the last letters he wrote to J.F. Kennedy before he resigned as prime minister, Macmillan invoked American intervention on Britain's side:

> There is … bound to be a most dangerous and unpleasant conflict unless Sukarno can be stopped at the last moment … All of this points to the absolute need for our two countries to stand together at this moment, in all respects. I cannot but feel that to allow Sukarno to drive a wedge between us in this matter of the oil companies would give him exactly the sign for which he is looking …

Macmillan, who thought that Kennedy had entered into unwise commitments to the American oil lobby, was disappointed with the president's reply and commented that it was 'not on an altogether happy note that my connection with the affairs of South East Asia was to terminate'.[58] As it happened, unlike his claim upon Western New Guinea (Irian Jaya), Sukarno's campaign against Malaysia failed to convince the American administration of its legitimacy. In January 1964, President Johnson sent Robert Kennedy to mediate between the contestants; unwilling to bring pressure to bear on the belligerents, the mission achieved nothing.

A third problem derived from the unresolved tension between Malaya and Singapore. Merger exacerbated communal tension. Resentful of Malay political privileges, the People's Action Party campaigned for 'multiracialism and Malaysian nationalism, offering the democratic socialist way to a more equal and just society'. In Kuala Lumpur the right wing of the United Malays National Organization interpreted such demands as a bid by Singapore to take over the Malaysian government. The crisis came to a head in August 1965. Pushed by extremists in his own party and out of touch with local developments on account of a prolonged period of sick-leave in London, the Tunku issued an ultimatum to Lee Kuan Yew which was tantamount to the ejection of Singapore from the federation.[59] It was in vain that Lord Head, Britain's high commissioner to Malaysia 1963–66, tried to dissuade the Tunku from this action. For the British government Malaysia's *raison d'être* lay in the merger of island and peninsula; their separation in 1965 made a nonsense of the original 'grand design'.

NOTES

This essay has benefited greatly from discussions with Dr Matthew Jones, my colleague at Royal Holloway, to whom I am indebted.

1. D.K. Fieldhouse, *Colonialism 1870–1945: An Introduction* (London, 1981), 8, see also 1, 2, 4, 9–10, 53.
2. D.K. Fieldhouse, *Black Africa, 1945–60: Economic Decolonization and Arrested Development* (London, 1986), 6. See also Nicholas J. White, *Business, Government, and the End of Empire: Malaya, 1942–1957* (Kuala Lumpur, 1997), 271.
3. Wm. Roger Louis and Ronald Robinson, 'The Imperialism of Decolonization', *Journal of Imperial and Commonwealth History*, 22, 3 (1994), 462–511.
4. Malcolm Caldwell, 'The British "Forward Movement", 1874–1914', in Mohamed Amin and Malcolm Caldwell (eds.), *Malaya: The Making of a Neo-Colony* (Nottingham, 1977), 34.
5. Ibid., 29.
6. Caldwell, 'From "Emergency" to "Independence", 1948–57', in Mohamed Amin and Caldwell, 251.
7. Brian Lapping, *End of Empire* (London, 1985), 187.
8. The Tunku gave his own account of the occasion in a newspaper article, reprinted in *Looking Back* (Kuala Lumpur, 1977), 77–89. Though he claimed to have electrified his audience, British officials had advance information about the speech, see British high commission to Commonwealth Relations Office, telegram, 26 May 1961, Public Record Office [PRO]: PREM 11/3418. Almost a year earlier the Tunku had suggested a 'Greater Malaysia' scheme to Lord Perth (minister of state for colonial affairs, 1957–62), though Macmillan had had expressed reservations: 'All this seems to me rather doubtful but I suppose it is worth considering.' Macmillan to N. Brook, 19 June 1960, ibid.
9. MacDonald, a former Cabinet minister, reported to the secretaries of state for foreign and colonial Affairs. Scott, a civil servant who later served as permanent secretary at the Ministry of Defence (1961–63), and Selkirk, who had been first lord of the Admiralty (1957–59) before his posting to Singapore, reported directly to the prime minister.
10. See Graham Saunders, *A History of Brunei* (Kuala Lumpur, 1994) and Vernon L. Porritt, *British colonial rule in Sarawak 1946–1963* (Kuala Lumpur, 1997).
11. See PRO: CAB 128/35, CC63(61)6, 16 Nov. 1961, and CC65(61)4, 23 Nov. 1961; CAB 129/107, C(61)190, 2 Nov. 1961; PREM 11/3420.
12. Lord Cobbold, a former governor of the Bank of England, was not the first choice for this job. The names of Malcolm MacDonald (then co-chairman of the international conference on Laos 1961–63), Lord Boyd (formerly Alan Lennox-Boyd and secretary of state for

colonial affairs 1954–59), and Lord Ogmore (formerly David Rees-Williams, under-secretary of state for colonial affairs 1947–50, and friend of Tunku Abdul Rahman) had all been mentioned, see PREM 11/3420 and 3866. The British nominated two commissioners: Sir Anthony Abell (governor of Sarawak 1950–59 and high commissioner for Brunei 1950–58) and Sir David Watherston (chief secretary of Malaya 1952–57). The nominees of the Federation of Malaya were Dato Wong Pow Nee and Mohamad Ghazali Shafie (permanent secretary of the Ministry of External Affairs 1958–70 and minister in the Malaysian federal government 1970–84).

13. *Report of the Commission of Enquiry, North Borneo and Sarawak, 1962*, Cmnd. 1794.
14. PREM 11/4346 and 4347.
15. See J.A.C Mackie, *Konfrontasi: The Indonesia–Malaysia Dispute 1963–1966* (Kuala Lumpur, 1974).
16. The British ambassador, Andrew Gilchrist, in a telegram giving a blow-by-blow account of the riots, reported: 'A further demonstration is now on its way. The charred corpse of my poor old Princess is causing an elegant traffic jam.' The prime minister noted in the margin: 'I hope the historian will not misunderstand this paragraph.' The reference was, of course, to the ambassadorial car. Gilchrist to Foreign Office, 4.39 am, 17 Sept. 1963, PREM 11/4310.
17. Gordon P. Means, *Malaysian Politics: The Second Generation* (Singapore, 1991), 91–2.
18. *The Observer* (London), 27 Feb. 1994, 22, c.8.
19. The author is currently engaged in selecting documents for a volume on the formation of Malaysia for the series, *British Documents on the End of Empire.*
20. *H of C Debs*, 463, c.2815, 13 April 1949.
21. A.J. Stockwell (ed.), *British Documents on the End of Empire: Malaya* (London, 1995) I, lxxvi, III, documents 378–81.
22. 'The outlook in Malaya up to 1960', note by the commissioner-general's office, [May 1957], PRO: FO 371/129342, no. 8, printed in Stockwell, (ed.), *BDEE, Malaya*, III, document 454. See also 'Future of the Alliance Government', March 1957, PRO: CO 1030/440, no. 1.
23. 'The outlook in Malaya up to 1960' [May 1957].
24. White, *Business, Government, and the End of Empire*, 272–79.
25. Selkirk to Macmillan, 3 Sept. 1963, PREM 11/4146.
26. PREM 11/3421.
27. 'The outlook in Malaya up to 1960' [May 1957].
28. Scott to Eden, 15 April 1956, PREM 11/2661.
29. Ibid., Scott to Eden, 1 June 1956.
30. Ibid., Scott to Eden, 18 Dec. 1956.
31. Selkirk to Macmillan, 17 Feb. 1960, PREM 11/3276.
32. Phillip Darby, *British Defence Policy East of Suez 1947–1968* (London, 1973), 214–43 ('Role defined 1962–1964').
33. Macmillan to Selkirk, 12 March 1963, PREM 11/4188.
34. Selkirk to Macmillan, 30 Nov. 1962, PREM 11/3869.
35. De Zulueta to Macmillan, 15 Dec. 1961, PREM 11/4189.
36. Though it is now accepted that the Brunei rising was easily suppressed, it is a mark of British lack of confidence in their power at the time that Selkirk could report to the prime minister on 20 Dec. 1962 that it 'came within an inch of being completely successful', PREM 11/4146.
37. Alistair Horne, *Macmillan*, II, *1957–1986* (London, 1989), 193.
38. Selkirk to Macmillan, 3 Sept. 1963, PREM 11/4146.
39. Horne, *Macmillan 1957–1986*, 395.
40. De Zulueta to Macmillan, 25 Feb. 1963 and 8 May 1963, PREM 11/4347.
41. Scott to Eden, 18 Dec. 1956, PREM 11/2661.
42. PREM 11/3422 and 3868.
43. PREM 11/4346, 4347, 4348, 4349, 4350.
44. Memorandum from Abell and Watherston to Cobbold, 21 June 1962, PREM 11/3867.
45. Rajah Charles Vyner Brooke to the prime minister, 16 July 1962, and Bertram Brooke to the prime minister, 20 Aug. and 13 Sept. 1963, PREM 11/4345.
46. H.P. Hall (commissioner-general's office) to W.I.J. Wallace (Colonial Office), 19 June 1962, PREM 11/3867.

47. De Zulueta to Macmillan, 19 March 1962, PREM 11/3866.
48. Macmillan to Brook, 21 June 1962, PREM 11/3867.
49. Ibid., telegrams between British high commission, Kuala Lumpur, and Macmillan, 4 July 1962. See also CAB 128/36, CC44(62)7, 5 July 1962, and CC53(62)2, 3 Aug. 1962; CAB 129/110, C(62)106, 4 July 1962.
50. Papers on these talks in May 19963 are at PREM 11/4347, 4348 and 4349. See also CAB 128/37, CC34(63)8, 23 May 1963. For the financial settlement in 1957 see Stockwell (ed.), *BDEE: Malaya*, III, document 441.
51. Sandys to Macmillan, 11 Sept. 1963, PREM 11/4350. Macmillan replied on 12 Sept. The three telegrams referred to at CAB 129/114, C(63)149 but retained under section 3(4) (viz LONSOS 171, SOSLON 109, OCULAR 651) are at PREM 11/4350. See also CAB 128/37, 52(63)1, 12 Sept. 1963.
52. Darby, *British Defence Policy*, 281–2.
53. Selkirk to Macmillan, 17 Jan. 1963, PREM 11/4346.
54. Macmillan to Home, 3 April 1963, PREM 11/4347.
55. Ibid., Sir Burke Trend (secretary to Cabinet) to Macmillan, 29 Mar. 1963.
56. Denis Healey, *The Time of My Life* (London, ed. 1990), 289–90.
57. De Zulueta to Macmillan, 20 Feb. 1963, PREM 11/4347.
58. Horne, *Macmillan 1957–86*, 415.
59. C.M. Turnbull, *A History of Singapore 1819–1975* (Singapore, ed. 1985), 286–93. See Mohamed Noordin Sopiee, *From Malayan Union to Singapore Separation* (Kuala Lumpur, 1974).

The Parting of the Ways: Britain and South Africa's Departure from the Commonwealth, 1951–61

RONALD HYAM

Since the autumn of 1950 British ministers and civil servants had contemplated the possibility that they might have to choose between their relationship with South Africa and their relationships with the rest of Africa and the world at large. It seemed increasingly obvious that British embarrassment, combined with South Africa's growing disenchantment, might at any time precipitate a 'parting of the ways'. A Conservative government was faced with precisely that choice in March 1961 at the Commonwealth Prime Ministers' Meeting. Yet more than ten years earlier a significant hardening of attitude towards South Africa had taken place under a Labour government.[1] The Commonwealth Relations Secretary, Patrick Gordon Walker, had laid it down that containment of the Union of South Africa was a policy equally important with political advancement for Africans. James Griffiths (as secretary of state for the colonies) had declared apartheid to be 'totally repugnant' and, supported by Aneurin Bevan, had foreseen a time when 'the United Kingdom might have to consider whether she lost more than she gained by her present association with the Union government'.[2] The joint deputy under-secretary at the Colonial Office, Sir Charles Jeffries, was clear before the end of 1952 that Britain was 'committed to the policy of a parti-coloured Commonwealth', and if a choice had to be made, would side with it against South Africa.[3] The high commissioner in South Africa, Sir Percivale Liesching (1955–58), wrote in 1957 that in the longer term the Union's continued membership of the Commonwealth was an open question. 'On our side,' he believed, 'it may be that we are moving towards a situation in which we might ourselves be content to see her outside.' When Sir John Maud took over from Liesching, one of the first things he did was to ask for an assessment of the economic factors which would influence a South African decision to leave the Commonwealth.[4]

South Africa's departure was more easily contemplated in theory than in practice, and in the meantime the dilemma for the British government was acute. On the one hand, Britain needed good relations with the Union not only because of their mutually beneficial and close economic connections, but also because of British defence requirements and the prestige of the Commonwealth – both important in the context of the Cold War. Good relations were also essential because of the vulnerability of the High Commission Territories, for which Britain remained responsible. So enmeshed were they in the South African orbit, in terms of geography and infrastructure, that Basutoland was regarded as completely dependent on South African goodwill, Swaziland as semi-dependent, and only Bechuanaland as semi-independent. On the other hand, it was vital to contain the expansion of the apartheid state northwards, and Britain needed a decent reputations as an enlightened colonial power who upheld racial equality. Any policy which could be represented as condoning apartheid put its relation with Afro-Asian states in jeopardy. Finding the right balance between co-operation and containment, between the demands of international reputation and national interests, was difficult. To suggest that some risks were undoubtedly taken in the hope that South Africa would see the usefulness of the Commonwealth connection perhaps understates the agony of the tightrope British ministers walked.[5]

The incoming Conservative government in October 1951 inherited authoritative advice from Sir Evelyn Baring, retiring after seven years as high commissioner. The three essential measures Britain had to take were, he wrote: to counteract the impact of the new Afrikaner nationalism in the territories north of the Limpopo; to protect and develop the High Commission Territories; and to maintain 'reasonably friendly relations' with the Union government.[6] The Conservatives also inherited three major pieces of unfinished business involving South African policy: what to do with Seretse Khama, whether or not to set up the Central African Federation, and how to settle the future of the Simonstown naval base. They decided to make the exclusion of Seretse from the Bangwato chieftainship permanent (1952). They determined to bring the Federation of the Rhodesias and Nyasaland into being (1953). They concluded an agreement over Simonstown (1955). It is frequently argued that all these policies were mistaken. There is a persistent belief that Seretse was sacrificed to appease the racial prejudices of South Africa.[7] This is not how the government (whether Labour or Conservative) saw it: to them, depriving him of the chieftainship was not appeasement, but a denial of a dangerous weapon to an unpredictable opponent. To recognize Seretse could provide South Africa with an excuse to make a determined push to take over the High Commission Territories in accordance with an administrative reversion provided for in the schedule to the South Africa Act (1909). It might of course be argued that Britain should have called South Africa's bluff, since the risks of the Union government's marching in militarily were negligible – but then people said the same thing about Argentina and the Falkland Islands. Be that as it may, the South African government could still make life in the Territories desperately difficult by economic sanctions and non-co-operation in the provision of services. The risk was real and Britain did not, in my judgement, exaggerate the threat to the Territories from the expansionist Union.[8] On the other hand, Central Africa was a different matter, and the Conservative government probably did over-react to the Afrikaner expansionist threat there. At any rate, the threat to the Rhodesians was not so serious as to justify imposing a highly artificial federal construct against the clearly expressed wishes of the African inhabitants.[9] As far as Simonstown is concerned, did the government put too high an estimate on getting South African defence co-operation and concede too much? – as has been repeatedly argued by G.R. Berridge, who speaks of 'a form of appeasement'. This interpretation has, however, been convincingly challenged by Peter Henshaw, who has shown that the balance of advantage was very far from being all on the South African side. In fact the Union was forced into two most significant concessions: guaranteed availability of the base in a war in which South Africa was neutral, and inapplicability of the colour bar at Simonstown.[10]

None of these three issues was handled in such a way as seriously to upset the South African government. So what drove the National Party and the Conservative government further part? Three things. First, it needs to be stressed that above all else it was the policy of apartheid, which British ministers and their advisers without exception thought was utterly wrong and retrograde. The Afrikaner state, commented Sir John Maud, had somehow managed to miss the spirit of the century: 'To a Western European, it seems to owe more to the seventeenth century than to the twentieth century – though there is an ominous Hitlerian smell about it.'[11] Secondly, there were problems caused by Britain's African policy. Indeed, the principal cause of post-war alienation – the new factor in Anglo-South African relations – was Britain's readiness to lead African territories towards self-government. As Sir John Le Rougetel (high commissioner, 1951–55) realized: 'They think our African policy is the most important factor in relations with them.' Malan reacted, he reported in 1951, with rage and terror to Britain's Gold Coast policy: it caused bitter opposition, a 'severe jolt', and led to a profound resurgence of anti-British feeling. To Malan, decolonization was 'a virus, at least as great a menace as communism', and Britain's Gold Coast policy 'signifies nothing less than undermining the foundations of the Commonwealth and its gradual liquidation'.[12] Strijdom (Malan's successor) was perhaps more pragmatic, and in the event he accepted an unpalatable inevitability and congratulated Ghana on its independence. However, this was not before he had complained bitterly to Prime Minister Eden that he had not been asked for his views on Ghanaian membership of the Commonwealth: he protested about being 'presented with a fait accompli' – to which he might consent, even though thinking it was 'premature and unwise'. Eden thought the draft official reply was too feeble: 'Strijdom sent me an offensive letter, even an insulting one – we require no lesson from him in how to treat blacks. We must send a firmer reply. We shall not be respected by these bullies if we do not.' Strijdom nevertheless repeated his complaint. Eden commented: 'still obstinate, rude and purblind'.[13] Thirdly, Britain and South Africa were driven apart by the friction caused by the continuing deadlock over the transfer of the High Commission Territories.

Within months of taking office, the Conservative government had decided it would take no initiative over the transfer issue, but sit tight and wait for Malan to make the first move. He seemed in no hurry to do so. Towards the end of his premiership, however, Malan at last in 1954 signified his long-awaited intention of making a formal request for transfer. He was persuaded not to do this, the British cabinet appealing to him not to disturb their existing reasonably co-operative contacts. Instead, Malan simply called for the resumption of negotiations where they had been left in 1939. Reply to this was given at once in the form of a statement by Prime Minister Churchill (in answer to a parliamentary question), expressing the hope that the Union would not 'needlessly press an issue on which we could not fall in with their views without failing in our trust', since there could be no question of agreeing at the present to transfer. It was the strongest and most uncompromising statement on the subject yet made by a British government. A written response to Malan was issued on 21 May 1954 stating that it would be futile to start negotiations because they would yield no practical result except to cause harm to Anglo-South African relations. Malan reacted in a threatening and most intemperate fashion, accusing Britain of finally closing the door on negotiations and repudiating its moral obligations to South Africa. The cabinet decided it had to be made clear to Malan that it was the current native policy of his government which had fundamentally changed the situation since 1939, but the point 'should not be made too directly or too hard'. It was important they should not say definitively that Britain would *never* transfer the Territories, because that would only precipitate a crisis. Equally, they could not say *consent* of the inhabitants was essential, though that was certainly the view of at least some Conservative ministers. Another accusatory memorandum was received from Malan in August 1954. It was ignored.[14]

Thereafter the transfer question was more or less dormant until the middle of 1958, when British proposals for constitutional reform in Basutoland prompted the new prime minister, Dr Verwoerd, to ask questions about the wider implications. He made public statements on the Territories in September and November, but these were fairly moderate. High Commissioner Liesching defined the British task as comparable to that 'of persuading a weary and exasperated traveller that a constantly receding horizon is the boundary of the Promised Land'.[15] The vulnerability of the Territories was re-examined, and found if anything to have increased.

Meanwhile there was the perennial problem of what degree of alignment to afford South Africa at the United Nations. Britain had reasons of its own as a colonial power for not wishing to encourage United Nations interference in the domestic concerns of African states. This explains much of Britain's apparent support for South Africa when the Union's policies were under attack. As British representative on the Trusteeship Council, Sir Andrew Cohen in 1959 was urging the need to put a greater distance between the British and South African positions. The Foreign Office supported him on this, but the Commonwealth Relations Office was anxious not to push South Africa to the 'parting of the ways'. The impending visit of Macmillan to South Africa, however, enabled a more radical position to be adopted. By November 1959 it was clear to the civil servants that the balance was not right between maintaining relations with the Union and securing international reputation. The prime minister would have to take this up with Verwoerd and make a public declaration of the new policy, even if it led to 'the parting of the ways'. Macmillan accepted that there was 'a very strong demand' for him to criticize apartheid. The crucial document in preparing the case originated as a draft cabinet memorandum, but the Commonwealth Relations Secretary, Lord Home, turned it into a personal minute to Macmillan. Its most striking proposition was that the Commonwealth 'would undoubtedly be happier and closer-knit were the ugly duckling out of the nest'. South African membership was described as an embarrassment, an anomaly, and a source of weakness. At the United Nations the British position was increasingly exposed, and voting against all resolutions on South African apartheid was harmful, upsetting the Americans, and damaging the Western cause in the Cold War. 'In the wider context of the battle against Communism for men's minds in the uncommitted countries, South Africa is a liability to the West.' Confidence in Britain was compromised and the sincerity of British thinking and purposes, especially about race, was called into question. However, if there was even a remote hope of a future South African state emerging with a different and happier complexion, it would be 'sad to destroy bridges now which may be invaluable later on'. But the central question remained: 'how long can we afford to support South Africa as much as we do?' Small changes in British voting procedures at the United Nations were proposed, but these were likely to be bitterly resented in South Africa as indicating that the Union could no longer count on Britain over issues regarded as vital to the maintenance of white supremacy. 'The parting of the ways' was thus almost certainly at hand. Home's conclusion was clear: 'our wider international interests and our relations with the new African states (especially Nigeria) are at stake', and it was therefore time to warn South Africa that Britain was going to start abstaining on issues where previously support had been given.[16]

Several senior ministers were asked to comment on Home's minute. The Foreign Secretary, Selwyn Lloyd, agreed that a change of some sort was required: 'our reputation for being progressive is going to be increasingly necessary as, while various territories achieve independence, the United Nations spotlight is more and more focused on those which continue to be British colonies'. Without a change of policy, British prestige would be further damaged and Britain would be regarded as standing amongst the retrograde. Iain Macleod for the Colonial Office lent his support, while Heathcoat Amory at the Treasury thought that despite the risks it was right to go ahead on these lines.[17]

Thus fortified, the speech-writers finalized the text of the speech Macmillan was to deliver in Cape Town on 3 February 1960. The key passage was not about 'the wind of change' but a declaration candidly rejecting 'the idea of any inherent superiority of one race over another': 'there are some aspects of your policies which make it impossible [to support you] without being false to our own deep convictions about the political destinies of free men, to which in our territories we are trying to give effect'. Coming to terms with nationalism was part of the all-important battle against communism: 'the struggle is joined and it is a struggle for the minds of men'. The speech was badly received by Afrikaners. Not only did Macmillan not mouth the expected platitudes, but he radically shifted the British position. One Dutch Reformed Church clergyman (G.J.J. Boshoff) denounced Macmillan as 'the Herod of England', who had said to Black Africa 'ask what you will', and when Black Africa demanded the head of White Man John, Macmillan replied with 'a note of sorrow in his voice as he apologetically agreed to the beheading'.[18]

In his private meetings with Verwoerd, Macmillan failed to establish any sort of rapport, and indeed he could not have been expected to do so. Sir John Maud had frequently warned that Verwoerd was an arrogant and ruthless intellectual, an authoritarian, enigmatic, doctrinaire fanatic of 'impregnable insularity', formidable, and 'frighteningly self-righteous'. Macmillan several times wrote the word 'depressing' on these reports. Once in South Africa, Macmillan was annoyed at being prevented from meeting any African National Congress leaders. He refused to be drawn into saying that a republic would make no difference to Commonwealth membership, carefully confining himself to describing the Commonwealth 'not as the setting sun of British imperialism, but as the dawn of an entirely new concept', one in which he hoped South Africa would be fully involved. He played 'a dead bat' on Verwoerd's representations over the High Commission Territories, giving no recorded undertaking even to consider the matter further. He made it absolutely clear that the Union could not have any kind of veto on constitutional advancement in the Territories.[19]

Some six weeks later came the horror of the Sharpeville police shootings, leaving 69 dead. The United Nations Security Council immediately took up the issue of censuring South Africa and calling for an end to apartheid. A special cabinet 'General' committee considered the dilemma this posed for Britain (objection to interference in domestic matters as against legitimate humanitarian protest). After two full discussions the cabinet decided that Britain would abstain from and not oppose the Security Council resolution. However, in April a General Assembly resolution condemning South Africa was passed with Britain voting *for* it. The precise reason for this major shift of policy is unclear, as the two further meetings of the 'General' committee remain closed for 50 years, but the American government had led the way by voting for the Security Council resolution, and the pressure of world revulsion was becoming stronger all the time. Sharpeville and its aftermath thus greatly increased the significance of the impending meeting of Commonwealth prime ministers.[20]

Following an assassination attempt on 9 April 1960, which he was lucky to survive, Verwoerd was not well enough to attend the Commonwealth Prime Ministers' Meeting in London in May 1960. Sir John Maud regarded this as deeply unfortunate, since it meant that Eric Louw (the foreign minister) attended in his stead. Maud regarded Louw as unfitted to the delicate task of retaining Commonwealth goodwill; he was embittered, spiteful, pedantic, self-righteous, vane, and dreary, an 'unpopular, unprepossessing and neurotic figure, so disturbingly reminiscent of Dr Goebbels'.[21] Macmillan and Home tried to dissuade Louw from raising the question of whether South Africa could expect to remain in the Commonwealth if it adopted a republican form of constitution, as it seemed unlikely there would be a favourable answer. Louw nevertheless not only put the question specifically but also most ineptly asked an additional question as to whether South Africa in its present form was still welcome.

This only irritated the prime ministers, although Macmillan was able to say that as far as Britain was concerned they hoped South Africa would remain, it being in the interests of the Commonwealth to keep united. The difficulty about giving an assurance over continuing membership, however, was that it was hypothetical, since they had no idea what the result of the South African referendum might be. The prime ministers agreed that such an assurance would amount to 'interference in an issue of domestic constitutional policy' and they unanimously refused to give it. In their view, a republic was not a nationally agreed policy in South Africa, but opposed by the official Opposition, quite apart from the fact that the majority adult population was excluded from the decision.[22]

In August 1960 Macmillan warned Verwoerd that it had become clear that South Africa's continuing membership as a republic would be opposed by some Commonwealth prime ministers. At best there would be a painful division along racial lines. Could the referendum not be deferred? 'Taking a long-term view, would it not serve your interests better to postpone it until times in Africa are calmer? To secure a breathing-space amid all these fast-flowing developments would be very valuable.' Verwoerd was unmoved.[23]

Although Abubakar Tafawa Balewa of Nigeria had made it plain he hoped to see South Africa 'squeezed out of the Commonwealth' (in order to strengthen it), Macmillan was more alarmed by reports that the Canadian Prime Minister, John Diefenbaker, might withdraw his support. Diefenbaker was under domestic pressure to make a stand against apartheid, and he felt personally resentful of the abusive treatment he had received from Louw at the previous meeting. Macmillan urged Diefenbaker not to take up any definite position in advance. All prime ministers, he argued, should come to the discussions uncommitted, and alive to the fateful effect on the majority population if South Africa were expelled: 'we can do more to influence the future of these people if they are within the framework of the Commonwealth than if they are outside it'. With a decision about a republic out of the way, Macmillan hoped there might be an opportunity for a resurgence of liberal thought within South Africa, encouraged by the Commonwealth. But to turn South Africa out would condemn the country to ever-growing apartheid bitterness. Moreover, expulsion of South Africa could create a dangerous precedent for the Commonwealth.[24] Six weeks later a similar letter was despatched to Nehru, making even more strongly the point that 'there is a real danger to the whole Commonwealth structure and the beginning of a break-up now'.[25]

Assessments of the likely effects of South African departure occupied officials from the summer of 1960. The Commonwealth Relations Office's brief for the prime minister stressed that bearing in mind the continuing need for good relations with South Africa, it was essential 'to leave Dr

Verwoerd convinced that we have done our utmost to keep South Africa in, and we should therefore argue to the last in favour of South Africa'. If the general sense of the Commonwealth meeting was against keeping South Africa in, 'we should, though still with every show of reluctance, be prepared to acquiesce'; not to do so would put at risk the cohesion of the Commonwealth and its significance as a multi-racial association. The departmental advisers were fairly certain no Commonwealth prime minister would want to take the initiative towards expelling South Africa and each would probably accept a majority decision to keep the country in. But no African state could afford to show itself as more accommodating than Diefenbaker, and so his role might become crucial. Officials seemed to agree that membership of the Commonwealth as such was not something to die in the last ditch for. Britain's more fundamental concerns were its economic links and its responsibility for the High Commission Territories. South Africa's membership of the Sterling Area was more important than membership of the Commonwealth. Most Treasury officials did not think that technically the withdrawal of South Africa even from the Sterling Area need matter too much, certainly less than it would have done ten years earlier. However, the Commonwealth Relations Office and the Bank of England were much more worried about prestige and the psychological impact of South Africa's withdrawal as 'a major crack' in the Sterling Area system, wondering whether it might not have a deleterious effect on the international position of the City of London as a financial centre if South Africa stopped selling through it the bulk of its gold.[26]

High Commissioner Sir John Maud's advice was consistently on the side of making maximum efforts to retain South Africa in the Commonwealth. Patience and forbearance were required, he thought. He was deeply concerned to uphold the interests of the disenfranchised majority, anxious not to damage the prospects of co-operation with a future *African* government of South Africa. They had to believe in the possibility of 'the Union's eventual redemption'. Retaining South Africa within the Commonwealth would give some chance of influencing it and laying foundations for the future, thus keeping faith with half the whites and all the non-Europeans, who might otherwise look for help elsewhere when their emancipation eventually came. Maud also warned that Verwoerd could well wish to be free of the moral pressures of membership; therefore, to expel South Africa might be playing his own game. He urged that Britain would have to sit it out with South Africa against the day of the collapse of the apartheid regime, just as Britain sat it out with the Russians in the Cold War. The National Party could not be in power for ever, since it was 'inconceivable that in this multi-racial state the criterion of advancement will forever remain the colour of your skin'. 'Verwoerdism' must eventually collapse, 'for the simple reason that it is not only evil but cannot be made to fit the facts: it is a policy for putting back in their shells eggs which were broken long ago when South Africa first began to become industrialised'. Maud's predictions were proved right: 'in the end the policy will have to be modified in the interests of economic good sense … it is likely to be bread and butter considerations which will win the day'. Equally perceptive was his insight that Christianity 'is a much more serious long-term threat than Communism to white supremacy'.[27]

As the Commonwealth prime ministers assembled in London for their decisive 1961 Meeting, Macmillan had a long talk with Verwoerd on 7 March. Verwoerd confirmed that South Africa hoped to remain in the Commonwealth, but recognized that discussion of racial policy was unavoidable.[28] There were fifteen conference sessions held between 8 and 17 March, the two dominant issues being South Africa and disarmament.[29] Discussions on South Africa began at the sixth session, on the morning of 13 March. Verwoerd made a short statement requesting acceptance of the wish of the Union government to continue as a member of the Commonwealth after the inauguration of the republic on 31 May. From the chair, Macmillan suggested that, treated purely as a constitutional matter, the issue should not present any great difficulty, since the precedents (India, Pakistan, Ghana, and – potentially – Ceylon) were clearly positive. But it would be disingenuous not to recognize that widespread anxiety about South Africa's racial policy would be a relevant consideration.

By prior arrangement, Nehru then opened the discussion, arguing for a clear declaration against racial discrimination and segregation, 'without which the Commonwealth association would be imperilled': there could be no effective co-operation between countries who did not recognize the validity of the concept of the multi-racial Commonwealth. After Nehru, each of the prime ministers made a prepared statement. Diefenbaker agreed that some public recognition of the multi-racial character of the Commonwealth was needed if the association were to be preserved. It might be necessary to identify some fundamental principles on which continuing association could be based. South Africa's racial policy could no longer be treated as a purely internal affair, since it had international repercussions and attracted such close and widespread concern: to accept South Africa's present request would be construed as approval of, or at least acquiescence in, South Africa's racial policy. President Ayub Khan of Pakistan supported the first two speakers, going on to express his country's sense of disillusion that the Commonwealth was an inadequate instrument of conciliation, for example in Kashmir. If it could not now even support the concept of racial equality, there would be further disillusionment about its value: 'the reputation and future influence of the Commonwealth, which it was necessary to maintain if emerging nations were not to fall prey to Communist influences, were at stake'. Next, Australia's Menzies said that it was wrong to link a discussion of South Africa's racial policy with continued membership of the Commonwealth. He opposed drawing up a declaration of basic principles, as this would destroy the character of the present association. Nkrumah, prime minister of Ghana, spoke after Menzies, delivering the shortest of all the statements, surprisingly moderate in tone. In his view, the principle of racial equality did not have to be formally declared, but members ought to subscribe to it as an underlying principle which could only grow in importance. Then Tunku Abdul Rahman, prime minister of Malaya, criticized South Africa for doing so little to help other Commonwealth countries, even refusing to accept accredited diplomatic representatives. South Africa appeared to him as wanting to remain in the Commonwealth because of the material advantage which it gave, but at the same time to pursue racial discrimination without modification, 'a policy which only strengthened the hands of Communists and other ill-wishers against the Commonwealth'. Did such a policy 'not offend the whole moral basis of the Commonwealth?' K.J. Holyoake of New Zealand believed South Africa would have been well advised to re-examine its 'intransigent' policy, but he counselled moderation in taking any irrevocable step which would deprive millions of people of the Commonwealth connection. Mrs S.R.D. Bandaranaike of Ceylon took up the reference to the battle for the minds of African peoples, for 'it was this that was at stake when considering apartheid'. The survival of the Commonwealth would depend on whether it was to become a truly multi-racial association based on equality; if these principles were compromised in order to retain South Africa in it, this could only encourage more extreme racialism in the Union. It was, she continued, being argued that expulsion of South Africa would split the Commonwealth, but 'equally there was the risk of a split if she remained'. They should make a stand and resolve to exclude South Africa unless its government undertook to make a change in racial policy. Finally, Sir Abubakar Tafawa Balewa, the newcomer to the circle, made play with the fact that Nigeria had just become a member in the belief that the Commonwealth stood for equality of the individual, regardless of race, colour, or creed. South Africa offended against this principle, and any arrangement by which it remained in the Commonwealth would merely be an encouragement to persist in its racial policies – something to be avoided at all costs.

At the afternoon session on 13 March, Verwoerd made a long defence of his position and the theory and practice of apartheid. He protested about 'unfriendly attitudes'. After Verwoerd parried a couple of needling questions, Nkrumah then took the initiative, declaring that the essential point appeared to have been missed: 'the Meeting should not waste time in mutual recrimination; the real issue was the whole future character of the Commonwealth'. Akubakar agreed: if members could not publicly subscribe to the principle of racial equality 'their association would be meaningless'. Chairman Macmillan then offered an interim summing-up, but he wanted mainly to emphasize that as this was a Commonwealth of nations, not of governments – which might come and go – the interests of the great population of South Africa, whether European or African, must not be neglected. He hoped they might agree upon a formula which would accept South Africa's continuing membership but also reaffirm the strong feeling of all other members against racial discrimination. The reaction to this appears to have been generally that it was possible but unrealistic, because its two halves seemed incompatible. This was plainly the moment for someone to sharpen the issue, and it was Nehru who did so: 'the eyes of the world were on this Meeting and the Commonwealth Prime Ministers should make it absolutely clear where they stood'. Nevertheless, Holyoake said he thought Macmillan had suggested the only practical course, and after a brief further discussion the proceedings were adjourned.

At the end of the first day it was uncertain what the outcome might be. Only Mrs Bandaranaike had so far used language which appeared to commit her to refusing consent to South Africa's continuing membership. The others had all stopped just short of such a commitment. That evening Macmillan sent a personal message to Verwoerd asking him, after 'a difficult day for us all', if he could not 'make a gesture' by agreeing to exchange high commissioners with other Commonwealth countries – the point raised by Abdul Rahman. This might be 'a small thing, but I think it might have great significance', since it really did not seem possible to maintain a Commonwealth where the prime ministers could only meet in London and were not prepared to receive each other's representatives in their capitals. He understood that Verwoerd based his policies 'upon a theoretical thesis which is very fundamental to you'; however, 'men are not ruled entirely by logic, but often by sentiment'. Verwoerd declined to be moved by this appeal, on several grounds: that it was unwarranted interference, attempting to lay down conditions of membership, when Ghana and Malaya had been admitted without conditions; that he had no particular reason to exchange representatives with New Zealand, Cyprus, or Sierra Leone; and that he was not prepared to make a friendly move towards countries which were actively hostile – Ghana, India, Malaya, Tanganyika, and Nigeria.[30]

On the following day Macmillan's draft communiqué was discussed.

Verwoerd at once admitted there was much in it he could not accept. Menzies disliked the way it 'constituted in effect notice to South Africa to quit'. Diefenbaker disputed this: 'it was rather a statement of the abiding principles to which the Commonwealth adhered'. Nehru insisted there should be no equivocation in stating that the Commonwealth could only hold together on the basis of racial equality: 'failure to do so would injure the Commonwealth irretrievably'. Discussion, he added, had revealed the true extent of divergence between the South African government and the rest. Nkrumah now made another moderate intervention, suggesting that perhaps the question of South Africa's membership should be postponed to give it time to reconsider its policies. Inevitably that provoked dissent, with Ayub Khan objecting. After a short break, Macmillan launched into a typically reflective excursus on the historical background and the value of the Commonwealth. Let them take a long view and not merely think in terms of an immediate solution. He would be reluctant to contemplate any change in their relationship with all the peoples of different race in South Africa. He realized nevertheless that all the prime ministers were subject to the pressure of public opinion on racial equality, and 'it was of great importance to make clear to the peoples of the Commonwealth and of the world where we stood on this issue'. Macmillan concluded this personal oration by offering to redraft their statement into two separate documents, constitutional and racial, during the lunch interval.

When discussion resumed on the afternoon of 14 March, Macmillan explained that the redrafted documents were intended to show that while the constitutional change did not provide any ground on which South Africa's application could properly be rejected, the other prime ministers still adhered to their objections to South Africa's racial policy. A communiqué would affirm a commitment by all members to build structures of society offering equality of opportunity for all. Nehru accepted that the documents fairly represented the course of discussion but they did not arrive at a reconciled conclusion. And what did Verwoerd think of them? Verwoerd replied tartly that the concept of the Commonwealth had changed in the course of the previous ten months, and it seemed that the intention was to lay down certain rules which might later be used to expel a member; the communiqué read to him as a deliberate motion of censure. Nkrumah underlined the difficulty for the rest of them: the communiqué must indicate that they had not changed their views in any way. To this Verwoerd responded that he would be prepared to consider a form of announcement which stated that whatever the views of individual prime ministers on South Africa's racial policies, it was the collective decision of the Meeting that South Africa would remain a member. Nkrumah's comment was that it would be difficult to accept this; the communiqué must contain a statement about agreeing that South Africa's racial policies were inconsistent with the ideals of the Commonwealth. Further redrafting was then considered, but as Nehru observed, the more they discussed the matter the more obvious was the difference of opinion. The session concluded with a powerful statement from Mrs Bandaranaike which reflected the day's hardening of attitudes:

> In her view, Dr Verwoerd had made it quite plain that he did not intend to change his racial policy. The question before the Prime Ministers therefore was whether they were prepared to compromise on an issue affecting human rights. She thought that most Prime Ministers would be unable to do this. She considered that the drafts circulated by Mr Macmillan had failed to bring out the salient point of the discussions which had taken place over the last two days. The real question was whether South Africa could be permitted to remain within the Commonwealth while her racial policy remained unchanged.

Nevertheless, the overall position now was that South Africa was confronted with the proposition that its membership would probably be continued if Verwoerd would accept the issue of a declaration by other members (to which he would not be expected to subscribe) recording their detestation of apartheid and affirming the principle of non-discrimination as basic to the multi-racial Commonwealth. Verwoerd, not unnaturally, found that hard to swallow. He asked to be allowed to consider his position overnight.

Next morning, after a private meeting with Macmillan, Verwoerd announced that he would accept such a formula and draft communiqué, provided he was given an opportunity to set out a summary of the arguments justifying his government's policy. Further redrafting was accordingly attempted, as Macmillan proposed. When these revisions were considered on the afternoon of 15 March, Diefenbaker and Nehru both complained that the revised communiqué gave too much emphasis to Verwoerd's views. But it was Abubakar who focused the crux of the debate: there was no indication that the South African government intended to modify its policies in any way, and in these circumstances he would have to consider whether Nigeria should remain a member of the Commonwealth if South Africa stayed in. Nehru seized on this leverage to speak again, insisting that the new draft was unbalanced, and giving notice that India would at the earliest opportunity raise the question of South African membership if her racial policy remained unchanged. Nkrumah now joined in with his hammer-blow, reserving the right also to raise formally at a later stage the expulsion of South Africa; alternatively Ghana would have to reconsider its own membership.[31] Whereupon Verwoerd retorted that he in turn must reserve the right to propose the expulsion of Ghana, since Nkrumah's policy was not in accordance with the principles of democracy. He also took exception to Nehru's remarks, and concluded, 'South Africa could not continue as a member-country if she was under the continual threat of expulsion': he must know that South Africa was welcome to remain, and if the present formula was merely a device to enable an unwelcome member to remain, then he would have to reconsider their position. Presumably there was then a moment of climactic silence, eventually broken by Macmillan, who merely said that his draft had been intended to settle the immediate issue, but if this called in question the continued adherence of several prime ministers to the Commonwealth association, they would all have to reconsider their positions during a short adjournment. After this tea-break, Verwoerd formally withdrew his request for South Africa to remain a member after 31 May 1961. He was, he said, 'amazed and shocked by the spirit of hostility and in this last meeting even of vindictiveness shown towards South Africa... the character of the Commonwealth has apparently changed completely during the last year'. There was no further recorded discussion or comment. Macmillan immediately produced a brief communiqué for publication forthwith, which was quickly approved. It was just three sentences long, little more than a simple statement that the prime minister of South Africa had withdrawn his application 'in the light of the views expressed on behalf of other member-governments and the indications of their future intentions regarding the racial policy of the Union Government'.

Later that evening, a highly despondent Macmillan chewed over the result with 'Rab' Butler and his Chief Whip, Martin Redmayne. He felt that a decisive factor had been the position of Abubakar, who might not politically have survived putting his name to a document agreeing to South Africa's continuing membership; at best he would have had to put down a formal motion (at the next Prime Ministers' Meeting) for South Africa's expulsion. All this meant that their present deliberations would have settled nothing finally, and they would 'get only the shadow and not the reality'. He was worried how the Conservative Party would take the news.[32] Lord Home was well aware of Macmillan's anguish and wrote him a sympathetic note:

> This is a very sad day for you and all of us but I don't see how with emotion overcoming reason it was possible to get a different result. Certainly you must not reproach yourself as you did everything which was humanly possible to keep South Africa in. I could see this morning when I talked to Ayub that the only alternative was the break-away of all the Asian and African members. That could not be faced.[33]

Home completely accepted Macmillan's own interpretation: the issue had been handled with restraint and if Verwoerd had only made 'one millimetre of concession the result might have been different'. This was the official gloss on the account immediately supplied to high commissioners. Ten days later, however, Duncan Sandys as Commonwealth Relations Secretary sent them a more positive interpretation: South Africa's departure made 'bridge building' easier, and provided the psychological climate for a new step forward in Commonwealth co-operation. 'The removal of any doubt about the acceptance of the principle of multi-racialism should enhance the prestige of the Commonwealth in the world as well as its own solidarity.'[34] The prime minister found it personally much harder to put such a brave face on events.

Macmillan's memoirs deployed emotive adjectives in describing the departure of South Africa from the Commonwealth: unhappy, painful, very sad, tragic, disastrous. He harped upon his sense of 'grief and foreboding': 'I felt almost a sense of despair' – was every problem to be met with such rigidity, incomprehension, and lack of compromise as Verwoerd had displayed?[35] Part of Macmillan's unhappiness was a realization that his own 'wind of change' speech had played its part in the outcome. To right-wing colleagues such as Lord Kilmuir, it was indeed Macmillan's fault, 'a direct consequence of one unguarded phrase in a single speech', though Macmillan had 'no conception of the mine he had unwittingly exploded'.[36] What Kilmuir could not know was that Macmillan had himself confided to Sir John Maud: 'The wind of change has blown us away'.[37] Macmillan never found it easy to forgive Diefenbaker (that 'woolly tub-thumper') for his 'holier than thou' attitude, but it is apparent from the record that it is unnecessary to invoke him as the prime mover of events.[38]

In any case, taking a wider perspective, it would be wrong to conclude that South Africa's departure arose simply out of pressure from the prime ministers. Verwoerd had more than sufficient reasons of his own for not particularly wanting to remain a member any longer. The Suez Crisis had shaken his confidence in Britain's capacity for independent action and military effectiveness. Decolonization made Britain less and less valuable to South Africa as an African 'ally'. Louw's cherished project for a joint African defence pact had definitively collapsed by 1960, and British automatic alignment behind South Africa at the United Nations had already gone. South Africa had very little interest in any other Commonwealth members apart from Britain itself. Verwoerd could reasonably expect that South Africa's economic links with Britain would remain intact.[39]

Those economic connections certainly persisted, although the cabinet determined at the outset of departure that 'it would be important to avoid giving the impression that after her withdrawal South Africa was to remain a member of the Commonwealth in all but name'. 'Commonwealth treatment' would not be given unless it was clearly in British interest to do so.[40] Nevertheless, the old imperatives to keep on terms with South Africa, despite apartheid, in a reasonable working relationship, remained. After the parting of the ways, the British government had to treat South Africa as half-ally and half-untouchable at the same time, equivocating on sanctions and continuing to pay such price in domestic political and international criticism as might be necessary to preserve its essential interests: arms supply for the strategic requirements of the Cape sea-route, discharge of its trusteeship for the High Commission Territories, and the promotion of trading interests which would encourage South Africa to remain in the Sterling Area. Geopolitics, long-term calculations, and moral obligations combined to ensure that it would continue to be British policy to 'keep a foot in this important door', as Sir John Maud put it, not only because if Britain withdrew entirely 'an enemy or rival would take her place', but because the British government wanted to 'keep faith' with the black majority which would surely one day form an African government.[41]

NOTES

I wish to thank most warmly Dr Peter Henshaw for his very great help in the preparation of this paper.

1. See generally on the Labour government, D.K. Fieldhouse, 'The Labour Governments and the Empire-Commonwealth', in R. Ovendale (ed.), *The Foreign Policy of British Labour Governments, 1945–51* (Leicester, 1984), 83–118; more specifically, P.J. Henshaw, 'Britain and South Africa at the United Nations: South-West Africa, Treatment of Indians, and Race Conflict, 1946–61', *South African Historical Journal*, XXXI (1994), 80–102.
2. R.Hyam (ed.), *The Labour Government and the End of Empire, 1945–51* (British Documents on the End of Empire Project, London, 1992) (BDEEP), intro, lxiv–lxviii.
3. D. Goldsworthy (ed.), *The Conservative Government and the End of Empire, 1951–57* (BDEEP, London, 1994), II, 174.
4. Liesching to H.J.B. Lintott, 14 March 1957, Public Record Office (PRO), London, Commonwealth Relations Office (CRO/DO), DO 35/6281, no 3A; CRO to Maud, 19 Dec. 1958, DO 8712, no 7.
5. Minutes, Sept. 1963, PRO, Foreign Office (FO), FO 371/167136.
6. Hyam (ed.), *Labour Government and the End of Empire,* IV, 355–6.
7. T. Tlou, N. Parsons, and W. Henderson, *Seretse Khama, 1921–80* (Braamfontein, 1955), 97–121, is unregenerate on this issue.
8. R. Hyam, 'The Political Consequences of Seretse Khama: Britain, the Bangwato and South Africa, 1948–52', *Historical Journal,* XXIX (1986), 921–47.
9. R. Hyam, 'The Geopolitical Origins of the Central African Federation, 1948–53', *Historical Journal,* XXX (1987), 145–72.
10. G.R. Berridge, *Economic Power in Anglo-South African Diplomacy: Simonstown, Sharpeville and After* (London, 1981), and 'South Africa and the Simonstown Agreements' (with J.E. Spence), in J.W. Young (ed.), *Foreign Policy of Churchill's Peacetime Administration, 1951–55* (Leicester, 1988), 181–205; P.J. Henshaw, 'The Transfer of Simonstown: Afrikaner Nationalism, Strategic Defence and British Global Power', *Journal of Imperial and Commonwealth History,* XX (1992), 417–44.
11. Cabinet memorandum, despatch from Maud to Lord Home, 14 May 1963, PRO, CAB

129/114, C(63)102.

12. Le Rougetel to CRO, despatch, 28 Dec. 1951, DO 35/4019, no 204; Hyam (ed.), *Labour Government and End of Empire,* IV, 297.
13. Minutes by Eden, July–Aug. 1956, PRO, Prime Minister's Office (PREM), PREM 11/1367; see also DO 35/5058, and Goldsworthy (ed.), *Conservative Government and the End of Empire,* document nos 147, 151–53.
14. Cabinet conclusions (1954), CAB 128/27/1, CC 17(54) 7, and CAB 128/27/2, CC 46(54); cabinet memoranda by Lord Swinton, March–Aug. 1954, CAB 129/69, C(54)115, 119, 135, 165, 216; 13 April 1954, *Parliamentary Debates* (Commons), Vol.526, 966–8.
15. Liesching to CRO, 14 May 1958, DO 35/7181, no 20.
16. Home to Macmillan, 17 Dec. 1959, DO 35/10621, no 39.
17. Selwyn Lloyd to Macmillan, 2 Jan. 1960, FO 371/145291, no 16; Heathcoat Amory to Macmillan, 17 Feb. 1960, PRO, Treasury (T), T 236/4873.
18. Newspaper report, *Die Burger*, 23 Feb. 1960, DO 35/10570 no 45. See also R. Ovendale, 'Macmillan and the Wind of Change in Africa, 1957–60', *Historical Journal,* XXXVIII (1957), 455–77.
19. Note on discussion between Macmillan and Verwoerd, 4 Feb. 1960, PREM 11/3070; Maud to CRO, despatch, 12 March 1959, DO 35/10559, no 169; Maud to Sir A. Clutterbuck, 15 Feb. 1960, DO 35/7181, no 86.
20. Minutes of Cabinet committee meeting, GEN 711, 28 March 1960, CAB 130/173, no 1; Cabinet Conclusions, 29 March and 1 April 1960, CAB 128/34, CC 21(60)3, and CC 22 (60)3.
21. Maud to CRO, despatch, 28 April 1960 (CRO confidential print, 4 May 1960), FO 371/146499, no 4.
22. Extract from minutes of Commonwealth Prime Ministers' Meeting, 10 May 1960, PRO, South Africa, High Commission, DO 119/1206, no 41A, PMM 8(60)3. Alistair Horne, *Macmillan,* II, *1957–1986* (London, 1989), 204, quotes Macmillan's diary during the conference: 'If we *do nothing*, the Commonwealth will seem to have no faith and no purpose. If we *do too much*, South Africa will secede and this may mean the beginning of a general break up.' J.B.D. Miller, *Survey of Commonwealth Affairs: Problems of Expansion and Attrition, 1953–69* (Oxford, 1974), 142–9, remains a valuable account of the 1960 conference.
23. Telegram from Macmillan to Verwoerd (via CRO to Maud), 2 Aug. 1960, DO 119/1206, no 62.
24. Letter from Macmillan to Diefenbaker, 18 Nov. 1960, PREM 11/3537, T 698/60.
25. Macmillan to Nehru, 6 Jan. 1961, PREM 11/3393, T 8/61
26. CRO minutes, 13 Aug. – 16 Dec. 1959, DO 35/10621; interdepartmental study, Oct. 1960, FO 371/152123, no 71; Treasury minutes, 5 Jan. – 12 Feb. 1960, T 236/4873; see also P.J. Henshaw, 'Britain, South Africa and the Sterling Area, 1931–61', *Historical Journal,* XXXIX (1996), 197–223.
27. Maud to CRO, despatches, 12 Oct. 1960, DO 35/10559, no 233; 22 Jan. 1960, DO 35/8712, no 11; 14 May 1963, CAB 129/114, C(63)102; CRO brief, July 1960, DO 119/1206, no 59.
28. Prime Minister's Office, note for the record, meeting between Macmillan and Verwoerd, 7 March 1961, PREM 11/3535.
29. Minutes of Commonwealth Prime Ministers' Meeting, March 1961, CAB 133/251, PMM 6–10 and 12 (61), withheld at PRO. I am most grateful to Dr Peter Henshaw for supplying a copy of the minutes from the South African Government Archives in Pretoria (BLO 449), together with a copy of a commentary sent to Norman Robertson of the Canadian External Affairs Dept, telegrams, 13–15 March 1961, National Archives of Canada, MC 30/E1/63, file, 18/1.
30. Letters between Macmillan and Verwoerd, 13 and 14 March 1961, PREM 11/3535. A draft communiqué was intensively discussed by Macmillan's advisers, notably Cabinet Secretary Sir Norman Brook, who rejected suggestions by Menzies for greater openness in setting forth the issues and the 'fundamental and vigorous criticism of South Africa'.
31. According to Macmillan's adviser on public relations (press secretary), 'strong, if not angry, words began to be used' at this session, and there were 'raised voices': Harold Evans, *Downing Street Diary: The Macmillan Years, 1957–63* (London, 1981), 141–3, which provides a well-informed account.

32. Note for the record, 15 March 1961, PREM 11/3535.
33. Home to Macmillan, 15 March 1961, ibid.
34. CRO telegram to high commissioners, 16 March 1961, ibid.; Sandys to high commissioners, 27 March 1961, cabinet memorandum, CAB 129/104, C(61)40.
35. Harold Macmillan, *Memoirs*, V, *Pointing the Way 1959–61* (London, 1972), 285–305. P.C. Gordon Walker, formerly the Labour government's secretary of state for Commonwealth relations, took a more robust view: the long, anxious, historic discussions had demonstrated the 'sense of reality and integrity of the Commonwealth', and given dramatic expression to the continuing will to keep it going: *The Commonwealth* (London, 1962), 379.
36. Earl of Kilmuir, *Political Adventure: Memoirs* (London, 1962), 315.
37. Macmillan, *Pointing the Way*, 302 (diary, 21 March 1961).
38. Horne, *Macmillan*, II, 204. F. Hayes, 'South Africa's Departure from the Commonwealth, 1960–61', *International History Review*, II (1980), 453–84, overestimates Diefenbaker's role.
39. P.J. Henshaw, 'South Africa's External Relations with Britain and the Commonwealth, 1945–56' (unpublished Ph.D. dissertation, Cambridge, 1989), ch.5, 'Relations with the Commonwealth Association, 1945–61'. For the African Defence Pact plan, see G.R. Berridge, *South Africa, the Colonial Powers and 'African Defence': Rise and Fall of a White Entente, 1945–60* (London, 1992), and Henshaw's review in *South African Historical Journal*, XXX (1994), 164–7.
40. Cabinet Conclusions, 21 March 1961, CAB 128/35/1, CC 15(61)7; see also PREM 11/3994.
41. Maud to CRO, telegram, 13 Aug. 1960, DO 119/1206, no 76. For an important summary (1963) of British policy towards South Africa, see the briefing despatch to Maud's successor, Sir Hugh Stevenson, 28 June 1963, CAB 129/114, C(63)109.

Waving Goodbye? Australia, Assisted Passages, and the Empire and Commonwealth Settlement Acts, 1945–72

STEPHEN CONSTANTINE

It is not surprising that the Empire Settlement Act of 1922 has attracted historical attention.[1] British government policy had traditionally left financial assistance for emigrants to philanthropic or commercial operators or to overseas governments keen to recruit labour from Britain. The free passage scheme for ex-service personnel and their families after the First World War had been an important precedent, but the Act of 1922 entailed a much more substantial commitment, authorizing the annual expenditure of up to £3m of British taxpayers' money over the next fifteen years to subsidize fares and for other schemes. The Act was renewed for a further fifteen years in 1937, but a reduction in the annual funding to a maximum of £1.5m seemed to indicate a decline in the British government's commitment. It is surprising therefore that the Acts were renewed in 1952, 1957, 1962, and 1967 – and expired only in 1972. It is well-known that the volume of emigration after the Second World War did hugely increase, and also that the governments of the white dominions (and Southern Rhodesia) did at different times and in different ways operate recruitment drives in Britain. However, the most sustained, ambitious, and expensive programme was launched by Australia, and it is too rarely noticed that the Australian scheme was part-funded by British taxpayers under the repeatedly renewed Empire and Commonwealth Settlement Acts. Post-war migration has received some academic attention,[2] but little historical consideration has been given to British government policy-making, except by Kathleen Paul whose recent important study is primarily concerned with concepts of nationality and the racist values implied by immigration as well as emigration policies.[3]

What makes post-war British policy initially so unexpected is the evidence of widespread disillusionment with state-assisted emigration by the 1930s; and this seemed to be based on sound economic and demographic reasoning. The push and pull forces favouring the Empire Settlement Act in 1922 were in reverse by the 1930s, and this shift appeared to become even more intense after 1945. Preoccupations with the apparent overpopulation of Britain had been replaced in the 1930s by concerns about the decline in the birth rate, further aired in the 1949 report of the Royal Commission on Population. A surplus of labour seemingly evident in high rates of unemployment between the wars was followed, during and after the war, not just by full employment but by often acute labour shortages. The bizarre notion that Britain was encumbered by a surplus of unmarried women in need of emigration to waiting males in the dominions had faded from the consciousness of all but the insensible by 1945. Even the long-standing idea that deprived or depraved children stood to benefit by transportation to the empire was seriously challenged by new concepts of child care exemplified by the Children Act of 1948.[4] The extension of other social services in Britain was also thought likely to reduce the incentive for emigration.[5] Moreover, the capacity of the dominions to absorb British migrants was seen to be grossly exaggerated when a hard look was taken at their climatic and geographical make-up following the collapse of international prices for their staple primary products in the 1930s.[6] Further population growth by immigration would seem to be dependent upon the maturing of secondary industries overseas, but this surely was incompatible with prevailing concepts of the empire-commonwealth: the natural harmony between industrial Britain and primary producers overseas would be disrupted by the emigration of skilled industrial workers to potential competitors.

However, the idea of state-assisted emigration was not entirely abandoned in official circles even in the 1930s. For example, the Oversea Settlement Board which advised the Dominions Office, having acknowledged all the difficulties, still saw merit in the idea in its final report published in 1938.[7] But revival was especially marked when state-assisted emigration to the empire featured in the British government's wartime reconstruction plans and post-war policies. As early as 1942, an interdepartmental committee began preparing a scheme to provide after the war free passages for ex-service personnel and their dependants. The dominions and Southern Rhodesia were consulted about more general migration proposals in April 1943. Empire migration was discussed in May 1944 at a meeting of the prime ministers of Britain and the dominions. In February 1945 there were further collective discussions with representatives of Australia, New Zealand, and South Africa. Bilateral negotiations between the British government and those of Australia and Southern Rhodesia on the free passages proposal concluded with agreements signed in March and October 1946 respectively. More importantly, an assisted passage scheme open to all

British citizens wishing to settle in Australia was also agreed on 5 March 1946.[8] This programme allowed adults to travel to Australia for £10 each, the remaining costs of fares being shared equally between the two governments. The British share would be paid for out of the £1.5m still notionally available each year under the Empire Settlement Act of 1937. It came into operation in March 1947 and was to run initially for two years, but at Australian request in March 1949 it was renewed for a further two years, without hesitation. There were even serious suggestions in the Commonwealth Relations Office (CRO) during 1949,[9] long before the expiry of the existing Empire Settlement Act, that its life should be extended forthwith for a further 15 years. It is important to note that the revival of state-assisted migration had been first approved by Churchill's wartime Coalition government but had been adopted and then extended by Attlee's post-war Labour government with barely a flicker of reservation.[10]

There is little to suggest that British governments in the 1940s were responding to demands from the empire-commonwealth. The initiative came from London, and indeed most of the reactions by overseas governments were initially cautious and in the end mainly unco-operative. Most of them during the war felt unable to predict their likely demand for new migrants until after their own troops had been demobilized and their own economies restored to peacetime conditions.[11] Southern Rhodesia never operated the scheme to which it had signed up, but in 1951 launched its own assisted passages programme; New Zealand declined British offers of financial involvement and similarly launched its own scheme in 1947; South Africa ran its own state-sponsored programme until after the Nationalist victory in the election of 1948; and Canada did not choose even to attend the 1945 conference and only launched its own scheme to encourage selected immigration at its own expense from 1951. Australia, however, responded with alacrity. The urgent need for a larger population had apparently been confirmed by fear of Japanese invasion in 1942 and by a growing anxiety about the decline in its birth rate. But these national security and economic development considerations only account for the positive nature of Australia's responses. They do not account for the British proposals.[12]

The plans coming out of the CRO were challenged by some officials and ministers, along lines which in the light of 1930s experiences seem entirely predictable. They pointed to the conflict of interests between Britain and the settler societies of the commonwealth. Lord Cherwell, for example, warned Churchill in April 1944 that population growth was declining, that the population was ageing, and that 'it would seem most ill-advised to export large numbers of young, fit and presumably fertile men and women ... With all the social services which we have promised to the old, we cannot afford deliberately to get rid of people of the age and type most likely to work and breed.'[13] In his turn, Attlee was similarly advised in December 1946 of the economic illogicality of encouraging emigration 'when an acute shortage of manpower and womanpower is at the bottom of nearly all our economic difficulties'.[14] Similar points were made by cabinet ministers. It was said in April 1945 that 'This country, with a diminishing population, could not afford to send its best stock abroad after the war', and in October 1945 it was more than rhetoric which prompted the question 'Was it desirable that any steps should be taken to encourage emigration from this country, in view of the prospective decline in the population?' Even the dominions secretary admitted in cabinet that the Australians 'might seek to obtain too many of our skilled industrial workers, whom we could ill spare'.[15] The Ministry of Labour repeatedly acknowledged that economic recovery was hampered by a shortage of skilled labour in key industries, and that assisting the emigration of British labour in such circumstances might seem perverse.[16]

Nevertheless, steps were taken to effect precisely such a transfer, and apparent conflicts of interest were denied. Since extensions of social security provisions consequent upon the Beveridge report might further discourage emigration from Britain, efforts were made to secure reciprocal agreements with commonwealth governments. Shipping shortages delaying departures might be dealt with by using ships of the Royal Navy. Ministers and officials were aware that the reduced rate of population growth in Britain and the needs of the British economy made it impossible for any commonwealth country choosing to boost its population by immigration to look solely to British sources, yet nevertheless they insisted that Britain should make a substantial contribution. Attlee also explained to the cabinet in 1942 that the war had boosted the development of secondary industries in the commonwealth and this 'may well offer a wider scope for the absorption in the Dominions of industrial workers from this country than has been offered in the past when land settlement has had a more prominent place in migration schemes'. While ministers acknowledged that this might lead to competition with the British economy for skilled and scarce labour, they asserted that commonwealth attempts to recruit workers of key importance for British economic reconstruction after the war could be moderated or diverted by consultation.[17]

The determination of British governments during and immediately after the war to reactivate the Empire Settlement Act owed something, although not much, to political pressure in Britain. There were two perceived sources. Frequent reports claimed that British troops had been prompted to consider emigration by their experiences overseas and by their contacts with commonwealth troops, and that they would expect government facilities to be made available to assist migration and settlement after the war, as had been provided in 1919. Free passages overseas for ex-service personnel were therefore offered as part of the demobilization programmes. But the problem about accepting this as a sufficient explanation is that commentators also argued that the government had to act quickly lest the current interest in emigration be dissipated and troops become reintegrated into civil society in Britain. Obviously, emigration, not demobilization, was the dominant priority. A second source of pressure for revived emigration came from surviving members of the pre-war emigration lobby whose mass migration fantasies had been challenged by demographic data but who continued to be exercised by the apparent over-population of Britain and the underdevelopment of the empire. Their arguments received an additional strategic twist during the war following the experience of aerial bombardment. Security for the British people lay in dispersal. That, they argued, might also require the extensive transfer overseas of industrial plant. However, although parliamentary questions required answers, there is nothing to link these representations to government initiatives. The wilder lobbyists, later formed into the Migration Council, were consistently dismissed by ministers and civil servants as extremists.[18]

With hindsight, we can see that those in government also pursued fantasies in their advocacy of emigration. State-sponsored emigration during the 1940s was promoted as both an immediate and a long-term political strategy designed to protect the economic and military interests of the settler societies of the British commonwealth, to sustain the power and prestige of the commonwealth as a whole, and to maintain thereby the pivotal role of Britain in a competitive world. Demographic and economic competition between constituent parts of the commonwealth was obscured by an atavistic notion that the British 'race' wherever located remained a single constituency. These perceptions are not just pre-Second World War in their flavour, but pre-First World War. Far from waving emigrants goodbye, British policy-makers assumed that they would remain integral to a British-dominated global system.

These points were repeatedly advanced in the wartime and post-war deliberations. Attlee told the cabinet in October 1942 that 'The war has shown the need for larger populations in the Dominions if the British Empire is to exercise a strong influence in the post-war period', and his 1943 despatch also emphasized their need for larger populations for defence purposes. The high commissioner in Australia, representing the British government, insisted in 1943 that 'to maintain the prestige of the British Commonwealth of Nations in the post-war world, increases in the population of the Dominions and more especially of Australia will be of the utmost importance'. Lord Cranborne explained to commonwealth representatives in 1945 that the falling birth rate and the labour needed for reconstruction in Britain meant that emigration could be seen as disadvantageous to Britain, but he assured them that 'if the Dominions were anxious to receive migrants from the United Kingdom, the immediate disadvantage to the latter of their loss would not be allowed to weigh against the wider considerations involved'. In April 1945 the Coalition government concluded that 'emigration from this country to the Dominions was a valuable means of strengthening the cohesion of the British Commonwealth', and in February 1947 the Labour government's dominions secretary and minister of labour together argued that the loss of manpower was 'outweighed by the overriding importance of a better distribution of population within the British Commonwealth on Defence and other grounds'. Commenting on the report of the Royal Commission on Population in 1949, the CRO feared that in Australia, as already in Canada and South Africa, the British component in the population might be swamped by other faster-breeding elements. The white commonwealth's ties of kinship and affection with Britain, it was judged, could only be maintained by a 'steady flow of fresh blood from this country'.[19]

The support of the Ministry of Labour for this strategy may seem surprising in view of its simultaneous efforts to cope with domestic labour shortages by, amongst other measures, the immigration into Britain of 'displaced persons' from continental Europe. However, officials gave unequivocal support since it was 'essential to the future of our relations with Australia that we should help her as much as we possibly can in the matter of providing suitable migrants'. They argued 'that even if the immediate loss of manpower and production due to emigration is considerable, the undoubted advantages to the Commonwealth as a whole, especially taking the long term view, are overriding'.[20] Considering how matters were subsequently to unfold, it is important to explain that the cabinet had agreed in 1944 that the Dominions Office and hence later the CRO would be responsible for policy and negotiations with commonwealth governments and the Ministry of Labour would administer agreed schemes.[21] Thus the Ministry of Labour with its regional and local offices advertised state-sponsored emigration, monitored the programmes, and, in co-operation with the Australian authorities, dealt with individual applications for assisted passage places. From the beginning the ministry always reckoned that its close involvement gave it influence over the selection of would-be migrants. As we shall see, the ministry considered itself uniquely placed to reconcile the apparently clashing manpower interests of Britain and Australia.

In view of the prevailing judgements of the 1940s it is surprising that official opinions became much more divided in the following decade and still more surprising that the principal critic of state-assisted emigration was the CRO. A review of policy was required because the assisted passage agreement with Australia was due to expire in March 1951 and the Empire Settlement Act itself in May 1952. In May 1950 senior officials in the CRO, prompted by the secretary of state, Patrick Gordon Walker, concluded that both the agreement and the Act should be allowed to lapse. Since the Ministry of Labour, the Ministry of Transport, the Home Office, and the Treasury were also involved, an interdepartmental committee chaired by an assistant under-secretary at the CRO (the Syers Committee) reviewed the issues. Views clashed, but on the whole the CRO, backed by the Treasury, prevailed. The committee recommended in December 1950 that the assisted passage scheme should be extended in March 1951 but for only one more year, when the CRO intended that it would be terminated just before the Act itself was allowed to expire. However, on further reflection, Gordon Walker decided that even the temporary extension of the assisted passage scheme should be refused.

The immediate stimulus was the need for economy in public expenditure. Originally, the cost of assisted passages to Australia after the payment of £10 by the adult migrant was to be shared equally by the two governments, but this had been based on the inaccurate assumption that the adult fare would be £75. When fares proved to be more expensive, the Australian government agreed that each British contribution should not exceed £32.50, and subsequently accepted that as an economy measure (when fares had risen to £120) the British contribution from 1 April 1950 could be restricted to £25.[22] Nevertheless, annual costs to British taxpayers had grown from £52,244 in 1947–48 to £607,987 by 1949–50, and were projected to rise to £1,435,000 by 1951–52. Therefore, in May 1950 the CRO began to argue for the ending of the agreement, and the case on financial grounds became more pressing when the need for increased defence expenditure led the Treasury in November 1950 to press fiercely for cuts in public expenditure elsewhere.[23]

However, CRO objections to state-assisted emigration derived from deeper considerations. Officials always assumed that there would be people who would independently choose to leave the United Kingdom, and even suggested that more might be done by way of publicity to steer such migrants to commonwealth destinations since such flows could help to sustain commonwealth solidarity and that, they always stressed, was desirable. However, the office expressed fundamental objections to stimulating such an exodus by subsidizing fares. Their objections adopted, at last, the critical appraisals of the 1930s, including, rather surprisingly given their responsibilities for the overseas commonwealth, a concern for the effects of emigration on domestic Britain. The demographic conditions which had once legitimized state sponsorship of migration had expired, they reckoned, now that the birth rate was below replacement level and the population was ageing. They also queried the use of public money to emigrate productive workers when taxpayers were burdened with the rising cost of social services and Britain had met the costs of education and welfare of those who left. Economically it made little sense to promote emigration since there was no longer unemployment at home but a labour shortage. Moreover, those being assisted to leave were industrial workers whose emigration would help Australian industry 'to compete against us'. There was, in addition, a specific objection to maintaining what was ostensibly a commonwealth migration policy which in practice merely subsidized with British taxpayers' money an Australian government able to afford to pay all the costs of its immigration programme – as did New Zealand. The Empire Settlement Act in practice gave Australia a privileged position within the commonwealth.[24]

Although a change of policy would be controversial, the CRO had not expected vehement opposition from the Ministry of Labour. As administrators of policy devised by the CRO, the ministry stressed the advantages which the assisted passage scheme gave in the management of the British labour market. Officials started from the premise that the white settler societies of the commonwealth would inevitably recruit much of their imported labour, especially of skilled labour, from Britain. Moreover, Australia's demands would be considerable because of the urgent need for population for defence and development. Furthermore, since it would be impossible to prevent the Australian authorities from actively seeking recruits, administrative co-operation was essential in order to prevent Australia's recruiting from damaging the British economy. Repeatedly, the ministry argued that the involvement of its officers enabled them to tone down advertising pitched at classes of workers in short supply, to restrict the numbers of workers in key occupations recruited, and to persuade Australia to take a broader social and occupational cross-section of the British people. In contrast, the ministry was less able to influence the advertising and selection processes of New Zealand with whom no jointly-funded assisted passage scheme had been set up.

These arguments were also based upon much broader concepts of British obligations to Australia and Britain's external interests in maintaining commonwealth integrity. These were not matters of administration but of policy. In an initial comment on the CRO's suggestions, ministry officials emphasized the defence needs of Australia and the importance of sustaining the British component in Australia's population. 'I am sure', wrote one, 'that on political and economic grounds it is a good thing to build up the working populations in the Dominions with British stock, and I believe too that on manpower grounds the policy is also a right one looking at the Commonwealth as a whole.' Officials claimed that the actual loss of labour through assisted emigration to Australia constituted only a tiny proportion of the British population but these migrants considerably contributed to the much smaller total population of Australia. The Minister of Labour, George Isaacs, also insisted that 'The fact that the British element in Canada tends to become more diluted makes it more, not less, important to maintain the British preponderance in those Commonwealth countries where it may still be practicable.' The issue needed to be considered as a commonwealth and not just British question.[25]

The paradox of this controversy was not lost on the participants. One official confessed that 'it looks as if we were opposing the expert Department (CRO) on grounds quite outside our own sphere', and another observed that 'we have been in the odd position of having to take the sort of line we might have expected CRO to take and find ourselves up against CRO opposition in doing so'.[26] Later, in the CRO, one official grumbled that the Ministry of Labour 'as usual tries to teach us our business'.[27] Syers, the chair of the interdepartmental committee, complained that he had faced considerable opposition from the Ministry of Labour. Certainly this explains why his committee had been unable to recommend unanimously that the Empire Settlement Act should not be renewed.[28] The Labour cabinet havered over a decision, but in June 1951 decided not to renew the assisted passage agreement with Australia beyond September 1951.[29] At this point the British government seemed certain to wave goodbye to its old empire migration policy.

However, there was another party to this debate – the government of Australia which was anxious to renew the assisted passage scheme since rapid immigration, preferably from British sources, was 'vital to national security' and could only be effected by state involvement. Moreover, the Australians warned, if the British government did not show support for the programme there would be 'political repercussions'. Gordon Walker returned to the cabinet still spluttering that renewal would retain 'the distasteful anachronism of paying our people to emigrate', but he suggested renewal of the agreement for a further three years but with a much reduced ceiling on annual British expenditure. The Minister of Labour insisted on a higher figure and again claimed that the policy of commonwealth migration would 'maintain the British connection in a society of nations from which this country derives much of its practical influence in the affairs of the world'.[30]

The cabinet had to choose. It was anomalous to finance emigration when there were manpower shortages in key industries, but it was important to preserve in the population of Australia and other commonwealth countries 'a due proportion of people of Anglo-Saxon stock'. What determined the decision was a concern that Australians would be offended if the British government withdrew its co-operation too precipitately. The compromise was to extend the programme until March 1954, to fix a ceiling of £500,000 a year on assisted passages, and to reduce the British subsidy on each ticket to a mere £10.[31] The Australian government resisted even these terms, and insisted on a British contribution of £25, though accepting the fixed annual ceiling. The implication of this capitulation was, of course, that the Empire Settlement Act itself would have to be renewed, to authorize expenditure on assisted passages beyond May 1952.[32]

Even this did not terminate the business, because the general election in October 1951 brought to power a new set of ministers who were at once confronted with rising defence costs and the need for cuts in public expenditure elsewhere. Conservative ministers inherited and espoused entrenched departmental positions. By December 1951, Lord Ismay, at the CRO, had identified the £500,000 just ear-marked for assisted passages to Australia as his office's largest single annual financial commitment, and offered it up to the chancellor for slaughter. He explained to cabinet that 'it is difficult to defend spending large sums of public money on helping some of the most productive elements in this country to leave it ... One can agree that the under-populated areas of the Commonwealth require a blood transfusion, which can best be supplied from this densely populated island; but there seems no reason why part of the cost of the operation should be paid by the impoverished donor.' The annual financial commitment to the assisted passage scheme should at least be reduced to £250,000 but preferably scrapped, although he suggested that the Empire Settlement Act itself might be renewed, to deflect criticism, to support child migration schemes, and to enable assisted passage arrangements to be resumed later if conditions changed.

None of this was acceptable to the Ministry of Labour and to its political chief, Walter Monckton. Once again the department claimed that the agreement with Australia enabled it to influence recruiting, and this time unregulated Canadian practices were held up as the behaviour to be avoided. The general advantages to the commonwealth as a whole of British emigration were re-asserted. Once again the cabinet gave priority to cuts in public expenditure. Ministers accepted the value of extending the Empire Settlement Act (to 1957), but authorized the secretary of state to negotiate with the Australian government for a release from the recently signed assisted passage agreement. Again the Australians stubbornly objected. The task of cajoling them into concession was devolved upon the Lord Privy

Seal, the Marquess of Salisbury. In an interview with the Australian high commissioner in January 1952, he stressed the British government's need for economy in public expenditure, argued that the justification for assisted passages from Britain had been eliminated by conditions of full employment, and hoped that nevertheless the Australian authorities would still co-operate with the Ministry of Labour in the selection of migrants. Salisbury had to report, however, that the high commissioner had been 'very annoyed' and had predicted that the proposal to end the agreement would be 'badly received'. He insisted that the flow of assisted migrants from Britain was integral to the economic development of Australia, and threatened serious consequences if the British abandoned their commitment. 'In the interests of Empire as a whole we desire to adhere to a high intake of our British migrants and to maintain our level of British stock rather than to divert to a preponderantly foreign intake', but, he noted pointedly, the Dutch and Italian governments were already more generous in their subsidizing of assisted passages to Australia. Some financial contribution from Britain was essential to demonstrate a continuing interest in Australia's well-being, and once again British ministers, the chancellor last of all, gave in. In June 1952, they agreed that the assisted passage scheme would be continued until March 1954 although with the annual maximum cost to the British taxpayer screwed down to a mere £150,000.[33] State-supported empire migration was a policy to which the British government was finding it difficult to bid goodbye.

Meanwhile, British ministers in April 1952 had been obliged to pass a new Empire Settlement Bill, extending its life, albeit for only five years and with an authorized total expenditure on all services of £1.5m a year. It would be hard to deduce from ministerial speeches that the CRO had wanted to abandon the policy of state-supported emigration. Ministers acknowledged that to avoid manpower shortages in key industries the emigrants selected for assistance should reflect a cross-section of society, but they claimed that the policy would actually help the balance of payments by boosting production inside the sterling area and reinforce the bonds of the commonwealth. Nor did Gordon Walker, speaking for Labour, do more than caution against the loss of too many migrants. Those in favour of a more vigorous depopulating of Britain had of course far more, and far more nonsense, to say.[34]

The problem with extending the assisted passage agreement only until March 1954 and the Empire Settlement Act only until May 1957 was that it made further debate imminent. Surprisingly, at this next stage none of the participants in the discussions attempted to argue against further extensions.

Rather than belief in the practical merits of extended commitments, this reflected a weariness of controversy and a conviction that the political repercussions of changing policy outweighed all objections. This was policy-making by inertia.

In October 1953 the CRO inserted an extension of the assisted passage agreement with Australia into its annual estimates for the following year. The following March the Treasury accepted this extension for one year but demanded a further review. In October 1954 an interdepartmental committee of officials (the Garner Committee) chaired by another CRO under-secretary reported unanimously in favour of continuing the agreement until 1957, when the further extension of the Empire Settlement Act and of schemes authorized under it would have to be reassessed. And in 1956 a similar interdepartmental committee (the Shannon Committee) unanimously recommended further legislation and continued funding of state-assisted migration.

Not unexpectedly, the Treasury, seeking economies in public expenditure, expressed opposition, but in December 1953 this merely obliged the CRO to present a case for a temporary extension.[35] Subsequently, however, the Treasury representative on the Garner Committee seems to have offered very little resistance to the proposed further extension until May 1957.[36] More predictably, the Ministry of Labour again trundled out its stock arguments in favour of the assisted passage scheme, insisting in June 1954, for example, that the arrangement enabled officials to moderate Australian recruiting, that the volume of emigration was too small to distort seriously the availability of labour in Britain (which was being increased in any case by immigration *from* the Commonwealth), and that the issue should be viewed as a commonwealth and not just a British issue. What surprised the ministry's representative, however, was that the CRO was not seriously hostile, and that the Garner report took 'full cognizance of the Department's point of view and suitable weight has been given to the considerations we were anxious to have stressed'.[37]

It is indeed arresting to find CRO officials and ministers once more expressing support for state-assisted migration. They were, it is true, subjected to political pressure from predictable quarters. In March 1954 the Australian high commissioner had stressed the need for continuing the assisted passage scheme, insisting that Australia was anxious to preserve the predominantly British character of the country, but he threatened an adverse reaction and dark consequences if a shortfall from desired immigrant numbers forced Australia to look instead to non-British sources.[38] Even more strident was the voice of the British high commissioner in Canberra. His views were sought at the insistence of the Ministry of Labour's representative on the Garner Committee, and once delivered the CRO had no option but to circulate his vigorous, even vicious, opinions. He warned that ending the assisted passage scheme would cause Australia to abandon attempts to sustain a high proportion of British people among its immigrant flows, and would be widely interpreted as showing that the British were no longer interested in maintaining the family relationship between the two countries. 'It will not be much use for the future if even white development of Australia means development by a polyglot collection of people, the surplus of uncontrolled breeding elsewhere, with a decreasing admixture of men and women from the United Kingdom.' Australia, and he meant 'white' Australia, deserved support because the world was becoming too unbalanced between 'Asians and whites', because Britain required a strong partner 'in this part of the world', and because Australia also needed protection by British immigration against 'Americanisation'.[39] Meanwhile, at home, the CRO had responded to parliamentary lobbying by setting up one of those advisory bodies which were designed by departments to absorb the energies of enthusiasts, but which could rebound upon their creators. The Oversea Migration Board, established in 1953, proved to be a more sensible body of persons than the CRO had expected, but the very caution of their judgements added weight to their conclusions, and their recommendation in July 1954 that the assisted passage scheme deserved renewal was hard to ignore.[40]

It is doubtful whether CRO officials were much persuaded by any of the arguments. What seems to have swept through the department was the conviction, derived from past experience and continued lobbying, that it would be unable to abandon the assisted passage scheme for fear of political repercussions. This was the essence of the CRO's response in December 1953 to the Treasury request for cuts. The following April an official, reviewing the bruising encounters at the Syers Committee in 1950 and subsequent developments, concluded: 'It seems unlikely that the proposed working party will be able to carry the matter further than their predecessor.' In May, even before his committee began its assessment of the merits of state-assisted migration, Garner accepted that 'In the last resort, Ministerial decisions will have to be taken on *political* grounds (i.e. whether the pressure for economy outweighs or not the political difficulties which would arise, both in Australia and in this country, if provision for migration were reduced).' At the first meeting of the committee in June, Garner condemned British financial aid for emigration as incompatible with the 'modern concept of the Commonwealth', but admitted that this view might have to be 'modified' because of the strength of support for the existing policy in Australia and on the government backbenches. The Garner report itself properly presented the economic and political arguments against

British-financed emigration, but then acknowledged the hostile political reactions which would follow the stopping of British financial support. It then tried to justify the renewal of the assisted passage scheme until May 1957 with the same maximum annual expenditure of £150,000 by repeating those assertions with which the CRO had been bombarded from other quarters – that the scheme gave some influence over selection and thus protected the British labour market, and that 'If the Commonwealth is to retain its British character, the life blood of the "old" Commonwealth should continually be reflected by the arrival of new settlers from this country and it is in the interests of the United Kingdom Government to foster the process'.[41]

What makes the Garner report so bizarre is that the objections of the Treasury and the CRO to the policy just endorsed remained afterwards unchanged. A Treasury official wrote in December 1954 that 'all of us at the Garner Committee – except the Ministry of Labour, whose reasons appeared to me to be trivial in relation to the sums and numbers involved – were unhappy about United Kingdom financial assistance to ordinary emigration to the Commonwealth, and recommended continuance in the case of Australia because of the impossibility of suddenly cutting it off in view of that country's attitude'. With this judgement a CRO official readily concurred, insisting that 'there is at present no demographic case for stimulating emigration to Australia, though there is no objection to letting such a volume of emigrants leave us as is likely to come forward without stimulation'. The question remained, he stated, 'a political one'.[42]

The way in which the CRO had responded in 1954 meant that it would almost inevitably react in the same fashion to the same pressures in 1956 when the renewal of the Empire Settlement Act and the assisted passage scheme had again to be considered. Once more the department would have liked to see the ending of state-assisted emigration. In February 1955 Garner even sounded out the British high commissioner as to whether it might be possible to 'soften up' Australian opinion so as to effect an escape from a policy commitment 'which is a relic of past Colonial days'. Once more the message from Australia warned that discontinuing the scheme would 'make a very bad impression on the Australian Government and public', since Britain's financial contribution 'was recognised as a token of the continuing interest of the United Kingdom in Australia's wish to keep up its British stock'. The high commissioner referred darkly to other strains in Anglo-Australian relations as an additional reason not at this time to cause fresh offence.[43] Once more the Oversea Migration Board was active, relaying the views of the Australian High Commission.[44]

Again, even before the Shannon Committee set to work, the CRO had accepted that renewal was unavoidable. Shannon opened the first meeting of his committee in May 1956 by explaining that the government was already committed to a policy of supporting emigration. In a memorandum of 5 June he compared the arguments for and against in the precise terms in which they eventually appeared in the report he signed in September, and with the same conclusion. State-assisted emigration was not a policy which would nowadays be initiated but the political repercussions would be too severe at home and abroad to be worth its ending. This judgement was endorsed on 6 June by his senior colleague: failure to renew 'would be bound to lead to political difficulties both with Australia and in this country'. Two days later the CRO representative on the Shannon Committee declared his department's support for the renewal of the Empire Settlement Act and of the assisted passage agreement. Thc Ministry of Labour representative was happy. The man from the Treasury bowed to the inevitable: 'If a strong political case was made out by the CRO and supported by other Departments he did not think the Treasury would advise the Chancellor of the Exchequer to contest the case.' So anxious were all participants to avoid these tedious repeated endorsements of seemingly inescapable commitments that they proposed, not only to renew the assisted passage scheme for five years and with the same maximum annual British contribution of £150,000, but to recommend re-enactment of the Empire Settlement Act for another fifteeen years and not just five, albeit with the same maximum annual expenditure on all provisions of £1.5m. Fearing House of Commons criticism of such a long-term pledge, however, ministers proposed instead to renew the Act for only five years. The cabinet endorsed the package with little discussion on 23 October 1956, thus ensuring that the whole exercise of review would have shortly to be repeated.[45] Parliamentary debate on the new Empire Settlement Bill early in 1957 was largely a simple-minded endorsement from both sides of the House, with a few demands for additional commitments. The only signal change was to insist that the new measure be titled the Commonwealth Settlement Act.[46]

It would be otiose to trudge in detail through another cycle of decision-making. Suffice it to say that in June 1961 another interdepartmental committee of officials (the Chadwick Committee) chaired by another CRO under-secretary set about gathering material to support that November another unanimous report in favour of extensions for a further five years from 1962 of the Commonwealth Settlement Act and the assisted passage agreement with Australia. This was approved by cabinet in December 1961 and the Act was passed in March 1962. State-assisted emigration still seemed a policy the British government was unable to abandon.

What is remarkable is that the case against providing British taxpayers' support for emigration was by now being articulated even more strongly. The recruiting in Britain of skilled, including professional, workers by commonwealth countries had become a subject of heated public concern by the beginning of the decade, made more alarming by the faltering British economy. There were official as well as press reports that the highly qualified were being especially targeted.[47] Even the Oversea Migration Board expressed unease, though its solution to the perceived deleterious effects on Britain was to call for more investment in higher education so as to increase supply.[48] Most remarkably, even the Ministry of Labour abandoned its former stance. A substantial review presented to the Chadwick Committee no longer echoed the confident assertion that co-operation with the Australian authorities enabled the ministry to moderate losses or that Britain ought to express through assisted emigration its commitment to commonwealth. Instead, there was first the assertion that 'The continuing shortage of skilled and professional workers in the United Kingdom is causing increasing concern because of its hampering effects on economic growth.' There followed a detailed occupational analysis of the migration figures, setting immigration against emigration, and a second stark conclusion that 'Emigration depletes United Kingdom manpower at certain sensitive points where there are persistent shortages and it includes some of the most highly qualified people.' The third point was an inescapable conclusion: 'the Ministry of Labour must question whether the policy of actively assisting persons to emigrate to the Commonwealth is now the right one'.[49] All this was acknowledged in the Chadwick report. In recommending the continuation of the existing policy, 'we add the rider that it may soon prove necessary to exercise more frequently our right to ask Commonwealth countries not to recruit skilled workers in short supply in this country'.[50]

The strength of the case against renewal was unable to affect the substantive outcome because, once more, that decision had already been made on political grounds even before the Chadwick Committee had begun its deliberations. The committee was not formally constituted until June 1961, but in March its subsequent chair was writing that 'In principle, and particularly in view of growing Australian criticism of our alleged lack of punch on migration policy, it would seem essential to extend the Acts, at least for a further five year period. This has been the decision reached at the end of previous quinquennial reviews and there seems no reason that that trend should change.' A senior colleague agreed that policy should continue as before 'out of regard for Australian susceptibilities'. Later that month, the parliamentary under-secretary (the Duke of Devonshire) even argued for an increase in Britain's financial contribution to the assisted passage scheme, for overtly political reasons, since a 'small increase would … bring with it a quite disproportionate amount of goodwill in Australia, and do something to satisfy the Government's critics on the subject in this country', and with this the secretary of state (Duncan Sandys) concurred.[51]

This justification accounts for the final judgement of the Chadwick report in November. Once again the political advantages of renewing the Commonwealth Settlement Act were paramount: 'Any lessening of our encouragement of emigration would be taken in Australia, and perhaps elsewhere, as an indication that we were not interested in maintaining those ties or in helping them to cope with their problems of manpower and defence.' The symbolic significance of the Act required its renewal. Similarly, the assisted passage agreement with Australia ought to be extended: 'Failure to renew the Agreement would be sharply resented and might adversely affect Anglo-Australian relations in other spheres.'[52] The secretary of state accepted the committee's arguments, and recommended to cabinet that both commitments should be extended for five years and that support for assisted passages should be increased from £150,000 to £300,000. True, in the light of the usual need for economies elsewhere in public expenditure the cabinet jibbed at that increase, but otherwise 'it was agreed that, while the emigration of skilled labour was likely to become more and more damaging to our economy, this would not of itself justify a departure from the five-year renewal period which had now become traditional'.[53] This curious appraisal was the essence of the case which ministers put to parliament, where the Commonwealth Settlement Bill was treated with unanimous approval and in terms hugely optimistic of the positive effect which British emigration was having on maintaining the proper character and integrity of the British commonwealth. There was little sign in those august assemblies that legislators were anxious to wave goodbye to past practice.[54]

The departmental records are not yet available to account for the further renewal in 1967 of the Commonwealth Settlement Act. However, the precise repetition in the terms of the Act – for a further five years, with an overall maximum allowed expenditure each year of £1.5m of which a maximum of £150,000 was dedicated to the assisted passage scheme – suggests that precisely the same decision-making practices had been followed.[55] One suspects that another under-secretary with colleagues in other departments laboriously assembled the economic case against renewal in the knowledge that the political arguments in favour would remain paramount. At least by the late 1960s price rises were rendering the financial contribution of the British taxpayer increasingly nugatory, but erosion by inflation is a peculiar method of changing policy.

Sometime, probably in 1971, the decision was at last presumably taken not to renew yet again, and in 1972 the Empire and Commonwealth Settlement Acts were allowed to lapse. By then, assisted immigrants to Australia from Britain under all post-war schemes totalled 1,011,985.[56] Before then, of course, since 1968, the Commonwealth Office itself had been merged with the Foreign Office, and the orientation of British external policy was shifting towards Europe. Only then, perhaps, could the British government bid goodbye, no longer to British-subsidized emigrants going out to Australia, but to the policy which for fear of political repercussions it had not dared before to abandon.

NOTES

1. Stephen Constantine (ed.), *Emigrants and Empire: British Settlement in the Dominions between the Wars* (Manchester, 1990) and references therein.
2. Julius Isaac, *British Post-War Migration* (Cambridge, 1954); Reg Appleyard, *The Ten Pound Immigrants* (London, 1988).
3. Kathleen Paul, *Whitewashing Britain: Race and Citizenship in the Postwar Era* (Ithaca, 1997).
4. Only reasons of space account for the lack of consideration given in this essay to this hugely important issue. The challenge of new ideas to past practice was acknowledged in each of the reports to be examined, and yet financial support for child emigration was on balance repeatedly endorsed and was authorized by the Acts largely for the reasons articulated more generally in this analysis. See Philip Bean and Joy Melville, *Lost Children of the Empire* (London, 1989), B.M.Coldrey, *Child Migration, the Australian Government and the Catholic Church 1926–1966* (Victoria, Australia, 1992), and Ann McVeigh, 'A History of the Child and Juvenile Migration Scheme to Australia' (unpublished Ph.D. thesis, Queen's University, Belfast, 1995).
5. Stephen Constantine, 'Empire Migration and Social Reform 1880–1960', in Colin G. Pooley and Ian D. Whyte (eds.), *Migrants, Emigrants and Immigrants* (London, 1991).
6. See, for example, W.D. Forsyth, *The Myth of Open Spaces* (Melbourne, 1942).
7. Report of the Oversea Settlement Board May 1938, *Parliamentary Papers*, Cmd 5766.
8. Post-War Migration: Proposed Free Passage Scheme, Public Record Office (PRO), London, Dominions Office (DO), DO 35/1134/M822/2; Committee on Overseas Settlement, PRO, Treasury (T), T 220/21; Attlee memo, 28 Oct.1942, PRO, Prime Minister's Office (PREM), PREM 4/42/1, WP(42)490, and War Cabinet minute, 19 Nov. 1942, WC155(42); Attlee to dominions governments, 2 April 1943, Migration Correspondence and Papers, DO 114/107; Prime Ministers' Meetings, minutes of 13th meeting, 12 May 1944, PREM 4/42/5; Post War Migration: Conference of Official Representatives of United Kingdom and Dominions, DO 35/1134/M822/127.
9. The Dominions Office, created 1925, became the Commonwealth Relations Office in July 1947, and the Department of Commonwealth Affairs in August 1966: it is called CRO for the sake of convenience throughout this essay.
10. WM(45)46th conclusions, 16 April 1945, PREM 4/42/1;CM(45)40th conclusions, 11 Oct.1945 and CM(46)2nd conclusions, 3 Jan.1946, PREM 8/1479; Assisted Passages-Australia, Renewal of the Assisted Passage Agreement, 1948–49, DO 35/3370; Renewal of the Empire Settlement Act 1922, DO 35/3394.
11. See correspondence collected in DO 114/107 and reactions to the 1945 conference in DO 35/1134/M822/127.
12. Andrew Markus, 'Labor and Immigration: Policy Formulation 1943–5', *Labour History*, 46 (May 1984), 21–33, stresses that it was Attlee's despatch of 2 April 1943 which prompted the Australian government to reconsider state-assisted immigration as a component in its population policies.

13. Cherwell to Churchill, 26 April 1944, PREM 4/42/1.
14. Gorell Barnes to Attlee, 17 Dec.1946, PREM 8/1479.
15. CM(45)40th Conclusions, 11 Oct.1945, ibid.
16. See, for example, Ministry of Labour and National Service, Report for the Years 1939–46, *PP*, Cmd.7225, 1947, 164–5, and Report for the Year 1948, *PP*, Cmd.7822, 1949, 30–1.
17. These issues are aired in Attlee memo WP(42)490, 28 Oct.1942, PREM 4/42/1; Attlee despatch of 2 April 1943 and Antrobus, British High Commissioner in Australia, to Dominions Office, 6 Sept.1943, DO 114/107; memo by Sir Patrick Duff Cooper, 26 Jan.1945, DO 35/1134/M822/127; Review of Emigration Policy in the Light of the Manpower Position in the United Kingdom, PRO, Ministry of Labour (LAB), LAB 13/281.
18. See, for example, Dudley Barker, *People for the Commonwealth: The Case for Mass Migration* (London, 1948), and numerous parliamentary speeches. For the membership, lobbying activities and publications of the Migration Council from 1952 to 1960 see DO 35/10220 and 10221.
19. The arguments are advanced in PREM 4/42/1; DO 114/107; DO 35/1134/M822/127; Migration within the British Commonwealth: Statement by His Majesty's Government in the United Kingdom, *PP*, Cmd.6658, 1945; and Trend of Population with Regard to Migration: Report of the Royal Commission on Population, CRO to Treasury, 12 Sept.1949, DO 35/3442.
20. Overseas Settlement in the Dominions, minute by Evans, 2 Jan.1947, LAB 13/199; Bevan to Veysey, 8 Dec.1947, LAB 13/281.
21. WM(44)139th conclusions, 20 Oct.1944, PREM 4/42/1.
22. Sedgwick to Syers, 24 Dec.1949, DO 35/3394; Future of Assisted Migration, CRO to Ministry of Labour, 4 Dec.1950, and 'Draft Report', LAB 13/835.
23. Papers Circulated to the Inter-Departmental Committee on Future Migration Policy, minutes of 1st and 3rd meetings, DO 35/3425; memo by Secretary of State for Commonwealth Relations, CP(50)306, 12 Dec.1950, PREM 8/1479.
24. Interdepartmental Committee on Migration Policy, minutes by Sedgwick and Syers and memo by Sedgwick, May 1950, DO 35/3424; minutes of meetings, DO 35/3425; Gordon Walker to Isaacs, 5 July 1950, memo 'Assisted Migration', CRO to Ministry of Labour, 4 Dec 1950, and 'Draft Report', LAB 13/835; 'Notes on Memo by Ministry of Labour', 16 Dec.1950, DO 35/3374.
25. 'Notes of Position of the Ministry of Labour on Expiring Empire Settlement Acts', 12 July 1950, minutes of Sept.1950, minute by Rossetti, 12 Dec.1950, LAB 13/835; memo by Minister of Labour, CP(50)320, 15 Dec.1950, PREM 8/1479.
26. Minutes of 10 Dec.1950 and 16 March 1951, LAB 13/835.
27. Minute of 13 Dec.1951, DO 35/3374.
28. Syers to Gordon Walker, 11 Dec.1950, ibid.
29. CM(50)87th conclusions, 18 Dec.1950, CM(51)47th conclusions, 28 June 1951, PREM 8/1479.
30. Memo by Secretary of State, 23 July 1951, CP(51)218, memo by Ministry of Labour, 26 July 1951, CP(51)225, ibid.
31. CM(51)55th conclusions, 26 July 1951, ibid.
32. Minutes and correspondence, July–Dec.1951, DO 35/3374 and LAB 13/835.
33. Reports, minutes and correspondence, Dec.1951 to June 1952, DO 35/3374 and LAB 13/835.
34. 21 April 1952, *Parliamentary Debates* (Commons), 5th Series, vol.499, 53–162; 20 May 1952, *Parliamentary Debates* (Lords), 5th Series, vol.176, 1197–226.
35. Inter-Departmental Committee on Migration Expenditure, correspondence of 2 Dec.1953 to 5 March 1954, DO 35/10212.
36. Agenda and Minutes of Meetings of the Inter-Departmental Committee on Migration Expenditure, DO 35/10214.
37. Future of Assisted Migration, 'Review of Long-Term Migration Policy', 15 June 1954, and minute by Cullingford, 21 Oct.1954, LAB 13/836.
38. Correspondence between the High Commissioner and the Secretary of State, 9–30 March 1954, ibid; Sedgwick to Holmes, 27 May 1954, DO 35/10212.

39. CRO to High Commissioner, 15 July 1954 and High Commissioner to CRO, 11 Aug. and 20 Aug.1954, ibid.
40. For the establishment of the OMB see DO 35/3426 and 6373; for the First Annual Report, July 1954, see *PP*, Cmd.9261 and 'The Assisted Passage Scheme to Australia', LAB 13/836; and for CRO reactions see minute by Costley-White, 16 March 1956, DO 35/6378.
41. Foster to Boyd-Carpenter, 14 Dec.1953, minute by Sedgwick, 5 April 1954, minute by Garner, 11 May 1954, DO 35/10212; report by Cullingford on 1st meeting of Inter-Departmental Committee, 1 July 1954, LAB 13/836; Inter-Departmental Committee on Migration Policy: Report 1954, DO 35/4879.
42. Drake to Morley, 24 Dec.1954, and minute by Morley, 30 Dec.1954, DO 35/10212.
43. Departmental Committee on Migration Policy, High Commissioner to CRO, 5 June and 29 June 1956, DO 35/6368; Interdepartmental Committee on Migration Policy 1956: Papers Circulated, Holmes to Garner 29 June 1956, DO 35/10215.
44. Minutes of OMB, 30 May 1956, ibid.
45. Interdepartmental Committee on Migration Policy 1956: Agenda and Minutes, minutes of 1st meeting, 30 May 1956, and of 2nd meeting, 8 June 1956, DO 35/10216; memo by Shannon, 5 June 1956, and minute by Garner, 6 June 1956, DO 35/6368; Report of the Interdepartmental Committee on Migration Policy 1956, copy of the report, minutes by Noble and Home, 18 and 21 Sept. 1956, and CP(56)240, 17 Oct. 1956, and CM(56)72nd conclusions, 23 Oct.1956, DO 35/10217.
46. 25 Jan.1957, *Parliamentary Debates* (Commons), 5th Series, vol.563, 541–630, 1088–128; 17 Feb.1957, *Parliamentary Debates* (Lords), 5th series, vol.201, 637–52; for drafts and amendments to the bill see Empire Settlement Acts...Question of Extension, DO 35/10224.
47. Interdepartmental Committee on Migration Policy 1961, Reports from High Commissioners, DO 175/27; Emigration of UK Skilled and Professional Workers to the Commonwealth, DO 175/110.
48. Seventh Annual Report of the Oversea Migration Board 1961, *PP*, Cmnd 1586; Overseas Migration Board, 'Training and Education', DO 175/110; Report, annex E, DO 175/38.
49. 'The Impact of Migration on Manpower Resources', DO 175/110.
50. Commonwealth and Empire Settlement Acts, 1922–1962: Extension for Five Years to 1967, 'British Emigration Policy: Report by Interdepartmental Committee of Officials, November 1961', DO 175/38.
51. Interdepartmental Committee on Emigration Policy 1961: Administrative Arrangements, minutes of 2 and 3 March 1961, DO 175/26; minutes of 30 March 1961, DO 175/27.
52. 'British Emigration Policy', DO 175/38.
53. 1 Dec.1961, PRO, Cabinet Papers (CAB), CAB 129/107,C(61)201; 5 Dec.1961, CAB128/35,CC67(61)6.
54. 1 March 1962, *Parliamentary Debates* (Commons) 5th Series, vol.654, 1557–87; 26 March 1962, *Parliamentary Debates* (Lords) 5th series, vol.238, 836–46; for ministerial guidance see Briefs for the Commonwealth Settlement Bill 1962, DO 175/39, and Note on United Kingdom Policy for Secretary of State April 1962, DO 175/24.
55. 5 April 1967, *Parliamentary Debates* (Commons), 5th Series, vol.744, 159–76; 24 April 1967, *Parliamentary Debates* (Lords), 5th Series, vol.282, 397–404.
56. Calculated from Appleyard, *Ten Pound Immigrants*, 160.

Mammon in Paradise: Economic Enterprise in Pacific Historiography

COLIN NEWBURY

The purpose of this paper is to raise questions about the place of business history in Pacific studies.[1] It has its origins in a comparative review of the evolution of colonial firms in Africa, published some years ago, and in my own use of business records for the mining industry in South Africa and plantations and mining in Papua New Guinea and French Polynesia. It will reflect reactions to a series of books and theses which have appeared over the past twenty years treating various sectors of Pacific economic history. Our debt to those who have wrestled with the source material peculiar to the operations of a firm is in no way diminished by a sense that we have, perhaps, failed to exploit these sources to the full, and, indeed, in some cases shied away from the challenge of accounting for the structure and function of a wide range of business in the Pacific islands.

This is partly because of the fragmented and often transitory nature of business records. Business history as developed in Europe, North America, and African and Asian studies is now a highly sophisticated (not to say esoteric) form with its own specialist journals and its own historiographical landmarks. Such model works fix on the big firms, typically those which diversified overseas and developed into multinational enterprises. For the Pacific Unilever, the Colonial Sugar Refinery in Fiji, perhaps Burns Philp and some of the Hawaiian 'Big Five', stand in the same league; and there are other candidates (*Société Le Nickel*, Maison Ballande, post-war New Guinea mining companies) which await their historians. There is the further difficulty that 'island-centred' history (the desirable goal of regional academic studies) can hardly be divorced from accounts of metropolitan-based enterprise and sources of capital, including the rim countries of the Pacific basin. This may not matter too much for a broad topic whose essential feature is entrepreneurial expansion and inter-regional financial and human factor flows. But it does mean that some selection within Australian, New Zealand, or American business history for enterprise relevant to the history of Pacific islanders has to be made; and this imposes an artificial division within the broad discipline of economic history which is seamless in cyclical themes of growth and decay and only incidentally concerned with parochial island case studies. Thirdly, there is a tendency among skilled practitioners of the craft to restrict the definition of what passes for 'business history' to meet a stern set of criteria including corporation decision-making, profitability measures, technological application, backward and forward linkages in local and foreign markets for which there may or may not be records. Judged in this way, even a well-developed historiography of economic enterprise may fail to pass muster according, at least, to one economic historian who has found New Zealand's business history to be 'uncritical, too personalised, focused on trivial details from individual firms and silent on relevant historical and theoretical debates'.[2]

This is not the place to enter the lists on the merits of company histories for one country whose historians are well able to defend themselves. The more general point worth making is that for the nineteenth-century Pacific few enterprises accumulated archives. Beside the big firms which became limited liability companies subject to law on public reports and disclosure of accounts is a larger category of single traders, partnerships, and early joint-stock enterprise across the mercantile, plantation, and extractive industries which are topics of generalization, rather than detailed analysis of performance. However imperfect their record they cannot be ignored; and by and large they will be the focus of the three main categories treated in this survey: mercantile and staple trades; commercial agriculture; and mining. For reasons that will become clear, the service sector will be subsumed in the first category, though in the post-colonial period, of course, there is a strong argument for writing about banking, insurance, tourism quite separately, especially where they have been treated as part of Australian, New Zealand, American, or other metropolitan studies of the clearing banks and other services. Local studies of construction and manufacturing feature in general economic surveys and country studies by the World Bank and academic institutes, and there are some valuable comparisons of more recent government and private enterprise for this sector in Fiji.[3] But for historical reasons, manufacturing, as a category of enterprise, is better subsumed under agricultural or mining processing in the nineteenth and early twentieth centuries until the appearance of light industries in Pacific island economies.

There is, too, a host of small-scale entrepreneurial activities – and not all of it of European origin – to be accounted for. Pre-colonial and non-immigrant entrepreneurial ventures pose special problems in explanation – not least because of their rarity outside of highly localized exchange systems. Indian, Chinese, and Japanese family business has been recognized, rather than explored in comparative depth, by a few anthropologists and students of ethnic settlement, while economic historians have failed so far to supply explanations of success or failure in enterprises undertaken by contrasting family structures.[4] Structures matter in business history where it is not sufficient to describe 'the history of economic activities' disembodied from the institutions which undertake the risks of organizing production and exchange.[5] The point is necessary, because it is relatively easy to describe the growth of early staple trades in island exchange systems, but it is much more difficult to provide the details of business organization at the metropolitan end of investment and processing, or the staple series required to measure market growth, or the operational record needed to account for the failure or survival of traders and merchants. Historical series are available for cotton and sugar, as early staples. But they are strangely inadequate for the Pacific's major export – coconut oil and copra. We now know much more about the market for labour and its recruitment and terms of service in Pacific islands' history than the market locally and overseas for the staple most commercial smallholdings and plantations employed labour to produce. Pacific historians could still learn something from works on the palm oil and palm kernel trade in Africa and, in particular, from the material now available on the development of vegetable oil brokerages and processing in England, Germany, and France in the nineteenth century.[6] Finally, it is in the demand side of Europe and America's consumption of raw materials that much of Pacific enterprise has its origins; and it is in this sector that the account of early business structures is particularly patchy.

This survey begins with alien 'big men' who were the products of American, Asian, and Australian 'country trades'. This term is chosen deliberately by analogy with the seaboard trade of India in the eastern archipelagos and the South China Sea. Unfortunately, those who have travelled in the wake of the East India Company have given us precious little on the structure and performance of chartered Spanish, Portuguese, or French companies in the northern Pacific.[7] After the end of monopoly ventures the country trades of the eastern seas were open to a wider variety of separate traders and partnerships coupled with the important agency houses whose structure, services and example spread well beyond Calcutta and Madras.[8] 'House of Agency' techniques deployed in early New South Wales trade are quite explicit from 1799; and the reasons for these techniques (warehousing for bulk cargoes and debt collection) continued to obtain throughout the period of weakening East India Company monopoly and the quest for profitable staples to relieve the outflow of sterling bills. These pioneer operations in colonial import-export trades and shipping provide the essential basis for the early 'hunter-gatherer' phase of Pacific islands commerce and the later establishment of shipping networks financed by brokers and wholesalers.[9]

The connection is made (though not always explicitly) in works by Margaret Steven, Harry Maude, D.R. Hainsworth, and D. Shineberg who have explored the operations and effects of staple ventures backed by shippers and wholesalers. Levels of capitalization were not high; operations looked more like mercantile ventures for immediate sale and profit of a staple – shell, hogs, sandalwood – rather than investment in shore stations. We also know that missionary settlers played a significant part in the establishment of local market-demand located in beach communities, rather than as a continuation of established periodic trade routes. In an important sense the Pacific islands country trade had to establish markets, whereas the East Asia trades utilized those already existing. Nevertheless, the agency system of the Australian colonies and California is the successor to the eastern system by the mid-nineteenth century.

The crucial difference between the 'hunter-gatherers' and their mercantile successors from the 1850s lay in the invention of the compound steam engine, as well as in improvements in raw material processing in Europe and North America. Sailing vessels remained useful for feeder services in the Pacific. But from mid-century the utilization of steamers on the long-haul routes and the application of a greater scale of capital investment and organization spread throughout the Pacific basin from mercantile agencies in Queensland, California, New Zealand, and the East Indies. For example, Buckley and Klugman make it clear in their study of the origins of Burns Philp that the partnership took no interest in the Pacific islands until they had acquired experience in general merchandizing and shipping from their bases in Townsville and Sydney. Long after they had exploited the natives of Queensland by domination of the retail trade of the Gulf of Carpentaria, they turned their attention tentatively, and speculatively, to the Gulf of Papua and ventured into pearl diving and a little blackbirding.[10]

But it is equally clear that the prototypes of Pacific enterprise had other features of Australian, European, American, and Latin American commercial practice. The typical 'company' of the first half of the nineteenth century was unincorporated, like its Asian and African counterparts. The partnership form of association by several principals, pooling private and/or borrowed capital was ubiquitous among British, French, German, or American entrepreneurs in the Pacific and capable of great adaptation. Records are few and precious, before the period of joint-stock formation, limited liability, and legal requirements on disclosure. But from the records we have of, say, Burns Philp prior to incorporation, German companies before about 1879, or American firms in Hawaii, several features can be discerned which have their parallels in other regions.

One which is not frequently emphasized is the specialization of such partnerships in particular commodity trades and their generalized functions at an operational level in island markets. This would seem to be true of firms in the pioneering commercial phase of Queensland's development, prior to railways, as it is for Melanesia and Polynesia. Thus, Burns Philp as a merchandizing firm in the 1870s and early 1880s, or J.C. Godeffroy & Sohn which pioneered merchandizing and produce buying by way of Valparaiso from the 1850s, concentrated on the most profitable credit lines in hardwares and textiles, in return for cash, wool, timber (in Queensland), and coconut oil and copra from Samoa to New Guinea and Micronesia. Burns Philp also built up a small coastal fleet and ventured into blackbirding; while for Godeffroys a large trading fleet gave a near monopoly of island agency work and bulking facilities. Like other Hamburg firms – Hennings, Ruge, Hedemann, A. Capelle, Eduard Hernsheim – they participated in the labour trade, as the plantation phase of commercial agriculture developed in the islands from the 1860s. Such firms also undertook services closer to banking, the organization of credit facilities, land sales, and the importation of specie, in the absence of such a sector in Pacific ports. The merchant was a money-lender; and the profitable transport of South American coin into nascent Polynesia markets parallels German importations of cowries into West African markets in the mid-nineteenth century.[11]

The long turnover period between collection, bulking, and final sale of staples accounts for merchant emphasis on high mark-up on merchandise through credit facilities. But much depended on the ability of island carriers to take advantage of the increased capacity of steam ships available by extension of lines from Europe to Singapore and Batavia and the Australian ports. It was not accidental, for example, that Burns Philp took a significant shareholding in the highly subsidized Queensland Shipping Company which operated Australian and Far Eastern mail contracts in the 1880s; or that the biggest challenge to the Queensland Company came from the combination of Mackinnon, Mackenzie and Company (from their base in Calcutta) and the Australian United Steam Navigation Company. And to these examples, one may add the linkage between Claus Spreckels – Californian sugar refiner and creator in 1881 of the Oceanic Steamship Company – and the Hawaiian sugar agencies he took over. In short, the techniques and finance of the Indian and Californian agencies, plus the development of coastal and long-haul lines, lay behind the cut-throat war of the second half of the nineteenth century over rates and contracts (assisted in the American case by cross investment from railway companies) Such was the essential background to the second phase of mercantile and agency investment in the south and north Pacific.[12] What is suggested here is that

Pacific mercantile and plantation development was transport-led from the 1860s and matched the demand for bulk staples. As a further proof one can point to Godeffroys' switch from coconut oil to sun-dried copra, once transhipment by Dutch steamship lines was available in Batavia from 1867; and to the cautious entry from a position of dominance in South Island ports by Union Steam Ship Company into Suva in 1880 to take advantage of bulk sugar cargoes, followed by rapid investment in vessels specially designed for Pacific conditions.[13]

At the beach and plantation end of production and collection, however, the generalized credit function of early partnerships deserves separate and comparative treatment in the history of Pacific business for a number of reasons. Apart from the lien established between merchant and borrower (whether trader, planter, or islander), extensive credit practices introduced rudimentary commercial legal practice through consular courts or occasionally through Australian or Californian courts. The spread of commercial law is very poorly documented in Pacific studies, in favour of a romanticized 'frontier' description of trading practices. But examination of more tedious correspondence in consular records – British, French, or American – soon reveals that a search for orderly litigation is one of the outstanding features of the growth of trade and settlement. The political consequences of legal conflict have been better charted than introduced notions of individualized property, mortgage and lease, interest rates and bankruptcy, accepted or contested quite early in Eastern Polynesia, Hawaii, Samoa, and Tonga.[14] It also needs to be remembered that early Pacific administrations – New Caledonia, Fiji, East Polynesia from the 1840s to the 1870s – unlike later administrations of the 1880s in territories with banking facilities, were among the indebted clients of merchants who negotiated drafts to meet local wages bills in periods of delayed remittances from Paris, London, or Sydney. A third feature is the restricted level of capitalization available for such ventures and reliance on reinvested profits, rather than further calls on capital or public subscription prior to the 1890s.

This feature requires more extensive documentation than can be given here; and it is fundamental to removing misconceptions prevalent in generalizations about European, Australasian, or American direct investment overseas.[15] In practice (and contrary to received wisdom about the availability of 'surplus' capital) it was quite difficult to raise speculative funding for distant ventures except from among those with a specialized knowledge of overseas markets. Consequently, restructuring into larger concerns which is a feature of mergers and commercial expansion from San Francisco, Sydney, Auckland, Hamburg, or Bordeaux into the Pacific from the late 1870s, as more capital was required, simply adapted elements of the partnership into a legally incorporated company with very limited shareholders. For example, when Burns Philp was incorporated in 1883 with a paid-up capital of £150,000, the two main partners and sixteen employees held most of the shares; and at the end of the 1880s there were still only seventy shareholders. Ventures were profitable and paid a dividend limited to 10 per cent till 1893, based mainly on sales of merchandise (55 per cent) and the rest from shipping and financial services. Similarly, when the Germany company – *Société commerciale de l'Océanie* – was formed out of Godeffroy interests in the late 1870s, with a limited capital of £116,000, shares were held by the Godeffroy family, the produce brokerage, Scharf & Kaiser, and C. Wilkens of Papeete. Tight control among family and associates remained a feature of both the Australian and the German companies and their cautious entry into plantation management, compared with more secure operations in banking, insurance, and shipping. As a result of such incorporations, of course, the measure of profitability becomes more accessible, rather than buried in partnership papers. Not many Pacific historians have faced up to the problems of accounting; but the few who have provided enough material for a revision of notions of 'monopoly'.[16] But as McLean notes (as author of one of the few Pacific business histories to supply profitability measures), 'statistics record success; they never adequately explain it'.[17] All of which raises the question why mercantile firms invested in plantations and what the financial advantage was, if any. It may be self-evident that sugar refiners and vegetable oil combines should do so. But they are relative late-comers to Pacific plantations, where the more usual form of investment was undertaken either directly by merchant houses or as form of sub-tenancy by planters who were staked by mercantile firms and merchants.

It emerges from studies of plantation agriculture that the basic reasons for investment in this form of production were really two. With regular steam communications, mercantile firms bought land and financed planters in order to assure supplies of cotton, copra, sugar for bulking and processing at regular intervals. This is a particular feature of early German land purchases in Fiji, Samoa, New Guinea; and it was carried over by Burns Philp, W.R. Carpenter, and others into Australian underwriting of plantations in New Guinea and the north Solomons. Such investment was also a hedge against future land and plantation values, of course, and an aspect of agency work. The latter diversification of services is a special feature of plantation management in Hawaii (to be examined later); but it was present earlier in acquisition of plantations and management by the *Société commerciale* in Tahiti and the Leeward Islands. The second reason is the more usual movement by refiners and vegetable oil processors vertically to sources of supply in the Solomons and Fiji (from Britain and Australia) and between California and Hawaiian sugar production as a movement by producers and agencies into refining.

The literature on mercantile and agency investment in plantations is quite extensive. The most detailed coverage of commercial agriculture is probably in Hawaii's history from the 1840s in the wake of the *Mahele* land sales (1849–51) and the 1876 Reciprocity Treaty which gave favoured entry to Hawaiian sugar. While the politics arising from those events have been well covered, the business history of capitalization and management of plantations by import-export agencies is less well-documented.[18] The aspect of concentration and bulking through Honolulu and many of the social linkages implicit in business relationships between planters and merchants are plain enough. But compared with studies of agency houses elsewhere – in Bombay, Calcutta, Madras, Zanzibar – many of the operational and financial aspects of this partial merger of interests are unclear. What is lacking are detailed accounts of the capital structures and levels of profitability of Brewers, Alexander & Baldwin, and Castle & Cooke in the older works by Sullivan, Dean, Taylor and others to match Michael Moynagh's study of the Colonial Sugar Refinery in Fiji.[19] The good news is that the Bishop Museum holds the papers of Theo H. Davies, sugar factor, and those of the Dillingham Corporation; and there are new repositories for the records of the Alexander and Baldwin Corporation and the Hawaiian Commercial and Sugar Company. Nevertheless, the history of plantation capital in Hawaii has serious gaps. It would be interesting to know the details of monopsony agreements, if any, on pricing for raw sugar, on labour recruitment and wages, and possibly on market shares in arrangements with Californian refiners, in the period before Hawaiian producers and agencies created 'C & H Sugar Refining' in 1906. Other features of this concentration follow established patterns: investment in transport and diversification into electricity, banking, Liberty House, and so forth. But so far the detailed history of the mergers and confiscations after 1898 through the 1930s is lacking and requires a composite study of the Big Five equal to Hawaii's excellent labour histories. Moreover, while monocultures attract historians, the diversification which has been a successful feature of Hawaii's business history has only recently been accounted for in Hawkins's unpublished thesis on the rise of canning and other industries.[20] While this is a valuable corrective, there are still questions unanswered about J.D. Dole's business record or the record of the pineapple co-operative association which only standard analysis of annual returns (if they exist) could answer.

The story, as we have it, of Papua's plantations is even less satisfactory. This is largely because attempts to write their history have concentrated on a sympathetic portrait of the smallholders and managers and avoided any analysis of the one complete set of plantation records we have for this area: the British New Guinea Development Company set up in 1910 as a political and commercial speculation with the blessing of Papua's administration by a limited number of Australian and British syndicates, single investors, and a few knighted capitalists.[21] Miraculously, it survived (we know not how) until relatively recently. In the case of German New Guinea we are better served and it is possible to account for the structure of plantation and agency companies during the Australian take-over as a vast rescue operation through the Expropriation Board with special terms for servicemen-planters set in place by Burns Philp, Carpenters, and the Commonwealth Bank.[22] By contrast with Hawaii, what emerges from the business history of commercial agriculture in Papua New Guinea is the failure of copra compared with sugar; the constant introduction of special measures for mortgage relief, mail subsidies, and protected navigation to rescue planters and their mercantile backers as an act of faith or patriotism; and the failure to diversify out of the strait-jacket of the Australian tariff system into local manufacturing through processing and exporting through the Far East direct to overseas markets.

The final plantation case study to be looked at briefly here is Moynagh's work on the CSR which is in many ways a model business history because of the quality of the sources available.[23] The features which contrast with Hawaii and Papua, however, reside more in the political influence of the company, its pressure against crop diversification, and manipulation of exchange rates, and its strategic withdrawal in 1973 at a favourable moment. Indeed, it has much more in common with other multinationals, as a sugar refinery, using planters in a form of *métayage*, practising transfer pricing and expatriating income on a large scale through debatable accounting (Head Office Expenses).

Histories of mining in the Pacific range from the romanticism of early alluvial gold in New Guinea to more ephemeral surveys of dramatic development led by some of the biggest conglomerates in the world. We shall have to wait for accounts of the operations of CRA, BHP or Placer and OK Tedi Mining Corporation in Bougainville and the Highlands.[24] So far, the one book we have on Ok Tedi by W.S. Pintz hardly takes us beyond the arrangement of contracts. In the meantime we shall have to make do with competent surveys which have the weakness that they make free with standard measures of company 'profits' and 'earnings' and the strength that they are good at seeking out political and banking linkages in Papua New Guinea or New Caledonia.[25] It is likely, however, that without better access to archives the emphasis will be, as in the past, on the labour content of mining costs and the social consequences, state taxation, and sources of revenue for developing economies. With the exception of some of the phosphate mining histories very little has been written so far to compare with works on major companies in Australia, Africa, or North America. And work on the Pacific Phosphate Company and the British Phosphate Commission has been particularly disappointing not to say anecdotal in its lengthy narrative of events and lack of analysis of business performance beyond export tonnages. It may be argued, of course, that the Phosphate Commission was not in the business of making 'profits', unlike its predecessor. But that is to dodge several important issues: namely, the acquisition at near-zero cost of phosphate-bearing lands on Nauru; the very high level of profitability enjoyed by the Pacific Phosphate Company which determined its purchase for £3.5 million;[26] and the need to provide the cheapest source of phosphates possible for Australian and New Zealand farmers compatible with running costs and miserable levels of royalties. The still unanswered question is how far was Antipodian agricultural production subsidized subsequently below world phosphate prices. Only a series worked out from the annual public reports of the Commissioners could go towards answering this question.[27]

An exception to these strictures – 'Atu Bain's thesis on Fiji gold mining – is both a model of what can be done with difficult source material and a cautionary tale on measures of profitability for the mines of the Emperor group. Rightly, from the author's viewpoint (with a labour theory of value in mind), considerable space is devoted to recruitment by group engagements, conditions of work, resistance and protest, and to the paternalism of the Fijian government towards the companies. The difficulty with this emphasis is that technology and the efficiency of the mines against the background of a fixed and then floating gold price are given little place; the usual measures are missing. But it is clear enough the mines were favoured to the extent of subsidies by government, though we are not given anywhere an analysis of labour costs as a percentage of total working costs (they were probably low). Measuring profits as a percentage of revenue, moreover, is a strange way of evaluating the performance of the group: it would be preferable to calculate profits as percentages of capital employed or of output.[28]

However, there are other features of great interest to business historians of the Pacific. One is a clear indication of a mining and merchant lobby headed by influential businessmen such as Sir Henry Scott and Sir Maynard Hedstrom whose activities in Fiji await further study. This oligarchy had great political and economic clout, and Australia's relations with the British colony can hardly be understood without work on their influence during and after the colonial period, especially as capital investment was institutionally rather than publicly subscribed (very few shares were offered on the Sydney Stock Exchange). The second feature is the very light taxation imposed – much lighter than in South Africa or Ghana, for example. One consequence has been the small contribution of gold mining to the Fijian economy; another is the total absence of a local small shareholder interest. Clearly, the topic has not been exhausted; but as in West Africa a study of the expatriate business community as a whole in the colonial and post-colonial periods is now called for.[29] A further possibility with parallels elsewhere is an account of Emperor Gold Mines activities in relation to the Alliance Party in patron–client terms, especially after the joint-venture with Western Mining in 1983 gave mining interests a greater stake in the stability of the political economy.

An understanding of businessmen beyond the general stereotypes depends, too, on biography and portraits of the Pacific entrepreneur set in perspective. So far the portrait gallery is richer in rogues from the hunter-gatherer phase of commercial ventures than revealing studies of decision-making at board level for major companies. Fortunately, hagiography seems to be limited to the Doles of Hawaii.[30] Governors fare better than businessmen in Pacific history;[31] and there are far fewer examples of biographical adulation than in African business history where Rhodes, Oppenheimer, Goldie, and Mackinnon have had to be revised downwards, as records have become available. Anne-Gabrielle Thompson's study of John Higginson (once compared with Rhodes) is a useful demonstration of the limitations of the genre, as historical explanation in business history, and a warning against taking such speculative ventures as the 'Caledonian Company of the New Hebrides' or the London Globe Mining Corporation (two of Higginson's inventions) at face value. In fact it turns out that he had very little to do with the centre piece of New Caledonia's economic history – *Société Le Nickel* – as he is sometimes supposed. Higginson, like Steinberger in Samoa, was more important for the people he duped than the firms he founded. He is the best example of a Pacific con man we have whose career yields hardly any information about the structures of plantation, land, and mining companies at an important period of New Caledonia's history – the change from plantations into cattle ranching and mining.[32] More usefully, the work that has been done on white planters in Papua New Guinea by David Lewis and Wendy Timms, or on Solomon Islands and Tanna trader-planters by Judith Bennett and Ron Adams, offers a firmer foundation for a typology of small-holder enterprise, but not a secure one for an evaluation of business success or failure.[33]

This survey suggests a number of themes to be followed up in teaching and supervising, if the Pacific field for business history is compared with other regions, or considered in relation to the political and social transformation which has dominated the literature. It might be conceded (as it was in African studies a couple of decades ago) that 'business' was unfashionable as an undertaking for the young historian – akin perhaps to consorting with the enemy in an academic climate inimical to 'capitalist' business culture.[34] Now (with an eye to the future job market?) this is less so; and a training in economic history, even an MBA, would not be thought strange for a Pacific historian.

Such investigators will find limitations in the source material. As in African business history, the content is heavy with 'economic activities' such as market trading, land concessions, and the politics of business lobbies, rather than the structure, performance, rise, decline, and economic importance of the enterprise. There is a further difficulty, more acute in Pacific studies than in Africa or Asia. That is the absence of pre-colonial business, apart from exchange cycles. In Pacific history, on a much smaller scale of accumulation and exchange of surplus, the problem, rather, is to explain the weakness of indigenous entrepreneurial activity in the colonial and post-colonial period. 'Bisnis' in the Highlands is not enough, compared with immigrant commerce and real efforts at commercial diversification in Tonga, Western Samoa, and the Cook Islands.[35] So far, island 'capitalism' lacks substantive comparative treatment at all levels of company formation. For the colonial period, there is a broad advance, strong on pioneers among the mercantile and planter groups, light on structures, mergers, profitability among the agricultural, forestry and extractive, transport and banking enterprises of the later nineteenth century and twentieth century. Sources for banking and the influence of chambers of commerce are not lacking. Perhaps a Pacific Business Archives Council is required to pull the references together.[36]

As we come to the end of Pacific empire, or its continuation by other means, one theme calls for examination – namely, the attitude of expatriate and local businessmen to the devolution of power to local politicians and parties. Historical examination of such attitudes has only just begun for Africa. But it has yielded the important result that, on the whole, reactions were tempered by the knowledge politicians could be managed in the initial phases of independence; and that most firms have adapted. In the Pacific the lines of communication used by companies for political ends bypassed much of the formal structure of the local secretariat, in the case of British territories, to gain a hearing in the Colonial Office. For Papua New Guinea there was also a direct route to Melbourne or to Canberra, but much more use was made of Commonwealth politicians. For the French territories a vigorous local press, chambers of commerce, and (at certain periods of representative government) the right to argue a commercial case directly with a colonial ministry have left a different set of records.

A second theme raises the more general question of a business, as well as an administrative, partition of Pacific territories. The question has been explored in the case of the partition of labour supplies in Melanesia and elsewhere which prefaced formal diplomatic division from 1885. But there is also the much larger carve-up by shipping companies of the trans-Pacific routes and bulk staple markets – an extension of the warfare for the Australasian and American coastal trades. Conversely, the history of rivalry and accommodation for the extension of commerce and services from the 'Anglo-Saxon' territories into French protected areas has yet to be written. Some of this duality of business and diplomacy is summed up, of course, in the history of that absurdity the New Hebrides Condominium which resulted from sustained Australian and French business and religious competition from bases in Melbourne, Sydney, and Noumea. But it is also present in the extension of tourist services, airline concessions and, in more subtle ways, in the scientific and aid-giving institutions of the post-war period of decolonization.[37]

Finally, there are larger problems implicit in Pacific business history, as elsewhere. One is whether the archetypal businessman as a risk-taker and combiner of the elements of production for profit has really survived into the age of managerial capitalism and the emergence of professionals in the operations of international companies. The topic of business leadership is bound up, moreover, with changes in methods of business finance through direct investment, joint ventures, curtailed repatriation, and complex tax concessions since the 1950s in all parts of the underdeveloped world. Political status matters in this area: Hawaii may look like an extension of Californian or Asian business, but Papua New Guinea or Fiji do not. Nor are they simply an extension of Australian business. What is not always recognized is that the 'metropole' as a source for finance is also multinational, less focused on several imperial capitals, and more open to funding through consortia, and less (in the British or Australian case) through the equity market.[38] In the long run the listing of public companies in Sydney, Melbourne, or London and Paris with interests in the Pacific islands may look exceptional, rather than the rule. The rule at the beginning (and now at the end of empire) was that private finance from banks, mortgage companies, and repatriated profits took the risk in uncertain markets for produce, land, transport, and other services. Nowadays, as earlier in Latin America or Africa, public issues are made to governments through banks or international fund-holders. The preference in business is for direct managed assets, not portfolio investment from a set of gullible institutions or private punters. Accordingly, since stock exchanges first appeared in Australia in 1871, there has been a rise and decline in South Sea bubbles, to the point where 'expatriate' investment is government negotiated at a diplomatic level with export credit guarantees and hopes of rescheduling later, rather than through the commercial venture at the level of the expatriate trader. That sea-change, too, has yet to be accurately charted in the Pacific.

NOTES

1. I am grateful to the editor of *Pacific Studies*, Dr Dale Robertson, for permission to reproduce this revised and extended version of an article which originated in surveys presented to the Pacific Islands Studies Occasional Seminar Series at the University of Hawaii and the Royal Society of New Zealand, Otago Branch, in January and April 1995. For a similar exercise, see A.G. Hopkins, 'Imperial Business in Africa, Part I Sources'; 'Part II Interpretations', *Journal of African History*, 18, 1, 2 (1976), 29–48 and 267–90; 'Big Business in African Studies', ibid., 28, 2 (1987), 119–40. Apart from the important omission of South African business studies, these surveys are the most perceptive commentary on areas of imperial business and can be read with Nicholas White, 'Government and Business in the Era of Decolonization: Malaya 1942–57', Ph.D. thesis, University of London, 1993. Stephanie Jones, *Merchants of the Raj*, (London, 1992); *Two Centuries of Overseas Trading: The Origins and Growth of the Inchcape Group* (London, 1986); and Stuart Rosewarne, 'Australian Imperialism in the Southwest Pacific, 1880–1940' (D.Phil. thesis, University of Sydney, 1985), for an indication of directions of research useful for Pacific historians.
2. Simon P. Ville, 'New Zealand Business History', *Business History*, 34, 2 (1992), 86–102. In mitigation for Ville's view it might be said we have had to wait until very recently for an account of the New Zealand Company as a business (see Patricia Burns, *Fatal Success*, London, 1989); it can be challenged, however, by the work of Gavin McLean, *The Southern Octopus: The Rise of a Shipping Empire* (Wellington, 1990), on Union Steamship Company and by older works, R.C.J. Stone, *Makers of Fortune* (Auckland, 1973). A concerted effort has been made to collect local business archives: see, for example, checklists, Hocken Library Extension, Archives and Manuscripts, Dunedin. Both the Australian National University and Melbourne University have considerable holdings of business records.
3. For the post-war period much can be gleaned on sectorial development from World Bank Country Studies: 1982 *Papua New Guinea Selected Development Issues* (Washington, 1982); *Papua New Guinea* (Washington, 1988), or from academic institutions specializing in the Pacific area such as the National Centre for Development Studies, Australian National University. For business development, banking surveys and company reports as well as the financial press are the most useful indicators of contemporary trends. See, too, *Asian Productivity Organisation, Corporate Culture and Productivity: Case Studies in Asia and the Pacific* (Tokyo, 1994) for an attempt to tackle the question of ethnicity and business from Fijian examples. Just how far 'developmental' studies have to go to include an account of business management in 'resource exploitation' can be seen in the recent overview by Stephen Henningham and R.J. May (eds.), *Resources, Development and Politics in the Pacific Islands* (Bathurst, 1992).
4. Richard U. Moench, *Economic Relations of the Chinese in the Society Islands* (Cambridge, MA, 1963) and David Wu, *The Chinese in Papua New Guinea, 1880–1980* (Hong Kong, 1982), are examples of the ethnic history genre without business records. For a different approach, see David Faure, 'The Lineage as Business Company: Patronage versus Law in the Development of Chinese Business', *The Second Conference on Modern Chinese Economic History* (Taiwan: The Institute of Economics, 1989), 347–76. For the beginnings of a vast post-war literature on the problems of island entrepreneurship, credit unions, 'companies', and co-operatives: V.D. Stace, *Report on Capital Formation Methods and Credit Facilities*

for Islanders in the South Pacific (Noumea: South Pacific Commission, 1962); T.S. Epstein, *Capitalism, Primitive and Modern: Some Aspects of Tolai Economic Growth* (Canberra, 1968).

5. J.A. Bennett, 'Wealth of the Solomons: A History of Trade, Plantations and Society, Solomon Islands, c.1800–1942', Ph.D. thesis, Australian National University, Canberra, 1979, iv; *Wealth of the Solomons: A History of a Pacific Archipelago, 1800–1979* (Honolulu, 1987).
6. Material relevant to Pacific staples can be found in Charlotte Leubuscher, *The Processing of Colonial Raw Materials: A Study in Location* (London, Colonial Office, 1951); and of course in the Customs Ledgers series of the Public Record Office, London, and territorial Blue Books. See, too, Catherine Snodgrass, *Copra and Coconut Oil* (Stanford University, Food Research Institute, 1928) for bibliography and statistics. A neglected source, apart from Rosewarne, 'Australian Imperialism', is the Australian Sydney Chamber of Commerce records and consulate records which provide a continuous commentary on Pacific staples and tariffs from the 1890s.
7. O.K.H. Spate, *The Pacific Since Magellan: Monopolists and Freebooters* (Canberra, 1983), 111–13; compare K.N. Chaudhuri, *The Trading World of Asia and the English East India Company, 1660–1760* (Cambridge, 1978).
8. Jones, *Two Centuries of Overseas Trading*; Margaret Steven, *Merchant Campbell 1769–1846: A Study in Colonial Trade* (Melbourne, 1965), 40–41, 100–2, 213, 242; D.R. Hainsworth, *Builders and Adventurers* (Melbourne, 1968), 37, 80, 106, 112–15, 165; Dorothy Shineberg, *They came for Sandalwood: A Study of the Sandalwood Trade in the South-West Pacific, 1830–1865* (Melbourne, 1967), ch.5.
9. Progression from 'hunter-gatherer' to company partnership and joint stock enterprise may be traced for example in Peter Slack and Dymphna Clark (eds.), *Eduard Hernsheim South Sea Merchant* (Boroko, Institute of Papua and New Guinea Studies, 1983). No one as yet has worked on the captured records of the Hernsheim company; and we do not know how successful his earlier partnership with Robertson was.
10. K. Buckley and K. Klugman, *The History of Burns Philp: The Australian Company in the South Pacific* (Sydney, 1981).
11. K. Buckley and K. Klugman, *The Australian Presence in the Pacific: Burns Philp 1914–1946* (Sydney, 1983), 118–19, for arguments against credit; Colin Newbury, *Tahiti Nui: Change and Survival in French Polynesia, 1767–1945* (Honolulu, 1980) 243–7.
12. Jones, *Two Centuries of Overseas Trading*, 139–42; Jacob Adler, *Claus Spreckels: The Sugar King in Hawaii* (Honolulu, 1966), 91; K. Schmack, *J.C. Godeffroy & Sohn, Kaufleute zu Hamburg: Leistung und Schicksal eines Wetlhandelshauses* (Hamburg, 1938).
13. McLean, *The Southern Octopus*, 37–40.
14. Deryck Scarr, 'Creditors and the House of Hennings: An Elegy from the Social and Economic History of Fiji', *Journal of Pacific History*, 7, 2 (1972), 104–7; Colin Newbury, 'Ho'o Tarahu: le crédit et le commerce en Polynésie orientale', *Journal de la Société des Océanistes*, 38, 74–5 (1985), 225–40; Bruce Knapman, 'Indigenous Involvement in the Cash Economy of Lau, Fiji, 1840–1946', *Journal of Pacific History*, 11, 3 (1976), 167–88.
15. Roger C. Thompson, 'Commerce, Christianity and Colonialism: the Australasian New Hebrides Company, 1883–1897', *Journal of Pacific History*, 6, (1971), 25–38; *Australian Imperialism in the Pacific: The Expansionist Era 1820–1920* (Melbourne, 1980); Rosewarne, 'Australian Imperialism'.
16. B. Knapman, *Fiji's Economic History, 1874–1939: Studies of Capitalist Colonial Development* (Canberra, 1987), ch.6; Buckley and Klugman, *The Australian Presence in the Pacific*, for measures of Burns Philp South Seas profits, but not for the parent company; McLean, *The Southern Octopus*; Newbury, *Tahiti Nui*, 242–54; Stewart Firth, 'German Firms in the Western Pacific Islands, 1857–1914', *Journal of Pacific History*, 8 (1973), 10–28; Rosewarne, 'Australian Imperialism', esp. ch.12 and table 9.5 which is unclear on basics such as net, gross, pre-tax and post-tax profits.
17. McLean, *The Southern Octopus*, 200.
18. The starting point for plantation business is still the rare work by J.A. Mollett, *Capital in Hawaiian Sugar: Its Formation and Relation to Labor and Output* (Hawaii Agricultural

Experiment Station, Honolulu, 1961). Business as part of agriculture is notably absent from the essays in Donald Denoon and Catherine Snowden (eds.), *A History of Agriculture in Papua New Guinea: a time to plant and a time to uproot* (Port Moresby, Institute of PNG Studies, 1981).

19. Arthur Dean, *Alexander & Baldwin Ltd. and the Predecessor Partnerships* (Honolulu, 1950); Josephine Sullivan, *A History of C. Brewer and Company Limited: One Hundred Years in the Hawaiian Islands, 1826–1926* (Boston, 1926); Frank J. Taylor, *From Land and Sea: The Story of Castle & Cook in Hawaii* (San Francisco, 1976); Michael Moynagh, *Brown or White? A History of the Fiji Sugar Industry, 1873–1973* (Canberra, 1981).
20. R.A. Hawkins, 'Economic Diversification in the American Pacific Territory of Hawaii, 1893–1941', Ph.D. thesis, London School of Economics, 1986.
21. David, Lewis, 'Planter Papua 1884–1942', Ph.D. thesis, The Australian National University, 1989.
22. We have little on companies' or planters' performance to compare with studies of labour recruitment and migration. But for the Expropriation Board period see Patricia Hopper, 'Kicking out the Hun', MA thesis, University of Papua New Guinea, 1980; Rosewarne, 'Australian Imperialism', ch.6; Newbury, 'The Long Apprenticeship: Labour in the Political Economy of New Guinea, 1915–1941', *Journal of Pacific Studies*, 18 (1995), 66–104; and for the post-war decline of some categories of Australian-managed plantations, Wendy Timms, 'The Post World War Two Colonial project and Australian Planters in Papua New Guinea: The search for relevance in the colonial twilight', Ph.D. thesis, The Australian National University, Canberra, 1996.
23. Moynagh, *Brown or White?* And compare, for example, Phillipe Chalmin, *Tate and Lyle: Géant du Sucre* (Paris, 1985), which also identifies the multinational features of the company.
24. Hank Nelson, *Black, White and Gold* (Canberra, 1976); A.M. Healy, *Bulolo: A History of the Development of the Bulolo Region* (Canberra, 1967); W.A. McGee and G.R. Henning, 'Investment in Lode Mining, Papua, 1878–1920', *Journal of Pacific History*, 24, 2 (1990), 244–59; C. O'Faircheallaigh, *Mining in the Papua New Guinea Economy, 1880–1980* (Port Moresby, 1982); W.S. Pintz, *Ok Tedi: Evolution of a Third World Mining Project* (London, 1984).
25. Michael C. Howard, *Mining Politics and Development in the South Pacific* (Boulder, CO, 1991).
26. Australian Archives, Canberra, CP 360/8, Hughes to Watt, 7 May 1919.
27. Maslyn Williams and Barrie MacDonald, *The Phosphateers: A History of the British Phosphate Commissioners and the Christmas Island Phosphate Commission* (Melbourne, 1985), 273–4 and *passim* for pricing arrangements, but no analysis of performance in what was a nationalized industry.
28. 'Atu Bain, *Labour and Gold in Fiji* (Cambridge, 1993).
29. See, for example, S.E. Stockwell, 'Political Strategies of British Business during Decolonization: The Case of the Gold Coast/Ghana, 1945–57', *Journal of Imperial and Commonwealth History*, 23, 2 (1995), 277–300; D.K. Fieldhouse, *Merchant Capital and Economic Decolonization: The United Africa Company, 1929–1987* (Oxford, 1994).
30. Rare examples outside short portraits in more general studies are: J.W. Davidson, *Peter Dillon of Vanikoro: Chevalier of the South Seas*, edited by O.K.H. Spate (Melbourne, 1975); Barry Rigby, 'Private Interests and the Origins of American Involvement in Samoa 1872–1877', *Journal of Pacific History*, 8 (1973), 75–87; Dorothy Shineberg (ed.), *The Trading Voyages of Andrew Cheyne, 1841–1844* (Canberra, 1971).
31. In this area J.K. Chapman, *The Career of Arthur Hamilton Gordon 1829–1912* (Toronto, 1965) requires revision for Gordon's (Lord Stanmore) later business career and connection with the Pacific Islands Company and the Pacific Phosphate Company.
32. Anne-Gabrielle Thompson, 'John Higginson 1839–1904: Patriot or Profiteer?', Ph.D. thesis, University of Queensland, 1982; 'The Use and Misuses of Capital: New Caledonia's Mining Industry, 1871–1901', *Journal of Pacific History*, 18, 1–2 (1984), 66–82.
33. Ron Adams, 'Les parias de la civilisation, négociants et planteurs à Tanna', *Le peuplement du Pacifiques et de la Nouvelle Calédonie au xixe siècle: Condamnés, colons, convicts,*

coolies, Chan Dang (Paris, 1993), 370–84; J. Bennett, *Wealth of the Solomons: A History of a Pacific Archipelago, 1800–1978* (Honolulu, 1987); Timms, 'The Post World War Two Colonial Project'.

34. A.A. Graves, 'The Abolition of the Queensland Labour Trade: Politics or Profits', in E.L. Wheelwright and Ken Buckley, *Essays in the Political Economy of Australian Capitalism*, vol.4 (Sydney, 1980).
35. Te'o Fairbairn, *Island Entrepreneurs: Problems and Performance in the Pacific* (Honolulu, 1988); Richard P.C. Brown and John Connell, *Entrepreneurs in the Emergent Economy: Migration, Remittances and Informal Markets in the Kingdom of Tonga* (Canberra, 1993); Richard P.C. Brown and John Foster, 'Remittances and Savings in Migrant Sending Countries', *Pacific Economic Bulletin*, 9, 2 (1994), 27–34; Doug and Teloma Munro, 'The Rise and Fall of the Vaitapu Company', *Journal of Pacific History*, 19, 3–4 (1985), 174–90; Knapman, 'Indigenous Involvement in the Cash Economy of Lau, Fiji, 1840–1946', ibid., 11, 3 (1976), 167–88; Ben R. Finney, *Polynesian Peasants and Proletarians: Socio-Economic Change among the Tahitians of French Polynesia* (Wellington, Polynesian Society Reprints Series No.9, 1965).
36. For example the archives of Westpac Corporation (the former ANZ Banking group), Melbourne, are open to researchers; and see the important thesis by Ganjo Yasuo, *The History of the Banque de l'Indochine (1875–1939); French imperialism in the Far East* (Tokyo, 1985), translated for the Comité pour l'histoire économique et financière de la France, Paris, 1993.
37. Stephen Bates, *The South Pacific Island Countries and France: A Study in Inter-State Relations* (Canberra, 1990). And see the competing agencies listed in Rosemary Cassidy, *Mind Your Business* (Suva, South Pacific Economic Commission, 1987).
38. It is possible the investment tide from Australia and New Zealand has ebbed: see the observations on this point in Ron Crocombe, *New Zealand's Relations with Other Pacific Islands/Aotearoa me Nga Moutere o te Moana Nui a Kiwa* (Christchurch, 1992).

David Fieldhouse and 'Imperialism': Some Historiographical Revisions

STEPHEN HOWE

Edward Said, in his *Culture and Imperialism*, offers a graceful little bow to David Fieldhouse as a 'distinguished conservative historian of empire'. He goes on, however, to quote Fieldhouse as advancing a proposition that is certainly central to Said's ideas about imperialism, but has been decidedly marginal to Fieldhouse's: that imperial authority depended finally on mental attitudes, rather than on economic clout or military might. The colonized's 'acceptance of subordination – whether through a positive sense of common interest with the parent state, or through inability to conceive of any alternative – made empire durable'.[1]

Fieldhouse's immediate reference point in the passage quoted was, as Said acknowledges, quite specifically to white settler colonists in the Americas. Said wishes to extend the point much more generally: it is by no means clear that Fieldhouse would agree. His work, from the earliest to the most recent, has featured collaborative or other attitudes among the colonized only as a very minor theme. Where the issue is touched upon, as at various points in his *Economics and Empire*, it is largely with reference to relations between pre-colonial states and informal imperialists; and generally stresses that such relationships were 'never entirely satisfactory or stable'. Their widespread breakdown in the late Victorian era is, indeed, the key to the 'peripheral' theory of colonial expansion for which Fieldhouse is known. Almost everywhere, 'indigenous collaboration ended in alien rule before 1914'.[2] So far as the attitudes of colonizers are concerned, Fieldhouse's earliest work placed great explanatory stress on the irrational popular imperialism or 'jingoism' of the late nineteenth century. Subsequently, however, he has been associated with – indeed identified as the strongest, most systematic proponent of – the view that neither the policy-makers nor the popular masses of Europe ever displayed much enthusiasm for imperial expansion. Empire-building is to be explained mainly neither by their desires nor by the calculations of economic advantage. Rather, it is to be found on the peripheries, in the areas of expansion themselves. In

Fieldhouse's most famous programmatic formulation, 'most men of power and responsibility found it necessary to build formal empires because the tide of events swept them past all alternative solutions to the rapidly worsening crisis on the periphery. Colonialism was not a preference but a last resort'.[3]

It may seem a little quixotic, then, to seek to bring David Fieldhouse and Edward Said into dialogue, to write about relations between Fieldhouse's work and the recent explosion of radical, leftwing, and post-colonialist theorizing about empires which Said effectively initiated. One could not well imagine two kinds of writing, ostensibly about the same broad subject, which have less in common. That, none the less, is what this article tries to do.

The great growth area in studies of empires and their aftermaths since the 1980s has been in cultural history and theory, fields fairly distant from Fieldhouse's primarily economic focus. Though much of this writing has been interdisciplinary, and has engaged growing numbers of historians (and indeed anthropologists and, now, political theorists), it has involved primarily literary critics and cultural theorists. It has been strongly shaped by post-structuralist, post-modernist, and discourse-analytical currents, none of which has had any place in Fieldhouse's writing. None of its gurus – Edward Said or Michel Foucault, Jacques Derrida or Jacques Lacan, Roland Barthes or Antonio Gramsci – has featured in his books: the very idea that they might have done so seems faintly absurd. More surprising is the converse; the sparseness of reference to Fieldhouse's work among cultural theorists of colonialism.[4] Our surprise at this may diminish, however, when we realize how many of these theorists appear not to have read *any* significant modern historical work about empire. Even stylistically, the gulf is huge. Fieldhouse's literary style is marked above all by its elegant austerity. That of many recent writers on colonial cultures, by contrast, is dense with allusion, metaphor, wordplay, and sometimes, for that matter, wilful obscurity. To move from his work to that of the colonial literary theorists is to travel from the savannah – a clear, hard-edged landscape, perhaps a little arid but with wide horizons and long views – to the exuberance, the profligacy, the density, and the murk of the rainforest.

Perhaps most obviously, the past decade or more's huge outpouring of colonial and post-colonial cultural history and theory has been, almost without exception, consciously and self-proclaimedly radical or anti-imperialist in intent. Fieldhouse, conversely, is usually identified as a conservative historian, one who has refused to see colonialism as either crime or conspiracy, has emphasized the honesty, efficiency, and selfless concern for their subjects of most colonial administrators,[5] and has offered nuanced but on overall balance favourable appraisals of colonialism's economic record. Empire, as Fieldhouse summarizes his case, was indeed 'economically conservative';[6] but this was by no means always a bad thing, as is indicated by the widespread post-colonial failure, especially in Africa, to achieve industrial takeoff through more radical, freespending policies.[7]

Here, in his assessment of empire's economic effects and legacies, David Fieldhouse's work is also sharply at odds with that of most radical, and especially Marxist, scholars: but in this case by way of sharp dispute rather than apparent mutual disregard. If there have seemed to be few obvious points of contact between his ideas and those of recent leftwing critics of empire, then by contrast his engagement with an older, mostly economically based, anti-colonialist literature has been lifelong and close. We shall make some brief comments on this engagement, before turning to ask what relationships there might yet come to be between Fieldhouse's work and the newer radical historiography of empire.

A great deal of David Fieldhouse's career has been spent in dialogue with Marxism. His most influential early article, and an equally influential collection which he edited, were devoted to dissection – and hostile critique – of the 'theory of capitalist imperialism' largely associated with Marxist thinkers and especially Lenin, though of course the radical-liberal J.A. Hobson was also exemplar of a slightly different version. All three of his broad surveys of colonial history, especially *Economics and Empire*, give considerable space to negative evaluation of Marxist and other radical views on the colonial record. An important historiographical overview of economic decolonization published in 1982, too, gave particular attention to changing Marxist interpretations of the phenomenon.[8] Major parts of his more recent books *Unilever Overseas* and *Merchant Capital and Economic Decolonization* seek to test specifically Marxist hypotheses about the character of capitalist overseas direct investment, its motivation, its effect on host countries, its relationship with colonial rule and decolonization, and the extent and direction of net transfers of resources between countries involved.[9]

His characteristic approach in this critical writing is to give brief, explicit presentation to one or more hypotheses, and then match them against the evidence. Frequently, he will insist on the inadequacy of the available evidence, or the extent to which historians' views remain bound by circumstance or the sheer shortness of time which has elapsed since the events discussed. On occasion, perhaps, he will over-insist on this: the opening paragraphs of both 'Decolonization, Development, and Dependence' and 'Multinational Corporations Reconsidered' appear to deny the intention or possibility of answering questions to which those articles' later pages *do* in fact propose answers. Sometimes, also, the presentation of the views being criticized might be thought *too* brief, so that where the hypotheses (or indeed dogmas and myths) concerned are ones he is predisposed to disprove, there is danger of their being caricatured through simplification. Arguably, he has sometimes done this with Marxist and dependency theories, underrating their internal variety.[10] Still, these procedures are vastly preferable to the undeniable tendency in much radical scholarship on empire – especially, as we shall see, among theorists of colonial culture and discourse – not to offer *any* testable propositions, as opposed to emotive affirmations, and to operate without any apparent guidelines as to what constitutes historical evidence.

Fieldhouse's organizing principle across more than thirty years' writing in this vein, then, was that proclaimed in a recent overview of the British imperial economic balance-sheet. 'There are two conflicting interpretations of empire – as a mutual self-help association or as an engine to enable capitalism to maximize the exploitation of colonies.'[11] He associated these views respectively with 'imperialist' and 'anti-imperialist' positions. Put in those stark terms, it hardly needs arguing that the 'anti-imperialist' economic case, in its old forms, has long since collapsed. It is almost self-evident, in the late 1990s, that the negative critique of the 'theory of capitalist imperialism' has won the day. In large part, though, one suspects that the rapid decline in popularity for the concept of capitalist economic imperialism is attributable less to the actual historical arguments involved than to the general political collapse of Marxism, and more especially of Lenin's legacy. Moreover, neither the Lenin-Hobson theory nor the vast body of rival and often more interesting Marxist-influenced theories have been interrogated and found wanting by contemporary cultural radicals. Rather, they have been discarded unexamined, as useless baggage encumbering the last decade or two's flight from Moscow, from structural Marxism. One result is that we still see reproduced today much of the characteristic rhetoric of an old metropolitan anti-colonialism, indeed often that of the 1920s Comintern, but now stripped of its Marxist clothing and reworked as a cultural nationalist and even, paradoxically, a post-modernist discourse.

In more recent years, therefore, anti-colonialist writing has shifted emphasis from economics to culture. The predominant negative view has been one depicting colonial empires not now as engines of economic exploitation, but of cultural alienation and oppression. Some writers in this vein still proclaim themselves Marxists; many more display strong if sometimes submerged Marxian influences; but very few engage in any serious way with economic analysis. Fieldhouse's work is, one could say with only a touch of irony, rather more Marxist than theirs. It is a more powerful, and single-minded, exposition of the 'logic of capital' and a 'modes of production narrative' than almost anything by latter-day Marxist or other radical critics of empire. Fieldhouse criticizes the specific economic arguments put forward by Marxists and indeed Hobsonians, but rarely if ever attacks such theorists for economic determinism or reductionism: the standard complaint against them in other quarters.

Without seeking to minimize the aspects of vicious exploitation or, at least as often, culpable neglect which characterized centre-periphery economic relations under colonialism, even radicals now might question whether colonial rule was not often, as Fieldhouse suggests, the lesser of two evils facing non-European societies in the nineteenth century: 'the out-thrust of Europe and North America was so strong and the capacity of most other societies to resist or make constructive use of that force so limited, that the realistic alternative to formal imperial rule was widespread anarchy'.[12] Or if not anarchy, then perhaps stagnation. Some Asian and African societies might have possessed, or had the potential to develop, state apparatuses capable of 'catching up' with Europe's economic, bureaucratic, and technological lead – Japan of course, maybe Egypt or Iran, Morocco, Turkey, even Benin. Most, however, probably did not; and it is at least plausible that they developed more rapidly under European rule than they would otherwise have done, as Fieldhouse has argued. That was, after all, Karl Marx's own view of the matter. Contemporary radical post-colonial writers have repeatedly denounced Marx's stance on empire for its Eurocentrism, its cultural arrogance, and its ignorance about non-European histories. All the charges are true enough: Marx was very much a Victorian western European in his assumptions. But a basic question has been systematically bypassed and even rendered unthinkable by the current hegemony among radicals of a highly moralistic kind of anti-colonialism: was his evaluation of the likely alternatives essentially correct? Those modern writers, like Bill Warren, who have responded in the affirmative and reiterated the case for imperialism's historically progressive role, have been marginalized in current debate.[13]

Many or even most aspects of Fieldhouse's critique of Marxist 'anti-imperialism', therefore, are no longer – at least for the present – in serious dispute. The opposition has abandoned the field, or completely shifted the ground of its attack on the colonial legacy. This is far less evidently the case for his more recent work, dealing with the more immediate past and present. Fieldhouse's qualified defence of multinational companies' operations in late colonial and post-colonial settings retains a considerable controversial charge. He posed the issues in dispute over multinationals as he had sometimes done with earlier, related discussions – in terms of an extremely stark opposition between what he called his own 'open-ended approach' (shared by 'most ideologically non-dogmatic economists') and 'Marxists, who believe that capitalism is exploitative under all possible conditions', but who further hold that 'while all capitalism exploits, direct foreign investment exploits absolutely'.[14] In fact the views which Fieldhouse counterposes to his own are, as he appears later to acknowledge, not those of Marx or ones to which Marxists as such are necessarily committed, but those of the 'dependency' and 'underdevelopment' theory of the 1960s and after. Yet since only non-Marxists, according to Fieldhouse, could consider even 'a theoretical possibility that a host country may stand to gain from direct foreign investment if this is properly handled by both sides', it is only with non-Marxists that debate is possible.[15]

More substantive and perhaps less problematic are Fieldhouse's arguments on economic decolonization. His crucial contention here is that, contrary to a view widely propounded on the left, 'decolonisation made a fundamental difference to the relationship between foreign capital and the host society because after independence the host government for the first time had the power, if it chose to use it, to regulate the activities of a foreign enterprise in any way it chose; and that in this new relationship even a very large company such as Unilever was weak by comparison with the government of even a small country, provided its function was to manufacture for the local market.'[16] Again, denial of such claims and insistence that political independence makes no real difference would appear to be something to which Marxists did not necessarily subscribe, though proponents of 'strong' or 'hard' versions of dependency theory tended to do so.

Yet radical analysts, even if not holding to the dogmas Fieldhouse attributes to them, would still most likely have difficulty with his discussion of post-colonial relations, especially those between new states and multinationals. In arguing that it is at best a gross overstatement to see multinationals as a new imperialist system, and that if their power is in any sense a third colonial occupation, then 'it must be said that the gates were opened from inside', he relies on highly suppositional claims about the power of state sovereignty. 'A determined state will normally act as it wishes and risk the consequences...it is the state that now holds most of the cards and can determine the rules of the game.'[17] This bold general claim, one might venture, needs more detailed substantiation than Fieldhouse has thought it relevant to provide.

In *Unilever Overseas*, Fieldhouse's main interest was 'to test some of the generalised statements made about the character of direct foreign investment in less developed countries'.[18] Why should a company choose to invest in production or establish manufacturing facilities overseas rather than exporting from its original home base? Were colonial status or its ending important factors in such calculations? A major subsidiary aim of *Unilever Overseas* was thus 'to investigate whether colonialism was attractive to a foreign firm contemplating overseas investment and, conversely, whether decolonisation deterred new investment and adversely affected the operations of existing enterprises'.[19]

His findings are more nuanced than the stark counterposition of worldviews cited above might have led readers to expect. The Indian case among others, in Fieldhouse's view, suggests that: 'There was nothing in colonialism as such to attract direct foreign investment in manufacturing for local consumption.' However, once established, colonial regimes of low taxation and weak local competition 'probably' meant conditions... peculiarly conducive to success'.[20] This appears a paradoxical 'conclusion. Little less paradoxical is that Unilever in South Asia appeared to flourish better in heavily planned economies with governments supposedly hostile to foreign business than in seemingly more welcoming political climates.

In relation to Nigeria, colonial status is accorded a different kind of significance. With the growth of nationalism and rapid political change there after 1954, 'Unilever had for the first time had to take account of political factors – which now meant the attitudes and aspirations of Nigerians rather than expatriate administrators – and also to think of regions rather than Nigeria as a whole. That is, business criteria were no longer conclusive. As in other countries... this marked the essential difference between colonialism and independence.'[21] The clear implication is that the peculiarity of colonial conditions for business was the sheer lack of necessity for political calculation. Otherwise, for black Africa in general, the basic problem for multinationals was quite simply the continent's poverty and thus limited consumer demand. This was compounded by the smallness of most African political units and thus of domestic markets. These inhibitions applied to both colonial and independence eras, and were relatively little affected by political change.[22]

From studying Unilever, Fieldhouse turned – in an even larger book – to its mighty and semi-autonomous subsidiary the United Africa Company. If Unilever's other colonial and post-colonial subsidiaries were largely manufacturing for local markets, the UAC was a key colonial instance of 'merchant capital' – trading in commodities and the products of pre-capitalist industry. This again underlines the 'Marxist' side of Fieldhouse's work, for the book's main organizing concept, merchant capitalism, is of course taken from Marx. With the rise both of modern industry and of 'finance capital', merchant capitalist enterprises were likely – as Marx had predicted – to be 'squeezed out'. And the kinds of activity of which UAC was the greatest modern example 'did indeed flourish best in economies which most closely resembled those of the West in its pre-industrial phase

– countries which had not yet developed modern industry and could not provide for themselves the financial and commercial services essential if they were to be linked by trade with the developed economies of the West'.[23] Until about the 1920s, these included a large part of Asia; but thereafter in places like India merchant capital found its role usurped either by local capitalists or by the growth of modern industry and finance.

Only in Africa, the most underdeveloped major region of the world economy, did merchant capital as represented by UAC still have the conditions to flourish – and there too developments of the 1950s and sixties gradually removed those conditions. The changes that limited (while not entirely removing) UAC's role were not so much political decolonization itself – indeed UAC, like Unilever, for some time saw independence as providing more new opportunities than new dangers – as what Fieldhouse labels 'economic decolonisation': 'by which I mean the process by which the African countries, once politically independent, used their sovereignty to cast off, or at least limit, the power of foreign merchant capital'.[24] Here again, Fieldhouse argues that political independence had real and major economic effects, even if these were by no means always the effects for which nationalists themselves had hoped. That failure of hopes, however, stemmed not mainly from colonial legacies, or continued dependence as such, or from the activities of the multinationals, but – as Fieldhouse had argued at length in his *Black Africa* – from the mistaken policies of the post-independence governments themselves, and their consequent inability to ensure either economic or political stability.

The upshot may appear, like Fieldhouse's view of the dominance of peripheral factors in causing imperial expansion, largely to absolve the metropolitan centres of responsibility. Whether in the 1880s or the 1990s, 'the gates were opened from inside', and conquerors or exploiters entered innocently, reluctantly. Subsequent disasters have been first and foremost the responsibility of indigenous colonial and post-colonial elites, of their incompetence, self-interest or malevolence. Leftist and post-colonial critics' disagreements with Fielhouse's recent writing are likely to centre here, on what Wolfgang Mommsen called 'the exculpatory effect of this theory'.[25] As yet, however, the ratio of genuine refutation to denunciation among such critics has been low. And on the other hand, Fieldhouse's arguments that the multinationals are weaker and even small states stronger than often thought, that the former's global reach is far less of a novelty than radicals tend to believe, has found powerful recent support from some leftwing scholars; while the dependency theory against which he polemicized has withered away in scholarly repute almost as thoroughly as has the theory of capitalist imperialism.[26]

In a broad survey article published in 1984, Fieldhouse asked whether imperial history could once again be constituted as a coherent subject. It had, he argued with evident truth, increasingly fragmented into disparate national and regional histories, as a direct consequence of political decolonization itself.[27] Although Fieldhouse concluded that imperial history *did* still exist, it was as not as a unitary state but as a loose federation with indeterminate boundaries and secessionary tendencies. In the subsequent decade or so, a major reintegrative move has taken place. It came from a quarter which Fieldhouse did not discuss, and clearly had not anticipated: from literary and cultural theory, with ever more vigorous offshoots into cultural history, and centred around the concept of colonial discourse. The main intellectual approach by which this new integration, or even homogenization, has been undertaken is thus what has become known as colonial discourse analysis. Colonial discourse theory sees colonial power everywhere, seeping into, controlling, transforming every aspect, every tiny detail of colonized societies. The writings and attitudes of those involved with empire are seen as constituting a system, a network, a discourse in the sense made famous by Michel Foucault. It inextricably combines the production of knowledge with the exercise of power. It deals in stereotypes and polar antitheses. It has both justificatory and repressive functions. And, perhaps above all, it *is* an 'it': colonial discourse and by extension the categories in which it deals (the colonizer, the colonized, the subject people, and so forth) can fruitfully be discussed in unitary, abstract, unsituated terms.

The polemical literature debating such approaches is already substantial – including some fairly sharp and sweeping dismissals from more 'traditional' historians – as is that of summary, synthesis, and selection, aimed at students on the mushrooming global industry of 'Post-colonial Studies' courses.[28] The reasons for negative judgement on much of this work are manifold. Theories of colonial discourse, and perhaps post-colonial cultural studies more generally, have often seemed quite unclear, apparently confused, as to what they have meant by colonialism. Partly for that reason, they have habitually greatly overstated the significance of colonialism for culture, and of culture for colonialism.

'Colonialism', the term itself, has been put to ever wider and more problematic uses: the concept has undertaken its own colonizing march. In some hands, colonialism appears to become coterminous with modernity, as in Timothy Mitchell's remarkable book *Colonising Egypt*, where 'Colonising refers not simply to the establishing of a European presence but also to the spread of a political order that inscribes in the social world a new conception of space, new forms of personhood, and a new means of manufacturing the experience of the real.'[29] Somewhat similarly, Nicholas Thomas relies on Foucaultian notions of governmentality to claim that 'In effect, modernity itself can be understood as a colonialist project in the special sense that both the societies internal to western nations, and those they possessed, administered, and reformed elsewhere, were understood as objects to be surveyed, regulated, and sanitized.'[30] At the most sweeping and worst, colonialism becomes identical with domination as such, as with Houston A. Baker's *Workings of the Spirit*, where the image of 'the colonizer' is introduced, as 'a sign that we shall employ for dominant and dominating authority' – thus emptying it of all specificity or analytical distinctiveness.[31]

Much current writing in this vein treats colonialism as homogenous and all-powerful, and uses the term to denote patterns of domination, or even merely of transregional contact, preceding, succeeding, or indeed substantially disengaged from periods of actual conquest, possession, and rule. Calling all these sorts of things 'colonial' not only denies or underrates historical variety and heterogeneity. It also teleologically projects kinds of Western dominance and non-European subalternity associated with the formal colonial period or even with late twentieth century images backwards – missing or misrepresenting a whole less formalized sphere of culture contact and interchange, and the very long periods when trading or other relations were *equal*, or when Europe itself was the 'periphery' and the 'backward' partner.

In part what is wrong has a disciplinary origin: the presumption that the tools and techniques of literary criticism can stand in for those of historical, social, and economic analysis. It is, to the historian, an evident methodological absurdity to base general claims about colonial mentalities on a single text. Yet the few individual colonial texts and incidents discussed – or more often merely mentioned – in work in this vein, too often function not, as in Geertzian 'thick description', as symptoms of wider social phenomena, but merely as perfunctory pegs on which to hang sweeping assertions about a generalized colonial situation. Claims initially made about the forms and reception of specific literary texts are then illegitimately generalized into claims about the historical and political situations from which such texts derive. The texts are often assumed to express a shared European mentality, the sentiments of a unified, conquering elite, its European agents as an abstract force. Historians, on their part, have long used snippets of literary material to support or illustrate historical arguments: almost inevitably in an impressionistic and almost haphazard way. The cultural studies of colonial discourse often effectively reverse the relationship without in any way improving it: using little odds and ends of historical evidence, or uncritical invocations of an extremely restricted range of historical writing, to provide ostensible support for arguments about literary texts.

There has been a tendency simply to assume that colonial expansion was both ubiquitously constitutive of metropolitan British culture, and equally crucially dependent on it – that culture was (and is) colonialist and colonialism cultural. So far as previous historians or cultural critics fail to recognize these taken-for-granted truths, they are damned both for insularity and for sliding into economic determinism. As Bruce Robbins notes in an acute critique, there is a kind of allegorical vulgar Freudianism in which empire becomes the universal unconscious of nineteenth-century culture, 'a repressed but definitive truth that is always already obliged to return'. This ignores both the 'non-cultural dynamics' of imperialism and the extent to which empire was *not* necessarily always present in metropolitan culture.[32]

In much contemporary writing, colonialism is seen as not only ubiquitous and all-powerful but as having literally and fully created that which it claimed to find in colonized societies. Such perspectives, probably most fully and powerfully argued for British India by Ronald Inden,[33] but with dozens of cruder expressions in less skilled hands, not only greatly overstate the inventive capacity of British rulers and understate that of their subjects, but make it impossible to investigate important continuities between pre-colonial and colonial history. Such a vision may be true to Foucault's programme, but it simply is *not* true to the colonial record itself. Colonized cultures were very often more resilient, and the colonial impact patchier, more superficial, less systematic, less effectual, than is assumed. The documents of colonial administration itself may sometimes create an image of unchallenged dominance, of utterly transformed social order. But – to take just one regional example, that of Anglophone West Africa – no reader of Chinua Achebe or Kwame Appiah, Kwasi Wiredu or Wole Soyinka, Adu Boahen or Ade Ajayi, could doubt either the strength of cultural continuities, or the richness of adaptive patterns which simply cannot be reduced to a simple dialectic of domination and resistance.

The relationship between knowledge and colonial power is either seen in crudely and ahistorically instrumentalist terms, or (sometimes, quite inconsistently, by the same authors) collapsed into indeterminacy by a vulgar-Foucaultian claim that knowledge and power are identical. Such rhetorical modes make it simply impossible to understand the widely varying relationships between intellectual predisposition and political project evidenced even among those who combined the roles of scholar and administrator – such as, for instance, the strikingly different understandings of their roles, and of African Islamic societies, taken by the remarkable succession of ethnologist-administrators in French West Africa: Francois Clozel, Maurice Delafosse, and Paul Marty.[34] Even more obvious, and deriving heavily from the disciplinary backgrounds and social milieux of the scholars concerned, is an overwhelming culturalist bias: indeed a cultural reductionism which is mirror-image of the economic reductionism typical of some parts of the Marxist tradition. There is no apparent interest whatsoever in the economics of colonial or post-colonial relations – and where passing references are made to these, they are most often by way of ill-understood claims derived from 'hard' versions of dependency theory.[35]

The ideas of David Fieldhouse and other, mostly older, political and economic theorists of imperialism can provide an important corrective to all these weaknesses. The corrective lies above all in their typical scepticism about the effective force of colonialist self-presentations. Ideologies of empire, as they insist, were far more often *ex post facto* rationalizations for acts of expansion undertaken for a very wide range of reasons, opportunistically driven by crisis, or by the availability of new means of domination (technological and other), rather than by the ideology itself. Understanding the colonialism of the nineteenth and twentieth centuries may in many ways be furthered more by attention to these means – for instance, the technological innovations which, for a time, produced a vast inequality of military, communications, and governing capacities between European and non-European societies – than by investigation of colonial ideologies or discourses. Colonial rule was indeed in large measure, as Fieldhouse puts it, 'a complex improvisation' rather than the putting into practice of a coherent plan.[36]

Fieldhouse provides, too, an important reminder to much colonial cultural theory in his frequent insistence that colonialism is very specifically a political phenomenon, a matter of the state. Any coherent analysis or even definition of it must bear this constantly in mind, retaining the recognition that its core is a juridical relation between a state and a territory; one in which the colonizing state took complete power over the government of the territory which it had annexed. Much contemporary theory silently abandons this focus, and inexplicitly (indeed, most often apparently unknowingly) substitutes at best a notion of a colonialism of civil society, at worst a purely discursive conception of colonial power. The former focuses on interest groups, religious bodies, educational institutions, and so on, whilst almost invariably failing to specify the relationship of their projects to colonial state power. Insofar as it is at all theoretically explicit, other than about its relations to earlier *literary* theory, it again takes much of its inspiration from the later Foucault, with his rejection of attention to the state as privileged source or instance of power. Within the general neglect of colonialism as a specifically political phenomenon, there has been an especial failure to retain due weight for what Fieldhouse called 'the imperialism of the statesmen', as well as that of the district officers, the permanent secretaries, and the colonels.

Much post-structuralist theory, of course, goes further, spurning not only the state but society as an object of analysis. Here colonial discourse analysis connects with the 'linguistic turn' in social and historical studies more generally in its rejection of social explanation and very often of totalizing explanation *tout court*.[37] Or rather, its ostensible rejection; for in fact very sweeping kinds of general claim about 'the colonial situation' are characteristic. In the more rigid kinds of colonial discourse analysis, colonialism is not only often homogenized and endowed with agency, rationality, ubiquity; it is granted a kind of transhistorical intentionality. Contemporary scholars, especially those in literary and cultural theory, very frequently assume that European colonialism was a wholly willed phenomenon (the main exceptions are traditional, orthodox Marxists who see it as an inevitable stage in the development of world capitalism). The assumption may seem natural enough; but it is made without argument or evidence. To indicate the problems with it, it may help to reiterate the Fieldhouse view:

> In the nineteenth century the out-thrust of Europe and North America was so strong and the capacity of most other societies to resist or make constructive use of that force so limited, that the realistic alternative to formal imperial rule was widespread anarchy. Many indigenous rulers recognized this clearly and invited foreign 'protection' to avert the danger ... Colonialism was thus a virtually automatic reflex on both sides of the relationship to acute problems of international relations.
>
> If colonialism is seen in this way, rather than as a deliberately constructed system of international servitude, it is not surprising that it should have been riddled with internal contradictions. On the one hand it came to be seen as an unwanted burden for the imperialists ... On the other hand it came increasingly to be regarded by subject peoples ... as an intolerable affront to the dignity of their own people ... This was the dialectic of colonialism as an historical phenomenon. In its beginning was its end.[38]

We have centred on weaknesses – not to say absurdities – widely present in the post-Saidian mushrooming of colonial cultural studies, and suggested that renewed emphasis on some of the dominant motifs in David Fieldhouse's work may act as much-needed therapy for its excesses. Yet the paroxysm of academic production in these areas has also had enormous strengths. By far the largest outpouring of new work has been in literary studies, from repeated dissection of such predictable figures as Conrad or Kipling to ingenious if not desperate efforts to register the supposed centrality of colonial themes in such unpromising *oeuvres* as those of Thomas Hardy, Elizabeth Gaskell, and Lewis Carroll. It is here, in literary criticism, that colonial cultural studies first took off; and here that much of the most derivative, historically ill-informed, and preposterous work has appeared. But there has been a substantial body of writing also on colonialism in relation not only to visual, musical, and other arts, but to almost every conceivable theme in cultural and social history: colonialism and sex, gender roles, science, technology, medicine, disease, madness, travel, education, religion, childhood, the press, geography, zoology, botany, time, crime, language, sport, photography, mathematics, archaeology ... up to and including postage stamps and public lavatories.[39]

Writing about empires is, surely, more varied and exciting than ever before, however problematic some particular emphases within it may be. The gains, even amidst the theoreticist excesses, cannot be doubted. To compare, for instance, the scanty and mostly already old references on which Fieldhouse was able to draw, in discussing the relationships between empire, psychology, and race in the 1960s and 1970s, with the very large and sophisticated literature on these themes now available, is to suggest how real the advance has been. Having stressed the continuing power of Fieldhouse's work as corrective to some more recent currents in imperial historiography, it is time to turn to areas of possible complementarity between these very different sorts of work.

One clear, if indirect, convergence lies in attention to the psychology of imperialism. Imperialism, Fieldhouse argued in his earliest relevant work, 'can properly be understood only in terms of the same social hysteria that has since given birth to other and more disastrous forms of aggressive nationalism'.[40] In a brief but suggestive discussion, he pointed towards this mass popular phenomenon as crucial to the 'new imperialism' of the late nineteenth century. This he called, echoing the language of Hobson and other late-Victorian critics, 'jingoism': it was something fevered, turbulent, insecure, and in the event short-lived. On further consideration, he came to reject it as a dominant line of explanation for aggressive expansion, and in later writings like *Economics and Empire* and 1981's *Colonialism* it plays only a minor part. Yet intriguingly, recent years have seen a major revival in psychoanalytic accounts of imperialism. This has mostly, of course, been in a vastly different idiom from Fieldhouse's. Although occasional reference has been made to the ideas of Joseph Schumpeter, on which Fieldhouse has drawn – as in Daniel Bivona's *Desire and Contradiction*[41] – the main theoretical resources used have been such recent French thinkers as Jacques Lacan, Gilles Deleuze, and Felix Guattari. Yet there is significant common ground with Fieldhouse's early ideas, in the widespread emphasis on anxieties and tensions of empire, on colonialist thinking as shot through with ambivalence and insecurity, in such writers as Homi K. Bhabha, Sara Suleri, Nigel Leask, Ann Laura Stoler, and Robert Young.[42] Much of this writing has been notable for its weak anchoring in historical knowledge; and indeed it is arguable that Lacanian theory, in particular, is inherently ahistorical.[43] It might thus be said that Fieldhouse's early arguments suffer from not being anchored in any psychological theory, while the more recent cultural studies work on colonial psyches has the opposite fault: failure to give any regard to historical specificity. There is clearly a potential basis for complementarity here.

Another area of possible dialogue lies in rejection of Eurocentric – or as Fieldhouse called them 'metrocentric' – approaches to the study of empires. Fieldhouse's 'peripheral' theory has been interpreted quite inconsistently both as a restatement of a 'Primat der Aussenpolitik' thesis and as an anti-Eurocentric one, as an argument *within* economic history and as a claim for the marginality of economic as opposed to political factors (in the last view, even as a rehabilitation of W.L. Langer's diplomat-centred view of imperial expansion).[44] Whatever it is – and it is not quite any of those things – it very evidently does not fall into the category so justly, if by now repetitively, denounced by radical and post-colonial writers, of 'Eurocentric' historiography. On the contrary, his work forms an important early strand, too often neglected, in the growth of a non-Eurocentric global history, alongside such more obvious names as Marshall Hodgson or Basil Davidson. Indeed, Fieldhouse's formulation of the peripheral theory, his repudiation of explanations centred on Europe, is not only more systematic but, at least in its fullest expression in *Economics and Empire*, more single-minded than other influential formulations like that of Robinson and Gallagher: the latter, as John Darwin has recently reiterated, 'rejects explicit reliance on peripheral factors as the prime cause of expansion'.[45] In this, and despite radically different idioms, influences, and political intentions, Fieldhouse's work offers more points of contact with contemporary post-colonial scholarship than does that of most other major European theorists of empire; and certainly more than does what is now the most challenging and influential 'metrocentric' reinterpretation of British imperialism, that of Cain and Hopkins.[46]

Fieldhouse's anti-metrocentrism might, however, be thought to have one significant (if ironic) limit: he has written very little about empire's impact on Britain itself. Could he be held to fall into the category, also in recent years almost routinely denounced by post-colonial critics, of British historians who, whether their focus was imperial or domestic, failed to recognize how profoundly and ubiquitously the imperial experience shaped Britain and British cultural-political identities themselves?[47] Certainly, when he came to list the ways in which even from a 'narrow metrocentric view of things', imperial history should be considered an integral part of metropolitan (that is, imperialist countries') history, his suggestions were all, as it were, from the centre outwards. They were 'the reasons and motives behind European expansion', the mechanics of empire-building, the organization of empire, and its costs and benefits.[48]

Was Fieldhouse, in common with almost all historians of his and earlier generations, therefore simply oblivious to the cultural drive for empire? Obviously not: but we might say that in his emphasis on short-lived 'jingo' furies, he failed to look enough at wider discursive, ideological, and public-opinion currents facilitating imperial expansion. His findings should, in retrospect, be modified under the force of Edward Said's startlingly simple, deceptively obvious statement that: 'the enterprise of empire depends upon the *idea of having an empire*'.[49] Thus Fieldhouse may underrate the extent to which the national imaginary had become 'imperialized', how far Britishness had become a global formation long before the age of the 'new imperialism'. A middle ground should thus be possible, as between his rejection of such currents' importance and much recent work's simple assumption of their ubiquity.

We can find elements of this middle ground in the shared emphasis, common to both Fieldhouse's work and much recent cultural history, on continuities across the nineteenth century, rejection of the idea of the late century as a wholly new, unique 'age of imperialism'. Indeed, we can come to see 'the idea of having an empire' – albeit never hegemonic, indeed very likely almost always the preserve of minorities, though often powerful ones – as having a much older lineage, extended through many mutations across a huge swathe of first English, then British history.[50] We certainly need not assume that 'global Britishness', a sense of collective identity which expanded the imagined national community right across the empire and beyond, became universal, hegemonic, or even dominant.[51] Much of the course of twentieth-century British history, not least the post-colonial turn to Europe and the semi-federalization of the United Kingdom itself, as realised in the 1997 Scottish and Welsh referenda, suggests how limited that sense was. Here too much of the new colonial cultural history has clearly been prone to gross overstatement.[52] The phenomenon may appear now, in its decline, far more powerful on the periphery than in the metropole, among those in places like New Zealand (or indeed Northern Ireland) which feel their affiliations to Britishness have been left stranded by a receding tide.[53] But we know enough, from recent scholarship, to recognize the possibility that such a sense had enough footholds, in enough disparate parts of a highly pluralist public sphere, to engage and influence policy-makers.

A rapidly growing body of work has, for instance, argued that the language of colonial missionary evangelism – though operating in an uneasy and sometimes oppositional relationship to colonial power itself – forged a new discourse of Britishness combining elements of providentialism, nationalism, and race theory.[54] If in the seventeenth and eighteenth centuries Protestantism 'at home' was crucial to the formation of Britishness (an argument most forcefully formulated in, though not originated by, Linda Colley's *Britons*),[55] then Protestant missionary endeavours abroad, and especially in colonial settings, contributed significantly to its remaking in the nineteenth.

Dispute between 'peripheral' and 'metrocentric' explanations may then come to be seen as based, in certain significant respects, on a false antithesis, at least so far as Britain's empire is concerned; for important constituencies in each partook of the same sense of global Britishness. Within this can be identified, at the very least, three rival conceptions of empire: seeing it respectively as a set of political forms, as a nexus of relationships (both 'formal' and 'informal') founded primarily on economics, and as an imagined or discursive creation. Fieldhouse's work has concentrated overwhelmingly on the first and second, and has said very little about the third. Yet unlike the theories of Hobson or Lenin (and indeed, that of most 'metrocentric' and political historians of empire) Fieldhouse's approach has openings to let us think of empire as, in historically illuminating ways, something constructed through collective imaginings.

We began with one invocation of David Fieldhouse's influence by Edward Said: an invocation across some seemingly very wide gulfs – from the Palestinian to the Englishman, radical to conservative, literary critic to economic historian. It is appropriate to close with another such. Elsewhere in the same book Said names Fieldhouse as among those in whose work 'one is made to see that the British empire integrated and fused things within it, and taken together it and other empires made the world one'.[56] It is in that spirit, perhaps, that Fieldhouse's writings can be brought into productive conversation with latterday radical and post-colonial scholarship. Like the best of such work, his is always about making connections, across broad reaches of time and of space.

NOTES

1. D.K. Fieldhouse, *The Colonial Empires: A Comparative Survey from the Eighteenth Century* (London, 1991 edn.), 103, quoted in Edward W. Said, *Culture and Imperialism* (London, 1993), 11.
2. Fieldhouse, *Economics and Empire 1830–1914* (2nd edn. London, 1984), 139, 83.
3. *Economics*, 462.
4. As a very crude indication, there sit on my own bookshelves rather over a hundred works that might be classified as 'colonial cultural studies', almost all published in the 1990s. Fewer than half a dozen of these have even bibliographical reference to Fieldhouse's work; though Edward Said, the effective founder of the genre, is an exception here.

5. Most forcefully, in *Colonial Empires*, 376–7.
6. 'For Richer, for Poorer?', in P.J. Marshall (ed.), *The Cambridge Illustrated History of the British Empire* (Cambridge, 1996), 146.
7. Fieldhouse has attempted balance-sheets of Africa's post-colonial development record in *Black Africa 1945–1980: Economic Decolonization and Arrested Development* (London, 1986), and 'Decolonization, Development, and Dependence: A Survey of Changing Attitudes', in Prosser Gifford and Wm. Roger Louis (eds.), *The Transfer of Power in Africa: Decolonization, 1940–1960* (New Haven and London, 1982).
8. 'Decolonization, Development, and Dependence'.
9. *Unilever Overseas: The Anatomy of a Multinational 1895–1965* (London and Stanford, 1978), esp. 15–16, 119–22, 576–98; *Merchant Capital and Economic Decolonization: The United Africa Company 1929–1987* (Oxford, 1994).
10. Though there is a considerable distance travelled between, say, the rather crude presentation of Marxist ideas in the 'Introduction' to Fieldhouse (ed.) *The Theory of Capitalist Imperialism* (London, 1967) and the far more detailed and nuanced discussion in 1982's 'Decolonization...', Fieldhouse would no doubt respond that this reflects, in large measure, the greater sophistication of the literature with which he was dealing in the latter.
11. 'For Richer…', 108.
12. *Colonialism 1870–1945: An Introduction* (London, 1981), 48. This remarkable, succinct overview of the phenomenon has only recently been matched in English by that of Jürgen Osterhammel, *Colonialism: A Theoretical Overview* (Princeton, NJ, and Kingston, 1997).
13. Bill Warren, *Imperialism, Pioneer of Capitalism* (London, 1980).
14. *Unilever*, 577–8.
15. Ibid., 579.
16. Ibid., 579.
17. '"A New Imperial System"? The Role of Multinational Corporations Reconsidered', in Wolfgang Mommsen and Jürgen Osterhammel (eds.), *Imperialism and After: Continuities and Discontinuities* (London, 1986), 237, 238.
18. *Unilever*, 2.
19. Ibid., 19.
20. Ibid., 243, 244.
21. Ibid., 363.
22. Ibid., 417–8.
23. *Merchant Capital*, vii.
24. Ibid., viii.
25. *Theories of Imperialism* (London, 1981), 108.
26. Instances of rethinking and recantation by former dependency theorists could be multiplied *ad nauseam*. For critique from the left of overblown claims about the power and novelty of multinational-sponsored globalization, see especially Paul Hirst and Grahame Thompson, *Globalization in Question,* (Oxford, 1996).
27. 'Can Humpty-Dumpty be put Together Again? Imperial History in the 1980s', in R.F. Holland and G. Rizvi (eds.), *Perspectives on Imperialism and Decolonization* (London, 1984).
28. The most extensive is John MacKenzie, *Orientalism: History, Theory and the Arts* (Manchester, 1995); others include Dane Kennedy, 'Imperial History and Post-Colonial Theory', *Journal of Imperial and Commonwealth History* 24, 3 (1996); Russell Jacoby, 'Marginal Returns: The Trouble with Post-Colonial Theory', *Lingua Franca* (Sept.Oct. 1995). Perhaps the best overviews are recent works by a literary critic and an anthropologist – though neither is sufficiently critical of the dominant trends in colonial cultural studies: Bart J. Moore-Gilbert, *Postcolonial Theory: Contexts, Practices, Politics* (London, 1997), and Nicholas Thomas, *Colonialism's Culture: Anthropology, Travel and Government* (Oxford, 1994).
29. *Colonising Egypt* (Berkeley, Ca, 1988; cited from 1991 2nd edn.), ix.
30. *Colonialism's Culture*, 4.
31. Houston A. Baker Jr., *Workings of the Spirit: The Poetics of Afro-American Women's Writing* (Chicago, 1991), 207.

32. Bruce Robbins, 'Colonial Discourse: A Paradigm and Its Discontents', *Victorian Studies*, 35, 2 (1992), 213.
33. 'Orientalist Constructions of India', *Modern Asian Studies*, 20, 3 (1986); *Imagining India* (Oxford, 1990). For the necessary counter-insistence that if modern India is indeed something imagined rather than handed down, it is a product at least as much of the nationalist as of the colonialist 'mind', see *inter alia* Sudipta Kaviraj, 'The Imaginary Institution of India', in Partha Chatterjee and Gyanendra Pandey (eds.), *Subaltern Studies VII* (Delhi, 1992); Sunil Khilnani, *The Idea of India* (London, 1997).
34. See Christopher Harrison, *France and Islam in West Africa, 1860–1960* (Cambridge, 1988), esp. Part III.
35. The work of Gayatri Chakravorty Spivak is a major case in point.
36. *Colonialism,* 42.
37. Space precludes even indicative citation here. Among historians of modern Britain, Patrick Joyce and James Vernon have been perhaps the most insistent evangelists for such a perspective. For a vigorous, if sometimes indiscriminate, counter-attack see Richard J. Evans, *In Defence of History* (London, 1997).
38. *Colonialism* , 48–9.
39. Any reader doubting this last entry on my list should consult Warwick Anderson, 'Excremental Colonialism: Public Health and the Poetics of Pollution', *Critical Inquiry*, 21 (1995), which might have been quite a good joke had it not apparently been written, as it were, po-faced.
40. D.K. Fieldhouse, '"Imperialism": An Historiographical Revision', *Economic History Review*, XIV, 2 (1961), 209.
41. Daniel Bivona, *Desire and Contradiction: Imperial Visions and Domestic Debates in Victorian Literature* (Manchester, 1990).
42. Major examples of what might be called the 'anxieties of empire' literature include Homi K. Bhabha, *The Location of Culture* (London, 1994); Frederick Cooper and Ann Laura Stoler, 'Between Metropole and Colony: Rethinking a Research Agenda', in idem (eds.), *Tensions of Empire: Colonial Cultures in a Bourgeois World* (Berkeley, 1997); Nigel Leask, *British Romantic Writers and the East: Anxieties of Empire* (Cambridge, 1992); Sara Suleri, *The Rhetoric of English India* (Chicago, 1991); Robert J.C. Young, *Colonial Desire: Hybridity in Theory, Culture and Race* (London, 1995).
43. Though see Teresa Brennan's ingenious effort to uncover a theory of history in the French writer's work: *History After Lacan* (London, 1993).
44. Roger Owen, 'Introduction' to idem and Bob Sutcliffe (eds.), *Studies in the Theory of Imperialism* (London, 1972). For dismissal of Fieldhouse as a latterday epigone of the German 'Aussenpolitik' theorists, and an astonishing claim that only ignorance of economic history could sanction such a view, see Hans-Ulrich Wehler, 'Industrial Growth and Early German Imperialism', in the same volume, 74.
45. 'Imperialism and the Victorians: The Dynamics of Territorial Expansion', *English Historical Review,* CXII, 447 (1997), 616, n.4.
46. P.J. Cain and A.G. Hopkins, *British Imperialism. vol.1. Innovation and Expansion 1688–1914; vol.2. Crisis and Deconstruction 1914–1990* (London, 1993). Conversely, one might register surprise at how small a place this work accords Fieldhouse's views among those the authors seek to supplant: see esp. their vol.1, 5–22; vol.2, 300–15.
47. Numerous instances could be cited. Fairly typical, if more sweepingly scornful than many, is Antoinette Burton, 'Rules of Thumb: British History and "Imperial Culture" in Nineteenth- and Twentieth-century Britain', *Women's History Review* 3, 4 (1994). Far more substantial critiques and alternatives are presented in the work-in-progress of Catherine Hall; for example, 'Rethinking Imperial History: The Reform Act of 1867', *New Left Review,* 208 (1994).
48. 'Humpty Dumpty', 10–11.
49. *Culture and Imperialism*, 10: emphasis in original.
50. For some of the signposts on that very long journey, see Rees Davies, 'The English State and the "Celtic" Peoples 1100–1400', *Journal of Historical Sociology*, 6, 1 (1993); John Gillingham, 'The Beginnings of English Imperialism', *JHS* (1992); Anthony Pagden, *Lords*

of All the World: Ideologies of Empire in Spain, Britain & France c.1500 – c.1800 (New Haven and London, 1995); David Armitage, 'The Cromwellian Protectorate and the Languages of Empire' *Historical Journal* 35, 3 (1992); Nicholas Canny, *Kingdom and Colony: Ireland in the Atlantic World, 1560–1800* (Baltimore, 1988); John Robertson (ed.), *A Union for Empire: Political Thought and the British Union of 1707* (Cambridge, 1995); C.A. Bayly, *Imperial Meridian: The British Empire and the World, 1780–1830* (London, 1989).

51. For nineteenth-century attempts to formulate, or urge, such a sense of global Britishness, see Charles Dilke, *Greater Britain* (London, 1868); idem, *Problems of Greater Britain* (2 vols. London, 1890); J.R. Seeley, *The Expansion of England* (London, 1883). For an argument that the effort had already been made, and had failed, a century earlier: P.J. Marshall, 'A Nation Defined by Empire, 1755–1776', in Alexander Grant and Keith J. Stringer (eds.), *Uniting the Kingdom? The Making of British History* (London, 1995). David Armitage, 'Making the Empire British: Scotland in the Atlantic World 1542–1707', *Past and Present,* 155 (1997), pushes the argument still further back in time. David Marquand, conversely, is among those emphasizing how long into the post-1945 era such ideas lingered: 'After Whig Imperialism: Can There be a New British Identity?', *New Community,* 21,2 (1995).
52. For some of the bolder – and perhaps less sustainable – claims in this sphere, see for example, Simon Gikandi, *Maps of Englishness: Writing Identity in the Culture of Colonialism* (New York, 1996); Ulf Hedetoft, *British Colonialism and Modern Identity* (Aalborg, 1985).
53. See the repeated recent cries of distress at this by the great New Zealand historian J.G.A. Pocock: for example, 'Conclusion: Contingency, Identity, Sovereignty', in Grant and Stringer, *Uniting the Kingdom?*, 297–302; idem, 'Deconstructing Europe', in Peter Gowan and Perry Anderson (eds.), *The Question of Europe* (London, 1997), 297–300, 316; 'Removal from the Wings', *London Review of Books*, 20 March 1997. For the more optimistic view of a younger New Zealand historian – and former student of David Fieldhouse – James Belich, *Making Peoples: A History of the New Zealanders From Polynesian Settlement to the End of the Nineteenth Century* (Auckland, 1996). Compare James Loughlin's argument on the shifting relationships of Ulster Unionists to Britishness: *Ulster Unionism and British National Identity since 1885* (London, 1995).
54. See, among others, Andrew Porter, 'Religion and Empire: British Expansion in the Long Nineteenth Century, 1780–1914', *JICH* 20, 3 (1992); Doug Stuart, '"For England and For Christ": The Gospel of Liberation and Subordination in Early Nineteenth Century Southern Africa', *Journal of Historical Sociology*, 6, 4 (1993), Jean and John Comaroff, *Of Revelation and Revolution: Christianity, Colonialism and Consciousness in South Africa, Vol.1* (Chicago, 1991).
55. Linda Colley, *Britons: Forging the Nation 1707–1837* (New Haven and London, 1992).
56. *Culture and Imperialism*, 4.

Taking Fieldhouse Further: Post-Colonizing Imperial History

PHILLIP DARBY

Except on the most literal reading of the term post-colonial, it can hardly be said to apply to David Fieldhouse's history. Certainly, few writers concerned with reconfiguring scholarship along post-colonial lines would admit much affinity between Fieldhouse's work and theirs. In *Culture and Imperialism*, Edward Said cites with approval a point made by 'the distinguished conservative historian of empire',[1] but references to Fieldhouse's writings are uncommon in the new literature, even to voice disagreement. This situation is emblematic of the relationship between imperial history and post-colonial studies: they pass like ships in the night. In this paper, I will argue that the two need to be brought into engagement. To this end, I propose to examine aspects of Fieldhouse's work on the history of empire and its aftermath to enquire whether the distance between traditional and emergent approaches is as great as appearances suggest. In doing so, I will concentrate on the significance of the dissolution of formal empire and look mainly at the case of Black Africa. My purpose will not be to pass judgement on substantive issues but to indicate the kind of areas where dialogue might prove fruitful.

The choice of David Fieldhouse's writings to ground this essay is intended as a personal tribute, but it is also highly functional in that it involves the negotiation of difference as well as the recognition of similarity and points of contact. The primacy that Fieldhouse has given to economic issues stands in marked contrast to their neglect in much contemporary post-colonial analysis. Related, he has shown little inclination to pursue the power of the discursive, which has become so central in post-colonial theory. A productive exchange, therefore, seems more likely to involve building bridges between different ways of thinking than might be the case if we took an imperial historian, such as A.P. Thornton, with a cultural and ideational orientation. Yet, in terms of where attention is directed, the ground is already prepared for connection. In large part, Fieldhouse's enquiries are articulated in spaces of primary concern to post-colonial theorists: between the then and now (empire and after), the here and there (the metropole and overseas) and the public and the private (the company). In these sites, engagement may be a matter of extending what is already in place; at best, a kind of translation exercise.

To foreground the work of a particular scholar does not, of course, offer an escape from the obstacles to intellectual engagement created by disciplinary domains and self-referential discourses. It may, however, concretize issues, enabling them to be seen in terms of problem-solving. This would represent a major step forward at a time when, for all the emphasis on interdisciplinary undertakings and a fuller recognition of the relativity of knowledge, it is arguable that a new kind of absolutism has emerged in the Western academy. At least in the humanities and social sciences, there is a deep divide between traditional disciplines and new formations of knowledge, with the foundational assumptions of the old being challenged by the ethics and theory of the new. Whereas, before, the separation of knowledges was largely on the basis of different realms, it is now about claims to legitimacy. Partly for this reason, there has been little trafficking between old and new. Each has clung to its own space and distinctive methodology, and very often insisted on its own language and publishing outlets.

Such is the case with imperial history and post-colonialism. What is more, post-colonialism is making the running. Empire, once the preserve of a sect of professionals, has become the stamping ground of students of literature, gender, culture, and more specialized fields such as medical discourse and museum studies. Clearly, for the moment, post-colonialism has captured the academic high ground. University courses are reconfigured; publishers' interest is keen; international conferences proliferate. At the same time, post-colonial themes and motifs have spilt into the performing and graphic arts, and they have been taken up by consumer capitalism.[2] Whether, however, post-colonialism's challenge to traditional disciplinary modes has more bite in imperial history than it does in (say) international relations or geography is perhaps arguable. For one thing, imperial history has had the experience of dialogue with historians of other (formerly colonized) cultures – in Africa led by scholars such as K. Onwuka Dike, B.A. Ogot, and A. Adu Boahen. While it is probable that this cross-cultural encounter has had a more profound impact on world history and on the general categories of historical explanation than on imperial history,[3] it has certainly narrowed the claims made in the name of European expansion. In many respects, post-colonial calls for an anti-foundationalist history of the Third World and for provincializing Europe represent an extension of the earlier challenges mounted by African historians and the Subaltern Studies Group.[4] There is, however, a more evident concern with the language of historical explanation and a fuller awareness of the politics of the construction of history – which, for traditionalists, is where most of the problems arise.

The emergence of post-colonialism as a discourse has brought in its trail new obstacles to international intellectual exchange. To some degree, the divide between old and new formations of knowledge appears to have been re-enacted between North and South. Despite the fact that many of the foremost post-colonial theorists have come from the non-European world, the discourse itself is based firmly in the West. This has been a source of unease in debates about the post-colonial intellectual and it has raised questions about the complicity of scholarship with dominant power structures. A related issue has involved the turn to post-structuralism. While on some accounts this has given post-colonial analysis more intellectual purchase,[5] it has also been seen as compromising the enunciation of oppositional politics. The established line of division between North and South have been unsettled by the process of decentring, the rejection of grand narratives, the rupturing of self/other binaries, and the neglect of material interest and structural determinants.[6] Coming as they do from those who have a voice in global academic exchange, such complaints are probably the tip of the iceberg. In the universities of Black Africa, for instance, post-colonial concerns with identity, subjectivity, and the symbolic are as likely to be greeted with hostility as with scepticism. It is not unusual to hear complaints that post-colonialism is the latest manifestation of the imperialism of Western scholarship.[7] No doubt this must partly be related to the limited access to Western monographs and international journals, but it also reflects a very different world view anchored in the materiality of imperialism, expressed through some variant of dependency. It is an ironic postscript to the times that the questions Fieldhouse poses resonate with the contemporary academic agenda in Africa in a way that post-colonial analysis certainly does not.

If in fact scholarship across the globe as well as in the West has taken such different trajectories, calls for a dialogue between old and new may all too easily become rhetorical. Dane Kennedy has recently presented a well reasoned case for a critical engagement between imperial history and post-colonial theory, arguing that this could broaden the methodological horizons of historians and check the theoretical excesses of literary scholars.[8] Presumably no one would take issue with the need for such an engagement. When the matter is put thus, it is perhaps natural to assume an openness to dialogue which we like to think of as a mark of academic enquiry. But can we assume that the problem is basically an intellectual one? Given the situation as outlined above, I do not think so. Closure is also a matter of interests, politics, and psychological predispositions. On the first point, there are issues of funding, jobs, and personal advancement tied to academic competition which encourage a disavowal of perspectives different from one's own. Politics becomes involved, not only in the debates about the partisanship of knowledge or otherwise, but also in the way the understanding and deployment of knowledge changes according to cultural context. The psychology of scholarship clearly requires more attention than it has received. Consider, for instance, the security associated with territorial preserves, the attraction of badges of distinctiveness and the wish to have no truck with the new (or it may be the old). John MacKenzie's argument that Said's work is of little value to historians might repay close reading on this score.[9] Even if we were to accept many of his criticisms, should it not be acknowledged that imaginative leaps above the 'facts' are very often what changes the course of scholarship? Dependency theory is a case in point. It is also useful to recall that at times those sharing a degree of commonality are the very people who have the greatest difficulty in connecting. Such issues cannot be taken up here, but they underline the need to focus on the viewer as well as on what is viewed. Of more immediate concern, it would seem that the kind of closures I have been discussing are better negotiated by starting with the particular, and the points where one approach might complement or lead into another, rather than with postulates at the core of disciplinary claims to distinctiveness.

Before proceeding in this way, a working outline of the field of post-colonial studies must be attempted. This is difficult because post-colonial theory – which I take to subsume colonial discourse analysis – has made a virtue out of changing ground and being open-ended. Moreover, its course has been set by a process of expansion in which other bodies of knowledge have been drawn into dialogue and become part of the discourse itself. In varying degrees, this is true of subaltern studies, gender analysis, and the writing on space and place. In the dominant view, the origins of the discourse lie in the writings of Fanon, Foucault, and Said, but a strong case can also be mounted that analysis grew out of the study of fiction written in ex-colonial countries and the attempt to discern commonalities in content and form.[10] If the latter position seems better to accord with a reading of the early texts, it is clearly out of step with the subsequent shifts in the centre of gravity of the discourse. Increasingly, there has been a movement from the personal and the contextual to more abstract analyses. Crucial here has been the incorporation of key elements of post-modernist thought. This has had its critics, but it has brought a mindfulness not to be entrapped by fixed and integrated conceptions of identity, culture, and place or the closures and binarisms of traditional social analysis. Associated, there has been a turn from resistance and recovery to ambivalence and hybridity. In other words, overtly oppositional politics have come to be replaced by a more nuanced reading of the colonial encounter and post-colonial predicament. Imperialism was not as secure and simple-minded as it had earlier been presented and the allegories of otherness need to be unsettled by a recognition of counter-movements and points of congruence. Although I have chosen to illustrate this shift to the 'in-between' by reference to the colonial encounter, analysis is no longer so closely tied to the formerly colonized world. Enquiry extends from the culture of domesticity in the metropoles to the construction of global cultural relations. It is as if the experience of colonialism is ubiquitous. What is now at issue is the whole nature of 'othering', meaning the way in which self and other are mutually constructed through discourse.

In all this, there has been one distinctive constant: post-colonialism and the sources upon which it draws have been self-consciously partisan. Rewriting the text is seen as an act of political intervention. When Chinua Achebe, for instance, is cited with approval, what is significant is not simply that he depicted the Ibo experience of the imperial encounter but that he did so in the belief that he was contributing to the making of a new Nigeria. So too, although more obliquely, Homi Bhabha presents his writing as directed to the creation of a different kind of world. His concern with the interstices of cultural engagement, with the 'beyond' as a space for action in the here and now, with the politics of the theoretical statement, all attempt to harness new forms of empowerment in the interests of social change.[11] The colonial past looms large throughout the literature and it is shown to be different from how we earlier imagined. Alternative ways of seeing denaturalize colonialism's categories; non-European identity, knowledge, and agency begin to appear in new forms. Hope lies at the heart of such reconceptualization in that presenting things differently may provide a basis for making a fresh start, for getting around discursive practices which had blocked challenge or change. At least implicitly, therefore, the understanding is that re-reading the past creates an openness about the future.

To position Fieldhouse's writing between the then and now may seem puzzling given his concern with the facts and with testing the validity of interpretative propositions by reference to the evidence in particular cases and places. It may also seem glib in so far as it connotes a sense of floating above events which might be taken to distract from his seriousness of purpose as an academic historian. What I am attempting to convey is that the present and even the future play an understated but formative role in his historical understanding. Fieldhouse has always been insistent that we cannot pass judgement on empire until we know what happened afterwards. As I read his work, this relates not only to interpreting source material but to orienting enquiry: both will be shaped to some degree by later happenings and values as well as by the events and thinking of an earlier era. Consider, for example, questions such as the effect of Unilever investments on the host country or why economic development in Black Africa was unsatisfactory after independence. In enquiring along these lines, are there not shades of Sir Keith Hancock's approach in his *Survey of British Commonwealth Affairs*? In these two volumes, Hancock – whom I take to be one of Fieldhouse's mentors – recreated the past in relation to the problems of the present.[12] I think something similar can be said of Fieldhouse's later work, not in the sense that the historical narrative might influence official policy but that it could contribute to a wider contemporary debate.

It is significant that, as empire became more distant, Fieldhouse came to develop a particular interest in its dissolution. Although decolonization is sometimes presented as a watershed – which of course is hotly contested – for the purposes of my argument the more appropriate metaphor is that of a bridge. That is to say, the processes taking place and the academic debate about them serve to link past, present, and future. Fieldhouse singles out the economic aspects for close attention and he naturally looks back to the record of and under empire. But I would suggest that it is the contemporaneity of this past that most engages him. There is one other area of temporal fluidity in Fieldhouse's analysis and that is the relationship between the processes of imperialism and the emergence of a global economic system. Starting with his observation in *Economics and Empire* that by about 1880 there was a profound change in the pathology of international relationships,[13] he moves on in subsequent work to engage with dependency, world systems theory, and the role of the multinational corporation. For the most part, these are discussed not so much in their own terms as in connection with other agendas as, for example, African development or the history of Unilever Overseas and the United Africa Company. Yet much is already in place for a broader study which might explore the role of empire in the economic transformations of the late twentieth century which are understood as a part of the phenomenon of globalization.

What I am suggesting is that elements of Fieldhouse's approach do not fit the model of the past as 'back there' (cut off from the present and from contemporary sensibilities) or the future as 'beyond here' (without contact with where we are now and our present ways of thinking). In other words, in some of its points of reference, Fieldhouse's history is not so dissimilar from post-colonial approaches that there can be no connection or cross-reference. The moment, however, we come to refocus our appraisal in terms of the categories of debate between knowledge formations, it is the differences which appear striking. Nowhere is this more apparent than with regard to whether it is appropriate for ideas about preferred futures to influence readings of what went before. On a post-colonial account, the process of retelling the colonial encounter from a counter-hegemonic standpoint undermines the constructs of Western universalism and creates a space where previously subordinate peoples can take control of their own destinies. It is precisely the imaginative dimensions of the project that enable the power/knowledge nexus of Western universalism to be broken and the subaltern empowered. Established historiography is much less sanguine about the imaginative recasting of the past, utilizing myth and invention. Eric Hobsbawm, for example, stresses the need to have regard to historical facts and warns of the dangers of the past being rewritten according to politco-ideological design.[14]

I do not consider it dodging the issues to say that in practice where the line is drawn is a matter of judgement. History cannot be insulated from politics. Discourse cannot be struck from the lexicon of power-broking. On neither count are we dealing with an either/or situation. Perspective probably comes easier at a certain distance from one's primary field of enquiry. There might be a considerable measure of agreement between imperial historians, for example, that both with respect to the imaginative reconstruction of history and to the politically enabling potentialities of the text, Achebe in *Things Fall Apart* got the balance about right whereas Ayi Kwei Armah in *Two Thousand Seasons* did not.[15] The primary point I want to make is rather different, however, and it relates to the debate about theory. It is far from clear that rehearsing more or less familiar positions is a productive way of proceeding. The possibilities of dialogue seem more likely to be enhanced by stepping outside the arena of theoretical contestation, at least for a time. In other words, like any conversation it is a matter of knowing where to begin. Mention of discourse has become like a red rag to the bulls of traditional imperial history; what Martha Hildreth calls objectivist history[16] would be regarded by most post-colonial scholars as a new kind of primitivism. In such a situation, the likelihood of admitting common ground seems slight.

Something similar may be said of many of those large propositions about the nature, course, and consequences of imperialism which, for all their suggestiveness, carry too much before them. Consider, for instance, the claim by many imperial historians that imperialism did not bite deeply into the life of colonized societies – or at least not as deeply as an earlier generation of historians thought. Some time back, Fieldhouse observed that the imperial factor had come to be seen as transitory.[17] According to MacKenzie, recent imperial historiography has tended to emphasize the ephemerality of imperial rule.[18] Such revisionism would win little support from post-colonial theorists. What stands out in their analysis is the continuing importance of changes associated with imperialism and the processes that it set in place, not only for colonized people but for the metropoles and relationships globally. This sense of relevance is probably part of the reason why post-colonial studies is a growth industry and imperial history is not.

Now certainly the distance between the two formations of thought is an expression of different understandings of the meaning of imperialism – in the mind and on the ground and whether or not it is indissolubly linked with its oppositions. This works to confirm what we have always known: that imperialism is too large and diverse a phenomenon to be captured by easy generalization. But clearly the problem is broader than this because wherever the ostensible boundaries are set, they are crossed with some frequency. There is something to be said for contrasting the categories of post-colonial analysis – modernity, identity, race, and culture – with the focus on politics and economics in their traditional mode. In the longer term, from a post-colonial perspective, the role of missionaries, decisions about education, the uprooting of colonial peoples were of greater significance than the diplomatic jostling or the ground rules for orderly partition laid down at the Berlin Conference in 1884–85. Many historians would probably agree, and they would point to research which supports this view. There is no shortage of studies on the influence of missionaries. Colonial education and the movement of people for reasons of labour have received their share of attention. More recently, gender and inter-racial sexual relations – so prominent on the post-colonial agenda – have received some airing. Another line of approach would relate to source material and the fact that, by and large, traditionalists have adopted a narrower view of what is admissible as evidence and placed a higher premium on its veracity than post-colonial theorists. Yet what lies in the background of these and similar exchanges is the difference in purpose of the two knowledge formations. For the post-colonial critic, the relationship between imperialism and its undoing is a continuing story. Through post-colonialism's concern with emergent identities, resituating displacement, and the recovery of agency it seeks to address where we are now and what might be done about it. On the whole, historians have taken a much more limited view of the utility of their narratives of the past and mostly they have been reluctant to draw out the implications of their work for politics in the making.

At least these are the flags that are flown. But if we look at what is done rather than what is said, the difference may not be quite so marked. At times, post-colonial analysis gives the impression of being oppositional to imperialism for its own sake.[19] The pursuit of historical guilt can distort understandings of the processes at work and mask the fact that, for some Africans, colonialism offered windows of opportunities. These need analysis, not least because of their relevance to debates about hybridity. It is also noticeable that, to date, Bhabha aside, post-colonialism has shied away from thinking too much about futures. To some extent this is understandable given the post-modern concern with indeterminacy and contingency. Still, considering how much attention has been devoted to the might-have-beens of history one might reasonably expect rather more on the what-might-yet-be. Along the same lines, for all the stress on self/other politics, there has been little attempt to relate theory to some of the hard issues of contemporary global relations, as for example human rights.

On the other side, occasionally and despite disciplinary conventions, historians have carried forward their studies of imperialism to relate to contemporary issues. This is true of MacKenzie's study of orientalism in the arts and, in the African context, of the writing of Basil Davidson and Terence Ranger. Mostly, however, there is not much more than hints and *obiter dicta* and it is left to readers to make connections – and since few post-colonial scholars read in the area the connections are not usually made. The situation is akin to the neglect in America after the Second World War of the material on colonial development in the inter-war years, an awareness of which might have qualified the extraordinary optimism about what could be accomplished through aid programmes. Returning to the question of transitoriness or otherwise of imperialism, one area of fundamental importance where connection needs to be made is the unevenness of imperial penetration within and between colonial societies. This is home turf for most imperial historians. Yet, despite its significance for thinking about identity, the nation, and material change, it is largely unfamiliar territory in post-colonial analysis. Mahmood Mamdani's challenging study, *Citizen and Subject*, which falls into neither camp but should engage both, would be an ideal point of reference.[20]

Writing in 1984, David Fieldhouse argued that there exists a lump of historical material which cannot properly be handled either in the context of the expansion of Europe or in telling the story of societies which for a time were under colonial rule. It is this area of interaction which constitutes the subject of imperial history. The historian, thus placed at the interstices, looks in two or more directions at the same time.[21] In outline, this schema is broadly similar to how post-colonial analysis might position itself and it is suggestive that much emphasis has come to be placed on the word 'interstices'. The metaphor of the lump, however, signals a concern with enclosure which is the antithesis of the approach of post-colonial studies. In fact, I think it must be said that in imperial history the tendency is to concentrate on particular issues and episodes whereas there is an openness about post-colonial understandings of the interaction between colonizer and colonized. In practice, it is not so easy to spell this out, partly because there is not much specifically post-colonial history of Africa. Postcolonial scholarship has preferred to look at colonialism in the broad. In any case, except with respect to literary texts, Africa has attracted much less attention than India. There is also the problem of deciding what is African history and what is imperial history. Where, for example, should one place Martin Chanock's Law, *Custom and Social Order: The Colonial Experience in Malawi and Zambia* or Michael Crowder's *The Flogging of Phinehas McIntosh: A Tale of Colonial Folly and Injustice?*[22] What weighting should attach to imperial intentions as against local consequences or is categorization more dependent upon political sensibility? I raise this because, as a rule of thumb, much African history seems more in tune with post-colonial perspectives than does imperial history.

Admitting the difficulties, it is worth attempting to identify characteristic features of a post-colonial approach. For a start, the process of interaction is invested with a dynamic or creative aspect, often particularly associated with the translation of imperialism from an ideology to behaviour and policy. This in-between space is not simply where the initiatives and responses of the colonized lead to an adjustment or rejection of imperial designs, but where new possibilities emerge through a process of give and take on each side of the encounter. The hinge of analysis is the idea of cultural difference but over time increasing recognition has been given to elements of borrowing and convergence. As Bhabha has put it: 'The place of difference and otherness, or the space of the adversarial ...is never entirely on the outside or implacably oppositional.'[23] On one reading of the direction of movement in contemporary post-colonialism, what emerges is the 'unnaturalness' of so much cultural difference. It could almost be said, for instance, that Bhabha's 'new internationalism' represents a new form of humanism. This accords with the shift of focus away from political aggregates – most notably the state – to people in their everyday lives – migration and displacement, the informal sector, gender, sexuality, and the body. On another tack, there are elements of similarity with Ashis Nandy's conception of a dialogue between cultures anchored in the notion that there is 'continuity between the victors and the victims'.[24]

Even where post-colonial theory is less psychoanalytically oriented and lacks the same sense of social optimism, the understanding of interaction extends outward from the interface of the colonial encounter to be refracted multitudinously within societies at home and overseas, and even globally. William Appleman Williams' celebrated phrase 'empire as a way of life', although developed in a different context and directed only to the metropoles, expresses the way the political is seen to be embedded in the ostensibly non-political. Culture, race, and gender become primary sites for plotting the processes of othering, the extent to which they converge and the way they are traversed. Culture is the slate upon which exchange is inscribed. Accordingly, source material needs to be drawn from new quarters and analytical tools borrowed from cultural theory – not that the cultural material is necessarily less reliable than the documents which preceded it, but there is now an awareness that all sources have multiple meanings and much depends upon how they are narrated.[25] Race is deeply implicated in the patterns of colonial rule, the construction of civil society, and the changing forms of capitalist penetration, but mostly not in ways recognized in official records or uncovered by historians.[26] The workings of race must therefore be brought to the surface especially since, with independence and the programmes of Africanization, racial legacies helped to fuel retribalization and the rise of ethnicity. Gender analysis led to questions being asked about whether men and women responded differently to the colonial encounter and what implications this might have for identity politics after decolonization. In the African context, a distinctive line of enquiry concerns the feminization of the continent at the hands of colonial writers and how this has come to be replaced by the 'Mother Africa' trope, promoted by male African politicians and novelists in a decidedly one-sided version of cultural recovery.[27] Material in each of these areas is sometimes brought together under the rubric of the extension of modernity to Africa, a process seen to be spearheaded by imperialism both formal and informal. Modernity tends to become a kind of 'hold-all' category and it has not proved easy to arrive at some accommodation with continuing notions of African distinctiveness. In other regions of the world the concept of colonial or counter-modernity has proved useful in exploring hybrid formations which look Western but in many respects are not. So far as I am aware, no such notion has been taken up by any of the discourses directly concerned with Africa – but assuredly we will not have long to wait.

The points I have been making about the breadth of the area of interaction are powerfully reinforced by the rethinking about spatiality which has been incorporated into post-colonial theory. Meeting places may still be important when considering personal relationships between colonizer and colonized, but as the categories of exchange have become more generic so the understanding of empire has begun to be deterritorialized. Elements of imperialism have been internalized in Africa.

In various ways, the idea of Africa has been domesticated in the metropoles. The process of deterritorialization is more pronounced after independence when interaction becomes increasingly global. Can it any longer be assumed that modernity is always located outside the continent? Given the part played by imperialism in the construction of tribalism and the contemporary role of arms supplies and the international media, can violence in the subcontinent be understood purely as an internal phenomenon? In other words, there are more connections between here and there than we have liked to think: the skins which attempted to keep apart the imperial and the colonial, the global and the local, are revealed to be porous. Mostly, post-colonial theory has restricted itself to the broad canvas, leaving the historical and empirical elaboration to others. One illustration of interest to imperial historians is the process by which the colonial grids of cities such as Nairobi and Harare have worked after decolonization to shift colonial social divisions, and the tensions which accompanied them, into the Black community and to situate them on a class rather than a racial basis.[28] Another is the argument that in Ghana the colonial practice of promoting the development of Accra and its environs by drawing resources from the north has been perpetuated by successive governments after 1957, acting in conjunction with the World Bank.[29]

Alongside the attempts by post-colonial scholars to extend the area of interaction outward is the attempt to work downward, to address processes at work in the lower echelons of colonial societies. Crucial here has been the project of bringing the subaltern out of the shadows of elitist conceptions of Third World nationalism and into history. Leaving to one side the work of the Subaltern Studies Group, I think it must be said that post-colonial theory itself has not managed to reach the lives of the people it wishes to recover because it has got stuck in the epistemological problems of doing so. There is, of course, a need to address questions of who can speak and whether the subaltern voice will be colonized the moment it is rendered into academic discourse. Yet there is also some bite in Arif Dirlick's argument that in terms of its discursive thematic, post-colonialism excludes from its scope most of those who inhabit post-colonial societies.[30]

Approached in the light of this material, what can be said about the shape of Fieldhouse's history? What is brought to our attention and what is not? Without doubt, it fulfils the brief Fieldhouse laid down for imperial historians: it looks in two directions at the same time; it is comparative and contextual; it is closely concerned with the processes which led to the creation of a world economic system. Ronald Robinson has observed that Fieldhouse's *Economics and Empire* realized the excentricity of *Africa and the Victorians*.[31] More than this, having set in place a geographical reorientation and marked out the channels through which agency flowed, he goes on to break new ground with regard to the economic dimensions of imperial and global intervention. But when it comes to matters of culture, race and gender, it is a different story. They are raised in the course of analysis, but cut short. Fieldhouse's reluctance to pursue these issues seems partly because of their subjectivity and the difficulty of drawing up a balance sheet. It is perhaps not coincidental that it is the economics of overseas involvement that Fieldhouse has made his own and it is economics which, more than any other discourse, is resistant to the politics of other cultures – unless it be Marxism cast in its orthodox mould.

Let me illustrate this contention by reference to *Black Africa 1945–1980*, which addresses the controversial question of why economic development was so disappointing after independence.[32] After carefully surveying the historical record, Fieldhouse discounts the role of the international economy and endogenous factors such as environment and fixes responsibility on African governments themselves. As he reads the evidence, it is the policy explanations which carry conviction. These include incentives for peasant food and cash crop production, excessive borrowing, high spending, and plain incompetence. Fieldhouse is persuasive when he argues that it was unrealistic to have expected rapid development in Africa, but is it not unrealistic also to imagine that politics might have run along the same lines as in the West? Achebe confronts some of the difficulties in *A Man of the People*,[33] but in *Black Africa 1945–1980* they are mostly sidelined by suggesting that had continuity with colonial practices been pursued more selectively things might have gone better.

The problem, as I see it, is that the cultural particularity of Africa's experience cannot readily be juggled to suit the supposed universalism of good economic management. To broaden the terms somewhat, Colin Leys has argued that the problem in Africa is not the state but the social formations on which it rests.[34] These issues are of political as well as scholarly importance. For over a decade, policy explanations have found favour in governmental circles in the West, and with international agencies like the World Bank, and they have been reformulated as prescriptions with more popular appeal such as good governance and democratization. If we are to believe the enthusiasts, the global divisions of the past are to be swept aside as more and more countries embrace neo-liberal economics and the pressures for democratization become irresistible. Whether, however, these new forms of one-worldism mesh with what is happening on the ground is quite another matter. One step in the direction of finding out would be to confront directly the cultural inheritance of the interaction between colonial rule and traditional social practices.

The space between the public and the private is also a space between imperial history and post-colonialism. It could easily be construed as contested terrain, but I want to argue that it is better approached as offering meeting places for productive exchange. Imperial history has mostly been associated with the official mind but this does not do justice to the work on missionaries, explorers, traders and the like. Post-colonialism has staked its claim to everyday life. Strategically situated in the middle is the trading company which serves as a connecting rod between the two. David Fieldhouse's studies of Unilever overseas and the United Africa Company are therefore of seminal importance to everyone concerned with the historical processes of linkage.[35] They are also of direct relevance to those concerned with the emergence of the contemporary political economy because they pay close attention to the changes associated with decolonization upon which so much turns and, so far as the multinational corporation is concerned, so little has been written.

In the first of these monographs, Fieldhouse asks why capital was invested in productive enterprises overseas rather than products exported from the home base, what was the character and profitability of the subsidiary companies, and what effects investment had on the host country. In the second, he examines the record of the United Africa Company and explores the reasons for its movement from general trading (merchant capital) to local manufacturing (industrial capital) and for its partial redeployment outside Africa in the 1960s and 1970s. The story he tells, primarily on the basis of company archives, is in many ways a microcosm of imperial history. The surplus capital argument gets short shrift. On many occasions, the actions of Unilever and the United Africa Company were defensive: it was a matter of responding to events on the periphery rather than calling the tune. Often the companies built on what was already in place. Chance played its part. The establishment of a soap-making venture in Nigeria in 1923 was a by-product of other considerations and property acquired for different purposes. It was 'almost accidental' that the United Africa Company owned plantations in Nigeria which, by the early 1950s, had expanded to about 37,000 acres. Above all, we learn that dominance was not necessarily durable; nor could it always be turned to advantage. In the end, the politics of decolonization redrew the economic possibilities. Independent states were prepared to exercise their sovereignty: profitability depended on the policies of host governments.

In largest part, these histories take their cue from the established categories of thinking about imperialism: trade and investment; the areas of tension and commonality between company and state; the relationship between the organization at home and its overseas arms. We learn much more, for example, about the companies' interaction with governments than we do about their relations with customers, actual or potential, in Africa. Both narratives begin in Europe but they recount the processes of decentring – the devolution of capital, manufacturing, control, and management to the outside world. In a sense, they are accounts of the end of empire in its traditional forms. They could also be read as signalling the way the process of globalization proceeds through localization. But there is another account to be given and it is about the rise of a new form of imperialism anchored in the commodity and involving the transformation of African cultures and very great changes in the identities of Africans. In this saga, the cake of Sunlight soap becomes the symbol of a new social order. Far from being reactive, Unilever and the United Africa Company are cast as key agents of change. In some measure, Africans become collaborators through their willingness to consume. It is not Fieldhouse's purpose to tell this story but in both volumes he hints in its direction. Writing, for instance, about the export of soap to West Africa in the first quarter of the twentieth century he observes: 'the very existence of this trade reflects a minor social revolution in West Africa, indicating that Africans adopted European attitudes to personal cleanliness as soon as supplies of soap at a reasonable price were available'.[36]

The task of mapping the role of commodification is taken up by Anne McClintock in her brilliant but brittle *Imperial Leather*, and more searchingly by Timothy Burke in *Lifebuoy Men, Lux Women*.[37] McClintock's study is mainly concerned with the function of commodity jingoism in Britain. Burke's book traces the commodification of cleanliness in Zimbabwe. The Unilever slogan 'Soap is Civilization' serves as an epigraph to McClintock's study and it signposts the centrality of Victorian advertising in the making of a new cultural system. By trafficking across the threshold of the public and the private, advertizing, McClintock suggests, began to subvert the very distinction it was entrusted with unholding. In a series of tantalizing vignettes, she sketches the way empire was domesticated, the functionality of the fetishization of the modern, and the emergence of commodity racism. Her text bristles with ideas but many historians will wonder about the connections. Burke's study is no less suggestive but more empirically and historically grounded. There are the 'kaffir trucks' and hawkers bringing the consumption of foreign commodities into the domestic space of Africans. We then learn that government officials encouraged such commercial penetration because it helped create 'new needs' – 'so long as the natives have no wants they will not and need not work'.[38] After the Second World War more sophisticated attempts were made to develop the African market which involved investigating African tastes and practices. Burke goes on to discuss the relationship between commodification and African selfhood, pursuing issues such as the body, status, and gender. It is of particular significance that women were widely believed to be the key to cultural change and on the evidence presented here this was probably well founded.

Drawing on Foucault, it might be said that recognizing the significance of the purchase of a cake of soap is bringing people into discourse. The act is both ordinary and extraordinary. It is not only that when people make this apparently inconsequential move they may be taking the first step into the culture of consumerism, but that they are imagining a different kind of life. We may debate whether this is good or bad, but we can hardly doubt its far-reaching consequences for global culture in the era of late capitalism. The cake of soap thus serves to draw together my overall lines of argument. The transaction may have taken place in the 1880s but it looks to the future and a different kind of world. It underlines the need to take a broad view of the interaction between colonizer and colonized. It indicates how compelling is the connection between the private and the public. In many situations, moreover, it can be taken to be a practical illustration of the power of the discursive.

Throughout the article, my emphasis has been on indicating areas of potential commonality between post-colonialism and imperial history in the interests of encouraging dialogue. These could be extended, in another context, by taking up the material on agency. In turn, I have attempted not to dwell on the obvious differences between the two formations, especially in the realm of theory. This is in line with what post-colonialism increasingly says about othering – but seldom puts into practice when confronted by ways of thinking different from its own. To build upon S.P. Mohanty, the hope is that by proceeding thus we might find that the other is not as different as we imagined.[39]

NOTES

It is a pleasure to acknowledge my indebtedness to Michael Dutton, Paul James, Edgar Ng, and Patrick Wolfe, all of the University of Melbourne and the newly established Institute of Postcolonial Studies. It was the first named who suggested the alternative title ‘Fetishizing Fieldhouse’.

1. Edward Said, *Culture and Imperialism* (London, 1993), 11.
2. For a sardonic account of post-colonialism’s successes see Russell Jacoby, ‘Marginal Returns: The Trouble with Post-colonial Theory’, *Linguafranca*, 5, 6 (1993), 30–7.
3. According to Steven Feierman, one of the first effects of the appearance of African history was to dissolve world history. See his ‘Africa in History: The End of Universal Narratives’, in Gyan Prakash (ed.), *After Colonialism: Imperial Histories and Postcolonial Displacements* (Princeton, 1995), ch.2.
4. See Gyan Prakash, ‘Writing Post-Orientalist Histories of the Third World: Pespectives from Indian Historiography’, *Comparative Studies in Society and History,* 32 (1990), 383–408 and Dipesh Chakrabarty, ‘Postcoloniality and the Artifice of History: Who Speaks for “Indian” Pasts’, *Representations,* 37 (1992), 1–26.

5. Patrick Wolfe, for instance, has argued that diasporan post-colonialism has derived much of its disruptive energy from a strategically provisional juggling of poststructuralism and Marxism. 'History and Imperialism: A Century of Theory, from Marx to Postcolonialism', *American Historical Review*, 102, 2 (1997), 388–420 at 408.
6. For representative critiques see Edward Said, 'Orientalism and after: an interview with Edward Said', *Radical Philosophy,* 63, (1993), 22–32 at 24–6; Aijaz Ahmad, *In Theory: Classes, Nations, Literatures* (London, 1992); Rosalind O'Hanlon and David Washbrook, 'After Orientalism: culture, criticism and politics in the Third World', *Comparative Studies in History and Society*, 34 (1992), 141–66.
7. A study of the reception of post-colonial theory in various parts of the Third World would be instructive. In Beijing in December 1996, a colleague and I were told by one of China's foremost post-modernist scholars that in China post-colonialism is seen as a conservative discourse, closely associated with the government.
8. Dane Kennedy, 'Imperial History and Post-Colonial Theory', *Journal of Imperial and Commonwealth History*, 24, 3 (1996), 345–63 at 346. I have argued a somewhat similar case for dialogue between international relations and post-colonialism in 'Bridging International Relations and Postcolonialism', *Alternatives*, 19 (1994), 371–97 (with A.J. Paolini), and *The Fiction of Imperialism: Reading Between International and Postcolonialism* (London, 1997).
9. John M. MacKenzie, 'Edward Said and the Historians', *Nineteenth-Century Contexts*, 18 (1994), 9–25. See also his *Orientalism: History, theory and the arts* (Manchester, 1995).
10. The latter view has been especially associated with B. Ashcroft, G. Griffiths, and Helen Tiffin, *The Empire Writes Back: Theory and Practice in Post-Colonial Literature* (London, 1989).
11. Homi K. Bhabha, *The Location of Culture* (London, 1994), especially introduction and ch.1.
12. Note, however, that after emphasizing that Hancock felt he had a normative role in writing the *Survey*, Fieldhouse states that in the post-colonial era the economic historian is relieved of this obligation. David Fieldhouse, 'Keith Hancock and Imperial Economic History: A Retrospect Forty Years On', ch.7 in Frederick Madden and D.K. Fieldhouse (eds.), *Oxford and the Idea of Commonwealth* (London, 1982), 162. This, of course, does not settle the issue I have raised.
13. D.K. Fieldouse, *Economics and Empire 1830–1914* (London, 1973), 461.
14. Eric J. Hobsbawm, 'The New Threat to History', *New York Review of Books*, 16 Dec. 1993, 62–4 at 63.
15. Chinua Achebe, *Things Fall Apart* (London, 1958); Ayi Kwei Armah, *Two Thousand Seasons* (Nairobi, 1973).
16. Martha L. Hildreth, 'Lamentations on Reality: A Response to John M MacKenzie's "Edward Said and the Historians"', *Nineteenth-Century Contexts,* 19 (1995), 65–73.
17. David Fieldhouse, 'Can Humpty-Dumpty be put together again? Imperial History in the 1980s', *Journal of Imperial and Commonwealth History*, 12 (1984), 9–23 at 15.
18. MacKenzie, *Orientalism*, 11.
19. See for example Linda Hutcheon, 'The Post Always Rings Twice: The Postmodern and the Postcolonial', *Textual Practice,* 18 (1994), 205–38.
20. Mahmood Mamdani, *Citizen and Subject: Contemporary Africa and the Legacy of Late Colonialism* (Princeton, 1996).
21. Fieldhouse, 'Can Humpty-Dumpty…' , 10, 18 and 9.
22. Martin Chanock, *Law, Custom and Social Order: The Colonial Experience in Malawi and Zambia* (London, 1985); Michael Crowder, *The Flogging of Phinehas McIntosh: A Tale of Colonial Folly and Injustice: Bechuanaland 1933* (New Haven, 1988).
23. Homi Bhabha, 'Signs taken for wonders: questions of ambivalence and authority under a tree outside Delhi, May 1817', *Critical Inquiry,* 12 (1985), 144–65 at 152.
24. See Ashis Nandy, *Traditions, Tyranny and Utopias: Essays in the Politics of Awareness* (Delhi, 1987), 26.
25. For some of the difficulties faced by cultural historians in incorporating new theoretical perspectives, see Elazar Barkan, 'Post-Anti-Colonial Histories: Representing the Other in Imperial Britain', *Journal of British Studies,* 33 (1994), 180–203.

26. Christopher Fyfe's article 'Race, Empire and the Historian', *Race and Class*, 33 (1992), 15–30 repays careful reading. Fyfe writes as an imperial historian but he could easily wear a post-colonial hat – except that his writing is so direct.
27. See Florence Stratton, *Contemporary African Literature and the Politics of Gender* (London, 1994), ch.2.
28. See for example Lovemore M. Zinyama, Daniel S. Tevera, and Sioux D. Cumming (eds.), *Harare: The Growth and Problems of the City* (Harare, 1993).
29. This is advanced in some detail in Jacob Songsore and Aloysius Den Kabe, *Challenging Rural Poverty in Northern Ghana: The Case of the Upper-West Region* (Trondheim, 1995).
30. Arif Dirlick, 'The Postcolonial Aura: Third World Criticism in the Age of Global Capitalism', *Critical Inquiry*, 20 (1994), 328–56 at 337.
31. Ronald Robinson, 'Oxford in Imperial Historiography', ch.2 in Madden and Fieldhouse, *Oxford and the Idea of Empire*, 47.
32. D. K. Fieldhouse, *Black Africa 1945–1980: Economic Decolonization and Arrested Development* (London, 1986).
33. Chinua Achebe, *A Man of the People* (London, 1966).
34. Colin Leys, 'Confronting the African Tragedy', *New Left Review*, 204 (1994), 33–47 at 46.
35. D. K. Fieldhouse, *Unilever Overseas: The Anatomy of a Multinational 1895–1965* (London, 1978), and D. K. Fieldhouse, *Merchant Capital and Economic Decolonization: The United Africa Company 1929–1987* (Oxford, 1994).
36. Fieldhouse, *Unilever Overseas*, 341.
37. Anne McClintock, *Imperial Leather: Race, Gender and Sexuality in the Colonial Conquest* (New York and London, 1995), and Timothy Burke, *Lifebuoy Men, Lux Women: Commodification, Consumption and Cleanliness in Modern Zimbabwe* (Durham and London, 1996).
38. Burke, *Lifebuoy Men*, 86.
39. S.P. Mohanty, 'Us and Them: On the Philosophical Basis of Political Criticism', *Yale Journal of Criticism*, 2, (1989), 5.

Notes on Contributors

C.A. Bayly is Vere Harmsworth Professor of Imperial and Naval History in the University of Cambridge. His books include *Imperial Meridian: The British Empire and the World 1780–1830* (1989) and *Empire and Information: Intelligence Gathering and Social Communication in India, 1780–1870* (1996).

Peter Burroughs, former Professor of History at Dalhousie University, has written extensively on nineteenth-century imperial administration and defence.

Stephen Constantine, Senior Lecturer in History at Lancaster University, is the author of *The Making of British Colonial Development Policy 1914–1940* (1984), and works on migration history including, as editor and contributor, *Emigrants and Empire: British Settlement in the Dominions Between the Wars* (1990).

Phillip Darby is Reader in International Relations at the University of Melbourne and Co-Director of the Institute of Postcolonial Studies, Melbourne. His most recent books are an edited volume, *At the Edge of International Relations: Postcolonialism, Gender and Dependency* (1997), and *The Fiction of Imperialism: Reading between International Relations and Postcolonialism* (1998).

Stephen Howe is Tutor in Politics at Ruskin College, Oxford, and author of *Anticolonialism in British Politics: The Left and the End of Empire, 1918–1964* (1993) and *Afrocentrism* (1998). Current work includes forthcoming books on Ireland and empire and on theories of colonialism.

Ronald Hyam is President of Magdalene College, Cambridge, and Reader in British Imperial History, author of *Britain's Imperial Century, 1815–1914* (new ed. 1993), *Empire and Sexuality* (1990), and editor of *The Labour Government and the End of Empire,1945–1951* (BDEEP 1992).

Howard Johnson is Professor of Black American Studies and History at the University of Delaware. His publications include *The Bahamas from Slavery to Servitude* (1996) and *The White Minority in the Caribbean* (1998) which he co-edited.

Bruce Knox, Senior Lecturer in History at Monash University, has written on various aspects of Australian and nineteenth-century British imperial history in journals in Britain, North America, and Australia. He is preparing an edition of Lord Carnarvon's diary from his Australian visit, 1887–88.

Colin Newbury, Emeritus Fellow of Linacre College, Oxford, former University Lecturer in Commonwealth history, is the author of works on Pacific and African history including *Tahiti Nui: Change and Survival in French Polynesia 1767–1945* (1980) and *The Diamond Ring: Business, Politics, and Precious Stones in South Africa, 1867–1947* (1989).

Jane Ridley is Senior Lecturer in History at the University of Buckingham. Her most recent book was *The Young Disraeli* (1995). She is currently writing a biography of Edwin Lutyens.

A.J. Stockwell is Professor of Imperial and Commonwealth History at Royal Holloway, University of London. He has published on British imperial history and modern Southeast Asia, and is editor of *British Documents on the End of Empire: Malaya, 1942–1957* (1995).

Sarah Stockwell is a lecturer in British imperial and commonwealth history at King's College London. With S.R. Ashton she edited *Imperial Policy and Colonial Practice 1925–1945* (BDEEP 1996), and is currently writing on British business and the end of empire in Ghana.

B.R. (Tom) Tomlinson, Professor of Economic History at the University of Strathclyde, has published extensively on Indian, Asian, and imperial history, including *The Political Economy of the Raj* (1979) and *The Economy of Modern India, 1860–1970* (1993).

Published Writings by David Fieldhouse

BOOKS

(with E.J. Hutchins and L.W. Stephens), *Two Centuries of Change: A History of Great Britain and the British Empire since 1688*, vol.II, 1815–1951 (Glasgow, 1964).

The Colonial Empires: A Comparative Survey from the Eighteenth Century (London, 1966; 2nd rev. ed. 1982).

The Theory of Capitalist Imperialism (London, 1967).

Economics and Empire 1830–1914 (London, 1973; 2nd ed. 1984).

Imperialisme (Bussum, 1975).

Unilever Overseas: The Anatomy of a Multinational 1895–1965 (London, 1978).

Colonialism 1870–1945: An Introduction (London, 1981).

(with F. Madden, eds.), *Oxford and the Idea of Commonwealth* (London, 1982).

(with F. Madden, eds.), *'The Empire of the Bretaignes', 1175–1688: The Foundations of a Colonial System of Government. Select Documents on the Constitutional History of the British Empire and Commonwealth, Vol.I* (Westport, CT, 1985).

(with F. Madden, eds.), *The Classical Period of the First British Empire, 1689–1783, Select Documents ..., Vol.II* (Westport, CT, 1985).

Black Africa 1945–80: Economic Decolonization and Arrested Development (London, 1986).

(with F. Madden, eds.), *Imperial Reconstruction, 1763–1840: The Evolution of Alternative Systems of Colonial Government, Select Documents ..., Vol.III* (Westport, CT, 1987).

(with F. Madden, eds.), *Settler Self-Government, 1840–1900: The Development of Representative and Responsible Government, Select Documents ..., Vol.IV* (Westport, CT, 1990).

(with F. Madden, eds.), *The Dependent Empire and Ireland, 1840–1900, Select Documents ..., Vol.V* (Westport, CT, 1991).

Merchant Capital and Economic Decolonization: The United Africa Company 1929–1987 (Oxford, 1994).

ARTICLES AND ESSAYS

'New Zealand, Fiji and the Colonial Office, 1900–1902', *Historical Studies Australia and New Zealand*, VIII, 30 (1958), 113–30.

'Sir Arthur Gordon and the Parihaka Crisis, 1880–1882', *Historical Studies Australia and New Zealand*, X, 37 (1961), 30–49.

'"Imperialism": An Historiographical Revision', *Economic History Review*, XIV, 2 (1961), 187–209.

'Autochthonous Elements in the Evolution of Dominion Status: The Case of New Zealand', *Journal of Commonwealth Political Studies*, I, 2 (1962), 85–111.

'British Imperialism in the Late Eighteenth Century: Defence or Opulence?' in K. Robinson and A.F. Madden (eds.), *Essays in Imperial Government, Presented to Margery Perham* (Oxford, 1963), 23–45.

'The British Empire', *Encyclopedia Britannica*, 1968.

'Colonialism', *Encyclopedia Americana*, 1968.

'Colonialism: Economic Aspects', *International Encyclopedia of the Social Sciences*, 1968.

'British Colonial Policy', in G.J. Abbott and N.B. Nairn (eds.), *Economic Growth of Australia 1788–1821* (Melbourne, 1969).

'The Economic Exploitation of Africa: Some British and French Comparisons', in P. Gifford and W.R. Louis (eds.), *France and Britain in Africa: Imperial Rivalry and Colonial Rule* (New Haven and London, 1971), 593–641.

'Decolonisation and the Multinational Company: Unilever in India, 1917–65', in P. Bairoch and M. Levy-Leboyer (eds.), *Disparities in Economic Development since the Industrial Revolution* (London, 1981), 58–64.

'Decolonization, Development, and Dependence: A Survey of Changing Attitudes', in P. Gifford and W.R. Louis (eds.), *The Transfer of Power in Africa: Decolonization 1940–1960* (New Haven and London, 1982), 483–514.

'Keith Hancock and Imperial Economic History: A Retrospect Forty Years On', in F. Madden and D.K. Fieldhouse (eds.), *Oxford and the Idea of Commonwealth* (London, 1982), 144–63.

'Can Humpty-Dumpty be put together again? Imperial History in the 1980s', *Journal of Imperial and Commonwealth History*, XII, 2 (1984), 9–23.

'The Labour Governments and the Empire-Commonwealth, 1945–1951', in R. Ovendale (ed.), *The Foreign Policy of the British Labour Governments, 1945–1951* (Leicester, 1984), 83–120.

'The Multinational: A Critique of a Concept', in A. Teichova, M. Levy-Leboyer, and H. Nussbaum (eds.), *Multilateral Enterprise in Historical Perspective* (Cambridge, 1986).

'"A New Imperial System"? The Role of the Multinational Corporations Reconsidered', in W.J. Mommsen and J. Osterhammel (eds.), *Imperialism and After: Continuities and Discontinuities* (London, 1986), 225–40.

'L'impero coloniale britannico', in N. Tranfaglia and M. Firpo (eds.), *La Storia, VI. L'Eta Contemporanea, 1, I Quadri Generali* (Turin, 1988).

'Ronald Robinson and the Cambridge Development Conferences, 1963–70', *Journal of Imperial and Commonwealth History*, XVI, 3 (1988), 173–99.

'Arrested Development in Anglophone Black Africa?', in P. Gifford and

W.R. Louis (eds.), *Decolonization and African Independence: The Transfer of Power, 1960–1980* (New Haven and London, 1988), 135–58.

'Colizzazione e Decolonizzazione', *Enciclopedia della Scienze Sociali*, Vol.I (Rome, 1989).

'Reappraisals in Early-modern New Zealand Political History', review article, *British Review of New Zealand Studies*, II (1989), 77–86.

'War and the Origins of the Gold Coast Marketing Board, 1939–40', in M. Twaddle (ed.), *Imperialism, the State, and the Third World* (London, 1992), 154–82.

'The Creation of the Colonial Empires', in M. Guidi (ed.), *Europa Moderna, 3, Electa* (Milan, 1992).

'British Merchants and French Decolonization: UAC in Francophone Africa, 1945–1960', in C.-R. Ageron and M. Michel (eds.), *L'Afrique noire française: l'heure des Indépendences* (Paris, 1992), 489–98.

'Gentlemen, Capitalists, and the British Empire', review article, *Journal of Imperial and Commonwealth History*, XXII, 3 (1994), 531–41.

'Imperialismo', *Enciclopedia delle Scienze Sociali*, Vol.IV (Rome, 1994).

'For Richer, for Poorer', in P.J. Marshall (ed.), *Cambridge Illustrated History of the British Empire* (Cambridge, 1996), 108–46.

'The British Model of State Exportation', in W. Blockmans, J. Borges de Macedo, and J.-P. Genet (eds.), *The Heritage of the Pre-Industrial European State* (Lisbon, 1996).

Index

Empire-Building and Empire Builders

Edward Ingram, *Simon Fraser University, British Columbia*

The twelve studies of empire-building and empire-builders which make up this volume range widely across the dream world that was the British Empire from the late eighteenth century to the Second World War. The essays re-interpret the work of imperial heroes, eminent historians, and fictional heroines. They illustrate the variety o techniques used by British empire-builders and the variety of explanations they gave to account for their sometimes infamous behaviour.

245 pages 1995 0 7146 46121 cloth

Ethnic Labour and British Imperial Trade

A History of Ethnic Seafarers in the UK

Diane Frost, *University of Liverpool and Merseyside Maritime Museum (Ed)*

> *'a significant contribution to our understanding of some of the non-Europeans who were increasingly significant in manning British ships from the mid-nineteenth century.'*
>
> *International Journal of Maritime History*

This collection of essays identifies a neglected but significant component of Britain's maritime and labour histor that of ethnic labour drawn from Britain's colonies in West Africa, the Middle East and Asia. The interdisciplinary nature of the volume raises a number of important issues: race and ethnicity, colonialism and migration, social class and the complex nature of racial hostility meted out by organized white labour.

178 pages 1995 0 7146 4185 5 paper

A special issue of the journal Immigrants & Minorities

Margery Perham and British Rule in Africa

Alison Smith *and* **Mary Bull** *(Eds)*

Margery Perham was an outstanding influence on official and academic thinking on British Colonial rule and decolonization in Africa during the middle part of the century. The book traces how the Second World War transformed her view of colonial rule and of the rate at which it would have to be relinquished.

248 pages 1992 0 7146 3451 4 cloth

A special issue of the Journal of Imperial and Commonwealth History

Emergencies and Disorder in the European Empires after 1945

Robert Holland, *Institute of Commonwealth Studies (Ed)*

Bringing together for the first time leading historians of European decolonization, this book is a landmark in the comparative analysis of the fall of the European empires, viewed both as a problematic of European policy-making and as a formative experience in the development of new states.

268 pages 1994 0 7146 4516 8 cloth 0 7146 4109 X paper

A special issue of the Journal of Imperial and Commonwealth History

FRANK CASS PUBLISHER
Newbury House, 900 Eastern Avenue, Newbury Park, Ilford, Essex IG2 7H
Tel: +44 (0)181 599 8866 Fax: +44 (0)181 599 0984 E-mail: info@frankcass.co
NORTH AMERIC
c/o ISBS, 5804 NE Hassalo Street, Portland, OR 97213 3644, US
Tel: 1 800 944 6190 Fax: 503 280 8832 E-mail cass@isbs.co
Website: http://www.frankcass.co